Be Like Adam's Son

Religions and Peace Studies

Series Editor: Alessandro Saggioro, Sapienza University, Rome

Peace and religion intertwine and, since they are crucial to all human cultures, they require a more and comprehensive analysis to be understood beyond all the clichés that portray religions either as warmongering or peace-promoting factors.

Dealing with peace and religion means navigating the concepts of border and boundary, identity, alterity, and diversity, questioning the role of historical narratives in conflicts and their resolutions.

This book series explores the nexus between peace and religion, providing a reference tool for interdisciplinary, diachronic, and comparative research approaches. Furthermore, it aims to collect and develop scientific analyses dealing with all types of sources, such as sacred texts, literature and art, symbols and musealized objects, official documents about peace issued by governmental and nongovernmental institutions, historical records, and many others. Also, a variety of sub-topics are included, all revolving around the peace-religion axis and ranging from ecology to sustainability, from migration to gender issues, and from economy to literature and art.

The interdisciplinary dimension of the book series is grounded in a discursive approach to conflict and (re)conciliation through the languages of history, philosophy, anthropology, sociology, law, literature, and arts. The time span covered is broad and encompasses past civilizations and empires and their legacy, up to the dislocation and crisis of their memory in the present.

Finally, one of the most significant challenges of this book series is to make room for a consistent reflection on the history of the study of religions and peace and the methodological approaches scholars have adopted over the centuries to shape the discipline.

Be Like Adam's Son

Theorising, Writing, and Practising Peace in the Arab Region

Edited by
Fernanda Fischione and Arturo Monaco

equinox

SHEFFIELD UK BR STOL CT

Published by Equinox Publishing Ltd.

UK: Office 415, The Workstation, 15 Paternoster Row, Sheffield, South Yorkshire, S1 2BX
USA: ISD, 70 Enterprise Drive, Bristol, CT 06010

www.equinoxpub.com

First published 2024

This volume results from the collective research project *Negotiating Stories in Cohabitation: Dynamics and Narratives of Peace in the Great Empires of the Past* (from Antiquity to Present Times), funded by Sapienza University of Rome, and is cosponsored by TRANSECT ("https://www.transect.eu/"), a project funded by the European Union's Horizon 2020 research and innovation program under the Marie Skłodowska-Curie grant agreement No 101027040.

British Library Cataloguing-in-Publication Data
A catalogue record for this book is available from the British Library.

ISBN-13 978 1 80050 384 7 (hardback)
978 1 80050 385 4 (paperback)
978 1 80050 386 1 (ePDF)
978 1 80050 465 3 (ePub)

Library of Congress Cataloging-in-Publication Data

Names: Fischione, Fernanda, editor. | Monaco, Arturo, editor.
Title: Be like Adam's son : theorising, writing and practising peace in the Arab region / edited by Fernanda Fischione, and Arturo Monaco.
Description: Sheffield, South Yorkshire ; Bristol, CT : Equinox Publishing Ltd, 2024. | Series: Religions and peace studies | Includes bibliographical references and index. | Summary: "The twelve chapters collected in the volume criticise, analyse, and discuss the issue of peace in Arab literature, philosophical and theological thought, and both institutional and grassroots practices of intercultural and interreligious mediation"-- Provided by publisher.
Identifiers: LCCN 2023031177 (print) | LCCN 2023031178 (ebook) | ISBN 9781800503847 (hardback) | ISBN 9781800503854 (paperback) | ISBN 9781800503861 (pdf) | ISBN 9781800504653 (epub)
Subjects: LCSH: Peace-building--Arab countries. | Peace (Philosophy) | Peace in literature. | Religion and politics--Arab countries. | Arab countries--Religious aspects. | Arab countries--Social conditions.
Classification: LCC JZ5584.A65 B45 2024 (print) | LCC JZ5584.A65 (ebook) | DDC 327.1/7209174927--dc23/eng/20231026
LC record available at https://lccn.loc.gov/2023031177
LC ebook record available at https://lccn.loc.gov/2023031178

Typeset by S.J.I. Services, New Delhi, India

Contents

Foreword vii
Isabella Camera d'Afflitto

Introduction 1
Fernanda Fischione and Arturo Monaco

Part 1. Theorising Peace and Nonviolence 15

1. From *Ǧihād* "until the Day of Resurrection" to Nonviolence: The Debate on War and Peace in the Mid-1960s Post-*Nahḍah* Arab Generation 17
Paola Pizzi

2. *Kun ka-ibn Ādam*: Nonviolence and Quranic Interpretation in Ǧawdat Saʿīd's Thought 45
Pietro Menghini

Part 2. From Literature of War to Literature of Reconciliation 75

3. The Iran-Iraq War in Iraqi Novels: Oblivion and Disappearance 77
Ronen Zeidel

4. The Painful Path towards Civil Liberties and Social Justice Followed by the Iraqi Ḥayāt Šarārah 102
Elvira Diana

5. Pluralism and Ethnoreligious Identities in Iraqi Fiction: ʿAbdullāh Ṣaḫī's Trilogy on Thawra City 126
Antonio Pacifico

6. In Search of the Virtuous City: Coexistence and (In)Hospitality in ʿAlī Badr's *ʿĀzif al-ġuyūm* 154
Annamaria Bianco

7. Literature as a Mirror: The Search for Peace and Pacification in Moroccan Society as Depicted in *Banāt al-ṣubbār* (2018) by Karīmah Aḥdād 179
Paola Viviani

8. Youssef Fadel's Trilogy: Testifying Violence to Negotiate Peace in Moroccan Literature 202
Cristina Dozio

Part 3. Practices of Mediation **227**

9. *Lā tuṣāliḥ* in the *Sīrat al-Zīr Sālim*: A Hymn to a Long-Term Peace 229
Daniela Potenza

10. Twofold Slavery: Slave in Malta, Slave to Love of his Beloved Master. The Peaceful Letter a Muslim Sent to Baldassarre Loyola Mandes SJ (1631–1667) 254
Federico Stella

11. Peace and Justice: A Catholic Palestinian Response to the Israeli-Palestinian Conflict 277
Paolo Maggiolini

12. A Thousand and One Jordans: The Story of Rafedìn 309
Odetta Pizzingrilli

Index of Names 338

Index of Subjects 346

Foreword

Isabella Camera d'Afflitto

"Ah, peace! How expansive peace is!"[1] These ironic words come from the mouth of the Pessoptimist, the famous character created by one of the most original and brilliant Arab writers of the 20th century, the Palestinian Imīl (Emil) Ḥabībī (1921–1996). An Israeli Arab, Ḥabībī refused to flee his hometown Haifa like many of his compatriots and chose to stay in a homeland that no longer existed, a homeland that had suffered through so many wars over the centuries while dreaming of the same peace everyone longed for. "So why am I depressed?"[2] is the question the Pessoptimist – the naïve protagonist who is not so naïve after all – always asks himself. He is depressed because, in the spring of 1948, he goes through the Valley of the Cross in Haifa and realises that the streets are empty. There is not even the sound of gunfire, which people were so used to before the fall of Haifa and the forced exile of its population.

It is the same depression of all those who, after various wars, live in the fear that it will all start all over again and that peace is only ephemeral. One can think here of the countless conflicts in the Arab countries in the Maghreb, such as Algeria, Libya, and the Western Sahara, or in the Mashreq, which witnessed the endless Palestinian-Israeli conflict and the more recent wars of Iraq, Lebanon, Syria, or Yemen. In addition, one can think of the conflicts that followed the Arab Spring, which gave us a brief glimpse of fragile successes and even more fragile reconciliations. Yet there is also the psychological and inner warfare that numerous Arab dictatorial regimes still carry out today. This war leaves casualties behind

1. Habiby 2003, p. 42.
2. Ibid.

almost everywhere, especially in the ranks of the intellectuals who pay a high price for openly denouncing the abuses of power. It is the same crushing power that ʿAbd al-Raḥmān al-Kawākibī (1849–1902) – a crucial 19th-century Syrian intellectual from Aleppo – denounced so clearly in his famous treatise on despotism, *Ṭabāʾiʿ al-istibdād wa-maṣāriʿ al-istiʿbād* (The Nature of Tyranny and the Devastating Results of Oppression). Al-Kawākibī stated explicitly: "[T]yranny cannot be resisted by force. It should be resisted by peaceful means in gradual steps"[3].

Many Arab writers yearn deeply for peace and feel the urge to present testimonies of wars, massacres, injustices, and persecutions in their works. They often speak out against today's oppression by setting their stories in the past, as is the case with the famous novel *al-Zaynī Barakāt* by the Egyptian writer Ǧamāl al-Ġiṭānī (1945–2015), set in the 16th century. Moreover, as some chapters of this volume show, recent outbursts of violence, war, and unrest are also pivotal themes of contemporary fiction. Violence and war are unleashed against the external enemy and increasingly against alleged internal enemies, wiping out women, men, and children's lives. The aggressor has a familiar face sometimes and embraces dangerous ideologies, confusing religion with oppression and fraternity with arrogance. And the peace everyone dreams of cannot be realized if clashing and manipulated doctrines within the same family tear the sons apart.

This is why the theme of peace in all its sociopolitical, philosophical, theological, and literary facets is key and universally relevant, as this valuable volume edited by Fernanda Fischione and Arturo Monaco highlights. Together, the twelve chapters of this book offer a compelling and comprehensive interdisciplinary view on topics ranging from theories of peace and non-violence to war and reconciliation literature and mediation practices. The editors have skilfully divided and grouped the chapters into three sections, according to these three main topics. This volume represents a significant step forward in our understanding of yesterday's and today's Arab world, where many dynamics seem to stay the same while the perpetrators do change. Dictators may appear invincible for some time, but they will eventually have to deal with history because in no part of the world will humanity ever stop seeking peace. And never

3. Al-Kawakibi (2021), Chapter: Getting Rid of Tyranny.

before has this word taken on such an increasingly pregnant and indispensable meaning.

References

Al-Kawakibi, A.R. (2021), *The Nature of Tyranny and the Devastating Results of Oppression*, trans. A. Chaikhouni, Hurst & Company, London, E-book edition.

Habiby, E. (2003), *The Secret Life of Saeed the Pessoptimist*, trans. S.K. Jayyusi, T. LeGassick, Interlink Books, Northampton (MA).

Isabella Camera d’Afflitto is a Honorary Professor of Modern and Contemporary Arabic Literature, Sapienza University of Rome.

Introduction

Fernanda Fischione and Arturo Monaco

The concept for this book was drafted within the framework of a collective research project funded by Sapienza University of Rome and titled *Negotiating Stories in Cohabitation: Dynamics and Narratives of Peace in the Great Empires of the Past (from Antiquity to Present Times)*. As part of this broader project, the chapters collected in this volume do not aim to provide a systematic overview of the theme of peace in today's cultural production in Arabic but aim to show a variety of approaches to peace as they emerge from literature, historiography, philosophy, and theology. The common feature connecting all the chapters is that each explores significant decolonialisation attempts by writers, thinkers, and clergy to tackle the intertwined issues of peace, transitional justice, conflict mediation, and peaceful society building. Digging into a huge reserve of previously neglected or understudied material, each chapter analyses texts, reflections, and practices produced in the Arab region, showing the vitality of the quest for peace and the originality of its articulations.

Peace studies provide an interdisciplinary framework that can fit the wide range of topics and approaches of the chapters. As many scholars specialising in peace studies highlight[1], the concept of peace is quite elusive, and it might be awkward to define unequivocally. Johan Galtung (1969) proposed making a distinction between "positive" and "negative" peace. Positive peace means the absence of structural violence and/or the realisation of social justice, while negative peace implies the mere absence of personal violence or war. In fact, peace is dialectical, as Charles Webel (2007), amongst others, states. It is more than the absence of war or

1. See, for instance, Galtung 1969; Webel, Galtung 2007; Cortright 2008; Barash 2018.

violence. It "denotes active individual and collective self-determination and emancipatory empowerment. Peace entails continuous peacekeeping and peacemaking. And peacemaking requires active and continual personal and collective transformation"[2]. According to this view, the opposite of peace is not conflict in general but terror and terrorism, which imply a kind of violence that "increases human pain and suffering and usually diminishes personal safety and peace of mind, without accomplishing 'higher order' political goals, such as national liberation and political or socioeconomic emancipation"[3].

Within this framework, the 12 chapters collected in the volume criticise, analyse, and discuss the issue of peace in Arabic literature, philosophical and theological thought, and both institutional and grassroots practices of intercultural and interreligious mediation. The volume consists of three parts: 1) Theorising Peace and Nonviolence; 2) From Literature of War to Literature of Reconciliation; and 3) Practices of Mediation.

The first part explores the theoretical development of peace and nonviolence in contemporary Islamic thought. The last decades have seen a growing concern for Islam and its interpretation of peace in scholarly publications. In a paper from 2000–2001, Mohammed Abu-Nimer suggested dividing the literature that focuses on the relation between Islam and the principles of war, peace, and nonviolence into three main categories: 1. Studies on war and *ǧihād* considering pacifism and nonviolence to be foreign concepts in Islam; 2. Studies on war and peace comprising a variety of approaches that tend to reconsider the role of peaceful and nonviolent means in the overall Islamic goal of establishing a just social reality; 3. Studies on peacebuilding and nonviolence focusing on the potential pacifist and nonviolent nature and characteristics of Islam[4]. A growing number of studies have been published since 9/11, when the dramatic association of Islam with violence in most media narratives and scholarly contributions led to attempts to explore and reconsider the peaceful aspects in Islamic theology and practice[5]. The two contributions

2. Webel, Galtung 2007, p. 8.
3. Ibid, p. 9.
4. Abu-Nimer (2000–2001, pp. 221–232) provides a significant set of references for each category.
5. One of the most recent attempts in this regard is Cole 2022.

in the first part of the volume can be included within the framework of these attempts.

In Chapter 1, Paola Pizzi outlines the main tendencies of the debate on war and peace in the mid-1960s post-*Nahḍah* Arab generation. She argues that Islamic literature attempted an early conceptualisation of war and peace on the basis of the Qurʾān. The cornerstone of this debate was the notion of *ǧihād*. Despite the polysemy of the term, its military interpretation was dominant in the first centuries of the Islamic conquests. However, a body of dissident literature did exist in mediaeval times, with the wide circulation of disputed *aḥādīṯ* exalting spiritual *ǧihād* as a tendency to non-belligerence and refusal to combat. With the *Nahḍah* movement in the mid-19th century, the debate continued between an apologetic concept of a "defensive *ǧihād*" and a radical, militant stance. Both positions were further developed by the post-*Nahḍah* generations, with a radicalization of the idea of armed *ǧihād* on the one hand and the ground-breaking steps towards an Islamic theory of nonviolence on the other. Pizzi provides an example of this debate through the analysis of three pivotal works published at about the same time in the 1960s by three prominent thinkers: the Syrian jurist Wahbah al-Zuḥaylī, the Egyptian thinker and member of the Muslim Brothers Sayyid Quṭb, and the Syrian theologian and preacher Ǧawdat Saʿīd. She concludes that, while al-Zuḥaylī and Quṭb confirmed the centrality of *ǧihād*, Saʿīd emerges as the first theorist of nonviolence in Islam.

The latter's nonviolent theories are further explored in Pietro Menghini's Chapter 2. Witness to a period full of change and turmoil for both Syria and the whole region in his long career as an Islamic religious thinker, Ǧawdat Saʿīd touched upon many central themes of Islamic philosophy, including nonviolence. The chapter focuses specifically on Saʿīd's book *Kun ka-ibn Ādam* (Be Like Adam's Son) – which inspired the title of this volume – published in 1997, and on the historicist exegetical methodology presented in support of nonviolence. In his analysis, Menghini inscribes Saʿīd's philosophy in the humanist current of thought theorised by the Lebanese thinker Chibli Mallat and described "as a deep cultural tradition defined by the centrality given by its members to nonviolence, opposition to unjust regimes, colonialism and imperialism, and the inclination to support nonviolent revolutions"[6]. Saʿīd's thought is

6. See below Chapter 2 and Mallat 2015, pp. 81–83.

therefore included in the long tradition of humanist thinkers in the Middle East, with the peculiar mark of focusing explicitly on nonviolence. The analysis of his theoretical contribution is relevant today as it highlights the existence of a consistent movement of nonviolent Islamic thinkers in the Middle East, therefore opposing the common representation of Islam provided in the media and popular culture. Moreover, it is also important because of the possible practical applications of Saʿīd's theories, given his strong connections to nonviolent activist groups at the beginning of the 2011 Syrian uprising.

The second part of the volume is completely devoted to literature. Arabic literature offers countless insights into war and peace. The dramatic changes that have shattered North African and Middle Eastern societies since the second half of the 20th century affected a large part of the literary production from and on the region. Writers and intellectuals expressed their dissent and their criticism of political choices that led to conflict. They contributed to voice memories of the past silenced by war, repression, and injustice. They thought of the possibilities of national and social reconciliation in torn communities and displayed new models of national belonging, pluralism and coexistence. The six chapters included in this part testify to the variety of attitudes to the theme of peace that novelists adopted in two specific case studies: Iraq and Morocco.

Ronen Zeidel's Chapter 3 is the first of the four chapters dedicated to Iraqi literature and provides an account of the literary production of the last forty years and how it portrays the Iran-Iraq war (1980–1988). Chapter 3 serves as a literary-historical framework for the following three chapters on Iraqi literature. The author suggests that writing about the war has gradually become marginal throughout the years, not because peace was implemented but because state repression and other urgent matters came to the fore. While the state sponsored the so-called *adab al-ḥarb* (war literature) or *adab al-Qādisiyyah* (the literature of Qādisiyyah) during the war, which was intended to glorify the war and Iraqi soldiers, the number of war novels decreased after 1988. Until 2003, state-sponsored novels were invited to address other hot topics of the time, such as the war on Kuwait, the Shiite and Kurdish rebellion, and the effects of the international sanctions on Iraqi society. Alternative writing did exist, but it seldom engaged with a critique of war and its effects. Dissident writers in Iraq and in the diaspora generally shifted attention from the front to the rear, choosing deserters as protagonists of their war novels instead of soldiers and focusing on the devastating consequences of war on the people. Few of them openly criticised the state and, when they did, they paid a high price for their positioning, as Chapter 4 below shows. After the fall of Saddam Hussein's regime, criticism of all aspects of life under the Baʿath, including the war, began to be expressed in novels. The post-2003 novels on war display some of the features typical of the alternative works of the 1990s, such as the focus on fugitives and marginal figures. This time, however, more emphasis is given to the connection between war and dictatorship. As Zeidel shows, war was considered the final outcome of the militarisation of society and the state, for which the Baʿath was responsible. The Party had shaped a deformed national identity that required revision. This led the intellectuals to open up new perspectives on the recent history of Iraq. They put the Iran-Iraq war into a historical narrative of a sequence of wars started in 1980. In addition, they highlighted the ethno-religious identities of Iraqi society, especially the Shia, as testified in Chapter 5 described below. In his concluding remarks, Zeidel takes into consideration the Iranian hold on Iraqi politics in recent years when writing a war novel became hazardous. Nevertheless, thanks to the new-found stability in Iraq, war has again appeared as a theme in some recent novels. Time will tell if this trend sheds new light on the troubled past of the country and opens up the possibility of reconciliation with it.

The other three contributions on Iraqi literature fit into the framework traced by Ronen Zeidel. As anticipated above, Elvira Diana's Chapter 4 sheds light on a writer who dared to challenge the regime and paid the consequences of her rebellion, the Iraqi scholar Ḥayāt Šarārah. By analysing the author's life trajectory as described in the biography written by her sister Balqīs as well as Ḥayāt's posthumous novel *Iḏā al-ayyām aġsaqat* (When the Days Grow Dark), the chapter engages in the rehabilitation of this committed scholar and writer, who fought for a peaceful society built on civil liberties and social justice. Through her academic activity and her writings, she denounced the dramatic effects of war and the Baʿathist repression in the country. In particular, her novel is an explicit protest against the humiliating practices carried out by the state against academia. The tragic consequences of the expression of this dissent led ultimately to Ḥayāt Šarārah's death, an alleged suicide behind which some saw the hand of the regime. Therefore, her case is exemplary of the destiny of any dissident voice who tried to confront the state inside the country until 2003.

Even after 2003, when the repressive Baʿathist regime was driven from power, speaking freely of past and ongoing events has not always been possible. This is why many intellectuals fled the country and publish their books abroad and express criticism about their society from the outside. The intellectual in exile, who is an extremely popular character in contemporary Arabic literature, has the advantage of looking at his country of origin and observing it from a "safe" distance. This gives him or her the opportunity to revise its history and deal with sensitive topics, such as memory, trauma, identity, coexistence, and pacification. At the same time, while maintaining the spiritual bond with the homeland, the exile loses the physical one and stands in a liminal position between the local and the international field. Chapter 5 by Antonio Pacifico focuses on one of these writers in exile, the Iraqi ʿAbdullāh Ṣaḫī. By analysing his trilogy published between 2008 and 2017, the chapter addresses the retrieval of ethnoreligious identities in the Iraqi literary production in recent decades. In particular, the analysis shows how the author rediscovers his personal Shia background in his fictional texts, both by recalling specific motifs of Shia religiosity and by asserting the importance of Thawra or Sadr City as a sacred place for the Iraqi Shia. As Pacifico argues, this choice is connected to a large (re)writing of history, which involves not only this particular place but also other elements of the social, cultural, and political imagination of modern Iraq. From Ṣaḫī's perspective, who stands in a liminal position with respect to the Iraqi literary field, the reference to ethnoreligious elements in the novel is not a threat to the ongoing peacebuilding process. On the contrary, they can contribute to reconfiguring, in a non-aggressive way, an inclusive national belonging that takes those ethnoreligious identities into account.

Such an inclusive identity and belonging may be questioned from the place of exile itself. Displaced to foreign countries, writers and intellectuals do not limit their insights to their country of origin but experience the limits of the alleged pluralistic societies where they find refuge. Chapter 6 by Annamaria Bianco looks at the themes of pluralism and peaceful coexistence in the European context, by adopting the perspective of another Iraqi exile, the writer ʿAlī Badr. In particular, she analyses his novel *ʿĀzif al-ġuyūm* (The Musician in the Clouds, 2016), a pseudo-fictional work, in which the author portrays the image of a cosmopolitan artist who lives in Belgium and aspires to universal recognition against the "identity blackmail" imposed by asylum. Via the fictional story, Badr reflects on displacement and scrutinises the very idea of Europe. The fictional tools of humour and utopia, represented by the meta-textual use of al-Fārābī's *al-madīnah al-fāḍilah* (the Virtuous City), help the author suggest an unorthodox reading of the refugee crisis in Europe. The image of the West as a "Gracious Heaven" that the protagonist expects to find in Europe before leaving Baghdad is replaced by a reality in which he experiences old forms of persecution and new practices of racism. This leads to the conclusion that no place in the world reflects the standards of the perfect city. But the author suggests that, by accepting the existence of dissonances and contradictions in the universe, we can create new possible scenarios of coexistence and solidarity in our contemporary transnational societies.

The Moroccan context is totally different from the Iraqi one and is characterised by the unwavering institutional stability granted by the Alawi monarchy. Nonetheless, such stability has constantly been challenged by processes and events which have marked the history of the country since the end of the French protectorate in 1956. Quite ironically, the term "pacification" labels one of the darkest pages of Morocco's modern history, namely, the French penetration into the country (1907–1934), which began long before the official birth of the protectorate itself. De Poli highlights that the establishment of the French protectorate in Morocco, while the result of a war lasting 25 years with at least 200,000 casualties, was called "pacification" to recall an irenic atmosphere that never existed[7]. As a French colonel stated in 1929, the difference between war and the French campaign was that "nous [the French] ne voulons pas la destruction de l'adversaire puisque c'est pour lui que nous travaillons et pour lui que nous travaillerons demain"[8].

Age-old issues of "territorial stress"[9] that have been affecting Morocco include the question of the Rif. The chronical peripheralisation of this

7. De Poli 2019.
8. Ibid., p. 480, footnote 8.
9. Naciri 1990, p. 13.

area – a mechanism that involved the neglect of local economies, education, and infrastructure and the lack of political representation – resulted in a regionalist protest movement whose legitimacy the Makhzen has constantly attempted to dismiss. The post-colonial phase of Moroccan history has seen the Riffians marginalised or even excluded from the broader definition of the nation. Kept at a distance from the centre – the "bled el-Makhzen," to recall the famous political-spatial divide characterising the country according to traditional political historiography – the Rif has been dealing with a heavy burden of injustice, humiliation (*hogra*), and consequent unrest. As Paola Viviani highlights in Chapter 7, Moroccan literature witnesses the fight of the Riffians to have their demands met and achieve fairer life conditions within Moroccan society. This chapter analyses Karīmah Aḥdād's *Banāt al-ṣubbār* (Cactus Girls, 2018), a choral novel that focuses on the story of a low-class family from al-Hoceima and especially on its female components as well as featuring several secondary characters acting as "sociological samples", each one exemplifying a social problem. The novel, in fact, stresses how numerous forms of oppression intersect in the Riffian society: besides the structural, state-driven combination of neglect and repression exerted on the region, violence hides in the obscurantist Islamist teachings increasingly permeating society and in the patriarchal norms oppressing women. *Banāt al-ṣubbār* – Viviani concludes – portrays the quest for a pacific society, which can only be achieved by means of a fierce fight against oppression and the struggle for self-liberation.

Among the factors of instability that Morocco has faced throughout its post-independence history, the infamous Years of Lead (1956–1999) covered more than four decades, although they cast their shadow way beyond the reign of Hassan II. The state-sponsored violence exerted in this period in fact weakened the social fabric of the country and caused deep trauma to many individuals and their families. The Makhzen attempted to regain social consensus and cohesion through the establishment of an Indemnity Commission that, however, understood restorative justice purely as a matter of financial compensation, a view rejected by the former victims and their relatives and heirs. The latter responded by establishing the Moroccan Forum for Truth and Equity in 1999, which paved the way for the Equity and Reconciliation Commission (2004). However, there is still much work left to do to fill in the gaps of incommunicability studding this traumatic collective experience which cannot be addressed by the official narratives. As Cristina Dozio highlights in Chapter 8, "What remains untold in the national archives has been voiced through a collective process of memorialisation, including testimonial writings, interviews, documentaries, and marches [...]". The chapter stresses the importance of going beyond the official national archives and digging into the unacknowledged memories of the former victims in order to voice the injustice they suffered at the hands of the state. Justice can have a chance only by including the victims' standpoint in the reconciliation process. As Dozio and other scholars argue, literary fiction is a privileged site of production of collective memorialisation. Chapter 8 analyses Youssef Fadel's trilogy comprising the novels *Qiṭṭ abyaḍ ǧamīl yasīru maʿī* (A Beautiful White Cat Walks with Me, 2011), *Ṭāʾir azraq nādir yuḥalliqu maʿī* (A Rare Blue Bird Flies with Me, 2013), and *Faraḥ* (Joy, 2016). The trilogy focuses on contested memories, such as political imprisonment, the Western Sahara conflict, and the construction of the King Hassan II Mosque. By fictionalising memory, Fadel's trilogy, as well as many other literary productions belonging to what Brahim El Guabli has called "the second wave of testimonial literature", appropriates the collective past and creates an unofficial archive offering a much-needed counternarrative.

The third part of the volume explores past and present practices of mediation as observed both through the lens of literature and in social, political, and theological lived experiences. In Chapters 9 and 10, mediation is key in attempting to reestablish a strong balance between the parties – a balance that can only be achieved when someone decides to refrain from using his power for the sake of peace. Chapters 11 and 12 account on experiences of religious (Christian) mediation by presenting two case studies: the Peace and Justice Commission in Palestine and the humanitarian project Rafedìn in Jordan.

In Chapter 9, Daniela Potenza analyses the conflict-avoidance strategies implemented in the *Sīrat al-Zīr Sālim al-Muhalhil*, one of the most important pieces of Arabic literature of all time. Although the legendary Basūs war is at the centre of the plot of the *Sīrah* and peacetime is only briefly and vaguely described as a pleasant time devoted to love, family, and leisure, Potenza notes how the war is waged only after the failure of many mediation attempts. Peace, therefore, does not mean reaching an irenic state of blissful delight but avoiding unleashing the tension, and mediation is the art of keeping a reasonable balance between the desire for vengeance and the need to prevent evil from spreading and destroying society – a pattern already unearthed by Ana Luengo[10] in an article devoted to another *sīrah*, that of Baybars. The attitude of the old Suʿād, who craves vengeance after the killing of her female camel, exemplifies the opposite of a rational attitude adopted for the sake of the common good. Suʿād, in fact, declares that she is ready to accept compensation instead of shedding Kulayb's blood but contemptuously states that the only possible compensation would either be given a bag full of stars or having her camel restored to life. Conversely, the *Sīrah* portrays King Kulayb's attitude as righteous and just: before his brother-in-law Ǧassās kills him, Kulayb and his fellow tribesmen try everything in their power to avoid a conflict. The thirst for vengeance is thus caused by blind rage, limitless ambition, and indifference to the common good, while justice is shaped around the idea of compensation, patience, and giving the enemy the chance to redeem themselves. If one considers that the attempt to achieve peace is so costly in terms of time, effort, mediation, and self-control, Kulayb's last wishes before dying come as no surprise: due to Ǧassās' despising his attempt to maintain peace, Kulayb cannot help but order his brother Sālim not to reconcile with Ǧassās without avenging his death. As Potenza highlights, the *Sīrah* has also a long history of adaptations. One of them is Amal Dunqul's poem *Lā tuṣāliḥ* (Do not Reconcile, 1976), written as a fierce criticism of Sādāt's politics and Egypt's peace agreement with Israel and eventually reused in graffiti during the 2011 uprisings in Cairo as a warning not to forget the martyrs and to do them justice.

Strength relations sharply appear in the text Federico Stella analyses in Chapter 10, a letter a Muslim slave in Malta sent to Baldassarre Loyola Mandes. The latter, a 17th-century Moroccan ruler, was captured by the Knights of St. John while on a pilgrimage to Mecca and kept captive in Malta, where he converted to Christianity and became a Jesuit. He was eventually freed and moved from Malta to Italy where he was ordained a priest and converted many slave Muslims to Christianity. The slave's letter to Baldassarre – who translated it into Italian for his spiritual guide – is heavily influenced by the style of homoerotic courtly poetry and, according to Stella, is an example of how potential conflicts can be

10. Luengo 2003.

fictionalised and thus mediated through writing. In this case, a potential interreligious controversy on Baldassarre's conversion to Christianity is transformed into a love letter from a slave to his master. The asymmetrical nature of their relationship is overcome by a mutual attempt to meet on common ground: against all odds, the slave does not blame Baldassarre for his conversion but, on the contrary, expresses all his longing for the master; for his part, Baldassarre's translation is an act of mediation in itself. Following the Jesuit practice of accommodation, he adopts a strategy of domestication of the Islamic content of the letter, simplifying it to make it more comprehensible and avoid othering his former Muslim co-religionaries.

In Chapter 11, Paolo Maggiolini focuses on an experience of mediation implemented by the Justice and Peace Commission in Palestine during the first Intifada. Israel has often tried to divide and coopt Palestinian Christian communities while maintaining good relations with the clergy – especially the Greek Orthodox Patriarchate – in order to benefit from the vast lands they possess. On their part, Christian churches in Palestine began to reflect on their identity in the 1970s by both questioning the political meaning and theological implications of being Christian in an occupied land. Their commitment can be deduced for the most part from the effort they put into indigenising the clergy in the Holy Land and countering the logic of Israel's colonial occupation of Palestine. One of the brightest examples of such indigenisation was Michel Sabbah, the first Arab Patriarch of the Roman Catholic (Latin) community, whose theological reflections influenced the work of the Commission and its efforts towards a just peace. The 1987 Intifada tested the new forms of grassroots activism born during the 1970s in opposition to the monopoly of the PLO on the national struggle for liberation. After the outbreak of the Intifada, the Commission – which had begun publishing its multilingual statements in 1980 – vocally supported Palestinian resistance, denouncing the economic neglect of rural areas, the evictions, the decline of education due to curfews and blockages, and many other issues affecting the daily life of Palestinians under the occupation. The Justice and Peace Commission and Michel Sabbah, as Maggiolini highlights, "sought to recompose the multidimensional and multivocal character of the Christian Palestinian presence, developing new individual and collective consciousness [...] and stimulating ecumenical and interfaith dialogue". By doing so, they travelled an original path towards liberation, a path where intra- and inter-religious coexistence, theological reflection, political commitment, and decoloniality could not be separated.

Another experience of Christian activism aiming to build a more peaceful society, although very different from the one described in Chapter 11, is the one Odetta Pizzingrilli explores in Chapter 12 about the story of Rafedìn. A humanitarian project conceived in Amman in March 2016 and addressing Iraqi refugee women, Rafedìn aims to facilitate the social and economic integration of a particularly weak component of Jordanian society through training these women for work in the tailoring sector. The project is currently run by the Habibi Valtiberina Association, founded and directed by Fr. Mario Cornioli, and contributes to the mushrooming of grassroots organisations that make up for the shortcomings of state institutions to guarantee fairer conditions for the many immigrant groups challenging Jordanian demography. As Pizzingrilli highlights, the presence of a large number of refugees in Jordan is both functional to and disruptive of the Jordanian official identity politics: selectively included or excluded at the political convenience of the moment, refugees are subjected to the "identity blackmail" mentioned above.

As the chapters of this volume show, peace and war are located at the two extremes of a continuum, and the full range of this spectrum deserves to be considered, refraining from overemphasising violence at the expense of peaceful attempts to solve conflicts on the one hand and idealising peace as an unattainable and abstract condition on the other. As argued above, peace is a dialectical process rather than a (hypo)static goal. Rephrasing the theologian and antiwar activist A. J. Muste, David Barash claims that "peace is never fully achieved; it can only be approached"[11]. In Kantian terms, perfect peace can be only "a 'regulative ideal', a norm [...] that ought to guide and regulate our behaviour but which is also unlikely to be universally observed"[12]. What is relevant is the process of negotiation and mediation that leads to it, namely, the attempts and continuous adjustments implemented with the purpose of getting closer and closer to it. And the chapters of this book aspire to give account of a number of such approaches.

11. Barash 2007, p. 1.
12. Webel, Galtung 2007, p. 12.

References

Abu-Nimer, M. (2000–2001), *A framework for nonviolence and peacebuilding in Islam*, in "Journal of Law and Religion", 15, 1–2, pp. 217–265. https://doi.org/10.2307/1051519

Barash, D. (2018), *Approaches to Peace: A Reader in Peace Studies*, Oxford University Press, New York and Oxford.

Cole, J. (2022) (ed.), *Peace Movements in Islam: History, Religion, and Politics*, I.B. Tauris, London.

Cortright, D. (2008), *Peace. A History of Movements and Ideas*, Cambridge University Press, New York.

De Poli, B. (2019), *La "pacificazione" del Marocco (1907–1934): Indagine preliminare sulle fonti storiografiche e documentarie di una conquista senza nome*, in A. Baldinetti et al. (eds), *Oltreconfine. Temi e fonti per lo studio dell'Africa. Volume in omaggio a Federico Cresti*, Aracne, Rome, pp. 477–491.

Galtung, J. (1969), *Violence, Peace, and Peace Research*, in "Journal of Peace Research", 6, 3, pp. 167–191. https://doi.org/10.1177/002234336900600301

Luengo, A. R. V. (2003), *Conflict Resolution in the "Sirat Baybars": A Peace Research Approach*, in "Oriente Moderno", Nuova serie, Anno 22, 83, 2, pp. 465–484. https://doi.org/10.1163/22138617-08302014

Mallat, C. (2015), *Revolution, Constitutionalism, and Justice beyond the Middle East*, Oxford University Press, New York and Oxford.

Naciri, M. (1999), *Territoire: contrôler ou developer. Le dilemme du pouvoir depuis un siècle*, in "Monde arabe, Maghreb Machrek", 164, pp. 8–35. https://doi.org/10.3917/machr1.164.0009

Webel, Ch., Galtung, J. (2007), *Handbook of Peace and Conflict Studies*, Routledge, London and NewYork.

Fernanda Fischione is a MSCA Fellow at Sapienza University of Rome – Université Internationale de Rabat with the project *Transnational Maghreb and the International Prize for Arabic Fiction: Pluralism, Inclusiveness, and Peaceful Coexistence in the Contemporary Maghrebi Novel*. She holds a PhD from Sapienza University of Rome, with a dissertation on literary space and place in the oeuvre of Jordanian writer and critic Ġālib Halasā. Since 2015, she has conducted two other projects: one on rap and protest music in the SWANA region in the aftermath of the 2011 uprisings, and one on nationalism and the novel in Jordan. She is an Arabic-to-Italian literary translator.

Arturo Monaco is a MSCA Fellow at Sapienza University of Rome – American University of Beirut, with the project *Digital Mythology and Arabic Literature: A Digital Archive to Study the Dynamics of the Reception of Greek Myths in Modern Arabic Literature*. He holds a PhD from Sapienza University of Rome. His PhD dissertation resulted in the book *Surrealismi arabi 1938–1970: Il Surrealismo e la letteratura araba in Egitto, Siria e Libano* (2020). His research interests include modern Arabic poetry, Arab literary press, intercultural exchanges between Arabic and foreign literatures. In the latter field, he translated Sulaymān al-Bustānī's Introduction for his own translation of Homer's *Iliad* (2022).

Part 1

Theorising Peace and Nonviolence

Chapter 1

From *Ǧihād* "until the Day of Resurrection" to Nonviolence: The Debate on War and Peace in the Mid-1960s Post-*Nahḍah* Arab Generation

Paola Pizzi

Abstract

Attempts to conceptualise about war and peace on the basis of the Qur'ān appear very early in Islamic literature, where we witness a marked tendency to resizing the polysemic Qur'ānic notion of *ǧihād* in favour of its military meaning. Peace is conceived either as the goal of *ǧihād* or as the absence of the grounds for waging it. Nevertheless, a dissenting stance has always existed: in modern times this led to the emergence of different interpretive paradigms according to which peace acquires a more autonomous status. This chapter analyses three works representing three different approaches to the doctrine of *ǧihād* adopted by the mid-1960s post-*Nahḍah* Arab generation. In particular, it highlights how different epistemological assumptions deeply influence both the discourse on peace and war in Islam and the doctrinal implications of such a debate, notably the emergence of an endogenous theory of nonviolence.

Keywords: contemporary Islam, *ǧihād*, *da'wah*, nonviolence, Qur'ānic hermeneutics

1. Introduction

It is well known that the concept of war is not alien to the Qur'ān. To some extent, one may argue that the alleged "combative nature" of Islam is a matter of course. Actually, the idea that *ǧihād* is one of the central axes of the religion founded by the prophet Muḥammad in the 7th century, if not its real cornerstone, is commonplace in public opinion. A certain essentialist approach, focusing on *ǧihād* as a predominant paradigm for interpreting Islamic doctrine and history as a whole, is not extraneous even to the academic field. According to the prominent peacebuilding scholar Mohammed Abu-Nimer, such an approach tends to apply "a *jihad*-lens" to Muslims' behaviours and discourses alike[1]. Yet, in the sacred text of Muslims and in Islamic religious discourse in general, the concept of peace is not less common than war. The word *salām* ("peace"), derived from the Arabic root *s-l-m*, appears 42 times in the Qur'ān and a dozen times in other forms with the same root and with a similar meaning, like *silm*, *salam* or *salm*[2]. As for the concept of war, the corresponding word in Arabic, *ḥarb* (from the root *ḥ-r-b*), appears only 4 times in the Qur'ān, and the same applies to the word *ǧihād* (from the root *ǧ-h-d*), literally "effort". The verb *ǧāhada*, "to strive (on the path of God, *fī sabīl Allāh*)'[3], is found 27 times[4], mostly in the third person plural, while its active participle *muǧāhid(ūn)*, "those who strive/fight", is found 4 times.

It is worth noting, however, that the Qur'ānic meaning of the lexeme *ǧihād* is not always clearly and unequivocally that of a violent, military effort: this is the meaning that can be attributed to the range of nouns deriving from the root *q-t-l*, "to kill", with 170 instances in the Qur'ān

1. See Abu-Nimer 2000, p. 222. According to the American scholar, this tendency can be found in the works of Bernard Lewis and Daniel Pipes, among others.
2. See http://corpus.quran.com/qurandictionary.jsp?q=slm. In all its derivations, which include words like *islām* and *muslim* (lit. *submission* and *to be submitted*), the root *s-l-m* appears 140 times. Slight differences may occur in the translation of these terms according to the context as well as the understanding of the translator himself.
3. Literally, *fī sabīl Allāh*, which often appears in the semantic field of the root *ǧ-h-d*, as is the case with the lexeme *ṣabr*, "patience", a fact which has been neglected by many scholars.
4. See http://corpus.quran.com/qurandictionary.jsp?q=jhd. Other nouns derived from the same root *ǧ-h-d* are *ǧuhd* (effort) and *ǧahda* (strongest), attested one and five times respectively.

(especially the ubiquitous third form infinitive *qitāl*, "struggle", "fight")[5]. Alfred Morabia points out that, despite the considerable number of occurrences of this root, the combat provisions contained in the Qur'ān are characterised by their generic nature, and nothing is said about the modalities or the precise aims of the fight, nor is it exalted as such. Instead, "l'accent est mis sur l'obéissance aux injonctions, souvent vigoureuses, du Seigneur, de soumettre les adversaires, qualifiés d''infidèles'"[6]. Moreover, as Fred M. Donner observes, while it is true that we find very harsh verses in the Qur'ān concerning the enemies of believers, "It is a distinctive feature of Qur'anic discourse, however, that many of its most uncompromising indictments of unbelief and impious behavior are conjoined with mitigating clauses that temper their apparent harshness and provide an opening for a more flexible approach"[7].

But the way Islam was spread by the prophet Muḥammad and his followers after the *hiğrah*, "emigration", from Mecca to Medina – namely, "also" through military campaigns – has progressively crystallised the meaning of *ğihād fī sabīl Allāh* in its military dimension, consequently overshadowing its polysemic value. Nonetheless, as Asma Afsaruddin observes, a diachronic survey of the existing material

> allows us to credibly exhume a repertoire of meanings assigned to *jihād* and martyrdom that were far more variegated, fluid, and contested in the early formative period (comprised roughly of the first three centuries of Islam) when compared with later centuries. The subsequent predominance of the legal/military dimensions of these terms attests to the eventual ascendancy of the scholarly juridical class and a powerful administrative/military bureaucracy, leading to the marginalization of important early perspectives[8].

Actually, the rapid territorial expansion in the first two centuries of Islam profoundly influenced the subsequent codification of the doctrine of *ğihād* and of the legal conditions of peace and war[9]. The 8th century already witnessed the development of a *ğihād* and *siyar* genre, which dealt first with

5. See http://corpus.quran.com/qurandictionary.jsp?q=qtl.
6. Morabia 1993, p. 142.
7. Donner 2012, p. 83.
8. Afsaruddin 2013, pp. 8–9.
9. Zappa 2002, pp. 48–49.

the law and rules of war, and second with the so-called "law of nations", that is, the whole of regulations which determine the nature of relations with non-Muslims in times of peace. According to Majid Khadduri, these regulations are indeed "only a temporary device to regulate the relations of Muslims with the outside world during non-hostile periods (i.e., when the jihād was in suspense), until the dār al-Islām should comprise the whole world"[10], but he observes at the same time that

> The Islamic state was compelled in practice to accommodate itself to the realities of surrounding conditions and to accept certain limitations, notwithstanding that in theory it recognised no state besides itself. Unable to incorporate the whole of mankind, the Islamic state tacitly accepted the principle of coexistence with others and conducted its external relations in accordance with principles derived from Islamic doctrine and from its long experience with other states[11].

Hence, the shifts that occurred in the concept of *ǧihād* are the result of both the particular perspective and position of traditionists and jurists, and the necessities of the context. Nevertheless, a "dissenting literature"[12] challenging the mainstream, military interpretation of *ǧihād* has always persisted. In other words, we also attest to a discourse intended to resize the military scope of *ǧihād* and to restrict its field of application. According to Leonardo Capezzone, the large-scale circulation in mediaeval times of some disputed *aḥādīṯ* (pl. of *ḥadīṯ*, i.e., oral tradition attributed to the prophet Muḥammad) that exalt spiritual *ǧihād* is a sign of a widespread tendency to non-belligerence and a refusal to combat[13]. In modern times, starting with the *Nahḍah* movement in the mid-19th century, an increasingly heated debate has been taking place between an apologetic and a militant position. The first tends to emphasise the concept of "defensive *ǧihād*" in order to scale down the use of force in Islamic action; the latter is both interventionist and radical in considering *ǧihād* as a privileged

10. Khadduri 1955, p. 145.
11. Khadduri 1966, p. 20.
12. Afsaruddin 2013, p. 4.
13. Capezzone 2016, p. 213. One of those *aḥādīṯ*, "We have returned from the lesser *ǧihād* to the greater *ǧihād*", is reported by the Persian jurist al-Bayhaqī (994–1066), but it does not appear in the six canonical collections. It is generally considered "weak" (*ḍaʿīf*).

means to establish an authentically Islamic society and pave the way to the creation of a truly Islamic state.

Both positions were further developed by what I call the post-*Nahḍah* generation, where we see either a radicalisation of the idea of armed *ğihād*, attempts at limiting its scope through new readings of the juridical tradition or ground-breaking steps towards an Islamic theory of nonviolence. The dialectic between these different positions and the increasing importance attributed to *ğihād* in the Islamic debate within Muslim societies is reflected in the abundant literature that appeared in the last century. An example of this debate is provided by three pivotal works published at about the same time in the 1960s which exemplify three different approaches to the theorisation of war and peace in Islam:

1. *Āṯār al-ḥarb: dirāsah fiqhiyyah muqāranah* (The Effects of War: A Comparative Juridical Study, 1962–1963) by the prominent Syrian jurist Wahbah al-Zuḥaylī (1932–2015), a ponderous juridical treatise that gained large popularity and critical success;
2. *Maʿālim fī l-ṭarīq* (Milestones, 1964) by the Egyptian thinker and prominent member of the Muslim Brothers Sayyid Quṭb (1906–1966), a manifesto that influenced generations of Islamists;
3. *Maḏhab ibn Ādam al-awwal: muškilat al-ʿunf fī l-ʿamal al-islāmī* (The Doctrine of Adam's First Son: The Problem of Violence in Islamic Action, 1966) by the Syrian theologian and preacher Ğawdat Saʿīd (1931–2022), one of the main theorists of nonviolence in Islam.

While the jurist Wahbah al-Zuḥaylī and the activist Sayyid Quṭb were concerned, though from different perspectives and with distinct purposes, to confirm the centrality of *ğihād*, the preacher Ğawdat Saʿīd was the first to theorise nonviolence in Islam. This is a fact that deserves deeper insight not merely into the general historical context in which these works arose but more specifically into their respective methodology and epistemology, a focus that existing academic studies often failed to emphasise in their outlook. Actually, most studies range from considering the bulk and early appearance of the material on military *ğihād* in Islamic literature as a proof of its "intrinsic" character as a doctrinal position[14] to emphasising the polysemy of this concept through a survey of the diachronic developments and the shifts of meaning that occurred in it[15].

A comparative analysis of the content of the above-mentioned works will help highlight some of the peculiarities of each approach in order to show the extent to which the involvement of different epistemologies impacts the ongoing debate on war and peace in Islam, thus determining its versatility and paving the way to further, potential doctrinal developments.

2. Wahbah al-Zuḥaylī and the juridical codification of *ǧihād*

The Syrian jurist Wahbah al-Zuḥaylī served as Dean of the Department of Islamic Law at the Faculty of Šarīʿah at Damascus University during the 1960s[16] and then as a professor in Syria and abroad. His major juridical treatise *Āṯār al-ḥarb: dirāsah fiqhiyyah muqāranah* can be considered a pioneering work at that time, especially due to the author's choice to

14. In addition to the authors cited by Abu-Nimer (see note 1), another example in this sense is provided by David Cook and his pivotal work *Understanding Jihad*, where he describes *ǧihād* as "warfare with spiritual significance" (Cook 2015, p. 2). Cook claims that the Qurʾān, with its abundant contents related to *ǧihād*, "presents a well-developed religious justification for waging war against Islam's enemies" and that, in summary, "the text provides the religious basis for the doctrine of jihad that would result in the great Muslim conquests of the seventh and eighth centuries" (ibid., p. 11).
15. Beside the already quoted study of Asma Afsaruddin, it is worth mentioning here the work of Māhir Šarīf, *Taṭawwur mafhūm al-ǧihād fī l-fikr al-islāmī* (The Development of the Concept of Ǧihād in Islamic Thought). Here, this Syrian historian presents a series of texts on *ǧihād* from the first appearance of the *siyar* literature to the present, focusing in particular on the *Nahḍah* period and describing the implications of the ruptures that occurred at the level of religious reform on the further developments of the doctrine of *ǧihād*. According to Šarīf, the emergence of new voices who question the predominant, belligerent interpretation of *ǧihād* represents "an attempt to reconnect what was broken in the path of religious reform and the revivification of the critical, rationalist and open tradition that it generated" (Šarīf 2008, p. 7).
16. The Faculty was founded in 1954 by a group of intellectuals of the reformist wing of the Muslim Brothers, among which Muṣṭafā al-Sibāʿī (1915–1964), the founder of the Syrian branch of the movement. Wahbah al-Zuḥaylī himself is considered to be a sympathiser of the movement. See Pierret 2013, pp. 36 and 39.

focus on the issue of war and peace in Islam from a comparative, juridical point of view. The text gained huge popularity and critical success all over the world. Zuḥaylī's main idea is that war – in Arabic, *ḥarb*, by which the author clearly means military *ğihād* – must not be understood as the normal and permanent condition of an Islamic state but only as a temporary one. The whole work is an attempt both to assess the juridical tradition on *ğihād* and to reinterpret it in light of the interest (*maṣlaḥah*), principles, and general purposes (*maqāṣid*) of Islam, thus creating the conditions for establishing a hierarchy of concepts in which the doctrine of *ğihād* is repurposed as a tool aimed to establish and safeguard peace when all other means are ineffective.

Muhammad Tahir Mansoori describes al-Zuḥaylī's legal theory on war and peace in Islam as providing a "very strong conceptual foundation for a peace-building approach" and "a strong basis in the *Sharīʿah* for promoting cooperation among the members of the world community"[17]. An analysis of the Syrian jurist's theoretical framework, however, reveals some aporias, which are not always resolved convincingly. A first observation concerns precisely the comparative perspective chosen by the author as the general approach taken by his study:

> Our research will demonstrate that Islam preceded the international law in many of its dispositions and principles, mainly with regard to the international principles of honour, human justice and global peace. Thereby, the false beliefs of some jurists that the provisions of Islamic law are deficient compared to those of modern international law – even though the provisions of Islamic law that coincide with the latter are many and of a general nature, and its sources are flexible – are dispelled. The fact is that international law is based on a regional foundation distributed among independent countries, while Islamic *šarīʿah* is based on human considerations. In fact, Islamic propaganda (*daʿwah*) is by its very nature a world propaganda and Islamic provisions are religious provisions, sanctioned from religion, and to implement them is the faith of the Muslims and the strength of their firm belief, as it is for all religious provisions, and their purpose is to reform the world[18].

17. Mansoori 2007, p. 435.
18. Zuḥaylī 2018, p. 29. Unless otherwise noted, all translations from Arabic are mine.

By comparing international law as a positive legal system to *šarīʿah* as a religious legal system, the author intends to show the ethical and moral superiority of the latter by virtue of its divine source and the universal vocation of Islamic *daʿwah*. Moreover, he presupposes that the classical elaboration of this system is still in effect today. In this way, al-Zuḥaylī establishes an axiom that makes the comparative approach a purely apologetic exercise, leading al-Zuḥaylī's discourse into the impasse of tautology, as we will try to show in the course of our investigation.

Another preliminary reflection concerns the title itself: the author refers to *ḥarb* and not to *ğihād*, and this implies an identification between the two concepts, and a clear stance towards the meaning he attributes to the Qurʾānic concept of *ğihād*, namely, that of armed combat. As al-Zuḥaylī states, "*ğihād*, war (*ḥarb*) and razzia (*ġazw*) in the origin of the Arabic language revolve around a single meaning, namely the fight against the enemy"[19]. As he observes shortly afterwards, "This is the meaning of *ğihād* among Muslims, as their jurists (*fuqahāʾ*) have conceptualised it"[20].

Zuḥaylī clarifies that the *fuqahāʾ* list three types of enemies – the external one, Satan, and the soul – thus confirming, at least in principle, the polysemy of the term *ğihād*. At the same time, he points to the military meaning as the one that has been developed in *fiqh*. The juridical *corpus* is thus handled as a source of authority for the understanding of primary texts: "Law establishes the way to achieve religious purposes, and religion gives law approval and acceptance"[21]. As al-Zuḥaylī acknowledges, it is true that the work of the *fuqahāʾ* consisted above all in codifying the context, thus legitimising the dominant vision of the world that produced it (namely, that of the rulers)[22], but, in his opinion, the consequences he derives from this consideration only apply to some specific aspects. This is the case, for example, with the division of the world into *dār al-Islām*, the "abode of Islam", and *dār al-ḥarb*, the "abode of war, which reflects a *Weltanschauung* according to which the foundation of *ğihād* is unbelief (*kufr*), an opinion that he rejects categorically. Nevertheless, such an

19. Ibid., p. 45.
20. Ibid., p. 47.
21. Ibid., p. 50.
22. As Morabia observes about the formation of the doctrine of *ğihād*, "la théorie n'a pas déterminé l'action des conquérants. C'est plutôt celle-ci qui a imprimé sa marque à la théorie, à tout le moins pour le premier siècle de l'Islam" (Morabia 1993, p. 184).

attempt to contextualise classical legal provisions does not concern the status of *ğihād*, which is immutable.

According to al-Zuḥaylī, while war is not to be understood as a permanent condition in Islam, it is unthinkable to imagine a world without war; therefore "none of the jurists of Islam has ever come to prohibit war, since it is a utopian and abstract opinion, whose invalidity has been proven by events"[23]. This excludes any theorisation about nonviolence from a juridical point of view but not a theorisation of peace, which Zuḥaylī regards as one of the essential purposes of *ğihād*. Even so, peace is hardly described as having its own ontological status, namely as being irreducible to and independent of any other conceptual category. Rather, it is conceived as the absence of motives for engaging in *ğihād*. But which are these motives? Here lies – in his view – one of the fundamental differences between the concept of war (*ḥarb*) in the Western legal definition and Islamic *ğihād*: if the aim of war is the pursuit of particular political ends, the motive for *ğihād* is

> to repel an aggression, protect the Muslim community, or eliminate the injustice of rulers who pose insurmountable obstacles to the Islamic *da'wah* and spurn it in order to eliminate the dissidence (*fitnah*) in religion so that the word of God and the truth are exalted, and the principles of justice, goodness, and moral excellence prevail, since Islam in reality is the great reforming message that is essential for the good of the peoples themselves[24].

In this sense, *ğihād* "is an obligation for Muslims to help Islam, after the enemy has created the conditions for it, contrary to war (*ḥarb*) [in international law] whose aim is to attack" in order to pursue "material goals"[25]. In this statement, however, we can identify another aporia: if, as al-Zuḥaylī says, *ğihād* is legitimised by the resistance that Muslims encounter on the path of the *da'wah*, the principle of "defence" applies only to Muslims, however, and does not seem to be valid for those people who resist the message. Indeed, considering *da'wah* to be the calling of Islam implies that a series of tools have to be put in place to protect it,

23. Zuḥaylī 2018, p. 38.
24. Ibid., p. 50.
25. Ibid., pp. 47 and 50.

including force: "It is obvious that the global *da'wah* necessarily implies a force to protect it and a shield that preserves it because truth and freedom subsist in the shadow of force and order, and the implementation of the juridical provisions and of the social rules is not realised without an authority, as well as the survival and power of the group do not subsist without a government"[26].

In these few lines, several decisive postulates are condensed: first of all, an organic link is established between religious propaganda and the use of force, even if only with a defensive purpose. In other words, *da'wah* requires strength. Thus, we witness a drastic redimensioning of the doctrinal autonomy of the phase of the peaceful and nonviolent preaching of the prophet Muḥammad at Mecca (610–622 AD), which in Zuḥaylī's perspective becomes functional to the subsequent phase, taking place in Medina (622–632 AD), when the Muslim community was allowed for the first time to resort to fighting through an *ad hoc* revelation[27]. Here, a second postulate can be identified: during the Meccan period, fighting was not allowed because the community was not strong enough. This is what al-Zuḥaylī clarifies shortly afterwards, when he states that, in Medina, "fighting was authorised in order to repel the aggressions and protect the *da'wah*, after the Muslims had become strong and after they had formed their own state and had become a nation"[28].

Thus, the Meccan *da'wah* is reduced to a mere "strategic" choice while waiting for the community to be strong enough to engage in armed combat, which must be waged within the legal and institutional framework of a state. Thus, the arbitrary use of force is discouraged, but, at the same time – and this is the third postulate – religious propaganda, *ǧihād*, and the creation of a state become inseparable, including all that comes with it in terms of the status of non-Muslims in the context of a hypothetical Islamic state. How does a similar state envision the principle of full

26. Ibid., p. 72.
27. Qur. XXII:39–40: "Those who have been attacked are permitted to take up arms because they have been wronged – God has the power to help them – those who have been driven unjustly from their homes only for saying, 'Our Lord is God'. If God did not repel some people by means of others, many monasteries, churches, synagogues, and mosques, where God's name is much invoked, would have been destroyed [...]" (trans. Abdel Haleem 2010).
28. Zuḥaylī 2018, pp. 79–80.

citizenship, implying the right for all to equally participate in political and institutional life, regardless of their religious affiliation? And how does a society based on the primacy of the *daʿwah* come to terms with the freedom of expression, opinion, and speech? Except for a general declaration of principles, these are all matters left to great uncertainty.

It is true that, for al-Zuḥaylī, the peaceful *daʿwah* has never been "abrogated", despite what some jurists claim by invoking the principle of *nasḫ*, that is, "abrogation" of one or more verses by another – mainly in favour of the more belligerent ones. But it can be carried out only as long as it is not threatened, that is, until the conditions for engaging *ğihād* are met. As al-Zuḥaylī explains, "it is very clear that Islam was not founded on fighting (*qitāl*) as an instrument for its spread, but combat was a natural development necessitated by the nature of the *daʿwah*, prepared by the situation and circumstances of the latter, from the position of Arab, Jewish and Byzantine unbelievers towards it, and [by the need to] protect the preachers (*duʿāt*)"[29].

Thus, *ğihād* is the tool for defending the *daʿwah*, which in turn is the tool for spreading Islam. At this point, one wonders where the boundary is between peaceful proclamation and the use of force whenever the *daʿwah*, even though not arousing violent resistance, does not produce the desired results, namely, the acceptance of Islam as a message that humanity – as mentioned – fundamentally needs. A solution to this aporia can be found in the "flexibility" that the *fiqh* applies to the regulation of relations with non-Muslims: in fact, not only do they "technically" have the possibility to choose between three options – Islam, protection (*ḏimmah*), or combat – but also "these three options do not exclude others"[30]. On the contrary, right from the early period of Islam, other forms of coexistence have also been implemented:

> Muslims agree that the competent authority (*walī l-amr*) can enter into any agreement that in his opinion fulfils the general interest (*maṣlaḥah*), and this demonstrates that the fundamental purpose of Islam is to achieve a stable state of peace and to ensure that *daʿwah* is practised freely. At that point, it is possible to make agreements with the Russians, Indians, and so on, depending on the interest, and

29. Ibid., p. 81.
30. Ibid., p. 102.

> without making the payment of the *ğizyah*[31] as a condition, so that the famous choice of one of the three previous options will have the sole purpose of inducing people to accept Islam externally[32].

Peace is therefore indeed a fundamental purpose of Islam, but it is at the ruler's discretion to deploy those tools that guarantee a peaceful coexistence with the "others", depending on the circumstances as well as his personal judgment. If this contractual flexibility paves the way for an extension of the forms with which peace between peoples can be agreed, there is still a fundamental asymmetry in the status of Muslims and non-Muslims[33], so that the concept of peace continues to be conceived as nothing more than the "absence of conflict".

In conclusion, if from a global perspective, al-Zuḥaylī's work represents a significant contribution to a reopening of the "door of the *iğtihād*" in the juridical field, and particularly with regard to the doctrine of *ğihād*, we see here the hegemony of the juridical paradigm which excludes the integration of new sources and new methods. As a consequence, the margin of interpretation, and therefore of renewal, of the juridical and doctrinal categories, is drastically limited.

Actually, according to my analysis, al-Zuḥaylī does not proceed to a real epistemological critique of the traditional juridical heritage whose normativity is largely still valid today. It is true that he adopts a restrictive meaning of *ğihād*, but this leads to some aporias which are difficult to overcome: the idea that the purpose of *ğihād* is not to spread Islam but to defend the *daʿwah*, which is itself the tool for spreading Islam, is a major

31. That is the tax owed by the members of the so-called "people of the Book" (*ahl al-kitāb*), i.e., Jews, Christians, and Zoroastrians, recognised in Islam by virtue of their possession of a revealed book, in return for the "protection" (*ḏimmah*) from which they benefit in an Islamic state, according to the classical legal codification.
32. Zuḥaylī 2018, pp. 102–103.
33. It must be said that al-Zuḥaylī seems to depart from such a traditional distinction, as he states that "the non-Muslim with whom there is a form of agreement is not considered a second-rate citizen as some claim, but he and the Muslim have the same degree of citizenship". Elsewhere, however, he describes – as "a natural thing and an expression of the majority" – the fact that, in an Islamic state, the ruler or the army chief is a Muslim, a principle that is inadmissible in a state based on full citizenship, as is the case for the concept of "nationality of the Islamic state" (ibid., pp. 142 and 144).

example of this dead end. The abundance of mitigating phrases serves the strongly apologetic and defensive structure of the text, which in my opinion, however, does not solve a basic problem, namely the absence, in Islamic legal codification, of an autonomous ontological status of the concept of peace, which is mostly defined in relation to *ǧihād* and as one of its fruits. Moreover, the concern to safeguard the centrality of *ǧihād* is made explicit in a clarification that the author makes at the end of his introduction to the second edition, dating back to 1965:

> To avoid misunderstandings and inferences that some of the readers of this book have fallen into, I want to draw attention to the fact that, analysing the question of *ǧihād* in Islam, I do not intend to affirm that it is only a defensive principle. On the contrary, Muslims can engage in combat if those authorised to do so see an interest in it or if there is some political opportunity in engaging in a battle and in managing the conflict, and if they have full control of the elements that determine the outcomes of a global conflict with the enemy. For us, this clarifies the nature of the battles and the conquests waged by Muslims in the past, so it is permitted to follow their method at present – yet avoiding aggression and injustice, as these are two things prohibited by the general principles of Islam, and provided that the purpose of *ǧihād* is that of reaching a supreme human end, the realisation of justice, and a true and positive peace[34].

Indeed, the urge to free himself from the accusation of aiming in some way at diminishing the combative dimension of *ǧihād* reveals how much the issue was debated at the time, so he adopted a polemic stance towards those contemporaries who labelled the theorists of "resizing" *ǧihād* as defeatists. Sayyid Quṭb played a prominent role among them[35].

3. Sayyid Quṭb and *Ǧihād* "until the Day of Resurrection"

The rejection of *defensive ǧihād* is just one of the aspects of the doctrine of *militant ǧihād* as theorised by the Egyptian thinker and activist

34. Ibid., pp. 21–22.
35. This debate is much more interesting if we remember, as explained above, that al-Zuḥaylī was a sympathizer of the Muslim Brotherhood, of which Quṭb was a prominent theorist.

Sayyid Quṭb in his *Maʿālim fī l-ṭarīq*. Quṭb was a prolific writer and the main ideologist of the Muslim Brotherhood. Among other works, he was the author of an commentary of the Qurʾān, *Fī ẓilāl al-Qurʾān*, which he wrote while in prison, between 1954 and 1964, following an alleged assassination attempt on the Egyptian president Ğamāl ʿAbd al-Nāṣir, for which the Islamist movement was held responsible. Like the commentary, *Maʿālim fī l-ṭarīq* was also written in prison and published in 1964, immediately gaining great public success but also inviting harsh criticism both by "official" Islam and from within Quṭb's own organisation. The head of the Muslim Brotherhood, Ḥasan al-Huḍaybī (1891–1973), distanced himself from its militant contents[36]. The radical ideas expressed in this work led to his further arrest in 1965, along with other members of the movement suspected of preparing a coup d'état, and his eventual death sentence. He was hanged a year later, on 29 August 1966.

The book *Maʿālim fī l-ṭarīq* develops a range of key ideological categories – such as that of "servitude to God alone" (*ʿubūdiyyah*), of "sovereignty of God" (*ḥākimiyyah*), of *ğāhiliyyah*, the pre-Islamic "ignorance", as a meta-historical concept applicable to those who do not submit to this sovereignty, and the practice of "anathema" (*takfīr*) deriving from it[37]. All these were going to become fundamental references for future radical Islamist movements. For the purpose of this study, I focus in particular on those elements that help us delineate his understanding of the doctrine of *ğihād*, which is "dogmatised" in its military sense to the detriment of all other meanings. Furthermore, its effectiveness is even extended regardless of any space-time context, thus becoming the standard of a true and sincere adherence to the Islamic method (*al-minhağ al-islāmī*) as Quṭb conceives it. By declaring the moral failure of Western ideologies such as Marxism, socialism, and nationalism, and hence of those governments that adopted them within the Muslim world, he declares the need

---

36. He later replied to the positions of Sayyid Quṭb with a pamphlet called *Duʿāh lā quḍāh* (Preachers, Not Judges), which was written in 1969 but published later in 1977. See Manduchi 2019, p. 51.
37. We are speaking of the "development" of such categories because they were already circulating in the Islamist discourse, which drew on contemporary sources, mainly the Pakistani theologian and politician Abū l-Aʿlà al-Mawdūdī (1903–1979). We describe this development as "ideological" because of Quṭb's ahistorical interpretation of the sources to corroborate his theoretical framework.

of "a new leadership for humanity"[38] to save it from the lack of values that characterises the Western system. This is why "the turn of Islam has come, the turn of the Islamic community (*ummah*)"[39], which, however, is far from ready to take a leading role, which was lost when Muslims abandoned the *šarī'ah*:

> It is necessary to ensure that this *ummah* exists once more, so that Islam can once again play the role that awaits it at the helm of humanity. What is needed is a "rebirth" of this *ummah*, which has an accumulation of generations, conceptualisations, situations and regimes behind it that have nothing to do with Islam, although it continues to claim to exist in the so-called "Islamic world"[40].

Thus, on the one hand, the West is rejected because it is considered to be morally unsuitable to play a role in world leadership. On the other hand, however, Islamic society in its current predicament is rejected as well as it is equally unsuitable to assume this role: immersed as it is in ignorance (*ğāhiliyyah*), it has moved away from the Islamic ideal embodied by the first generation of Muslims. The latter had understood the inseparable link between faith in the one God and the activity of spreading it, which is now to be restored by a chosen *avant-garde* (*ṭalī'ah*): the book was written for this *avant-garde* to indicate the "milestones" of its duty[41]. What we observe here is an attempt to make a clean sweep to establish a new and unique paradigm for interpreting the goals of Islam and the duties of the *ummah*. Indeed, not only does Quṭb dissociate himself from the reality that surrounds him, he also breaks with the past in favour of an archetypal and mythical vision of it, which – as we will see – is functional to his conception of a dogmatic *ğihād* that transcends time and space, thus escaping any further interpretation. In this sense, one must refrain from theorising on religious matters:

> When we want to make Islam a theory to be studied, we alienate it from the nature of the method of divine creation and from the nature of the method of divine thought, and we submit it to human methods

38. Quṭb 1979, p. 4.
39. Ibid., p. 5.
40. Ibid., p. 6.
41. Ibid., pp. 9–10.

> of thought! As if the divine method were inferior to human methods! And as if we wanted to advance God's method in terms of concept and action, so as to equate it with the methods of human beings! The issue, from this point of view, is dangerous, and the [resulting] defeat is lethal[42].

This method establishes the primacy of action over rational theorisation: any attempt to apply human reason to revelation is explicitly equated to a real threat to God's method. Accordingly, there is no room for hermeneutics, much less for reflection on its epistemological foundations. Any activity of interpretation is thus delegitimised and a real methodological competition – if not a conflict – is established between God and humans, from which the "divine method" comes out on top by virtue of its dogmatic, universal, and hence coercive, value. This is expressed by means of a perfect tautology: "The 'method' is equivalent to the 'truth' and there is no conceptual separation between the two: any extraneous method cannot lead to the realisation of Islam"[43]. In such a system, the only function accorded to human beings is that of total submission and obedience to God:

> Submission (*islām*) to God is the global foundation to which all human beings must return, or reconcile with, so as they don't put any political system or material force as an obstacle to the *da'wah*, and leave the field open so that every individual can choose it or not according to their free will, but without resisting it or fighting it. And if someone does that, *islām* has the duty to fight him until death or until he surrenders[44].

Islam has indeed come to free people from mutual enslavement and to transfer to God alone the prerogative of being served (*'ubūdiyyah*), but this implies a "total revolution against the sovereignty (*ḥākimiyyah*) of men" with the aim to "destroy the kingdom of men and establish the

42. Ibid., pp. 42–43.
43. Ibid., p. 45. The late prominent Egyptian theologian Naṣr Ḥāmid Abū Zayd (1943–2010) describes brilliantly, and even ironically, this tautological approach when he defines Quṭb's concept of *ḥākimiyyah* as "the institution of the authority of the text on the basis of the authority of the text" (Abū Zayd 2017, p. 107).
44. Quṭb 1979, pp. 58–59.

kingdom of God on earth"[45] by means of *ǧihād*. The *da'wah*, therefore, is not sufficient to make God's religion triumph on earth, and the experience of the prophets is a proof of this: action is required to eliminate any form of human government in order to establish God's, which is based on the *šarī'ah*. In other words, "*ǧihād* is a requirement of the *da'wah*"[46] and cannot be reduced to a purely defensive action, which is the stance of the defeated (*mahzūmīn*), who seek in this way to reject the accusations made by the West against *ǧihād* as a means of spreading the faith through violence. Actually, according to Quṭb, this is where the decisive difference between religion and faith lies:

> the meaning of religion (*dīn*) is wider than that of faith (*'aqīdah*): religion is the method and system that governs life, which is based in Islam on faith but in general is broader than faith. In Islam, different communities can be submitted to the general method which is based on the principle of God's sovereignty (*ḥākimiyyah*), even if some communities have not embraced the faith in Islam"[47].

Religion is hence the dimension containing faith and in which the latter can be exercised "freely". Therefore, freedom of belief is guaranteed only *after* the religion of God is established throughout the earth: Islam is the only framework in which religious pluralism sanctioned by Qur. II:256. "There is no compulsion in religion", is implemented, with all that derives from that in terms of the status of non-Muslims – as we have already pointed out above. Consequently, the concept of the "sovereignty of God" reveals an essentially political significance from which derives that of *ǧihād* as a political struggle: "There [will be] no compulsion in religion only after the liberation from the power of men and after the establishment of the principle according to which everything belongs to God, namely, that all religion belongs to God"[43].

Actually, Quṭb clarifies, in the Qur'ān we see a progression towards the generality of *ǧihād* and not a contraction of it. After the initial forbidding

45. Ibid., pp. 59–60.
46. Ibid., p. 66.
47. Ibid., p. 64.
48. Ibid., p. 74. Thus, as Abū Zayd observes, the role and general purpose of Islam is reduced to "the liberation of men from reciprocal enslavement in order to subject it to another type of enslavement" (Abū Zayd 2017, p. 112).

of violence during the Meccan and early Medinese period, armed combat will later be authorised to cope with opponents, until it takes on the character of a general command:

> This refraining from fighting in Mecca was nothing more than a phase in a long plan, and the same applies to the very first period of the *hiğrah*. What prompted the Muslim community in Medina to expand after the first period was not simply the protection of the city: this was an indispensable initial goal, but it was not the final goal. It was a goal to guarantee the tool and ensure the basis to expand in order to free people and to eliminate the obstacles that prevent them from expanding[49].

It is evident here that the normativity of the Meccan nonviolent method is overcome by the Medinese period so that the search for peace can only be accomplished through *ğihād*: "When Islam seeks peace (*silm*), it does not mean a cheap peace, that is, the simple guarantee of a space in which the Islamic faith can be practised. No, it wants a peace in which all religion belongs to God, that is, in which all men are subservient to God, and in which men do not take others as their masters in the place of God"[50]. In essence, *ğihād* is the tool for realising the universalistic project of Islam in a metahistorical dimension characterised by the archetypal struggle between Islam and *ğāhiliyyah*, which overcomes – by radicalising it – the historical-juridical opposition between *dār al-Islām* and *dār al-ḥarb*[51]: "The battle is constant, and *ğihād* goes on until the day of Resurrection"[52].

In conclusion, a fundamental epistemological problem arises in Sayyid Quṭb's thought with regard to *ğihād*, the premise of which is the total identification between his theoretical framework and the "truth." By refusing any historical and hermeneutical approach to the interpretation of revelation, Quṭb's method seems to be based on a series of ideological assumptions aimed at legitimising a totalitarian political project, which is assimilated with God's project *tout-court*. In this sense, *ğihād* serves not only as the means established by God to remove any opposition to His sovereignty – which is, by the way, something very anthropomorphic

49. Quṭb 1979, pp. 68–69.
50. Ibid., p. 66.
51. Manduchi 2019, p. 61.
52. Quṭb 1979, p. 119.

– but it is considered *immanent* to Islam as it remains in force until the end of time. In contrast, peace has no autonomous status, it is not an end, and it is not even a means but only the condition of passive quiescence obtained through fighting, in which God's sovereignty is exercised.

4. Ǧawdat Saʿīd and Islamic Nonviolence between the "Method of the Prophets" and the "Death of War"

The thought of the third author examined in this study is based on a completely different register, and not only in comparison with the previous ones but also more widely with respect to the general religious debate around *ğihād* in contemporary Islam. Known significantly in the Middle East as the "Gandhi of Muslims", the Syrian Sunni theologian and preacher of Circassian origins, Ǧawdat Saʿīd (Biʾr ʿAǧam, 1931-Istanbul, 2022), can be considered a pioneer in promoting a radical refusal of violence in Islamic action. His first book, *Maḏhab ibn Ādam al-awwal: muškilat al-ʿunf fī l-ʿamal al-islāmī*, written in 1966, was a pioneering attempt to shed light on this issue at that time. Hence, focusing on this work is crucial both in investigating his peculiar interpretation of the doctrine of *ğihād* and in evaluating his hermeneutical approach to the reading of the Qurʾān[53]. Indeed, according to Saʿīd, the holy book of Islam drastically limits the use of violence and promotes peaceful change in social and political life in view of establishing an era of global peace and justice on earth. This approach has been at the core of Saʿīd's reflection on revelation throughout his life, up until his proclamation of the "death of war" and the adoption of radical nonviolence as the supreme ethical goal of humankind in his later works.

In continuity with the thought of the awakening movement (*Nahḍah*) and its reformist trend (*iṣlāḥ*) – represented by its pioneer Ǧamāl al-Dīn al-Afġānī (1838–1897) and his disciple, Muḥammad ʿAbduh (1849–1905) in Egypt, and by Muhammad Iqbal (1877–1938) in India – as well as with scholars of the post-*Nahḍah* generation such as the Algerian

53. His contribution in this sense is still underestimated, and no comprehensive study on his thought has appeared yet. Among the scholars who have dealt with his ideas, it is worth mentioning Muller (2009) (in particular, pp. 562–577), Belhaj (2017), Dumairieh (2017), Menghini (2019), and Schiavo (2019), among others.

Malek Bennabi (1905–1973), Saʿīd believes that Muslim societies must bridge the gap separating them from modernity and development which prevents them from coping with the challenges they face and hinders their efficiency so that they are unable to play a constructive role on the world scene. The novelty of his thought, however, consists in having identified the very origin of the malaise of Muslims in resorting to violence in Islamic activism as an instrument to change the *status quo*.

Actually, in his view, the only way to reform Islamic societies is by peaceful means. Indeed, the rejection of violence – which he elaborated over time in increasingly radical terms, both through preaching and an intense intellectual activity in Syria as well as abroad – is the common thread of his thought. According to Saʿīd, peaceful action is the only method for achieving the transition from a society based on compulsion, force, and violence to a society based on justice, the rule of law, peace, and human dignity. Such considerations would lead him to a theory of nonviolence as a historical development of the doctrine of *ǧihād*.

Maḏhab can be considered the first of Saʿīd's efforts to provide a doctrinal foundation and legitimacy to this theoretical framework, which is deeply influenced by his interpretation of the Qurʾān and the *ḥadīṯ* corpus in relation to (and in their interaction with) reality and history. Published one year after Saʿīd's first imprisonment by the Syrian Baʿaṯhist authorities in 1965 for his open criticism of the coup government, which came to power in 1963[54], this book was intended to be an announcement (*iʿlān*) of his unilateral adherence to the "method of Adam's first son", Abel, who refused to raise his hand against his brother Cain killing him. The particular Qurʾānic account of this primordial and symbolic story, in which Abel declares his conscious refusal to commit the same fault as Cain[55], demonstrates, in Saʿīd's view, that the problem of violence lies at the very origin of human existence. At the same time, it clearly indicates the right way to face violence: that is, the radical rejection of reacting to violence with violence to the point of abstaining from self-defence. Thus, Abel becomes the archetype to which people are destined to conform.

54. Between the 1960s and the mid-1970s, Saʿīd was imprisoned five times due to his opposition, which gave rise to suspicions that he could be linked to fringe elements of the Islamist movement.

55. "If you raise your hand to kill me, I will not raise my hand to kill you. I fear God, the Lord of the worlds" (Qur. V: 28).

Moreover, according to Saʿīd, this was the method of all the prophets, who patiently and peacefully announced their message of social change, despite the hostility of the people to whom they were sent.

The purpose of Saʿīd's "announcement" is not to challenge the violent and undemocratic shift of the regime: rather, he wants to distance himself clearly and unequivocally from any improper understanding and use of *ǧihād* by Muslims as a legitimate Islamic means to overthrow an unjust ruler or to spread an idea – whether political or religious – by force. This was probably the accusation that had been levelled against him by the Syrian authorities, but it is also the one that he himself made against the Islamist movement, of which the organisation of the Muslim Brothers could be considered the main incarnation at that time. Indeed, during his stay in Egypt between 1946 and 1958, where he graduated at al-Azhar University in Cairo, he witnessed the emergence of a violent political commitment by some elements of this movement, even by means of secret activism[56], and its identification with a legitimate *ǧihād* – a development in which Saʿīd, with particular clairvoyance, identified the risk of a dangerous drift to come:

> What worries me the most and makes me insist on the matter is what I foresee will happen in the next decades, that is, the possibility that the conflict escalates, that the battle will intensify, that Muslims will be more and more powerless and that they will multiply their difficulty and incapacity to face it. This is why the preachers (*duʿāh*) must

56. Suffice it to recall the murder, by a member of the Muslim Brotherhood, of Prime Minister Maḥmūd al-Nuqrāšī in December 1948, one year after his decision to ban the organization, and the consequent murder in retaliation of the founder of the Brotherhood, Ḥasan al-Bannā, in 1949 (Guazzone 2016, p. 214). After that, the movement faced an alternation of political fortunes and misfortunes until the Free Officers' Revolution (23 July 1952). It soon came into a collision with this Revolution, which led to a harsh repression of the organisation for the years to come – as mentioned above, Sayyid Quṭb was executed in 1966, the same year that *Maḏhab* was published. As for the secret activism of the Muslim Brotherhood, it was embodied by the so-called "special regime" (*niẓām ḫāṣṣ*) that appeared in the 1940s. The latter was "[i]nspired in the first instance as an idea by the concept of jihad, formalized into an organization under the pressures of nationalist agitation", and "almost immediately rationalized as an instrument for the defence of Islam and the Society" (Mitchell 1969, p. 32). Through time, it gained an increasingly operational independence.

> think for the Muslims because the days to come will be more violent than the previous ones, unless we renew the preaching (*da'wah*) on the basis of the unchanging law (*sunnah*) with which the prophets descended into the arena of conflict and their strength was: "Our Lord is God!" (Qur. XLVI:13)[57].

This "unchanging law" is the same one that the prophet of Islam complied with, in perfect continuity with all his predecessors: during the Meccan period, Muḥammad's preaching was rigorously peaceful, as he totally abstained from violence, even in self-defence, and also prohibited his followers from using it, despite the harassment they faced by their fellow tribesmen. This "strategy" was not motivated by an alleged weakness of the early Muslims but by the goal of spreading God's message only in virtue of its truth. As Saʿīd puts it,

> The goal is that the Muslim should not be guilty of preaching (*da'wah*) to kill, that is, of inducing people to do so. The goal is that the Muslim has no other fault than that of believing in God, who is powerful and worthy of praise, and that of saying "My lord is God". The goal is that the Muslim has no other fault than the free answer of people to his call (*da'wah*) to believe in God. The goal is that no one imposes his opinion on others by force, and that no one should give up his opinion out of fear of force. The goal is that the preaching of the Muslim does not take any other path than that followed by the prophets, from beginning to end. The goal is to endure suffering because of one's principles and not to impose one's principles by making others suffer[58].

After the *hiğrah* to Medina, with the creation of a first nucleus of Islamic state following a consensus-based agreement – the so-called Constitution of Medina, which regulated the relations between the prophet Muḥammad and the local tribes – *ğihād* was permitted but only to defend the newly established community, as Qur. XXII:39–40 clearly states. This method was preserved during the era of the four Rightly Guided caliphs who succeeded Muḥammad after his death in 632 AD, but soon after, that is from ca. 661 AD on, political violence and the usurpation of power, including

57. Saʿīd 1993b, p. 210.
58. Saʿīd 1993b, p. 93.

the enforcement of dynastic succession, got the upper hand, and Muslims still live in this situation up to the present. A critical study of the sources reporting the emergence of the Islamic society in Medina, as well as an evaluation of its political development, need separate research: what matters here is the dramatic consequence that Saʿīd draws from this interpretation of proto-Islamic history, namely that there is no such Islamic society today that satisfies the criteria of "democracy" that would make it eligible to endorse and implement *ğihād*, as was the case for the first Islamic society. With this statement, he is de facto declaring that *ğihād* is not viable nowadays. Addressing his interlocutors, Saʿīd argues:

> Do you think that God has prescribed this duty for you – the duty to fight in a society not subject to Islam – while you are incapable of doing what God has commanded you to do in all situations, that is, to speak the truth wherever you are, without fear of criticism? Telling the truth is what God has commanded you, and this is how Islamic society is formed. Once the Islamic society is formed and whoever has received the delegation calls you to *ğihād*, if you back down, that's when you have failed in one of the great obligations of Islam[59].

Saʿīd is very careful to reassure his co-religionists that he has no intention of abolishing the doctrine of *ğihād*, but at the same time he firmly believes that *ğihād* has very specific conditions, which Muslims have forgotten:

> We do not say that fighting is absolutely forbidden [...] indeed we believe that *gihād* always remains in force, but Muslims must know when it is lawful to implement the sanctions established by God. I can say with great certainty that Muslims have been harmed equally by the fact that they tried to engage in *ğihād* and combat without being an Islamic society distinct from the others, and by the inadequacy of those who claim to represent the so-called "Islamic" nations as well as by their excesses in following God's order to carry out *ğihād*. Indeed, the damage caused by these excesses is even greater[60].

What we observe in Saʿīd's thought is hence a rehabilitation of the normativity of the Meccan experience, that of the reform of *ğāhiliyyah* society

59. Ibid., p. 97.
60. Ibid., p. 101.

through peaceful proclamation. This method is elevated to the status of *sunnah* in its sense of "unchangeable law", enjoying its own autonomy with respect to any further "legal" development envisioned in the Qur'ān, and *a fortiori* any human juridical codification. In this sense, preaching (*da'wah*) is not simply a "first warning" to non-Muslims to accept Islam unconditionally before being forced to accept it under some conditions – best-case scenario an agreement (*'ahd*). Nor it is a "temporary device" in the absence of the propitious conditions to engage *ǧihād*. Instead, it is the "only way" to restore a true Islamic society. In other words, *da'wah* is conceived as totally released from *ǧihād*: "Islam does not need the truth to be established by force" because "falsehood simply vanishes with the coming of truth, falsehood persists only in the absence of truth"[61].

A distinctly hermeneutical perspective is outlined here, insofar as the need to define the truth leads Sa'īd to critique the traditional exegetical approach. Muslims – he argues – are no longer able to interpret and understand the Qur'ān correctly due to a prevailing literalist approach to the text. Indeed, the Holy Book is not sufficient on its own to provide answers but must be read in the light of social and historical reality, as the text itself urges its readers to do: "We will show them Our signs in the universe and in themselves [or "in their souls"], until it becomes clear to them that this Qur'ān is the truth" (Qur. XLI:53). As Sa'īd explains,

> the scarce capacity of texts to find a cure [for problems] manifests itself when they lose the support of the signs of God in the universe and in the souls [of men], especially in moments of trial like the one we are experiencing. In order for the texts to play their positive role, it is necessary that the signs in the universe and in the souls also take a role [...]. What allows the texts to take the right direction, orienting them and defining their purposes, without leaving room for doubts about them, comes only from the signs of God in the universe and in souls[62].

The implications of this hermeneutical approach to the interpretation of the revelation as a whole, and to the doctrine of *ǧihād* in particular, are huge: establishing that the confirmation of truth must be sought "outside" the Qur'ān implies that the text is not self-sustaining and that its

61. Ibid., pp. 158 and 160.
62. Ibid., pp. 221 and 225.

significance is not established once for all. On the contrary, it increases together with "history", which, for Saʿīd, is the dimension in which reality is manifested in all its forms, and that has to be recognised as essential for the exegetical work.

This idea will find its mature expression in Saʿīd's later works, where he declares that "history does not replace the Qurʾān; rather, it is the source of the Qurʾān, its support to show its truth". Furthermore, unlike the Qurʾān, which was revealed through a human medium, i.e., language, "history is the book that addresses humans without any intermediary, in a direct way"[63]. Indeed, what is envisioned here is a critical broadening of the epistemological horizon, which opens up to new perspectives in exegesis and contributes to free the field from unavailing stratifications and to make sense of the ever-evolving meaning of revelation.

In this perspective, it is history that shows people that war and violence are no longer legitimate tools for solving problems; it has demonstrated the inadequacy of violence: paradoxically, the highly destructive potential reached by the modern military industry has invalidated any residual legitimacy of war. In other words, the time of war and violence has been "abrogated" once and for all, by history:

> Today, war is no longer a tool to resolve conflict. […] War is dead with the invention of the atomic bomb. Today, war is carried out only by foolish men and evildoers who exploit the ignorance of those devoid of knowledge. Those who use reason solve problems by means of science, intelligence, justice, and goodness. Although war continues in many places, we declare that war is dead, and this means that it no longer has any role in the solutions of crises and problems that men try to solve in this way. We mean that it has been abrogated, just like horses and donkeys have been abrogated, just like hunting and the sword have been abrogated, and it is no longer an option or a possible means to reach any goal[64].

As we can see, the doctrinal instrument of abrogation acquires a new and innovative application here in a complete rupture with the one attested in the tradition, where it is used to limit – at various degrees – the

63. Saʿīd 1998, pp. 83–84.
64. Dumairieh 2017, pp. 53–54. The original Arabic text from which this quotation is taken is an unedited document which I translated into Italian for Dumairieh's book.

normativity of those Qur'ānic verses promoting peace and tolerance. In Sa'īd's epistemology we therefore find the foundation of a teleological vision that identifies the very essence of the divine eschatological project in the overcoming of the "primordial problem" of humankind, that of violence, and in the establishment of "a new world, a dignified future that is worthy of human dignity, a future that most people despair of being able to achieve, and that not even angels have been able to imagine or believe possible, that is global peace"[65].

In the end, the recognition of the epistemic pre-eminence of history in Qur'ānic exegesis is what will allow Sa'īd to take a decisive step towards overcoming the "legal" impasse inherent in the idea of "conditioned *ǧihād*" to which he was still limiting himself in his first book, and which leads at best, as we have seen, to a mere "moratorium" on *ǧihād*, and not to its doctrinal redefinition. Thus, the problem of a correct understanding of *ǧihād* is not simply juridical but eminently hermeneutical and requires a close interaction with reality. This early, fundamental intuition expressed in *Maḏhab* will be at the core of all of Sa'īd's further doctrinal developments, paving the way to a decisive shift from a *ǧihād* bound to a highly restrictive principle to the call to revive the "method of the prophets", up until his theorisation of the "death of war" and radical nonviolence.

5. Conclusion

A comparative survey of the specific approach of these three works to the doctrine of *ǧihād* has allowed us to highlight for each of them the peculiar epistemic premises for an Islamic discourse on peace and war and their implications. As emerged in the course of the analysis, both Wahbah al-Zuḥaylī's rigorously jurisprudential stance and Sayyid Quṭb's militant one imply the exclusion, in varying degrees, of other interpretive paradigms, thus significantly reducing the potential for a renewal of the sense and the scope of *ǧihād* or for granting the concept of peace an ontological independence.

As for Ǧawdat Sa'īd, we observe in his works a progressive epistemological opening that allowed him to overcome the legal and ideological

65. Sa'īd 1993a, p. 217.

crystallisations of the meaning of *ğihād*, not by repudiating it but rather by recovering its Qurʾānic polysemy. Moreover, by establishing a dialectical relationship between revelation and reality, the place of humans, their responsibility, and their function in history are emphasised, thus conferring to peacebuilding and nonviolence a new, autonomous status as both the supreme ethical duty of humankind and the real essence of God's eschatological project.

References

Abu-Nimer, M. (2000), *A Framework for Nonviolence and Peacebuilding in Islam*, in "Journal of Law and Religion", 15, pp. 217–265. https://doi.org/10.2307/1051519

Abū Zayd, N. Ḥ. (2017), *Naqd al-ḫiṭāb al-dīnī*, Muʾassasah Muʾminūn bi-lā Ḥudūd, Bayrūt, 1st edition 1994.

Afsaruddin, A. (2013), *Striving in the Path of God: Jihad and Martyrdom in Islamic Thought*, Oxford University Press, New York.

Belhaj, A. (2017), *Jawdat Saʿid and the Muslim Philosophy of Peace*, in H. Shadi (ed.), *Legitimate and Illegitimate Violence in Contemporary Islamic Thought*, Nomos Verlagsgesellschaft, Baden-Baden, pp. 229–245.

Capezzone, L. (2016), *Medioevo arabo: Una storia dell'islam medievale (VII–XV secolo)*, Mondadori Università, Milan.

Carré, O. (1984), *Mystique et politique: Lecture révolutionnaire du Coran par Sayyed Qutb, frère musulman radical*, Les Éditions du Cerf, Paris.

Cook, D. (2015), *Understanding Jihad*, University of California Press, Oakland, 1st ed. 2005.

Donner, F. M. (2012), *Muhammad and the Believers: At the Origins of Islam*, The Belknap Press of Harvard University Press, Cambridge (MA).

Dumairieh, N. (ed.) (2017), *Jawdat Said: Vie islamiche alla non violenza*, Zikkaron, Marzabotto.

Guazzone, L. (2016), *Storia contemporanea del Mondo arabo: I Paesi arabi dall'impero ottomano ad oggi*, Mondadori Università, Florence.

Khadduri, M. (1955), *War and Peace in the Law of Islam*, The Johns Hopkins Press, Baltimore, 1st ed., 1941.

Khadduri, M. (1966), *The Islamic Law of Nations. Shaybānī's Siyar*, The Johns Hopkins Press, Baltimore.

Manduchi, P. (2019), *La riscoperta del ğihād: la lettura rivoluzionaria di Sayyid Quṭb*, in P. Manduchi, N. Melis (eds.), *Ğihād. Definizioni e riletture di un termine abusato*, Mondadori, Milan, pp. 37–68.

Mansoori, M. T. (2007), *The Questions of War and Peace in Contemporary Islamic Legal Discourse: The Contribution of Wahbah al-Zuḥaylī*, in "Islamic Studies", 46, 3, pp. 417–435.
Menghini, P. (2019), *Nonviolence in Islam: Jawdat Sa'id and the Path of Adam First Son*, in "Afkar. The Undergraduate Journal of Middle East Studies", 1, 1, pp. 49–59.
Mitchell, R. P. (1969), *The Society of the Muslim Brothers*, Oxford University Press, London.
Morabia, A. (1993), *Le Ǧihād dans l'Islam médiéval: Le « combat sacré » des origines au XIIème siècle*, Albin Michel, Paris.
Muller, J. M. (2009), *Désarmer les dieux: Le christianisme et l'islam au regard de l'exigence de non-violence*, Les Éditions du Relié, Gordes.
Pierret, T. (2013), *Religion and State in Syria: The Sunni Ulama from Coup to Revolution*, Cambridge University Press, New York.
The Qur'an, trans. M. A. S. Abdel Haleem, Oxford University Press, New York, 2010 (1st ed. 2004).
Quran Dictionary, https://corpus.quran.com/qurandictionary.jsp (last accessed 23 March 2021).
Quṭb, S. (1979), *Ma'ālim fī l-ṭarīq*, Dār al-Šurūq, Beirut, 1st ed., 1964.
Sa'īd, Ǧ. (1993a), *Iqra' wa-Rabbu-ka al-Akram*, Dār al-fikr al-mu'āṣir, Beirut.
Sa'īd, Ǧ. (1993b), *Maḏhab ibn Ādam al-awwal: muškilat al-'unf fī l-'amal al-islāmī*, Dār al-Fikr al-Mu'āṣir, Beirut, 1st ed. 1966.
Sa'īd, Ǧ. (1998), *al-Tafsīr al-sunanī*, in "Qaḍāyā islāmiyyah mu'āṣirah", 4, pp. 58–122.
Šarīf, M. (2008), *Taṭawwur mafhūm al-ǧihād fī l-fikr al-islāmī*, Dār al-Madà, Damascus.
Schiavo, V. (2019), *Jawdat Said: l'Islam della nonviolenza*, in "Oasis", available at: https://www.oasiscenter.eu/it/nonviolenza-nell-islam-jawdat-said (last accessed 23 August 2021).
Zappa, F. (2002), *Jihād e martirio nella tradizione islamica*, in "La società degli individui", 14, 2, pp. 45–60.
al-Zuḥaylī, W. (2018), *Āṯār al-ḥarb: dirāsah fiqhiyyah muqāranah*, Dār al-Fikr, Damascus, 1st edition 1962–1963.

Paola Pizzi is a PhD graduate of Sapienza University – EPHE (2022). After graduating in Arabic Language and Literature at 'Ca' Foscari' University in Venice and in Islamic Studies at PISAI (Rome), she was Lecturer in the Arabic Language at "Unint" University (Rome) and a professional translator for international news agencies and publishers. In her doctoral research, she analysed the thought of the Syrian preacher and theologian Ǧawdat Sa'īd (1931–2022).

Chapter 2

Kun ka-ibn Ādam: Nonviolence and Quranic Interpretation in Ğawdat Saʿīd's Thought

Pietro Menghini

Abstract

This chapter explores the nonviolent theories of the Syrian thinker Ğawdat Saʿīd presented in his work, *Kun ka-ibn Ādam* (Be Like Adam's Son). In this book, Saʿīd develops a historicist method of exegesis of the Quran to support his nonviolent interpretation of Islam. This chapter will analyse how Saʿīd outlines his exegetical method and his conception of history. Thus, it investigates the relationship between historical exegesis and Saʿīd's nonviolent theory, and contradictions in Saʿīd's thought are highlighted. His work is analysed within the framework developed by Chibli Mallat, i.e., comparing the ideas of the Syrian thinker with those of other Muslim thinkers included by Mallat in a Middle Eastern humanist tradition. In this way, the chapter argues for the integration of Saʿīd's work into a long humanist tradition in the region, supporting his nonviolent theory.

Keywords: Ğawdat Saʿīd, nonviolence in Islam, Quranic interpretation, Islamic reformism, Islamic humanism

1. Introduction

Ǧawdat Saʿīd was born in the Syrian village of Biʾr ʿAǧam in 1931[1]. In 1946, he moved to Cairo to study at al-Azhar University, obtaining a degree in pedagogy and Arabic. In Cairo, he was able to meet thinkers such as Malek Bennabi (Mālik Bin Nabī), whose influence on his work are examined in this chapter, and to participate in the lively intellectual life of the Egyptian capital, which probably influenced the development of his ideas. He later taught Arabic in Saudi Arabia for two years and then returned to Syria just to be called up for conscription a year later. Following his service, he started teaching Arabic and spreading his ideas about nonviolence. His activism led to his arrest and imprisonment five times over the years. He was finally banned from teaching in 1973 and returned to Biʾr ʿAǧam where he restored the family farm and became a farmer and a preacher at the local mosque. At the end of the 1990s, he and Abd al-Akram al-Saqqa (ʿAbd al-Akram al-Saqqā), one of his followers, founded a Quranic study group based on his ideas of nonviolence. The group later became known as *Šabāb Dārayā* (the Youth of Daraya) and played an important role at the beginning of the Syrian nonviolent uprising in 2011. He lived in Istanbul after being forced to flee his village because of bombardments by the regime in 2013 until his death in January 2022[2].

The work of Ǧawdat Saʿīd, from the 1960s to the present, covers half of the 20th century, a period full of change and turmoil both for Syria and for the whole MENA region. The contents and preoccupation expressed in his books mirror the historical period Saʿīd worked in. In his long career as an Islamic religious thinker, Saʿīd touched upon many central themes of Islamic philosophy, starting from nonviolence with his first

1. In this chapter, I have transliterated the names of authors of works quoted in Arabic, along with the titles of their works, followed by the translations of the titles. I have done the same for placenames and terms not found in the Cambridge Online Dictionary (https://dictionary.cambridge.org/). For terms found in the dictionary, such as Islam or Quran, the spelling provided is followed. The names of the authors whose works are quoted in English, Italian, or French are transliterated only at the first occurrence in brackets. Nevertheless, terms referring to specific concepts, even if present in the Cambridge Dictionary, like *jihad* or *signifier*, are in italics.
2. Dumairieh 2017, pp. xv–x. Ollivry-Dumarieh 2016, p. 133. al-Qādirī 2006, pp. 17–18. Trombetta 2017, p. 220.

book, *Madhab ibn Ādam al-awwal* (The Way of Adam's Upright Son), published in 1966[3]. He later published, in 1972, *Ḥattà mā yuġayyirū mā bi-anfusihim* (Until They Change What's in Their Souls) on free will and, in 1988, *Iqra' wa-rabbuka al-akram* (Read! And Your Lord is the Most Bountiful), focusing on the importance of knowledge[4]. In this chapter, I analyse *Kun ka-ibn Ādam* (Be Like Adam's Son), published in 1997, which is presented as a summary of all the themes the thinker touched on in his other books. In this work, Sa'īd focuses on free will, knowledge, nonviolence and introduces history as a new component to his thought, connecting all these different elements[5].

Only a small number of authors have analysed Sa'īd's thought. Dumairieh and Pizzi are among them, and, in *Vie islamiche alla nonviolenza* (a Italian translation of and commentary on excerpts from Sa'īd's works), they thoroughly analyse the different themes Sa'īd dealt with[6]. Ollivry-Dumairieh has also dedicated an article to Sa'īd's thought, giving interesting insights on his general view of nonviolence while also providing precious information on his life and studies[7]. Similarly, Jean-Marie Müller dedicated a chapter of his book on nonviolence and religions to Sa'īd, focusing on the role of the latter's ideas in a possible interfaith debate on nonviolence[8]. Abdessamad Belhaj has also written an article on Sa'īd's conception of nonviolence and is the only author to approach Sa'īd's conception of historicist epistemology. In his very accurate article, Belhaj highlights the limits of Sa'īd's work by pointing out how he

3. Sa'īd has published 11 books, along with many articles, interviews, and videos. Here I mention only four of his works, those most relevant – in my opinion – to the understanding of the essay I analyse.
4. Sa'īd 1993; Sa'īd [1972]; Sa'īd [1988]. For this chapter, I used the PDF file of the fifth edition (1993) of *Madhab ibn Ādam*. Thus, even if the book was initially published in 1966, the year noted in the footnotes and bibliography is 1993. As for the other two books, I used PDF downloadable files from Sa'īd's website. Since the years of publication are not marked in the latter, I cite the dates of the first editions of the two books in square brackets.
5. Sa'īd 1997. The PDF file of the first edition of *Kun ka-ibn Ādam* has been used in this chapter.
6. Dumairieh 2017.
7. Ollivry-Dumairieh 2016.
8. Müller 2010.

ignores the historical use of violence in the period of Muhammad's prophetic mission[9].

This chapter focuses specifically on Saʿīd's book, *Kun ka-ibn Ādam*, and the historicist exegetical method presented in support of nonviolence. It engages with Belhaj's critique and argues in favour of the possibility of a different interpretation. Furthermore, Saʿīd's thought is inscribed in the humanist current of thought theorised by the Lebanese thinker Chibli Mallat and defined as *insāniyyah* (humanism)[10]. This current is described by Mallat as a deep cultural tradition defined by the centrality given by its members to nonviolence, opposition to unjust regimes, colonialism and imperialism, and the inclination to support nonviolent revolutions[11]. Mallat relies on an Erasmian conception of humanism with its emphasis on freedom of conscience, free will, and faith in humanity's capacity for self-improvement[12]. In this way, connecting Saʿīd's thought with those of other thinkers included by Mallat in *insāniyyah*, I argue for the integration of Saʿīd's thought in a long tradition of humanist thinkers in the Middle East. This chapter presents Saʿīd's work as an expression of this current, except for his explicit focused on nonviolence, unlike other thinkers for whom nonviolence was more of a tacit consequence of their ideas[13]. The presence of nonviolent thinkers in the Middle East is often presented as a surprise and, even though the number of thinkers focusing openly on nonviolence is relatively small, if their work is conceived as part of the *insāniyyah* tradition, their existence is by no means casual or exceptional[14]. Nevertheless, the importance of the nonviolent and humanist tradition in the Middle East must be highlighted, considering the common focus on violence when approaching cultures of the region, and Islam in particular, in the media, the press and popular culture[15].

9. Belhaj 2017.
10. Mallat 2015, pp. 81–83.
11. Ibid., p. 83.
12. Ibid. On pp. 81–98 Mallat lists many possible members of the current of thought that he retrospectively describes, including philosophers, Sufis, poets, historians, and political dissidents. The ideas of free will and faith in humanity's ability for self-improvement are also central to Saʿīd's thought, as I argue in this chapter.
13. Ibid., pp. 83–84.
14. Belhaj 2017, p. 229.
15. Said 1996, p. 10. It is interesting to remark that Ǧawdat Saʿīd himself focuses, as I highlight in the chapter, on the presence of violence in the region and its history,

Furthermore, Mallat's understanding of nonviolence as a philosophy of history rather than a method of revolt is used to analyse Saʿīd's work, observing the development of his ideas between these two conceptions of nonviolence[16]. Thus, this chapter presents a comparison between Saʿīd's ideas and some of the thinkers quoted by Mallat as part of the *insāniyyah*, trying to highlight possible influences on Saʿīd's work. Among those thinkers, I refer to Muhammad Abduh (Muḥammad ʿAbduh, 1849–1905), ʿAbd al-Raḥmān al-Kawākibī (1855–1902), Muhammad Iqbal (Muḥammad Iqbāl, 1877–1938), Amin al-Khuli (Amīn al-Ḫūlī, 1895–1966), Malek Bennabi (1905–1973), Mahmud Muhammad Taha (Maḥmūd Muḥammad Ṭaha, 1909–1985), Muhammad Khalafallah (Muḥammad Ḫalaf Allāh, 1916–1991), Ali Shariati (ʿAlī Šarīʿatī, 1933–1977), Nasr Abu Zayd (Naṣr Abū Zayd, 1943–2010) and Abdolkarim Soroush (ʿAbdulkarīm Sorūš, b. 1945).

The analysis presents quotes from *Kun ka-ibn Ādam* following a thematic order to facilitate the examination since the book approaches the different topics at different stages, going back and forth from one to another. Other titles of Saʿīd's works are mentioned as well. This chapter focuses in the first place on Saʿīd's idea of decadence, then on the presentation of his theory of separation between a *language of letters* and a *language of meanings*. Moreover, I present Saʿīd's historicist exegetical method. Ultimately, I aim to investigate the consequences of the application of this method for his nonviolent interpretation of the Quran. Throughout the analysis, I also highlight some critical points of Saʿīd's thought as well as his backing away from the application of historicist exegesis. Thus, I provide some possible interpretations, relating Saʿīd's ideas to the historical context of his work and life.

Even though this chapter focuses only on two aspects of Saʿīd's thought expressed in *Kun ka-ibn Ādam* and is only an attempt to interpret his multifaceted thought, the analysis of Saʿīd's work is of great

---

finding in it one of the causes of the decadence he highlights. Nevertheless, Saʿīd also finds the solution to the use of violence within the cultural heritage of Islam, implicitly refusing any of the stereotypes highlighted by Edward Said (1996) on the allegedly violent nature of Islam.

16. Mallat 2015, p. 31. The fact that Mallat defines nonviolence as a philosophy of history is particularly significant to understand Saʿīd's idea of historical exegesis, as I argue below.

importance. Reflections and analyses on his thought are much needed to highlight the Middle Eastern nonviolent cultural production, often understudied in favour of more visible topics regarding the history and culture of the region. Furthermore, Saʿīd's involvement with nonviolent activists' groups at the beginning of the 2011 Syrian uprising gives his work particular importance for its possible practical applications that still need to be properly examined.

2. Decline

As highlighted in the introduction, Ǧawdat Saʿīd can be inscribed in the current of thought of the *insāniyyah*, a current in which Mallat includes many thinkers of the *nahḍah* (Revival). As part of the *insāniyyah* tradition, Saʿīd is also influenced by the reformist movement and, in line with the ideas of such a current, *Kun ka-ibn Ādam* opens with a description of the decline the *ummah* (the Islamic Nation) has fallen into[17]. "How have we abandoned the straight path? [...] We see the rest of the world building democracies and following the straight path, while we drifted away from that path and now we do not even know how to return to it"[18]. Such an argument is not new to the works of Muslim reformists. Nevertheless, as I argue below, the originality of Saʿīd's ideas must be highlighted by pointing to the reason he outlines for the decline of the *ummah*[19].

17. A strong connection between this worldly reality and religious truth can be found in Islam. Following this logic, material loss or defeats are understood as a loss of divine favour, itself a consequence of disobeying God's laws (Hourani 1983, p. 228). Thus, works of reformist thinkers often start from noting a state of material decline of the *ummah*, mirroring a moral decay and estrangement from God's path. The need for reform is postulated on the basis of such observations (Black 2011, pp. 290, 293, 324, 325). For an interesting analysis on the necessity of the idea of decline, see Fieni 2012.
18. Saʿīd 1997, p. 295. He returns to this point on pp. 72, 295. In his work, when Saʿīd says "we," he refers to Muslims or Islamic society in general, which, in his thought, corresponds to the *ummah* (Saʿīd 1997, p. 72). The translations of quotes from *Kun ka-ibn Ādam* are mine. An English synopsis of the book is available on Ǧawdat Saʿīd's website (https://www.jawdatsaid.net/en/index.php/Main_Page).
19. The idea of the decline of the *ummah* is a recurring theme in many reformist Muslim thinkers, including several thinkers that could be considered outside Mallat's *insāniyyah*. Saʿīd shares the preoccupation with the decline of the *ummah* with thinkers

ʿAbd al-Raḥmān al-Kawākibī, in his book *Umm al-qurà* (Mother of Cities), also focuses on the historical process of the degeneration of the *ummah* and describes how the acceptance of tyranny brought Islamic society to such a state of decline[20]. From this starting point, he states the need for a reform of Islamic society[21]. Muhammad Iqbal begins his argument in a similar way. He states that the original potentiality of Islam needs to be rediscovered and the thick bark of wrong interpretations that has covered its true meaning removed[22]. Proposing this view, Iqbal suggests that the *ummah* is in a state of decline, just as Saʿīd and al-Kawākibī did. Furthermore, the idea of an original essence of Islam that had been covered up by wrong interpretations can also be found in Saʿīd's work. Bennabi also focuses on the decline of Islamic society. He develops the concept of *colonisabilité*, which highlights the importance of recognising decline as the first step to fighting it and liberating the *ummah* from the conditions that brought it to its decline and colonial dependence[23]. This liberation has to be achieved through a far-reaching cultural revolution as an attempt to fight decline and ultimately gain salvation[24]. The same need for cultural reform can be observed in Saʿīd's work, as he calls for a profound change in Muslims' mentality and the way they interpret the Quran, as I argue here[25]. Bennabi, just like al-Kawākibī, sees the decay of the *ummah* as part of a long historical process, suggesting two of the

---

such as Mawdūdī or Quṭb but poses their solutions, in particular, those of Quṭb. Dumairieh states that Saʿīd's first work, published in 1966, was a response to Quṭb's *Maʿālim fī al-Tarīq*, which was published in 1964 (Dumairieh 2017, p. xv). The difference between thinkers such as Mawdūdī or Quṭb and Mallat's *insāniyyah* is defined by the importance given to nonviolence by the latter. Finally, Saʿīd's relation with Mawdūdī is difficult to define clearly, as, for instance, the former often quotes the latter. Even though Mawdūdī would probably not be included in *insāniyyah*, Saʿīd still builds on his thought. This highlights Saʿīd's openness as a thinker. He draws on different sources, without letting strict definitions as Islamist, reformers or Salafī limit his possible sources of inspiration.

20. Weismann 2015, pp. 74; al-Kawākibī 1941; al-Kawākibī is also mentioned as one of the most important members of *insāniyyah* by Mallat 2015, pp. 84–87.
21. Weismann 2015, p. 73.
22. Iqbal 2012, p. 124.
23. Bennabi 2006, p. 134.
24. Roberts 1994, p. 22.
25. Saʿīd 1997, p. 195.

possible sources for Saʿīd's analysis of the historical dimension of the Muslims' decay and their estrangement from God's path[26].

Considering the works of these three thinkers, it can be understood how Saʿīd focuses on some main topics of the reformist tradition in defining decline The Syrian thinker emphasises the historical dimension of decay and the existence of a true form of Islam that needs to be brought back to light. These two ideas, which he uses to define the symptoms of decline, are also central to the solution he proposes for it. Even though many of his ideas are shared by other reformist thinkers, the main reason he gives for the origin of decline of Islamic society is different from those usually offered[27]. He concentrates on the problem of the widespread use of violence. Saʿīd highlights his originality by focusing on an issue only a few other Muslim thinkers have seen as the main problem of the reform of Islam, although some considered it marginally, as previously pointed out in the introduction[28]. Saʿīd argues "When I wrote about the *maḏhab* of Adam's son, I chose this title because I felt this topic [the problem of using violence] is the main problem of humanity since the time of the Upright Son of Adam"[29].

Saʿīd notes how violence is a constant element in the history of humanity and the history of the *ummah* since the ancient times of Abel. In line with this observation, he connects his theory to the decline of Islamic society, asserting a causal relationship between the use of violence and the decline of Islamic society, conceived as an estrangement from the path God has set out for the Muslim community[30].

26. Walsh 2007, p. 237.
27. Said 1996, pp. 44, 47, 91.
28. Saʿīd 1997, pp. 66–67. In the section entitled "Reconstructing Nonviolent Culture in the Humanist Tradition" in his book *Philosophy of Nonviolence: Revolution, Constitutionalism, and Justice beyond the Middle East*, Mallat mentions many thinkers who contributed to the humanist tradition he outlines. The only one he mentions in direct reference to nonviolence is Ǧawdat Saʿīd (Mallat 2015, pp. 81–98). Another thinker that could be added to Mallat's list is Abd al-Ghaffar Khan (d. 1988), the Pakistani nonviolent activist and philosopher.
29. Saʿīd 1997, p. 66. *The Upright Son of Adam* is a reference to Abel, a central figure in Saʿīd's thought to whom he dedicated his first book published in 1966. The *maḏhab* of Adam's son is the school of thought of Abel, supporting absolute nonviolence.
30. Ibid., pp. 15, 182.

Furthermore, the Syrian thinker relies on Quran 2:30 to highlight how, when God created humankind, angels worried more about the possibility that humans would indulge in violence than the possibility of their disbelief. "This [the preoccupation of the angels] demonstrates that doing mischief and spilling blood is the mother of all evils"[31]. In Saʿīd's opinion, this is yet another element proving how violence is the main reason for the decay of Islamic society. Thus, the question that immediately follows in Saʿīd's reasoning is: How is it possible that people abandoned God's path for that of violence when they had been given the Quran to guide them on the straight path[32]?

3. Interpretation

To answer this question, Saʿīd approaches the problem of the exegesis of the Quranic text by asking rhetorically if a correct interpretation of the text could lead to violence and subsequent decline[33]. Quoting a *ḥadīṯ*, Saʿīd affirms that the prophet Muhammad had foreseen the moment when Muslims would read the Quran but would no longer understand it, exactly as what happened to Jews and Christians with the Bible[34]. In Saʿīd's thought, the loss of the ability to understand the Quran is equivalent to the loss of the capacity to interpret its text[35]. To explain how Muslims lost

31. Ibid., p. 67. "'Surely I am making in the earth a successor.' They said, 'Will You make therein one who will corrupt in it and shed blood while we (are the ones who) extol (with) Your praise and call You Holy?' He said, 'Surely I know whatever you do not know.' Quran 2:30." The English translation of Quranic verses is taken from Saʿīd's webpage (https://www.jawdatsaid.net/en/index.php/Main_Page), where the verses quoted in the chapter are presented in English as well. It is in this way that I respect Saʿīd's translations.
32. Ibid., p. 19.
33. Ibid.
34. "The Messenger was once mentioning a certain future event, when he commented: 'This will take place when men have deserted knowledge.' One companion, Ziyād bin Labīd, objected: 'How can this be, Messenger of Allah, when we learn the Quran and will have our children recite it, and they will have their children recite it, and so on until the Day of Judgment?' 'Oh, Ziyād! I used to think of you as better than most in Madīnah! Do you not see how the Jews and the Christians still have the Bible, yet it does them no good at all?'" (ibid., p. 19).
35. Ibid., p. 20.

this ability, Saʿīd emphasises the separation between what he calls the *language of letters* (*luġat al-ḥurūf*) and the *language of meanings* (*luġat al-maʿānī*)[36].

Drawing on Saussure, Saʿīd describes the difference between the physical expression of a word, both in vocal and written form (*luġat al-ḥurūf*), and its meaning (*luġat al-maʿānī*)[37]. He states: "Those who think they can find truth in words will remain far from reality [...] for words can indicate reality and can also indicate its opposite"[38]. It starts to be clear that such separation entails the loss of the idea of an absolute connection between a word and its meaning, respectively defined, using Saussure's terminology, as *signifier* and *signified*. On the contrary, Saʿīd argues, connecting these two aspects is the responsibility of human beings[39]. Even though he draws on Saussure, Saʿīd tries to reconnect with the Islamic tradition, calling on one of the thinkers Mallat places in the *insāniyyah* intellectual tradition, quoting al-Ghazali (al-Ġazālī, 1058–1111) as the first source for the concept of separation between *signifier* and *signified*[40]. Saʿīd traces this idea back to the famous Muslim philosopher, probably trying to give legitimacy to his theory by quoting such a well-known intellectual and inserting his own ideas into a long Islamic trend. Abu Zayd's work substantiates Saʿīd's claim by tracing the idea of separation between *signifier* and *signified* back to the work of al-Tabari (al-Ṭabarī, 839–923), al-Qadi Abd al-Jabbar (al-Qāḍī ʿAbd al-Ǧabbār, 935–1025), al-Ǧurǧānī (1009–1078), and the already mentioned al-Ghazali, thus placing Saʿīd amongst this group of thinkers[41].

Further exploring this separation of *signifier* and *signified*, Saʿīd explains how the distinction between these two aspects in the Islamic

36. Ibid., pp. 17, 249.
37. Saussure 2005, pp. 83–85; Saʿīd 1997, p. 249.
38. Saʿīd 1997, pp. 249–250. In this passage, Saʿīd mentions Saussure, tracing a parallel with al-Ghazali.
39. Ibid., p. 204.
40. Ibid., p. 250.
41. Abū Zayd 2002, p. 45. The works and approaches of al-Qadi Abd al-Jabbar and al-Ǧurǧānī differ profoundly, both because the former is a *muʿtazilī* and the latter part of the school of thought of *al-ašʿariyyah* and because their approaches to the differences between *signifier* and *signified* diverge strongly. Nevertheless, they both reflect on the connections and separations between form and meaning (Larkin, 1988).

context coincides with the division between the physical text of the Quran and its interpretation, the first one being the *signifier* and the second the *signified.*

> The Messenger of God, when addressing the Qurayš with the Quran, did not have problems caused by the language he was announcing his message in, for they knew the language. He had problems because they did not understand the meaning of what he was saying. What is not understood through the language of meaning cannot be understood. Thus, there must be another source[42].

Relying on the example of the prophet Muhammad, Sa'īd argues that the Qurayš in Mecca did not understand what Muhammad was saying since they did not understand the *signified* (the meaning of the Quran) attached to the *signifier* they knew well (the Arabic language of the Quranic text). This separation can be found also in the debate on the *i'ǧāz* or inimitability of the Quran, to which Abu Zayd refers[43]. One of the two main approaches to this debate establishes a dichotomy between *lafẓ* (form or letter) and *ma'nà* (meaning), to understand which of the two aspects of the Holy Book was inimitable[44], even though he is not dealing directly with the problem of *i'ǧāz*, Sa'īd draws on the separation created by this debate to explain the reason why Muslims could not interpret the Quran anymore

42. Sa'īd 1997, p. 20.
43. Vasalou 2002, p. 24. The debate on *i'ǧāz* starts in the Quran itself, when detractors of Muhammad's prophetic mission are challenged to produce verses as perfect as those of the Holy Book. The debate continued and, in particular between the 9th and the 11th centuries, provided, on the one hand, the conception that the inimitability of the Quran resides in its style and its content and, on the other, the idea that inimitability of the Quran resides in its content more than in its style. This second position traces a separation between thought and expression and thus between the letter and the spirit of the Quran, finding in the latter the true location of its inimitability. This debate about the inimitability of the Quran is also connected with the debate surrounding the uncreated or created nature of the Quran. The first position described above supports the idea of an uncreated Quran, where the form of the book is also an expression of its eternal and inimitable nature. The second position supports the idea of the Quran as created in time, thus its language is "temporal speech of God," as defined by Larkin (1988, p. 32), and cannot be the site of the Quran's inimitability as it was the form given to the inimitable and eternal content of the Quran to create them in time.
44. Abu Zayd 2003, pp. 11–12.

and thus the *ummah* fell into decay. By following the idea that the form in the Quran is separate from its meaning, Saʿīd theorises that the *signifier* and the *signified* of the Quranic text are not indissolubly connected, and thus Muslims lost the true *signified* of the Quran and read only the *signifier*, attaching wrong meanings to it. In this way, they cover the Quran – and, according to Iqbal, Islam at large – with wrong interpretations, using the wrong tools to approach the text, just as Belhaj highlights[45].

Drawing on a long tradition of modern thinkers that focused on the problem of separation between meaning and form in the Quran – as well as on a more ancient philosophical tradition, as mentioned above – Abu Zayd explains how a literary approach to this text is necessary to understand it properly[46]. He explores the importance of reading the text in its historical context to understand it. This assertion stresses the importance of historicising the *signifier* of the text. Muhammad Abduh, Amin al-Khuli, and Muhammad Khalafallah have all focused on the importance of understanding the formulas used, the stories told, and the narratives of the Quran as shaped by the historical context of the Arabian Peninsula of the 7th century AD and are thus not to be read and interpreted literally[47]. Saʿīd's assertion that "they [Muslims who refuse to recognise the importance of history] are not capable of understanding or believing that the events of history are the source of the Quran" could be read within the framework of Abu Zayd's thought[48]. Using such an understanding of Saʿīd's ideas implies that he holds that the *signifier* of the Quran is historically determined. This entails the necessity of reading it in the context it was produced in and thus the impossibility of a literal reading.

On the other hand, Saʿīd's conception of the *signified* in the Quran does not seem to be relative or historically determined. In *Kun ka-ibn Ādam,* Saʿīd refers many times to "the truth" or "reality" in the Quran, revealing that, in his understanding, the Quranic *signified* is to some extent an absolute concept, as Belhaj also points out[49]. It is interesting to note here that even though Saʿīd uses the theory of separation between *signifier* and

45. Belhaj 2017, p. 234.
46. Abu Zayd 2002, pp. 16–17.
47. Ibid., p. 20.
48. Saʿīd 1997, p. 22.
49. Ibid., pp. 24, 45, 85, 195, 127; Belhaj 2017, p. 234.

signified, he does not abandon the idea that there is a true *signified* for the Quranic *signifier*. This exposes one of the contradictions of his thought.

Furthermore, the Sudanese thinker Muhammad Mahmud Taha explains how two messages can be found in Islam: the first is a historical one, and the second is the eternal and true one[50]. The first is historically connected to the time the Quran was revealed in, cannot be separated from it, and it is determined by it[51]. But this message, in Taha's opinion, is a superficial expression of the second, which expresses the eternal and true meaning of Islam, which is still *in fieri*[52] (in progress).

Taha's thought is particularly enlightening and useful when reading Sa'īd's ideas about the existence of an absolute meaning of the Quran, corresponding to his *language of meanings* or *signified*. Thus, following this interpretation, Sa'īd asserts the existence of the separation in the Quran between a *language of letter* (the *signifier*) historically determined and as such not to be read universally or literally, and a *language of meaning* (the *signified*) conceived as the universal and eternal meaning of the Quran.

Having theorised about this separation, Sa'īd states he needs a tool or source to reconnect the *signified* to the *signifier* so that Muslims can benefit once again from the guidance of the Quran[53]. He states that "they [Muslims who refuse to recognise the importance of history] are not capable of understanding […] that history is our source for grasping the truth of the admonitions in the Quran", pointing to history itself as the source of the knowledge to interpret the holy text[54].

50. Taha 1996, p. 46.
51. Ibid., p. 21.
52. Ibid., p. 147.
53. In the excerpt I quoted (Sa'īd 1997, p. 20) Sa'īd hints at the existence of another source for understanding the meaning of the Quranic text: mastering the *language of meanings*, as he calls it. Also, Belhaj (2017, p. 234) points to Sa'īd's research for a tool for understanding the Quran. In this context, understanding means connecting the *signifier* and the *signified* as I emphasised.
54. Sa'īd 1997, p. 22.

History

Saʿīd thus theorises about the existence of a source of knowledge outside the Quran which can help reestablish the connection between the *signified* and the *signifier* in the Quranic text[55]. Saʿīd argues that the Quran mentions inheritance or ablution just a few times, but it also stresses the importance of history by narrating many episodes of the past. "Indeed, the Quran, despite its size, does not mention inheritance or ablution more than twice but mentions historical events, past catastrophes, and consequences for those who did not pay attention to history many times"[56]. Then Saʿīd affirms that the Quran itself points to history as the tool for understanding it properly. Furthermore, he states that "indeed, those who understand history kneel humbly before the door of this holy place, which is the sources of understanding of the Quran [...]"[57].

As I argued, interpreting the Quran in terms of Saʿīd's theory means connecting the *signifier* of the text with the absolute *signified*. According to Saʿīd, history allows Muslims to make this connection. On the one hand, the *signifier* is determined by history, which, as was shown, gives form to it. On the other hand, regarding the relation between the *signified* and the *signifier*, history gives examples properly interpreting the *signifier* and thus finding the true *signified* of the Quran. These examples should be used to read the *signifier* and understand its true *signified*.

For instance, Saʿīd refers many times to the story of the Son of Adam, which provides the title for his first book and the one being analysed here[58]. This story, which assumes a historical dimension in Saʿīd's thought, sees Abel taking an absolutely nonviolent stance in confronting his brother Cain, to the point of refusing to use force even as a tool of self-defence. In this example Saʿīd finds a key to the reading of the Quranic *signifier* and thus to understand the true meaning, or the *signified*, of the text. In his opinion, the *signifier* must be read using the nonviolent example of Abel, deducing from it a nonviolent *signified*. In the following paragraphs, I examine which method the Syrian Islamic religious thinker uses to choose examples to follow in history.

55. Ibid.
56. Ibid., p. 24.
57. Ibid., p. 165.
58. Saʿīd 1997, pp. 20, 66, 93, 97.

The knowledge of the true *signified* is thus given by observing historical events. The *signifier* is fixed since it was determined in a particular moment of history, and the *signified* has been established as well since it is the true and eternal meaning of the text. What needs to be constantly determined and what is related to the examples of history is the connection between the two, which determines the knowledge of the true *signified*. As I argued, connecting these two aspects means interpreting the Quran[59].

Such a vision entails profound knowledge and attention to history, which makes Saʿīd insist, several times in his book, on the importance of knowledge in the process of the reform of the *ummah*[60]. The centrality of knowledge is one of the main aspects of Saʿīd's thought, deeply connected to his vision of history as the tool for restoring the relationship between the *signifier* and the *signified*. The importance of history as the source of human knowledge is also highlighted by Iqbal[61]. The Pakistani philosopher states that the Quran, which constantly appeals to reason and experience, points to history as a source of knowledge. Nevertheless, Iqbal refuses a historical approach to the Quran, highlighting how its message could thus be reduced to its historical context and lose its universality[62]. To avoid the possibility of the universality of the Quran being limited by its historicisation, Saʿīd turns repeatedly to the separation between *signifier* and *signified*. Even though he does not follow Iqbal's refusal of the historical approach to reading the Quran, he draws on his idea of a universal meaning of the Quran, just as he did with Taha's ideas[63]. Such a universal meaning is the *signified* that needs to be connected to the *signifier* with the help of historical examples.

This tension between eternity and temporality, the absolute and the relative – the former expressed by the universal meaning and the second identified with the historical form of the text – can often be found in Saʿīd's works. As remarked by the Iranian intellectual Abdolkarim Soroush, reconciling eternity and temporality is one of the goals of

59. Belhaj argues that Saʿīd's historicist method entails that "History evolves and so should also the reading of the book [the Quran]" (Belhaj 2017, p. 234).
60. Saʿīd 1997, p. 28. Saʿīd [1988].
61. Iqbal 2012, p. 101.
62. Sevea 2012, p. 119.
63. Ibid., p. 120.

Islamic reformism[64]. Thus, Saʿīd's attempts to connect the historically determined *signifier* and the absolute *signified* of the Quran parallels the reformists' effort at reconciling eternity and temporality, further integrating the Syrian thinker into this current of thought and, in turn, in Mallat's *insāniyyah*. This attempt also marks one of Saʿīd's contradictions, trying to combine absolute and relative aspects of his thought.

The problem Saʿīd poses in his book, after setting history as the source of knowledge for interpreting the Quran, is that the separation between *signifier* and *signified* can be applied to history as well[65]. Thus, how can Muslims understand the meaning of a historical event and use this meaning to interpret the Holy Book? Any meaning can be attached to a historical event since there is no absolute connection between the historical event as *signifier* and the meaning of it as *signified*. How can Muslims determine whether Abel's behaviour is a just example to follow? Saʿīd is well aware of this problem and tries to propose a solution by further explaining his conception of history and historical events.

5. Consequences

By declaring that "no event has a meaning on its own if we do not look at the consequences of that event" and thus that "Everybody can explain events as he wishes and can give to words the meaning he wants"[66], Saʿīd is admitting that looking at historical events is not a sufficient principle for understanding the Quran. This is due to the application of his theory of separation between the *signifier* and *signified* to historical events as well.

Consequently, Saʿīd tries to define another principle that can help Muslims understand how to interpret a historical event and hence how to interpret the meaning of the Quran. He invites Muslims to look at the consequences of an event to understand how to interpret it. He states: "Indeed, America's history is not what Americans write about themselves, nor what people who hate them write, nor what is written by those who admire them. America's history is the destiny they build now, it is the vision that people will have in five hundred years about America and

64. Soroush 2010, p. 30.
65. Saʿīd 1997, p. 87.
66. Ibid., p. 205.

Americans and the results of their actions"[67]. Saʿīd demonstrates that he is well aware of the role of people in the construction of the interpretation of history and its misrepresentation, just as with the Quranic interpretation. He tries, then, to find a real historical dimension behind the human constructions and interpretations, parallel to his search for the true meaning of the Quran. To understand the real meaning of an event, Saʿīd relies on the flow of time as an element revealing the true nature of an event, discovering its meaning through its consequences. Iqbal also highlights a similar concept. Referring to Quran 13:17, he points out how time divides what is useful from what is detrimental[68]. Another Syrian thinker, Muḥammad al-Būṭī, is similarly focused on the idea of truth as a self-revealing force that will inevitably show itself[69]. Saʿīd is relying on a similar concept to understand the meaning of historical events. He hopes that the true meaning of an event will become apparent and reveal itself, just as truth would do in al-Būṭī's thought. In this vein, we can understand Saʿīd's conception of history as a progression towards what is better[70]. While this idea explains why Muslims should look at the consequences of events to understand which examples to follow and which not, it poses a problem for Saʿīd's idea of the decline of the *ummah*. How could the *ummah* fall into decay if history is advancing towards what is better? This is yet another of Saʿīd's contradictions that remains to be solved.

Even though Saʿīd relies on the principle of self-revealing truth, he ends up setting up another principle to understand the true meaning of a historical event and the example that we should deduce from it. He states that "justice is to give to others in the same way you would give to yourself and the opposite, he who refuses that is truly unjust [...]. The subtle point here is that justice will not be realised unless we follow the example of Adam's son"[71]. Setting this principle for understanding which

67. Ibid., p. 81. In the Arabic text, Saʿīd uses the word *Amrīkā*, probably referring to the United States of America.
68. Iqbal 2012, p. 13: "As for the scum, it is to be thrown away, while that which benefits people remains on the Earth. This is how Allah brings out the parables". Cf. Qur. XIII:17).
69. al-Būṭī 1994, p. 59.
70. Saʿīd 1997, p. 112: "Indeed, I have no doubt that history is progressing towards what is better".
71. Ibid., p. 63.

interpretation is right and which is wrong implies that Saʿīd recognises the fallacy of his principle of looking at consequences. He probably realises, even though he does not openly admit it, that his theory of separation between *signifier* and *signified* can be applied to the consequences of a historical event as well. Human misinterpretation can also apply to consequences and so on. This consideration should suggest the impossibility of determining the right interpretation of a historical event and thus of the right interpretation of the Quran as well and the true *signified* of the text, without a proper tool. Nonviolence, then, is the touchstone by which one can discriminate between a righteous and an unrighteous historical event, and the key Saʿīd utilises to interpret the Quran.

As I hinted while explaining history's role in connecting *signifier* and *signified*, such a principle means that the criteria for understanding which examples Muslims should follow and which they should not follow is given by Adam's son's nonviolent stance. Thus, an example of nonviolence that should be used to interpret the Quranic *signifier* and understand that its true *signified* is a nonviolent one. By setting nonviolence as the principle by which the Quran should be interpreted, Saʿīd closes the circle he opened by highlighting violence as the problem causing the decadence of the *ummah*. In this way, Saʿīd finds in history the principle he was looking for to interpret the Quran. The fact that he finds such a principle in history is noteworthy since history was already highlighted as the dimension where the decline of the *ummah* could be observed. Thus, the solution to this decline is to be found in the same dimension as the decline itself.

Nevertheless, the conception of history in Saʿīd's thought presents two contradictory aspects. The first sees history as the product of human choices: people can abandon God's path or stick to it while looking at examples in history. The second sees history as a progression toward what is better, as is made clear by the principle of self-revealing truth, which would entail a loss of free choice for humans in determining the course of history with their choices. In his introduction to Saʿīd's *Ḥattà mā yuġayyirū mā bi-anfusihim*, Malek Bennabi highlights how an opposition can be outlined in Saʿīd's thought between an absolute vision of history as a chain of cause and effect stemming from God himself moving towards what is better and a more relativistic vision of history as shaped by the possibility of change through human action[72].

Furthermore, as already highlighted by analysing Saʿīd's attempt to reconnect the eternal *signified* with the historically determined *signifier*, his thought illustrates another conflict: that between eternity and temporality, between the absolute and the relative. Such a conflict, which Soroush also points out, runs parallel to the opposition between an absolute aspect to history and a relative one in Saʿīd's thought.

Saʿīd' whole work is an attempt to reconcile these two contradictions. He thus strives to support the connection between the *signifier* and the *signified.* He tries to reconcile the historical interpretation of the Quran, which permits the metaphorical interpretation he supports, with the existence of the Quran's true meaning, which supports the universality he wants to give to nonviolence. On the other hand, he tries to combine these two views to also solve the opposition between his vision of history as absolute (determined by God) and history as relative (determined by humans). To reconcile these two contradictions, Saʿīd defines a principle that can unite the two dimensions of history and the two aspects of the interpretation of the Quran. The principle that he finds, as it was shown, is nonviolence, which permits combining the *signifier* and the *signified* and interpreting the Quran. Moreover, this can also solve the contradiction between relative and absolute history.

In his lecture "The Philosophy of History: Cain and Abel"[73], Ali Shariati describes the contradiction that runs throughout history and pervades it[74]. This contradiction is the one intercurrent between the absolute nature of God and the becoming and changing essence of humankind, and it started with the story of Cain and Abel. This contradiction gives rise to a dialectic between relative and absolute which Shariati calls the Philosophy of History, starting from the nonviolent example of Abel[75]. Mallat also describes nonviolence as the philosophy of history, supporting Shariati's vision of the importance of the nonviolent example of Abel

72. Saʿīd [1972], p. 10. See Bennabi's introduction to the book.
73. This lecture (pp. 98–111) is part of a collection by Shariati, published in 1979 with the title *On the Sociology of Islam*.
74. Ibid., p. 98.
75. Ibid., p. 99.

as a point of departure of a dialectic between the absolute and the relative running through history[76].

Thus, Saʿīd's thought might be interpreted in light of these considerations. The Syrian thinker might propose nonviolence as the principle for solving the oppositions that were highlighted in his thought. The story of Abel represents the starting point between the relative and the absolute, and thus going back to this principle could solve this conflict, as articulated in Saʿīd's thought in the dialectic between the relative *signifier* and the absolute *signified* and the dialectic between the absolute and the relative view of history[77]. This archetypical moment works perfectly as a key to resolve this tension as it is part of sacred history where the relative and the absolute can be combined. Many of the problems and contradictions of Saʿīd's thought stem from the attempt to build a historicist exegesis drawing on examples from both sacred and profane history without distinction.

6. Nonviolence

Rather than being only the element that connects the two aspects of absoluteness and relativity in Saʿīd's thought, he also chooses the story of Cain and Abel as the representation of nonviolence and the example by which Muslims should understand the Quran. In this sense, nonviolence becomes the key to the interpretation of the Quran in all its parts. It must be read and understood in light of this principle, even if a literal reading would seem to suggest different meaning. This historical methodology for the exegesis of the holy text, developed by Saʿīd, could have helped the thinker overcome the limits of his nonviolent theory described in his first book on nonviolence in 1966.

In *Maḏhab ibn Ādam*, one of the main problems in Saʿīd's argument was that he had to account for the violence the prophet Muhammad used during his prophetic mission. In his first book, Saʿīd built his nonviolent model on the basis of Abel's example and then looking at Muhammad's

76. Mallat 2015, p. 5. Shariati 1979, p. 99.

77. Webel 2007, p. 7. It is noteworthy that, in the introduction to the volume *Handbook of Peace and Conflict Studies* as well, peace is defined as dialectical and as a historical idea, a very similar definition to that given by Saʿīd.

leadership[78]. He argued that prophets carried a message of nonviolence, and so did Muhammad[79]. Nevertheless, Saʿīd had to take into the account the fact that Muhammad used violence during his prophetic mission. Thus, he theorised that nonviolence was the method that had to be followed by Muslims during the process of the creation of an Islamic society. After the creation of such a society, violence was not prohibited any longer but could be used as a tool of self-defence[80].

The fact that Saʿīd sees the creation of Islamic society as subordinate to the previous free agreement of all the people participating in it as probably difficult to reach makes one wonder if this was not a quick solution to relegate the possible use of violence to a moment in the far future while outlawing it in the present[81]. With the exegetical tools developed in *Kun ka-ibn Ādam*, Saʿīd could have solved the problem of Muhammad's use of violence by applying the tool to the prophetic mission to read its true meaning[82]. As such, he could have argued that the actions of the prophetic mission are nothing more than the *signifier* and their *signified* as found in the light of the same historical examples used to interpret the Quran. In this way, applying his theory of historical exegesis, Saʿīd could have supported his nonviolent reading of Islam, overcoming the problem

78. For an analysis of Saʿīd's first work, see Menghini 2019.
79. Saʿīd 1993, p. 12.
80. Ibid., pp. 28–29.
81. For a detailed argumentation on such considerations, see Menghini 2019. The free agreement at the basis of Islamic society in Saʿīd's thought is similar to Rousseau's social contract, as also remarked by Dumairieh 2017, pp. xxx–xxxii. Nevertheless, the idea of the social contract in Saʿīd could also be adopted from the Islamic tradition, drawing on thinkers such as al-Māwardī. In his work *al-Aḥkām al-Sulṭāniyyah*, al-Māwardī defines the *Contract of the Imamate*, or the ways an Islamic state can be formed. Among the different theories described by the writer, there is also the possibility of the creation of the state by an agreement either between the majority of those in power and of influence in each country or by a group of five people (al-Mawardi 2000, p. 13). This could have provided an initial source for the idea of social contract that we find in Saʿīd's thought.
82. Belhaj rightly remarks that this problem remains unsolved, as I show below. Furthermore, Saʿīd states that "All the prophets invite humankind to abandon violence and to embrace a different way of living. 'There is no compulsion in Religion, and the straight path is well distinguished from the error' (Qur. II:256)." This seems to imply that the Quran's message of nonviolence is also to be found in prophetic missions.

of justifying the use of violence by the prophet Muhammad by explaining the true interpretation of his actions. Despite what could have been expected, Saʿīd declares that:

> Indeed, they do not understand *Badr* and *Ḥunayn*, and neither do they understand *Dāḥas*, *Ġabrāʾ* or the War of *Basūs* and they produce confusion when they say that *Badr* and *Ḥunayn* were like the two Gulf Wars[83]. They do not differentiate between the cut opened by the surgeon to carry out surgery and the wound inflicted by a criminal with the intention of killing somebody[84].

Thus, it would seem that Saʿīd does not apply the tool he created to the prophetic mission. Instead, he goes back to the positions he supported in his first book, justifying Muhammad's use of violence as self-defence[85].

Furthermore, Saʿīd starts discussing the conditions in which defensive *jihad* is acceptable or the conditions for the use of violence are applicable[86]. "Ask whomever you wish, what is the difference between the *muǧāhidīn* and the *ḫawāriǧ*, ask him about the conditions for *jihad*, or who can kill and what is the legal condition for that"[87]. This quote seems to entail that there are conditions in which *jihad* can be waged, a violent one in which killing is considered. This again seems a step backward to the theories developed in 1966 in *Maḏhab ibn Ādam*. In this view, violence is not always prohibited; rather, it would be allowed as a method of self-defence. Such a step back is confirmed by Saʿīd himself when he

83. *Badr* and *Ḥunayn* are the battles fought by the newly formed Islamic community during Muhammad's lifetime. *Dāḥas*, *Ġabrāʾ* and the War of *Basūs* are wars in the pre-Islamic period.
84. Saʿīd 1997, p. 217.
85. Dumairieh 2017, p. xxv.
86. On the debate of defensive *jihad* versus an aggressive one, in his first book Saʿīd supports the idea that only in defensive *jihad* is the use of violence acceptable. "When, however, the existing society is a Muslim one, which accepts the codes and norms of Islam, the act of force to sustain those rules becomes necessary" (Saʿīd 1993, pp. 28–29). For a general account of the debate over aggressive and defensive *jihad*, see Cook 2005.
87. Saʿīd 1997, p. 218. In Saʿīd's thought, the *jihad ḫawāriǧ* is the *jihad* of those who want to impose their view of religion on others by force. He elaborates this distinction already in his first book (Saʿīd 1993, pp. 57–58) and the fact that in *Kun ka-ibn Ādam* he also goes back to this concept is telling of how he falls back on his older theories.

states, "Some of us rely on reason and say, 'Intellect accepts self-defence if attacked.' Others rely only on the law and say, 'What is your opinion on the battle of *Badr*, *Uḥud* and *Ḥunayn*?'"[88] This quote seems to express Sa'īd's acceptance of violence in self-defence over against the nonviolent example of Abel and the idea of the need for a new historically determined way of expressing the absolute nonviolent *signified* of the Quran and the prophetic mission.

Thus, from what seems to be a shift from the conception of nonviolence as a method supported in *Maḏhab ibn Ādam* to nonviolence as a philosophy of history and a principle in *Kun ka-ibn Ādam*, Sa'īd goes back to supporting the use of violence as a tool of self-defence in Muhammad's case. This would bring the thinker back to the conception of nonviolence as a method to reach a precise goal that he first presented in 1966. Mallat argues that nonviolence is more than a method for the revolutions in the region: it is a philosophy of history, as previously explained[89]. *Kun ka-ibn Ādam* seemed to confirm Mallat's intuition and thus substantiate the argument presented in this chapter about Sa'īd's connection to the *insāniyyah* described by the Lebanese scholar. The argument of *Kun ka-ibn Ādam* partly confirms this shift and partly contradicts it, failing to account for the use of force during Muhammad's prophetic mission in line with Sa'īd's idea of nonviolence and leaving yet another contradiction to be resolved in Sa'īd's work. This internal division of Sa'īd's thought mirrors the division in the debate about the possibility of the use of violence in Islam. Leaman, who retraces this debate, highlights the existence of two main schools on this topic, the absolutist one and the consequentialist one[90]. The similarity of these terms to the division between absoluteness and relativity in Sa'īd's thought deserves comment. On the one hand, the absolutist current believes in an absolute prohibition of violence, based on an ethical reading of the Quran. On the other hand, the consequentialist view supports the idea that violence can be used in certain situations, especially an instrument of self-defence[91]. These two ideas seem to express the two different positions supported by Sa'īd in *Kun ka-ibn*

88. Ibid., p. 174.
89. Mallat 2015, p. 5.
90. Leaman 2017, p. 70.
91. Ibid., pp. 69–70.

Ādam, as also highlighted by the terms used, and thus Saʿīd's backing away from his historicist exegesis can be read as a return from an absolutist stance to a consequentialist one, already supported in 1966 in *Maḏhab ibn Ādam*.

Why then does Saʿīd back away from the theories elaborated in *Kun ka-ibn Ādam*? In his critique of Saʿīd's thought, Belhaj accuses him of having a romantic idea of Muhammad's prophetic mission[92]. Belhaj argues that Saʿīd is convinced that the early period of Islam was dominated by peace, following this idea shared by many reformists[93]. In Belhaj's critique, that would be the reason for Saʿīd's lack of a clear explanation of the use of violence during the prophetic mission. As this chapter has shown, however, Saʿīd seems to be conscious of the use of violence by the prophet Muhammad and consequently tries to find a way to justify it and integrate it into his theory of nonviolence. In his first book, he does that by relegating the use of violence to a specific time. In his book analysed here, he constructs the exegetical tools that could help him overcome the problem of the use of violence by Muhammad, but, as has been shown, in the end, he goes back to his first theory. This approach seems to show how much attention he devotes to the question of the use of violence during the prophetic mission. Nevertheless, a question still remains. Why would Saʿīd back off from the absolutist theories, using Leaman's definition, developed in *Kun ka-ibn Ādam* and move toward the consequentialist theories of his first book?

There is no clear answer to this question, but some hypotheses can be provided. First, it is important to look at Saʿīd's historical context. This was briefly outlined in the introduction to this chapter, and it was a context of repression, in reference to both his personal experience and his times in general in the region. He lived in Egypt during the 1950s, where he probably witnessed the persecutions against the Muslim Brotherhood. He also experienced Assad's repression in Ḥamāh in 1982 and the legal case against Abu Zayd's theories in 1992[94]. As seen from this analysis, Saʿīd's ideas and Abu Zayd's are quite close. Thus, Saʿīd might have

92. Belhaj 2017, p. 237. What is true in Belhaj's critique is that Saʿīd does not deal at all with the aggressive use of violence by the prophet during his mission.

93. Ibid. 2017, p. 243.

94. Kepel 2006, p. 18. Trombetta 2017, p. 117.

worried about facing the same fate as Abu Zayd or repression in general by using his theories to interpret Muhammad's life and actions – especially since Muhammad's behaviour is traditionally seen as a perfect role model and thus not easily subject to question[95]. This could be a probable interpretation if Saʿīd had not faced repression from the Syrian regime several times, being imprisoned various times and forced to leave his job as a teacher but never abandoning his ideas and principles[96]. Then, another explanation may relate to what could be the true goal of his work. Looking at his life experience, it can be argued that his main preoccupation was the spread of the violence he was witnessing. Saʿīd dedicated his life to fighting the idea that problems could be solved by using violent methods and argued that the true meaning of the Quran was a nonviolent one. He probably wanted his ideas to spread and be accepted by everybody, from philosophers to lay believers. To do so, Saʿīd might have preferred to explain his nonviolent reading of Muhammad's actions in a more traditional way, focusing on the importance of the Prophet as a role model and highlighting how such a model could be interpreted and followed in a nonviolent way. Saʿīd probably thought that his ideas about a separation between *signifier* and *signified*, when fully applied, would create problems for the general acceptance of his theories, as happened in the case of Abu Zayd's ideas. Hence, such considerations could have motivated him to not put his theories about the separation between *signifier* and *signified* into practice. Even more, he was accused by ʿĀdil al-Tall, a strong critic of his ideas, of being a materialist and of polluting the interpretation of the Quran even before the publication of *Kun ka-ibn Ādam*[97]. Such critiques might have pushed him to stick to a more traditional interpretation to raise fewer perplexities in his readers and to allow his ideas to spread more easily.

7. Conclusion

In this chapter, I explored the development of a historical method of exegesis of the Quran and its use in support of a nonviolent interpretation

95. On the *Imitatio Muhammadi*, see, for instance, Schimmel 1975.
96. Dumairieh 2017, pp. xv–xx.
97. al-Tall 1995, p. 92.

of the text. I was also able to examine the ideas of the Syrian thinker Ǧawdat Saʿīd, starting with his ideas about the decline of Islamic society. Moreover, I analysed Saʿīd's diagnosis of the origin of this decay, highlighting his idea of decline as stemming from the use of violence, which comes from wrong interpretations of the Quranic text. The separation between the *signifier* and the *signified* in the Quran was pointed out as the cause of these wrong interpretations and the historicist approach used by Saʿīd was described to reconnect these two aspects. I examined how these ideas could be applied to support the nonviolent reading of the Quran and the prophetic mission, overcoming the problems encountered by the author in this first work from 1966. Finally, I provided a possible interpretation for the thinker's retreat from the historicist exegesis applied to Muhammad's mission.

The chapter conducted an in-depth analysis of the use of history as an exegetical tool and its consequences on nonviolent interpretation of the Quran in *Kun ka-ibn Ādam*. Such an investigation was missing from the literature on Ǧawdat Saʿīd's works and proposed a possible interpretation for his approach to the use of violence in the prophetic mission. This suggested an alternative to Belhaj's explanation.

Furthermore, using the framework of analysis outlined by Mallat, I have been able to highlight Saʿīd's similarities with many other thinkers included by the Lebanese scholar within *insāniyyah*. Consequently, Saʿīd's thought could be inscribed into this current, and, although his open focus on nonviolence is a marker of his originality, the ideas he draws on make him a clear expression of this humanist line of thinking. As such, his nonviolent ideas should not be read with surprise or as an outright exception but as the expression of a long trend of thought that gives proper support and builds foundations that could be used to support ideas and interpretations of the Quran and Islam such as those proposed by Saʿīd. Moreover, Saʿīd focuses on humanity as the receiving end of the Quranic message. Its role in changing the destiny of the *ummah* by learning from history points to the humanism that is deeply rooted in Saʿīd's thought. Still relying on Mallat's framework, I showed the partial shift from nonviolence as a method to nonviolence as a philosophy of history.

In light of this analysis, it can be argued that Saʿīd is part of an Islamic humanist current of thought that, even if it does not focus directly on developing nonviolent philosophies, built the epistemological tools that could be used for this. Hence, nonviolence in Islamic thought is not an exception per se but the product of a long philosophical development within the *insāniyyah* tradition. Furthermore, it can be argued that Saʿīd is well aware of all the implications and the shortcomings of his theories, especially concerning the use of violence during Muhammad's prophetic mission, but nevertheless tries to deal with them to reach his objectives.

Finally, the analysis of the contents of Saʿīd's works on nonviolence outlined in this chapter can be the starting point for further investigations on the overall reception of his thought and the use that has been made of it by nonviolent activists, such as those involved in the 2011 Syrian uprising. Indeed, without a clear knowledge of the themes and methods he approached in his works, of which an initial analysis has been provided here, an investigation of their reception and their possible application would be impossible.

References

Abu Zayd, N. (2002), *Islam e storia*, Bollati Boringhieri, Torino.

Abu Zayd, N. (2003), *The Dilemma of the Literary Approach to the Qur'an*, in "Alif: Journal of Comparative Poetics", 23, pp. 8–47. https://doi.org/10.2307/1350075

Belhaj, A. (2017), *Jawdat Sa'id and the Muslim Philosophy of Peace*, in H. Shadi (ed.), *Islam Peace Ethics*, Nomos Verlag, Baden-Baden, pp. 229–245.

Bennabi, M. (2006), *Vocation de l'Islam*, Albouraq, Beirut.

al-Būṭī, S. R. (1994), *al-Ǧihād fī l-islām*, Dār al-fikr, Damascus.

Black, A. (2011), *The History of Islamic Political Thought: From the Prophet to the Present*, Edinburgh University Press, Edinburgh.

Dumairieh, N. (2017), *Introduzione*, in Saʿīd, Ǧ., *Vie islamiche alla non violenza*, trans. P. Pizzi, Zikkaron, Bologna.

Fieni, D. (2012), *French decadence, Arab Awakenings: Figures of Decay in the Arab Nahda*, in "Boundary 2: An International Journal of Literature and Culture", 39, 2, pp. 143–160. https://doi.org/10.1215/01903659-1597916

Hourani, A. (2013), *Arabic Thought in the Liberal Age, 1798–1939*, Cambridge University Press, Cambridge-New York.

Iqbāl, M. (2012), *The Reconstruction of Religious Thought in Islam*, Stanford University Press, Stanford.

al-Kawākibī, A. (1941), *Umm al-qurà*, al-Maṭbuʿah al-miṣriyyah bi-l-Azhar, Cairo.

Kepel, G. (2006), *Il profeta e il faraone. I Fratelli musulmani alle origini del movimento islamista*, trans. F. Galimberti, Laterza, Roma-Bari.

Larkin, M. (1988), *The Inimitability of the Qur'an: Two Perspectives*, in "Religion and Literature", 20, 1, pp. 31–47.

Leaman, O. (2017), *Peace and Violence in Islam: Philosophical Issues*, in H. Shadi (ed.), *Islam Peace Ethics*, Nomos Verlag, Baden-Baden, pp. 69–82.

Mallat, C. (2015), *Revolution, Constitutionalism, and Justice beyond the Middle East*, Oxford University Press, New York and Oxford.

al-Mawardi, H. (2000), *The Ordinance of Government*, Garnet Publishing, London.

Menghini, P. (2019), *Nonviolence in Islam: Jawdat Sa'id and the Path of Adam's First Son*, in "Afkar: The Undergraduate Journal of Middle East Studies", 1, pp. 49–59.

Müller, J. (2010), *Désarmer les dieux: Le christianisme et l'islam face à la non-violence*, Les Editions du Relié, Paris.

Ollivry-Dumairieh, F. (2016), *Jawdat Saïd: Penseur de la non violence en Islam*, in "Ultreïa!", 9, 1, pp. 132–136.

al-Qādirī, Ġ. (2006), *Ǧawdat Sa'īd nubḏah 'an sīratihi wa-fikratihi wa-a'amālihi*, in Salim M. A. (ed.), *Ǧawdat Sa'īd: Buhūṯ wa-maqalāt muhdà ilayhi*, Dār al-fikr, Damascus, pp. 17–27.

Qutb, S. (2006), *Milestones*, Islamic Book Service, New Delhi.

Roberts, H. (1994), *From Radical Mission to Equivocal Ambition: The Expansion and Manipulation of Algerian Islamism, 1979–1992*, in Marty E. M. (ed.), *Accounting for Fundamentalisms: The Dynamic Character of Movements*, University of Chicago Press, Chicago, pp. 428–489.

Said, E. (1996), *Covering Islam. How Media and the Experts Determine How We See the Rest of the World*, Vintage Books, New York.

Sa'īd, Ǧ. (1972), *Ḥattà mā yuġayyirū mā bi-anfusihim*, available at https://www.jawdatsaid.net (last accessed 28 February 2021).

Sa'īd, Ǧ. (1988), *Iqra'! Wa-rabbuka al-akram*, available at https://www.jawdatsaid.net (last accessed 24 February 2021).

Sa'īd, Ǧ. (1993), *Maḏhab ibn Ādam al-awwal: Muškilat al-'unf fī l-'amal al-islāmī*, Dār al-fikr al-mu'āṣir, Beirut.

Sa'īd, Ǧ. (1997), *Kun ka-ibn Ādam*, Dār al-fikr al-mu'āṣir, Beirut.

Saussure, F. (2005), *Corso di linguistica generale*, trans. T. De Mauro, Laterza, Roma-Bari.

Schimmel, A. (1975), *And Muhammad Is His Messenger: The Veneration of the Prophet in Islamic Piety*, University of North Carolina Press, Chapel Hill.

Sevea, I. S. (2012), *The Political Philosophy of Muhammad Iqbal: Islam and Nationalism in Late Colonial India*, Cambridge University Press, Cambridge.

Shariati, A. (1979), *On the Sociology of Islam: Lectures by Ali Shariati*, Mizan Press, Berkley.

Soroush, A. (2000), *Reason, Freedom & Democracy in Islam*, Oxford University Press, Oxford.

Taha, M. M. (2006), *The Second Message of Islam*, Syracuse University Press, Syracuse.

al-Tall, A. (1995), *al-Naz'ah al-māddiyyah fī l-'ālam al-islāmī*, Dār al-bayyinah, Damascus.

Trombetta, L. (2017), *Siria, dagli ottomani agli Asad. E oltre*, Mondadori, Milan.

Vasalou, S. (2002), *The Miraculous Eloquence of the Qur'an: General Trajectories and Individual Approaches*, in "Journal of Qur'anic Studies", 4, 2, pp. 23–53. https://doi.org/10.3366/jqs.2002.4.2.23

Walsh, S. J. (2007), *Killing Post-Almohad man: Malek Bennabi, Algerian Islamism and the Search for a Liberal Governance*, in "The Journal of North African Studies", 12, 2, pp. 235–254. https://doi.org/10.1080/13629380701235251

Webel, C. (2007), *Introduction: toward a Philosophy and Metapsychology of Peace*, In Webel, C., Galtung, J. (eds), *Handbook of Peace and Conflict Studies*, Routledge, London and New York, pp. 4–13.

Weismann, I. (2015), *Abd al-Rahman al-Kawakibi: Islamic Reform and Arab Revival*, Simon and Schuster, New York.

Pietro Menghini is a PhD candidate at the Scuola Superiore Meridionale, Naples. His work focuses on the history of the Sadrist Trend during the 1990s, and his research interests concentrate on Islamic political thought and the history of the Middle East. He previously graduated in Islamic and Arabic Studies from the University of Naples "L'Orientale" with a dissertation on the nonviolent Syrian thinker Ǧawdat Sa'īd.

Part 2

From Literature of War to Literature of Reconciliation

Chapter 3

The Iran-Iraq War in Iraqi Novels: Oblivion and Disappearance

Ronen Zeidel

Abstract

This chapter discusses the writing on the Iran-Iraq war in Iraqi novels. It divides the period into three sub-periods: the war (1980–1988), 1988–2003, and 2003–present. During the war, literature was used to justify the war and the number of war novels published was in the thousands. After the end of the war the number declined. Little by little, dissident writers in Iraq and in the diaspora shifted attention from the front to the rear. They chose deserters as protagonists in their war novels instead of the soldiers in the state-sponsored literature. After 2003, this trend became the hallmark of writing on the war. Another recurring motive was that Baʿath repression and war were intertwined. War was the imminent outcome of a process of militarisation masterminded by the Baʿath. With the increased hegemony of Iran and Iran backed political factions in Iraq since the 2010s, it became more complicated to write about the war and to commemorate it. Two recent novels may show a new path.

Keywords: Iran-Iraq War, Iraq, novels, Iraqi literature, Saddam Hussein

1. Introduction

On 8 April 2021, the International Committee of the Red Cross (ICRC) inspected the delivery of the remains of 68 Iraqi soldiers, formerly considered missing in battle, to Iraq. Thirty-three years after the end of the war, Iraq and Iran still engage in similar exchanges. But most commentators on social media resort to the term used by state-owned *Al Iraqiya* TV channel to describe the eight-year war as, namely, an *armed conflict* (*nizāʿ musallaḥ*), as if the war was only a temporary "conflict"[1].

For various reasons, the Iran-Iraq war, is being forgotten in Iraqi official and unofficial memory. Concentrating on the Iraqi novel, this chapter outlines the attitude towards the war from the 1980s through the fall of the Baʿath regime in 2003 to the present, during which the war declined in significance until its almost total disappearance from literature. This chapter traces the change, dividing the period into three sub-periods: the war (1980–1988), 1988–2003, and 2003–present. It also discusses state-sponsored "official" literature and the alternative literature before 2003. After 2003, the previous division lost its relevance, yet writing about the war continued to decline. Contextualising novels in the period of their writing and publication provides explanations of this process. In terms of discipline, this study is a historical outline that uses literature as source material. It reflects the representation, or lack of representation, of the war in Iraqi novels and explains it through historical events and personal reasons of the writers. While acknowledging and discussing the exceptions, the study focuses on the general trend.

Very little was written about the Iraqi novel and the Iran-Iraq war. Muhsin al-Musawi's *Reading Iraq: Culture and Power in Conflict* is more about how the Iraqi spirit is expressed through art and prose. Fabio Caiani and Catherine Cobham's *The Iraqi Novel: Key Writers, Key Texts* reviews the history of the modern novel in Iraq and focuses on "key writers", including an analysis of the war in Mahdī ʿĪsà al-Ṣaqr's novels. Eric Davis' *Memories of State: Politics, History, and Collective Identity in Modern Iraq* contributes to the debate on hegemony, regime, and their role in the production of culture in pre-2003 Iraq but does not cover the period after 2003. A collection of articles edited by Stefan Milich, Friederike Pannewick, and Leslie Tramontini, *Conflicting Narratives: War, Trauma and Memory in Iraqi Culture*, not only deals with novels or the Iran-Iraq war but also introduces the term "trauma" to describe the cultural

1. https://m.facebook.com/photo?fbid=3877167459029133&set=a.669645503114694&_rdr

production in the 1990s and the first decade of the 21st century as the result of a cumulation of wars. Ikram Masmoudi's *War and Occupation in Iraqi Fiction* focuses more on the impact of wars on the Iraqi individual, using Agamben's concept of *homo sacer* (the sacred man) to describe the life of the Iraqi individual who serves as the hero of the novels she analyses. This individual is an outcast, excluded from both divine and human law and reduced to being a living dead person. In the first chapter, Masmoudi investigates in-depth some novels on the Iran-Iraq war written after 2003, but she barely discusses many novels written during the war and before the American invasion.

This chapter is not about how wars affected the Iraqi individual; rather, it is about writers and their choice to write or not to write about the Iran-Iraq war. I argue that opposition writers chose to illuminate different sides of the war or not to write about it at all[2]. This chapter is not about the devaluation of Iraqi lives from the 1980s onward; it is about the devaluation of the Iran-Iraq War and its memory.

More relevant is Amir Moosavi's dissertation, *Reimagining War*[3]. Moosavi compares Arab Iraqi and Persian literary works on the war, claiming that soldiers and writers on both sides essentially experienced the same event. He charts a process by which state-sanctioned official literature on the war on both sides turned into literature expressing loss and agony and later into a vehicle of protest. He concentrates on the post-war period. My study covers the war and post-war periods and, in the Iraqi case, it also covers post-2003. Not able to read Persian, I could not compare Iraqi works with Persian works. Moreover, I present a general look at Iraqi literature on the war rather than an individual look at each and every writer or text. My perspective is more historical and political than literary. I argue that, because the two countries have followed completely different paths during and after the war, comparing their literatures misses a crucial point: Iraq changed dramatically after 2003, whereas change in Iran was minor.

2. al-Musawi 2006; Caiani, Cobham 2013, particularly chapter 6, pp. 163–194; Davis 2005; Milich, Pannewick, Tramontini 2012; Masmoudi 2015; Zeidel 2020.
3. Moosavi 2016. The dissertation will be published as a book called *Dust that Never Settled: Afterlives of the Iran-Iraq War in Arabic and Persian Literatures*.

Some of the above-mentioned books are more useful than the others in discussing the Iran-Iraq war. For the discussion of pre-2003 literature on the Iran-Iraq War, however, the most useful study is Salām ʿAbbūd's *Ṯaqāfat al-ʿunf fī l-ʿIraq* (The Culture of Violence in Iraq), published in 2002[4]. ʿAbbūd, a literary critic and Iraqi émigré, focuses on the relation between a dictatorial regime and its intellectuals. He accurately describes the dilemmas faced by the intellectuals living under such a regime and the ease of achieving conformity[5]. Unlike Masmoudi, ʿAbbūd does not ignore the "War Novels" and refers to them often. He looks at a large number of novels written during the war that glorify it and use his sometimes intimate acquaintance with the authors to provide a context for why they served the regime. For some, an early arrest or admonition was enough to achieve total cooperation. For others, that was not even needed: prizes, remunerations, and prestige were enough for co-optation and compliance. Significantly, ʿAbbūd does not see any difference between authors writing on the war in Iraq and outside of it. On the contrary, some Iraq-based writers, such as Mahdī ʿĪsà al-Ṣaqr and Muḥammad Ḫuḍayr, were more daring by their refusal to write on the war than writers in the diaspora. ʿAbbūd published his book in 2002, one year before the American invasion. His book, thus, does not cover the changes in Iraqi literature after 2003 and their implications on the writing on the Iran-Iraq war.

Remembering the war in Iraqi literature is not separate from the tribulations of Iraqi history between 1980–2021. Accordingly, this chapter divides the period into three sub-periods: the Iran-Iraq war (1980–1988), the post-war era and the 1990s (1988–2003), and post-2003. The last period is one in which a totally different literature on the war emerged for the first time.

This essay is based on a reading of over 300 Iraqi novels written and published between 1980 and 2021. Not all of them are about the Iran-Iraq War. I argue that reading a large number of novels gives a better idea of the scope and true weight of an event than an analysis of a few hand-picked and iconic novels. Every relevant novel is analysed according to a set of questions: How central is the war in the novels? Does the plot take

4. ʿAbbūd 2002.
5. An article on the disposition of Iraqi novelists during the 1990s and the change after 2003 is Zeidel 2017.

place at the front or the rear? Who are the heroes? Are red lines – whether imposed by the Baʿath regime or others[6] – respected? If written before 2003, was the novel sponsored by the Saddam regime or not? Finally, I compare the number of novels on the war written before and after 2003 and in every sub-period.

2. The War Period

Throughout its history, the Iraqi regime under Saddam Hussein attached particular significance to literary output and the novel. This proclivity began during the Iran-Iraq War. In later periods, Saddam ordered novelists to fashion their state-sponsored literature along similar lines set during the war[7]. The state-sponsored campaign to glorify the war started once the war stalled, around 1981 and seriously threatened Saddam's regime. It continued to the last day of the war, involving most writers in Iraq. The campaign was called *adab al-ḥarb* (war literature) or *adab al-Qādisiyyah* (the literature of Qādisiyyah), named after the battle in which the Muslims defeated the Persians in 636 AD. The official name of the Iran-Iraq War was *Qādisiyyat Ṣaddām* (Saddam's Qādisiyyah). The number of titles published during the war by the official press of the Ministry of Information in this campaign is estimated to be in the thousands.

Salām ʿAbbūd divides this literature into two periods. In the first period, well-known writers who did not take an active part in the war glorified the war. They wrote about ordinary soldiers as if they were "Rambos" annihilating the Iranian enemy by hand. These books are replete with sadistic descriptions of killing the enemy[8], and such writing continued well into the last years of the war. ʿAbbūd differentiates between young

6. Red lines are invisible borders of subjects that should not be discussed in the novel. I will outline the red lines for each period and examine whether novels and authors respect them. Red lines are not only imposed by totalitarian regimes, such as Saddam's. Post-2003 red lines have also been set by Iran and its proxies in the Iraqi political arena and the streets or, in contrast, by Iraqi patriotic nationalism.
7. For a discussion of the regime and literature in Iraq in the last years of the Baʿath see Zeidel 2017. This is the only research focusing on the interaction between the regime and literary circles. Other studies focus on the texts, the content, and the writers along with their life experiences.
8. ʿAbbūd 2002, p. 28.

writers who served on the front and older writers, who were not mobilised, who wrote about the war, usually glorifying it in supernatural terms. Nevertheless, in most cases, the younger generation wrote prose that was completely detached from their experiences at the front because nothing else was permitted. ʿAbbūd calls the distance between what the writer would like to write and what he is expected to be writing "the killing distance" (*al-masāfah al-qātilah*) that kills creativity. This inner struggle produced a change toward the end of the war. Young and gifted writers who fought on the front had to comply with literary norms imposed by the regime and write about the war in heroic and supernatural terms.

ʿAbbūd traces the change in the writer Ǧāsim al-Raṣīf, who served about eight years on the frontlines and won several literary prizes for his prose at the time. His last war novel *Hiǧābāt al-ǧaḥīm* (The Gates of Hell), published in the last year of the war, is a more realistic presentation of the front. The detailed description of the front and the battles and the more realistic protagonists serve as a contrast to the previous style of war novels, including those by al-Raṣīf himself. ʿAbbūd notices that, not only did al-Raṣīf start writing differently about the war in 1988, but other writers, such as Fayṣal ʿAbd al-Ḥasan, adopted the same more realistic style as well. Both al-Raṣīf and ʿAbd al-Ḥasan served on the front and were laureated by the regime for their later novels. ʿAbbūd does not believe that this change could have occurred without official encouragement. In his mind, these novels were commissioned by the regime towards the end of the war. In other words, preparing for peace necessitated a rough description of war. Because peace – or rather the end of the war – was not expected, I am not convinced that this is the right explanation[9].

3. State-Sponsored Novels: Examples of *adab al-ḥarb*

Following the American and Russian examples of war literature contributing to the war effort, the Iraqi regime invested a great deal in the writing and publication of war literature (prose, poetry, etc.) during the war and its distribution to the units at the front. It came to be known as *adab al-ḥarb*. Most of this literature was of very low literary quality, and

9. Ibid., p. 36.

scholars tend to underestimate its significance[10]. Yet, the sheer volume of this literature – hundreds of novels by leading writers and upstarts – leaves little doubt that the State invested seriously in this field. Nothing similar on this war was published in later periods, including after the regime change in 2003. Out of an ideological necessity to justify a war which was being prolonged, a literary campaign emerged with its own rules and red lines dictated by the censor.

I will focus on a sample of novels written and published during the war. These are ʿĀyid Ḫiṣbāk's *al-Qamar al-ṣaḥrawī* (Desert Moon), Saʿd Muḥammad Raḥīm's *Hākaḏa istanṭaqnā al-fulāḏ* (This Is How We Made the Steel Speak) and Hišām Tawfīq al-Rikābī's *Aʿdād al-Midfaʿ 106* (Battery 106), all published in 1983; Ǧāsim al-Raṣīf's *Ḫaṭṭ aḥmar* (Red Line), published in 1985, and *Abǧadiyyat al-mawt ḥubb*[an] (The Alphabet of Dying of Love), published after the two Gulf Wars in 1991[11].

All these novels were written and published in crucial times during the war, which became defensive from 1982 onward. All these novels won prizes in literary contests of war novels. Significantly, all the novels are set at the front and their protagonists are soldiers. In fact, the real protagonist of the novels from 1983 is the small military unit serving at the front. It serves as a microcosm of Iraq, with soldiers representing a variety of geographies (the city and the rural areas), social categories (e.g., the educated, the uneducated, and students – a sector known for its reluctance to be recruited), and ethnicities (mainly Arabs and Kurds). All of them are like a family. They face an enemy preparing an offensive.

Although the plot is set at the front, the protagonists carry memories of their civilian lives. In particular, relations with the women they love or – if they are married – with their families. These are often painful memories of romantic disappointments: in Ḫiṣbāk's novel, for instance, the hero discovers that the woman he loves works as a prostitute. The masculine camaraderie at the front serves as a compensation to the failures of romantic life at home.

10. Masmoudi (2015) does not use this literature in her book. The only scholar who refers to this genre is Salām ʿAbbūd (2002) to bash the contributors and show the lethal damage by the dictatorship to Iraqi culture.
11. Ḫiṣbāk 1983; Raḥīm 1983; al-Rikābī 1983; al-Raṣīf 2002; al-Raṣīf 2000.

The novel *Ḫaṭṭ aḥmar* by Ǧāsim al-Raṣīf takes place in Basra and the nearby southern front. It was written when Basra was being heavily bombarded by Iran, thus al-Raṣīf turns the city into a protagonist of the novel. The positive figures volunteer to serve at the front. One of them, a combat pilot, continues his mission into Iran to destroy more targets than needed. The other novel, *Abǧadiyyat al-mawt ḥubb*[an], is located in Fao, the remote Iraqi hamlet on the Gulf, occupied by the Iranians in 1986 and retaken by the Iraqis in 1988. Using polyphony as a narrative technique, he again makes the town his real protagonist. The novel has two other main protagonists: a local woman, who fights along with the other soldiers and is taken prisoner, and a fresh recruit, an anti-hero who does not know how to shoot yet insists on taking part in the Iraqi offensive. His friend is shot, but he ignores it and continues running. Like all the main protagonists of these novels, he is killed in the end. In al-Rikābī's novel, three out of four soldiers die in battle. One of them, Nāẓim, who loses both legs during the battle, evades being captured by Iranian troops by killing himself. The implicit message is that dying a martyr's death in battle is preferable to survival in captivity[12]. This motif will be repeated in novels on captivity published in the late 1990s. In contrast, the woman in al-Raṣīf's *Abǧadiyyah* is convinced by her fellow soldiers not to die in battle and is thus "allowed" to be captured. By doing so, al-Raṣīf uses his female protagonist to demonise the enemy, which is another hallmark of this genre. Thus, in *Abǧadiyyah*, the author describes Iranian atrocities committed on Iraqi prisoners of war (POWs)[13]. In Raḥīm's novel, the Iranians are labelled "insects"[14]. In ʿĀyid Ḫiṣbāk's novel, there is both dehumanisation and contempt of the Iranian enemy: their planes never hit the targets, their soldiers (unlike Iraqi soldiers) surrender without fighting, and their tanks "go like sheep to the slaughter"[15]. In al-Rikābī's novel, Iranians are portrayed as criminals, murderers, and aggressors and are held responsible for the prolongation of the war. This combination of dehumanisation and contempt follows ideological guidelines and could also be seen in other products of Iraqi war propaganda at the time, specifically cartoons.

12. For more on commemoration of the war see: Baram, Rohde, Zeidel 2012, p. 116.
13. al-Raṣīf 2000, pp. 114–115, 138.
14. Raḥīm 1983, p. 214.
15. Ḫiṣbāk 1983, p. 142.

Despite the limited space for freedom to describe the horrors of war, all these novels obey the ideological guidelines set by the Iraqi regime. None of the novels in my sample contains overt praise for the regime and Saddam Hussein. Instead, they do it in subtler ways. In al-Rikābī's novel, the political guidance officer, the Baʿath party's representative in every unit, insists on accompanying the soldiers to the front lines in order to raise their morale[16]. This is the only overt reference to the party, whilst Saddam Hussein is never mentioned directly or indirectly. The subtlety is expressed by not crossing the red lines. The novels justify the war, which is presented as a patriotic and defensive war but also as fate (*qadar*)[17]. There is no mention of deserters and the possibility of deserting. In Rikābī's novel, the commander warns his soldiers that retreat in battle is treachery and will be punished by public execution[18]. In contrast, the protagonists even enjoy returning to their small unit at the front after their leaves. In fact, some of them even escape their troubles back home by joining the troops. As shown before, the Iranian enemy is dehumanised but is also accused of prolonging the war[19].

When the main Iranian demand to end the war was the removal of Saddam Hussein, the novels never question the legitimacy of the Saddam regime and never consider that to be a proper way of ending the war. The novels glorify the war by presenting it as something that transcends normal life and fabricates heroes[20]. Inexplicably, all the novels end with the death of the main characters. This probably reflects the war situation at the time and lauds the value of self-sacrifice in defence of the homeland. However, death – as in Raḥīm's novel – is not the end of life but its continuation.

4. State-Sponsored Literature in the 1990s

Following the end of the war in 1988, the number of war novels decreased. Ǧāsim al-Raṣīf's novel *Abǧadiyyah* (1991) is probably the last war novel

16. al-Rikābī 1983, p. 147.
17. Ibid., pp. 148, 219.
18. Ibid., pp. 303–304.
19. Ibid., p. 329.
20. This is a central motif in Saʿd Muḥammad Raḥīm's novels as well as in other.

in the style of the 1980s. After another war in 1990–1991 and the imposition of international sanctions, the emphasis in the novels turned from the front to the rear, portraying the suffering under the embargo. The Iran-Iraq war was presented now as part of a sequence of wars imposed on Iraq which still continues despite the ceasefire.

In most state-sponsored novels, the war faded into the near past in the plot. The protagonist typically reminisces about the war while suffering from sanctions. One exception appeared toward the end of the 1990s and was embraced by Saddam Hussein in a meeting with writers in 2000. These are novels about the experiences of Iraqi POWs in Iranian captivity. There were multiple reasons for the publication of POWs novels at that time. Most of the POWs returned to Iraq in exchanges during the 1990s, and there was a need to reintegrate them into society. Their stories also showed perseverance – facing torture and record-long captivity – and this was a value that the Iraqi regime intended to promote[21]. POWs' novels share some aspects with state-sponsored war literature. The Iran-Iraq war is the formative experience and the present tense of the plot. Being captured was the worst scenario and – like the protagonists of the war novels – the POWs preferred to die in battle rather than live in prolonged agony. The experience of captivity enables the writers to present a dehumanised and demonic enemy. Captivity also enables the prisoners to be steadfast as Iraqis and as Baʿathists. This literature differs from war novels, however, in the change in location from the warfront to prisoner camps in Iran.

Writers were now instructed to write about other events such as the Kuwait war (1991), the Shiite and Kurdish rebellions, and the hardship of the sanctions. Consequently, the Iran-Iraq war lost its primacy to be "the great patriotic war" that it actually was. Yet the sheer volume of the literature produced during the war contributed to the preservation of its memory in later periods.

21. These novels include *Makān aswad* (A Black Place) by Muḥammad Mazīd (1999); *Ḍuyūf fī qafṣ* (Guests in a Cage) by Fāḍil ʿAbbās al-Kaʿbi (1999); *Madinat al-ḏiyāb* (The City of Wolves) by ʿĀdil al-Šawiyyah (1999); *Bustān ʿAbbūd* (ʿAbbūd's Orchard) by Ṭāriq ʿAbd Allāh al-Mašhadānī (2000). On POW novels, see Zeidel 2008.

5. Alternative Writing on the War in Pre-2003 Novels

Alternative writing on the war in Iraq and the diaspora started with a delay. Aside from *adab al-ḥarb* and its contributors, other writers in Iraq and the emerging diaspora did not write about the war during the 1980s. There may be various reasons. In Iraq it was extremely dangerous or even impossible to defy the official line. Outside Iraq, opposition writers or writers who fled for political reasons found themselves in a sensitive position and may have opted not to write critically on a war waged against their homeland. Some, especially those who were members of the Iraqi Communist Party, were still shocked by pre-war events that forced them to emigrate and preferred to concentrate on the loss of political power before the war. Since all of them were out of Iraq, the war was not part of their daily reality and they preferred to write about life in exile.

Salām ʿAbbūd noticed that location alone does not explain how one writes on the war. Interestingly, the seeds of change started in exile and in Iraq (albeit more modestly) at the same time in the first half of the 1990s. This never became a trend, and the number of novels is small. In the 1990s there were other experiences to write about: the Gulf War, the 1991 Shiite Intifada, the sanctions, repression, and, for many, also the hopelessness of life during the 1990s – a common subject in post-2003 literature on that period. Well-known writers who contributed extensively to the war literature and fled Iraq during the 1990s – notably al-Raṣīf and ʿAbd al-Sattār Nāṣir – did not write about the war from exile and preferred to write about repression.

Aside from being anti-Baʿathist, alternative writing on the war has two characteristics: shifting the location from the front to the rear and choosing deserters as protagonists. The front is where all the battles took place, and being there meant active engagement in warfare. However, the road to the rear was also very dangerous and any soldier who made it could run across Baʿth party patrols, literally hunting deserters. This is where Agamben's concept of *homo sacer* – namely, someone who is not sacred enough to be accepted by the gods and can still easily be killed by humans – can be useful. As clarified above, Masmoudi applies it to this genre of the novel. By writing about deserters, the authors defied some of the red lines set by the regime. Their heroes choose not to be part of the war machine and undermine the justification of the war. In addition, the act of desertion does not save them. Writing about deserters would figure more in post-2003 novels on the war. The rear is another battlefront between the deserters and the forces of repression representing the regime. Thus, by shifting from the front in which Iraqis fight an external foe, the writers focus on the internal conflict, within Saddam's Iraq, between totalitarian repression and its victims.

Apparently, the first to write an alternative novel on the war was Berlin-based Naǧm Wālī. Wālī left Iraq in 1980, deserting the army after a very short military service at the beginning of the war. The manuscript of *al-Ḥarb fī ḥayy al-Ṭarab* (War in Ḥayy al-Ṭarab) was written in Germany between 1983 and 1985 but was only published in 1993[22]. Ḥayy al-Ṭarab is the red-light district of Basra, so close yet so far from the front. It is the "other Iraq", a microcosm, just like the military unit in the war novels of the regime. This location is another protagonist of the novel, along with its three heroes, and a special chapter is dedicated to it. Ḥayy al-Ṭarab is the realm of the gypsies, foreign workers, and other outcasts. It is a centre of prostitution, drinking and dancing, and the place where the three persons at the centre of the plot find shelter. Two of the three protagonists are deserters, and one of them even killed his commander. They arrive at a place where people have heard about the war but do not really know where it is. While there, the heroes are in limbo since staying is not an option and they do not have anywhere to escape to. Eventually, the district is besieged by the regime forces. The novel ends with a battle between the deserters and the regime forces – a battle for their lives. In the final lines, Wālī draws a parallel between this battle and the front: "[the military police] deployed there [around a terrace of a house in Ḥayy al-Ṭarab] just as they deploy along the front lines"[23]. Just as in the war novels, Wālī's heroes face a dead end.

A different alternative novel, penned this time by a well-known Iraq-based author, is *Bayt ʿalà nahr Diǧlah* (A House on the Tigris River) by Mahdī ʿĪsà al-Ṣaqr[24]. The novel was published in 2006 in Damascus, but the manuscript was written in Baghdad in 1991 and 1992. Wālī wrote his novel in Germany during the war, but al-Ṣaqr wrote this daring manuscript

22. Wālī 1993.
23. Ibid., p. 135.
24. al-Ṣaqr 2006.

in Baghdad, risking his life and knowing that it might not be published. The fact that some alternative novels were written by well-known writers in Iraq – even if they were only published after 2003 – is evidence that not all writers were willing to comply with the dictates of the regime[25].

The novel is about a soldier who returns home from Iranian captivity. He is mentally ill and constantly evokes memories of his imprisonment, and his return disrupts the life of his family. A pyromaniac, he eventually sets the house on fire. The novel is set in 1991–1992, four years after the war and one year after another war. The novel is not about the war or captivity, it is about a family in Baghdad having to rehabilitate a war victim. In one of the central scenes, the atrocities of the war are seen from the angle of the military morgue in Baghdad. During the war, the hero was presumed missing in battle, and his sister goes to the morgue to check if his body has arrived. Al-Ṣaqr mentions the large number of trucks carrying dead bodies. He also criticises the vulgarity of the staff there: "The gang [*al-ǧamāʿah*, a reference to Tikritis close to Saddam] asks about the quantity of onions for this week". "Onions" was code for bodies: this scene breaks a taboo on the number of casualties in the war and therefore could have never been published under Saddam[26]. This is how the war is seen from the rear: morgues, a mentally ill former POW, and a disrupted family life. This is the impact of war rather than the war itself.

Al-Ṣaqr continued writing about these themes in a later novel, *Ṣirāḫ al-nawāris* (The Seagull's Cry) in 1997[27]. Significantly, this novel was published in Beirut but under the Baʿath, which surely knew that the book was issued. Here again, one of the main characters returns from captivity mentally ill. He tries to commit suicide by drowning himself in Ḥabbāniyyah lake, but it is not clear whether he committed suicide or was murdered. The main suspect for the alleged murder is his brother who evaded conscription. Al-Ṣaqr conveys his solidarity with the war's collateral victims in their difficulty to adjust to normal life through the narrator – the son of the deceased. Here again the war is present in the background. The present tense is the 1990s and the location is a tourist resort on Ḥabbāniyyah lake, west of Baghdad. The Iraqi regime allowed

25. For more on the atmosphere in literary circles during the 1990s, see Zeidel 2017.
26. al-Ṣaqr 2006, p. 174.
27. al-Ṣaqr 1997.

its publication possibly because of its affinity for ex-POWs and the negative depiction of the draft-dodging brother.

Another novel written before the fall of Saddam is *al-Ḥikāyah al-sādisah* (The Sixth Story) by Ṭāhā Ḥāmid al-Šabīb[28]. The novel was written in Baghdad in 2001 and published shortly after in Cairo. Al-Šabīb was already known as a dissident writer in Iraq. To avoid problems with the censor, none of his novels make any reference to a specific time or place. Again, the novel focuses on the rear and on the margins of society. The main characters are a group of children who make their living by begging and being supported by some benevolent civilians. The background is a dictatorship in a continuous war. The children, who are mentally retarded, do not understand what war is. They know it is bad and liken it to a monster. One of their benefactors, an old woman, loses her son in the war. Another, a teacher, who refuses to sing nationalistic songs during the morning call at school, is recruited and will be killed in the war. His funeral will serve as an expression of protest against the war and dictatorship. This novel is a protest against the culture of militarism, in which war and repression are intertwined.

Another rare example of an alternative novel is Ḥayāt Šarārah's *Iḏā al-ayyām aġsaqat* (When The Days Grow Dark), published in Beirut in 2000[29]. The manuscript was completed before 1997 in Baghdad, and the writer committed suicide soon after. This novel is about the work routine of a professor at the University of Baghdad who is approaching early retirement. It is emphatically anti-Baʿathist and portrays an ultra-depressing picture of Iraq in the 1990s. It takes place the 1990s, and the main features of life are repression, hopelessness, and economic hardship under sanctions. The war is in the near past. Interestingly, it is more vivid in memory than the more recent Gulf War, which is not mentioned at all. The narrator reminisces on the obligatory military training of staff[30], on students who died during the war[31], on the air raids on Baghdad and the horror they produced[32]. But the most powerful invocation of the war is

28. al-Šabīb 2009.
29. Šarārah 2000. On the author, see a long introduction to the novel by her sister Balqīs Šarārah. See also Chapter 4 in this volume.
30. Šarārah 2000, pp. 187–197.
31. Ibid., p. 282.
32. Ibid., p. 173.

in a recurring dream the narrator has in which he marches with columns of soldiers under the monstrous Victory Arch (Saddam's monument celebrating victory in the war) to their bitter and fateful death. This dream happens again in the last lines of the novel: "The soldiers march in tight lines … under the two swords held by two giant fists and they end with their vanishing. … and I follow them… and become part of this human block […]"[33]. The hallmark of alternative literature on the war is highlighted in this novel: war and totalitarian repression are intertwined.

These were some rare examples of alternative writing on the war before 2003. Unlike official literature on the war, they focus on the rear and on marginal figures in Iraqi society, notably the fugitives. In general, the war lost its central place in both official and unofficial novels, emphasising other issues. Many novels from that period referred to the war in passing. The most common reference, found in many novels, was that everything was painted black due to the proliferation of casualties in every family and corner[34]. Here is how Batūl al-Ḫuḍayrī describes the end of the war in *Kam badat al-samāʾ qarībah* (Heaven Seemed so Close): "The war ended. Some of the prisoners returned. Some of the missing in battle appeared. Some of those present disappeared"[35].

6. The War in Post-2003 Novels

After the removal of Saddam Hussein and the Baʿathist regime, it became possible in Iraq to publish critical books about all aspects of life under the Baʿath, including the war. Yet, the total number of books that mention the war remained low, while books dedicated to the war were uncommon. The new period preserved some of the features of writing on the war from the alternative writing of the 1990s. Fugitives and marginal figures were again at the centre of the plots. In clear reaction to the Baʿathist *adab al-ḥarb*, the heroes were anti-heroes or, in the words of Agamben and Masmoudi, *homo sacer*. The novels are set at the rear rather than the front: in cities, red-light districts and shabby hotels or military training camps from which the hero escapes, instead of real battle fields.

33. Ibid., pp. 103, 316–317.
34. See, for example, *al-Tānkī* (The Water Tower) by ʿĀliyah Mamdūh (2019).
35. al-Ḫuḍayrī 2003, pp. 150–151.

The post-2003 novels on the war elaborated more on the interrelations between war and dictatorship. War was considered the final outcome of a process of the militarisation of society and the state. The Baʿth era was the "khaki-coloured era" (*al-ʿaṣr al-zaytūnī*) in the words of novelist Naṣīf Falak. This militarisation was diagnosed by writers and intellectuals as one of the main deficiencies of Baʿathist Iraq. It was used to shape a deformed national identity and therefore required revision. This was also part of the process of de-Baʿathification which accompanied the transformation of the political regime in Iraq.

The events of 2003 enabled intellectuals to have a historical perspective on the recent history of Iraq. Consequently, the innovation of post 2003 writing on the Iran-Iraq War of the 1980s was that it fit into a historical narrative of a sequence of wars that started in 1980. Recent Iraqi history is characterised by an almost never-ending chain of destructive wars which enabled the dictatorship to survive and prosper and ruined the individual and civil society. The intellectuals place the responsibility for the wars solely on the Iraqi regime of Saddam Hussein.

Post-2003 literature highlighted sectarian identities – especially the Shiite identity[36]. This tendency was more prominent in the first decade and faded gradually as a result of the sectarian civil war of 2006–2007. In Ḥamīd al-ʿIqābī's *al-Ḍilʿ* (The Rib) from 2007, some of the war experiences of the narrator are painted in sectarian colours[37]. This daring novel is the first to employ many Shiite motifs. In a scene during the war, the soldiers of an Iraqi armoured unit are under fire at the front. Al-ʿIqābī names the soldiers, and many have unmistakably Shiite names. At a later point in the novel, one of the soldiers whispers Shiite invocations in fear[38]. This novel highlights the fact that most of the Iraqi soldiers who fought in the war were Shiite. Stressing such a detail was taboo before 2003.

Sectarianising the war brings us to the subject of deserters. There were two kinds of deserters in post-2003 literature on the war: those who fled to the rear and those who deserted to Iran during the war and committed treason in the eyes of the Iraqi regime. Al-ʿIqābī's hero belongs to the second type: he considers deserting during the battles and identifies much

36. See Chapter 5 in this volume.
37. al-ʿIqābi 2007.
38. Ibid., pp. 293, 306.

more with the Iranian soldiers than with the Iraqi regime who sent him to fight. This should be compared with the representations of the Iranian enemy in the war literature from the 1980s. He eventually deserts to Iran, but the suffering he endures there convinces him that Iran is not a place to live, so he decides to leave for Denmark.

Another deserter who escapes to Iran is the hero of Naṣīf Falak's *Ḫiḍr Qad wa-l-ʿaṣr al-zaytūnī* (Ḫiḍr Qad and the Khaki-Coloured Era), also from 2007[39]. Ḫiḍr, the hero, serves in the Kurdish areas on the northern front and from there decides to desert to Iran. His desertion is ceremonial: he climbs the highest mountain and rids himself of all vestiges of his former national identity. He gets rid of his uniforms and throws away his beret. In that magical moment he declares the establishment of a "nation of his own". He then descends to Iran and is taken to a prison camp. Here again, staying in Iran would only accentuate his problems[40]. Post-2003 literature could make their heroes desert to Iran. Yet the authors did not do it out of pro-Iranian inclination; rather, desertion was presented as a pacifist act of protest against the Iraqi regime. Only after reaching Iran, do the fugitives discover that the Iranian regime, both as an ideology and an identity, is just as evil as the Saddam regime.

Other deserters fled to the Iraqi rear, especially to Baghdad. We already met three of them in Naǧm Wālī's novel from the 1990s, when writing about desertion to Iran was unthinkable. Such are the heroes of ʿAlī Badr's *Asātiḏat al-wahm* (The Masters of Illusion) from 2011[41]. The time frame of the novel is 1987 – the last year of the war – and the location is the centre of Baghdad. This is where the three fugitive protagonists are being sheltered, but even there they are not safe. The fugitives are poets and – as Masmoudi correctly claims – poetry for them is one more shelter from the dreadful reality that surrounds them[42]. In this anti-Baʿathist novel, repression is present in the background, not at the centre, and is simply usually implied. Instead, Badr portrays an alternative world existing in downtown Baghdad under the watchful eye of the dictatorship. He served in the Iraqi army, but his novel is as far from the front as possible.

39. Falak 2007.
40. Ibid., pp. 72–75.
41. Badr 2011.
42. Masmoudi discusses this novel at length; cf. Masmoudi 2015, pp. 36–58.

All these novels on deserters share some similarities. The deserters in post-2003 war novels are intellectuals and men of letters, reflecting on the situation. They are poets, writers, and others who find shelter in the act of artistic creation. In part, they resemble the writers themselves. They desert out of political motives and as part of their rejection of the Baʿathist dictatorship. In most cases, they will be killed by the regime. Interestingly, this was the fate of the protagonists of the state-sponsored *adab al-ḥarb*. Iraqi prose leans towards the tragic. Whereas the deaths in battle of such protagonists could be interpreted as martyrdom (*šahādah*) in the sense of sacrifice for sublime principles, the deaths of the former are the fate of the *homo sacer* and touch the essence of the Iraqi tragedy. They die in vain.

In all these novels, war is used to highlight militarism, repression, and bigotry, which were hallmarks of the previous regime. But post-2003 novels also fit the war into a narrative of the first in a sequence of wars in which 2003 was not the final. In Nawzat Šamdīn's *Suqūṭ sirdāb* (Falling into a Cellar) from 2015, the hero is locked by his mother in a cellar (*sirdāb*) to avoid conscription in the Gulf war of 1991[43]. He spends twelve years in that hidden cellar where he feels, rather than experiences, the American invasion of 2003. His father, a brigadier in the army, allegedly died in battle during the Iran-Iraq War. While hiding in the cellar, he discovers that his father was hidden in the same place after escaping from the army. His father committed suicide in the cellar, and his son discovers the remains of his body there. The hero realises that he is in the same situation his father was: they both escaped, were hidden, and feared for their lives. Despite their differences – the father loved the army, and the son loathes it – they both end up in the same humiliating state. For the purposes of this study, it is important to show that the self-imposed incarceration symbolically started during the 1980s. Since the 1980s, wars and repression prevented the Iraqis from living normal lives. Ironically, it does not stop with the removal of Saddam: after 2003, the hero decides to leave the cellar. He takes a ride in his city, Mosul, and finally decides to return to the cellar, shutting the door after him in the final scene.

Most writers who participated in *adab al-ḥarb* and retained their literary career in Iraq and the diaspora neglected the war in later novels. This

43. Šamdīn 2015.

was the case for ʿAbd al-Sattār Nāṣir and Ǧāsim al-Raṣīf, for example. One writer, however, Saʿd Muḥammad Raḥīm, the author of one of the state-sponsored novels discussed before, did write about the war after 2003. It is interesting to read a writer who, liberated from the chains of dictatorship, writes a completely different novel on the war. In 2018, his novel *Fusḥah li-l-ǧunūn* (A Space for Madness) was published in Baghdad[44]. The novel is set in the writer's hometown Saʿdiyyah during the first years of the war, when the town was on the front (central sector). Yet his protagonist is not a soldier but a civilian who refuses to be evacuated like the rest of the population. He is a marginalised figure and politically suspect. Throughout the novel it is not clear whether the hero is sane. Undoubtedly, however, his presumed madness saves his life. He organises a group of other outcasts, including a deserter. He is a gifted poet, and, like most of the heroes of the novels I analyse in my study, he dies in the end. These are elements which could not appear in Raḥīm's writing during the 1980s. The real turning point that distinguishes this period from his writing in the 1980s[45] is found in this short scene in which the hero speaks with some looters:

> The hero: May the one who sparked the war be cursed!
> The looters: They [the Iranians] started the war. Don't you listen to Radio Baghdad?
> The hero: Curse them, curse you, curse on the leaders and the pimps… Curse on the president and [all] the presidents![46]

By cursing Saddam, he actually scares the looters and protects property. But breaching this taboo is permitted only to a character who may not be sane. When a group of Iraqi reporters who visit the town are confronted with the same incident, they become wary and change the subject[47].

Nevertheless, other aspects make it differ from post-2003 literature about the war. The hero is a civilian who refuses to leave his hometown despite the risk. Is he more patriotic than heroes in other novels? He is not

44. Raḥīm 2018.
45. His contributions to *adab al-ḥarb* are omitted from his bibliographies and biographies.
46. Ibid., pp. 32–33.
47. Ibid., p. 243.

persecuted by the army or the party, despite his shadowy past and disobedience. Raḥīm was possibly trying to recreate the atmosphere of the war years in 2018 and shaped the dialogues accordingly.

During the 1980s, the enemy was Iran. In alternative literature since the 1990s and in post-war novels, the enemy was the Iraqi Baʿathist regime. With the strengthening of the Iranian hold on Iraqi politics in recent years, pointing to the Iranians as the enemy and, to some extent, even writing a war novel became hazardous. Some of the most powerful political personalities in Iraq today, particularly commanders of Shiite militias served either in the Iranian army during the war or in auxiliary forces and almost all spent the war years in Iranian exile. In the second decade of the 21st century, the number of novels in which the war is mentioned was considerably reduced.

Since 2018, Iraq has experienced a serious wave of demonstrations of protest, the main sentiment of which is anti-Iranian. Occasionally, especially on special dates associated with the war, Iraqi social media shows pictures of victorious Iraqi soldiers at the front or posts celebrating the Iraqi "victory" over the Iranians as an expression of national pride. But the first Iraqi novel celebrating the victory in the war and the perseverance of people, army, and state after eight years of aggression is yet to be written.

In recent years, however, especially with new-found stability in Iraq following the defeat of ISIS and the almost total disappearance of terror attacks from the streets, it appears that some writers are rediscovering the war in their novels. One such novel is Aḥmad Ibrāhīm al-Saʿd's *al-ʿIrāq sīnimā* (Iraq Cinema) from 2020[48]. The author was too young to serve in the army during the war; thus, war figures in the novel as a childhood experience. Located in Basra, this novel is set at the rear. The protagonists, a group of three boys, used to play near the military hospital in Basra. Reminiscent of al-Ṣaqr's *Bayt ʿalà nahr Diğlah*, they try to estimate the number of casualties reaching the morgue and are arrested for that. The boys do not have fathers. One of them, not the narrator, was conscripted to the war, deserted, and was caught. The writer depicts a scene from childhood under the shadow of the war which is macabre and often shocking and disgusting. Characteristically, war and repression are

48. al-Saʿd 2020.

intertwined. Beyond that, the protagonists think about their lives as a film. They dream about making a film about their lives and one of them would be the director. The second half of the novel implies that all Iraqis had been living their lives as a film. Here again, we encounter the narrative of a sequence of wars in which the Iran-Iraq War was the first and most significant. This is the theme of the film which the narrator makes. It is about different stations in the life of the director, and the connecting motif is that of a train moving from station to station, each station represents a war. In this novel we find all the characteristics of the post-2003 writing on the war: location in the rear, the intertwining of war and repression, desertion, and the narrative of a sequence of wars, which is recent Iraqi history.

The second novel, Ḥamīd Qasim's *Ẓahr al-samakah* (The Fish's Back) is a return to the style of the war literature of the 1980s, albeit with a completely reversed message[49]. It is located in a small unit at the front serving as a microcosm for Iraq. The soldiers do not justify the war; they detest serving at the front and desire to go back home. Their greatest fear is the Iraqi execution squads and not the Iranians. The unit includes many soldiers who are considered "suspicious" by the Baʿathist regime. Then, on a small hill called "The Fish's Back", the small Iraqi unit meets its Iranian counterpart. The two units do not fight each other; instead, they spend time together, getting to know each other and even becoming friends. This is the main innovation of the novel. On a small hill at the front, a handful of Iraqi and Iranian soldiers, both fearful of their own regime, establish their own haven. For the first time, the Iranians are not vilified and do not solely bear the responsibility for the prolongation of the war. The writer creates a parallel between two dictatorial regimes who equally bear responsibility for the longest war in the 20th century.

7. Conclusion

This chapter followed the evolution of Iraqi prose on the Iran-Iraq War since the 1980s. During the war (1980–1988), the regime produced an unprecedented number of novels to justify and glorify a controversial

49. Qāsim 2021.

war. Naturally, the number declined after the end of the war and even more under the Saddam regime. This trend continued after 2003, with yet another drop in the 2010s. Since the beginning of the 2020s, the war is again appearing in Iraqi novels and it is too early to know if this trend is going to last.

Yet, the decline in numbers fails to explain why this war is referred to as "an armed conflict" by the Iraqi media or not referred to at all. Why isn't it called the "great patriotic war" that it actually was[50]? The official name of the war under the Baʿath was *Qādisiyyat Ṣaddām*, and obviously this corollary, with its Saddamist connotations, could not be maintained. In daily usage, Iraqis now call the war "the Iran war" (*Ḥarb Iran*) or "the 1980s war" (*Ḥarb al-Ṯamānīnāt*). These names lack glory and romanticism – so necessary for making a "great patriotic war". They signify weariness from wars and not yearning for a return to militarism and spirit of battle.

Since the war was presented as Baʿathist propaganda, anti-Baʿathist novelists tended to show the other side of it: deserters rather than soldiers and officers, the rear rather than the front, were at the centre of an alternative writing on the war that started in the 1990s. The real enemy was not the Iranians but the Iraqi regime. Later, after 2003, this line of writing became part of a cultural and political phenomenon called "de-Baʿathification". Some post-2003 writers, dismantling what they perceived to be Baʿathist "national chauvinism", even legitimised the act of deserting in wartime to Iran. In doing so, they conveyed a message that the war was yet another crime against the Iraqi individual and not a "great patriotic war". In a way, most prominent writers failed to combine anti-war sentiments with their patriotism. They felt that writing about the war from a patriotic angle would brand them Baʿathists, and they opted for the former option. The sole exception is Saʿd Muḥammad Raḥīm, a former

50. This requires clarification: I do not mean to judge the Iraqis for not referring to the war as the "great patriotic war". Iraqis have the right to consider this war a folly, a crime committed by the Saddam regime, and a waste of human lives. I am simply reflecting on the lack of reference to the war by the authorities for their own calculations and by intellectuals. And I also try to explain it. Nor do I mean that Iraq should emulate Iran where the war is still celebrated as the "great patriotic war". Iran is still ruled by the same regime that waged the war.

collaborator with the Baʿath, who managed to successfully combine the two sentiments in his last novel (2018).

During the 2010s, the increasing hegemony of Iran and its allies in Iraq became a major hazard for the literary commemoration of the war. Some of Iraq's main writers left the country and from the safety of exile aired their criticism on politics but did not write about that war. Despite that, the growing Iranian hegemony produces a sense of Iraqi patriotism from below in which the war plays a major role. In this case, literature failed to capture the sentiment of the population. Authors continued to play the strings of anti-Baʿathism when public sentiment was increasingly patriotic and anti-Iranian. The introspective nature of post-2003 Iraqi literature, with its emphasis on the faults of the Iraqi regime and Iraqi history, explains the discrepancy.

In the absence of a strong government and censorship in contemporary Iraq, it is now the role of intellectuals to shape the future memory of the Iran-Iraq war. The intellectuals should take the role of the state and substitute its distorted version of the war from the past with a more valid one. The war still plays an important role in the lived memory of many Iraqis. Failing to write about the war would possibly entice other agents of memorialisation (clerics, politicians) to formulate their own versions, either eradicating the war from the collective memory or justifying it and boasting of victory. The last two novels in my account may signal a new approach.

References

ʿAbbūd, S. (2002), *Ṯaqāfat al-ʿunf fī l-ʿIraq*, al-Ǧamal, Kūlūniyā [Köln].

Badr, ʿA. (2011), *Asātīḏat al-wahm*, al-Muʾassasah al-ʿArabiyyah, Beirut.

Baram, A., Rohde, A., Zeidel, R. (2012), *Between the Unknown Soldier Monument and the Cemetery: Commemorating Fallen Soldiers in Iraq 1958–2010*, in Milich, S., Pannewick, F., Tramontini, L. (eds) (2012), *Conflicting Narratives: War, Trauma and Memory in Iraqi Culture*, Reichert Verlag, Wiesbaden, pp. 109–124.

Caiani, F., Cobham, C. (2013), *The Iraqi Novel: Key Writers, Key Texts*, Edinburgh University Press, Edinburgh.

Davis, E. (2005), *Memories of State: Politics, History, and Collective Identity in Modern Iraq*, University of California Press, Berkeley (CA).

Falak, N. (2007), *Ḫiḍr Qad wa-l-ʿaṣr al-zaytūnī*, Dār al-Sabāḥ, Baghdad.
Ḫiṣbāk, ʿĀ. (1983), *al-Qamar al-ṣaḥrāwī*, Dār al-Ḥurriyah, Baghdad.
al-Ḫuḍayrī, B. (2003³), *Kam badat al-samāʾ qarībah*, al-Muʾassasah al-ʿArabiyyah, ʿAmman.
al-ʿIqābi, Ḥ. (2007), *al-Ḍilʿ*, al-Ǧamal, Cologne.
al-Kaʿbi, F. ʿA. (1999), *Ḍuyūf fī qafṣ*, Dār al-Ḥurriyah, Baghdad.
Mamdūh, ʿĀ. (2019), *al-Tānkī*, al-Mutawāssit, Milan.
al-Mašhadānī, Ṭ. ʿA. (2000), *Bustān ʿAbbūd*, Dār al-Ḥurriyah, Baghdad.
Masmoudi, I. (2015), *War and Occupation in Iraqi Fiction*, Edinburgh University Press, Edinburgh.
Mazīd, M. (1999), *Makān aswad*, Dār al-Ḥurriyah, Baghdad.
Milich, S., Pannewick, F., Tramontini, L. (eds) (2012), *Conflicting Narratives: War, Trauma and Memory in Iraqi Culture*, Reichert Verlag, Wiesbaden.
Moosavi, A. (2016), *Reimagining War: Negotiating Ideology and Disenchantment in Literary Narratives of the Iran-Iraq War*, PhD thesis, New York University.
al-Musawi, M. (2006), *Reading Iraq: Culture and Power in Conflict*, Tauris, London.
Qāsim, Ḥ. (2021), *Ẓahr al-samakah*, Nābū, Baghdad.
Raḥīm, S. M. (1983), *Hākaḏa istantaqnā al-fulāḏ*, Dār al-Ḥurriyah, Baghdad.
Raḥīm, S. M. (2018), *Fusḥah li-l-ǧunūn*, Sutūr, Baġdād.
al-Raṣīf, Ǧ. (2000²), *Abjadiyyat al-mawt ḥubb^an*, al-Muʾassasah al-ʿArabiyyah, Beirut.
al-Raṣīf, Ǧ. (2002²), *Ḫaṭṭ aḥmar*, al-Muʾassasah al-ʿArabiyyah, Beirut.
al-Rikābī, H. T. (1983), *Aʿdād al-midfaʿ 106*, Dār al-Šuʾūn al-Ṯaqāfiyyah al-ʿĀmmah, Baghdad.
al-Šabīb, Ṭ. Ḥ. (2009²), *al-Ḥikāyah al-sādisah*, Faḍāʾāt, ʿAmman.
al-Saʿd, A. I. (2020), *al-ʿIrāq sīnimā*, Dār al-Muʿqidīn, Basra.
Šamdīn, N. (2015), *Suqūt sirdāb*, al-Muʾassasah al-ʿArabiyyah, Beirut.
Šarārah, Ḥ. (2000), *Iḏā al-ayyām aġsaqat*, al-Muʾassasah al-ʿArabiyyah, Beirut.
al-Ṣaqr, M. ʿĪ. (1997), *Ṣirāḫ al-nawāris*, Dār al-Ādāb, Beirut.
al-Ṣaqr, M. ʿĪ. (2006), *Bayt ʿalà nahr Diğlah*, al-Madà, Damascus.
al-Šawiyyah, ʿĀ. (1999), *Madinat al-ḏiyāb*, Dār al-Ḥurriyah, Baghdad.
Wālī, N. (1993), *al-Ḥarb fī Ḥayy al-Ṭarab*, Dār al-Ṣaḥrāʾ, Budapest.
Zeidel, R. (2008), *The Painful Return: Prisoners of War and Society in Iraq 1988–2007*, in "Anthropology of the Middle East", 3, 2 (Winter), pp. 57–75. https://doi.org/10.3167/ame.2008.030205
Zeidel, R. (2017), *On Dictatorship, Literature and the Coming Revolution: Regime and Novels in Iraq 1995–2003*, in "Nidaba", 2, 1, pp. 62–75.
Zeidel, R. (2020), *Pluralism in the Iraqi Novel after 2003: Literature and the Recovery of National Identity*, Lexington Books, Lanham.

Ronen Zeidel is an Iraq analyst in the Moshe Dayan Center, Tel Aviv University. He has published dozens of articles in leading academic journals in the West and also in Iraq. His book *Pluralism in the Iraqi Novel after 2003* was published by Lexington Books in 2020.

Chapter 4

The Painful Path towards Civil Liberties and Social Justice Followed by the Iraqi Ḥayāt Šarārah

Elvira Diana

Abstract

Ḥayāt Šarārah (1935–1997) was an Iraqi academic who fought the imposition of the regime culture inside and outside the university classroom. She firmly opposed all forms of oppression – cultural or political. In her posthumous novel *Iḏā al-ayyām aġsaqat* (When the Days Grow Dark), she denounces the difficulties of university life in Baghdad under the regime of Saddam Hussein, when academia was humiliated, oppressed, and deprived of its independent voice. On 1 August 1997, a gas pipe exploded in her home in Baghdad, in the historic *Madīnat al-salām* (City of Peace), killing her and one of her two daughters. Although it was officially classified as suicide, the regime was thought to be hehind these violent deaths. This chapter aims at analysing the painful private and professional path towards a peaceful society built upon civil liberties and social justice travelled by this researcher, writer, and translator persecuted in life and neglected for many years even after her death because of conspiratorial political censorship.

Keywords: Saddam Hussein, narrating resistance, contemporary Arab women writers

1. When the Personal Story of a Woman is the Story of a Whole People

A charming girl from the alleys of Naǧaf echoing with poetry
from the dawn of their foundation heard a voice telling her
to carry in one hand a cornerstone of the great gardens of Babylon
while the other hand spread a perfume between the sinuosity of the
consonant without the diacritical points present in the *Iqrāʾ* sura[1].
Behind the desert infested with nacre-skinned snakes,
the peoples cried out:
this is a woman of rejection
possessed by red *ginn*
who sows evil in the minds of the ruling authority.
[...]. Nobody knows who set her on fire
except the regime[2].

Maḥmūd Ḥamad, 11/01/2007

These are some lines from the poem *Wa "Iḏā al-ayyām aġsaqat". Lā tansaw Ḥayāt Šarārah* (And "When the Days Grow Dark". Do not Forget Ḥayāt Šarārah) written by Maḥmūd Ḥamad[3]. He celebrates the value and strength of Ḥayāt Šarārah as a woman and a political militant through metaphorical and profound images. An Iraqi academic and translator, Ḥayāt Šarārah was persecuted in life and neglected for many years even after her death because of a silent but suffocating political censorship. She fought the imposition of the regime culture, an instrument of political propaganda, inside and outside the university classroom by opposing all forms of oppression, cultural or political. A champion of civil liberties, she was convinced that only fundamental freedoms, together with social justice, are able to generate peaceful and inclusive societies. This type of society is essential, on the one hand, for reducing all forms of violence, corruption, and abuse of power and, on the other, for ensuring that everybody's rights and duties are fully respected. Therefore, we could consider

1. Sura *al-ʿAlaq* (The Clot), also known as sura *Iqrāʾ* (Read), is chapter XCVI of the Qur'ān. The traditional view is almost unanimous: verses 1–5 are supposed to be the first revelation received by Muḥammad.
2. See Sulṭān 2016, p. 74. See also Ḥamad 2007.
3. An Iraqi poet residing in the United Arab Emirates.

her a herald of the targets expressed in the United Nations 2030 Agenda for Sustainable Development. This well-known universal agenda is based on five key concepts, one of which is peace viewed simultaneously as a tool and as a goal "to foster peaceful, just and inclusive societies which are free from fear and violence. There can be no sustainable development without peace and no peace without sustainable development"[4].

Born in 1935 in the holy city of Nağaf, Ḥayāt Šarārah came from a cultured family of Lebanese origin who had immigrated to Iraq in the 1920s. Her biography is known to us thanks to the long and touching *Muqaddimah* (Introduction) to her posthumous novel *Iḏā al-ayyām aġsaqat* (When the Days Grow Dark)[5], written by her sister Balqīs, also a writer, who emigrated to the United States years ago. This *Muqaddimah* is dated November 1999 and, with its almost 80 pages that also include private letters sent by Ḥayāt to her family, it is actually a precious testimony of Iraq's history in the last century. It describes the personal events of the author contextualising them in the historico-political realities of the country. Balqīs Šarārah follows her sister's life through childhood, womanhood, marriage, and motherhood, intertwining her story with the conflicting historical path of Iraq from the years of the monarchy to those of Saddam Hussein (1937–2006), as well as the multiple political figures who, in the meantime, had taken turns at governing the country. Everything is handled with the sensitivity and involvement typical of eyewitnesses[6].

Balqīs tells us that the sisters grew up in a very open and stimulating cultural context: from her father, Muḥammad Šarārah, a poet, writer, and teacher, Ḥayāt, the third daughter, inherited a love for Arabic poetry and the Arabic *fuṣḥà* since he used to speak in standard Arabic even in daily

4. See the Resolution adopted by the General Assembly of the United Nations on 25 September 2015, *Transforming our World: the 2030 Agenda for Sustainable Development*, p. 2.
5. al-Mu'assasah al-'arabiyyah li-l-dirāsāt wa-l-našr, Beirut 2000. The novel has been republished by the publishing house Dār al-Madà, Damascus 2011. The quotations in this article refer to the 2011 edition. For the *Muqaddimah*, see B. Šarārah, 2011, pp. 9–84.
6. Some pages of this *Muqaddimah* have been translated into English by the magazine "Banipal", 63, 2018. See B. Sharara 2018, pp. 14–25. See also Saeed 2021.

conversation. When the family moved to Baghdad in the mid-1940s[7], their home became a veritable literary salon frequented by the most prominent Iraqi littérateurs and thinkers of the time, even from different political positions. These weekly meetings were attended by young people destined to leave an indelible mark on Arabic literature: Muḥammad Mahdī al-Ǧawāhirī (1899–1997), Ḥusayn Muruwwah (1910–1987)[8], Badr Šākir al-Sayyāb (1926–1964), Buland al-Ḥaydarī (1926–1996)[9], Lamīʿah ʿAbbās ʿAmārah (1929), Akram al-Watrī (1930–2013), and Nāzik al-Malāʾikah (1923–2007), often accompanied by her father Ṣādiq al-Malāʾikah or by her brother Nizār[10]. It is perhaps superfluous to mention that these are the most important names of a long list of Iraqi poets who rescued "Arabic poetry from its rhythmic and structured approach to make it a place of experimentation and transgression, which mirrored all the political, artistic and intellectual trends and concerns of the time, from existentialist thought to committed literature"[11].

Ḥayāt, still a teenager, witnessed the wave of violence that hit the country in 1949, a year after the popular protests against the Portsmouth Treaty[12] and the pro-British policy of Nūrī al-Saʿīd (1888–1958), while demonstrations of solidarity for the Palestinian cause also increased. Martial law was imposed, political parties were outlawed, and newspapers were suppressed. A massive campaign of arrests was waged against opposition party members and their leaders, university students, and left-wing intellectuals. Actually, starting in the 1920s, many intellectuals not aligned with the government suffered persecution and oppression, resulting in arbitrary imprisonment and torture that made no distinction between male and female intellectuals[13]. This was because Iraqi intellectuals have

7. In 1936, the family first moved to Nassiriya, where the father started working as an Arabic language teacher.
8. Lebanese journalist, author, and literary critic, with Iraqi citizenship.
9. Poet of Kurdish origin.
10. B. Šarārah 2011, pp. 13–14.
11. Ǧabbār et al. 2006, p. 52.
12. Known as the Anglo-Iraqi Treaty of 1948, it was a treaty between Iraq and the United Kingdom signed in Portsmouth on 15 January 1948. It was a revision of the Anglo-Iraqi Treaty of 1930 and provided for the abolition of the British military bases in Basra and Habbaniya. Indeed, it confirmed British privileges and their supremacy in the country. For more on Iraqi history, see Tripp 2007.
13. See Kashou 2013, pp. 62–66.

always played an active role in the social and political life of the country, expressing their dissent against any form of imperialism, foreign or domestic. The same al-Ǧawāhirī, for example, together with the other exponents of neoclassical poetry, Maʿrūf Ruṣāfī (1857–1945) and Ǧamīl Ṣidqī al-Zahāwī (1863–1936), "acquired prestige with the general public not only because of their talent as poets, but also thanks to the important role they played in the political arena"[14]. In fact, as Balqīs writes, in 1949 al-Ǧawāhirī and al-Sayyāb were arrested, along with her father and her uncle, while Ḥusayn Muruwwah and his family were deprived of Iraqi citizenship[15].

These ordeals, both in the family milieu and in the country as a whole, remained etched in Ḥayāt's memory so as to emerge later in her unpublished novel *Wamīḍ barq baʿīd* (A Distant Glimmer)[16], the book Balqīs mentions in her sister's biography. They probably also influenced her life choices: when she was still very young, Ḥayāt joined the Iraqi Communist Party, which sent her to a peace conference in Prague in 1952, although she was not even seventeen years old. It is worth remembering that, among the political parties that operated almost exclusively underground, "the most relevant was the Communist Party founded in 1934 and which organised almost all the mass demonstrations and strikes in the 1940s and 1950s. It was the most important opposition party, present throughout the land and whose members were predominantly Kurds and Shia Arabs"[17]. Meanwhile, internal tensions were also being fuelled by the deteriorating economic situation in the country. Shortly after her departure for Prague, on 23 November 1952, the so-called *Intifāḍat tišrīn* (November riot) broke out with popular protests going hand in hand with mass arrests. In the following months, her father was arrested once again and sentenced to a year in prison for

14. Caiani, Cobham 2013, p. 3.
15. B. Shararah 2011, pp. 18, 20.
16. Ibid., p. 19.
17. See Galletti 2011, p. 55. Unless otherwise noted, all translations from Arabic and Italian are the author's.

belonging to the *Anṣār al-salām* (Partisans of Peace)[18] organisation and for writing a number of dissident articles[19].

After graduating from high school, Ḥayāt could not attend Baghdad University because she had not obtained the *šahādat ḥusn al-sulūk* (certificate of good conduct). In those years, denying access to university was one of the tools employed by the government to punish students active in the Communist Party and in other left-wing movements. This greatly reduced their future employment opportunities. For this reason, the country saw a significant number of high school graduates leave for Syria and Egypt. Ḥayāt was one of them, and she enrolled in the English Language Department at Cairo University. There she met many Iraqi students, including her future husband, Muḥammad Ṣāliḥ Sumaysim, who had fled to Egypt to escape persecution by the Iraqi monarchy[20].

Meanwhile, new political events awaited Iraq: a group of officers, led by General ʿAbd al-Karīm Qāsim (1914–1963) and Colonel ʿAbd al-Salām ʿĀrif (1921–1966), probably inspired by the Egyptian example, organised a coup that overthrew the monarchy and proclaimed a republic. It was 14 July 1958: Ḥayāt and her father returned to Baghdad, along with many other exiles. There, she was finally able to enrol in the university[21], from which she graduated in 1960. While continuing her militancy in the Communist Party, she began to disagree with some of the positions taken by the Party, which, according to her, were contrary to the principles of the Party itself[22]. A year after graduation, she left

18. "Announced at the end of the August 1954, Decree 16 required that all non-governmental organisations to re-register with the Ministry of the Interior; members of organisations, 'whether direct or through organizations aimed at serving the above-mentioned purposes [i.e. 'propagation of communism, anarchism, or immorality'] or doctrines under the screen of any name, such as the Partisans of Peace, the Democratic Youth, and so forth', were threatened with seven years' imprisonment". See Bishop 2013, p. 320.
19. B. Šarārah 2011, p. 24. Afterwards, her father moved to Lebanon for a time, having lost all hope of being able to continue working and living in Iraq without suffering persecution and control. This was especially after his name appeared on the government's blacklist. Ibid., p. 26.
20. Ibid., pp. 26–27.
21. She enrolled in the English Language Department at the College of Arts.
22. B. Šarārah 2011, p. 28. At the end of 1960, her father was arrested again and sentenced to three months in prison for writing an article in which he contested the integrity of the elections in the teachers' union. Ibid., p. 34. On the disillusions of the

for Moscow, where she received a doctorate in Russian literature from Moscow University:

> Ḥayāt spent six years in Moscow. Her scholarship was for five years and so, to be able to complete her thesis on *Tūlstūy fannān* (Tolstoy as an Artist), she had to apply for a one-year extension. The Soviet authorities, however, rejected her request because she refused to cooperate with the Communist Party responsible for Iraqi students. So, to support herself financially that year, she was forced to take a job as translator at the TASS Agency[23] and to sell most of her clothes[24].

During her stay in Russia, Iraq underwent other political changes: in 1963, another military *coup* supported by the Baʿath Party eliminated ʿAbd al-Karīm Qāsim and appointed ʿAbd al-Salām ʿĀrif President of the Republic. All parties were dissolved, and the repression against the Communist Party and other progressive forces was spearheaded by the violent *Ḥaras qawmī* corps (National Guard), an oft-repeated name in Balqīs Šarārah's biography[25]. In 1968, after further political events, another *coup d'état*, supported by the moderate wing of the Baʿath Party, appointed Aḥmad Ḥasan al-Bakr (1914–1982) President of the Republic. That was the same year in which Ḥayāt returned to Iraq, but – as her sister writes – she kept herself out of politics and dedicated herself to writing and doing research. She began teaching Russian literature at Baghdad University's College of Arts.

The 1970s brought additional suffering and pain on both the private and the national level. In 1970, Ḥayāt's mother died, and the ensuing grief marked her profoundly: "although Ḥayāt had spent most of her life away

---

Iraqi intellectual class, the so-called *al-ǧīl al-ḍāʾiʿ* (the lost generation), following the authoritarian turn of the 1958 revolution, see Ruocco 2014–2015, p. 525.

23. TASS is the largest Russian news agency and one of the largest in the world. It was founded in 1904.
24. B. Šarārah 2011, pp. 38–39. When Ḥayāt was in Moscow, her father decided to leave Iraq once again for political reasons and went to China. There he taught at Peking University. Ibid., p. 36.
25. From 15 to 21 February 1965, right in the Baghdad of ʿAbd al-Salām ʿĀrif, the fifth Conference of Arab Writers was held on the topic *Dawr al-adab fī maʿrakat al-taḥrīr wa-l-bināʾ* (The Role of Literature in the Battle for Liberation and Construction). See Ruocco 1999, p. 145.

from home, she was aware that her mother had sacrificed her entire existence for her children. After becoming a mother herself, she thoroughly understood that motherhood carries with it duties and renunciations"[26]. On the national level, political instability and repressive measures persisted. The people remained in a state of poverty and kept suffering hardships even though, after the 1973 war[27], Iraqi oil revenues had increased significantly. But "most of [those revenues] were used to pay for armaments to make Iraq a powerful warrior state in the region, while only small sums were allocated for infrastructure, culture and health, and then, almost exclusively in the capital"[28]. In 1970, her only moment of joy was her marriage to Doctor Muḥammad Ṣāliḥ Sumaysim. Theirs was an unconventional and untraditional union: they married in front of a judge, and there were no celebrations afterwards. They rented a house which was quite modest compared to the family home she was accustomed to, "but Ḥayāt was satisfied and sure that it was the right thing"[29].

According to Balqīs Šarārah, during Aḥmad Ḥasan al-Bakr's presidency, the government was actually already in the hands of Saddam Hussein who was Vice-President at the time: he "used to visit every corner of the country and distribute gifts to the people, from refrigerators to televisions. He thus gained the trust of the masses and increased his popularity"[30]. Meanwhile, the discrimination and harassment of those who refused to join the Baʿath Party increased. Ḥayāt herself was a victim of this intimidation campaign: when she failed to join the Party, she was removed from her position as professor at Baghdad University. By order of the administration of the College of Arts, she was transferred to the Ministry of Industry and eventually to the city of al-Diwaniya[31], where she worked as a translator on a Russian project[32]. It goes without saying that, in those years, academia in Iraq was totally politicised and

26. B. Šarārah 2011, p. 39.
27. The allusion is to the war against Israel in which Iraq participated by sending troops to the Syrian front and using the threat of cutting off oil supplies as a weapon.
28. B. Šarārah 2011, p. 40.
29. Ibid, p. 39.
30. Ibid., pp. 40–41.
31. A city in south central Iraq, about 160 km southeast of Baghdad.
32. Ḥayāt Šarārah later returned to university but was transferred to the Language Department.

the Baʿath Party controlled all state institutions, including public education, and acted as the legitimate representative of the ruling authorities[33]. The arrest campaigns continued and also involved Ḥayāt's husband who was taken from his home one night. Like the entire educated and intellectual class of the country, he was treated in a non-violent way, at least at the time of his arrest. On his release a month later, however, he was a different person: tired in body and soul, he was a broken man (*šaḫṣ muḥaṭṭam*), who attempted to forget the physical and psychological torture he suffered during his incarceration by drinking whiskey constantly. Ḥayāt immersed herself in her studies and academic activities, helpless in the face of her husband's malaise, which affected the whole family[34].

In the 1980s, new fatal events upset both her life and that of the whole country. On the private level, Ḥayāt's father died in 1979, while on the national level Saddam Hussein replaced Aḥmad Ḥasan al-Bakr as President. Upon consolidating his power, the new *raʾīs* attacked Iran in September 1980. At the outbreak of that bloody war, which also caused all schools and universities to be closed, Ḥayāt expressed her fears and concerns for her two daughters, Zaynab and Mahā, aged seven and eleven respectively, to her sister Maryam in a letter[35]. While the war against Iran dragged on, blocking the country's development both economically and culturally, another bereavement marked her family in 1982: the sudden death of her husband, victim of a cerebral embolism. She thus found herself alone raising and educating her daughters since all her relatives were outside the country. Those were years of profound solitude, as she wrote in the aforementioned unpublished novel *Wamīḍ barq baʿīd* and in some of the letters sent to her sister Maryam[36].

The constant humiliations suffered at the hands of the regime notwithstanding, her studies and writing activities were a source of comfort for Ḥayāt and a sort of refuge against the violence and injustice oppressing the country. The 1980s were undoubtedly the most prolific for her literary production. First of all, she collected the research material left by her father, and used it to publish a number of books in his name, such

33. *Ḥayāt Šarārah... ʿirāqiyyah min zaman al-tawahhuǧ* 2010.
34. B. Šarārah 2011, pp. 42, 44–45.
35. Ibid., p. 50.
36. Ibid, pp. 52–53.

as *al-Mutanabbī bayna l-buṭūlah wa-l-iġtirāb* (al-Mutanabbī Between Heroism and Alienation, 1981) and *Naẓarāt fī turāṯinā al-qawmī* (Glances at Our National Heritage, 1982). Furthermore, despite the difficulty in finding available publishers, she managed to publish various articles on Arabic literature. Her essay *Ṣafaḥāt min sīrat Nāzik al-Malā'ikah* (Pages from the Biography of Nāzik al-Malā'ikah)[37] is considered one of the best critical texts on the free verse poetry movement in Iraq. As an expert in Russian literature, she also translated some Russian classics into Arabic during that time, including Gogol's play *al-Mufattiš al-'āmm* (The Inspector-General) and a number of novels by Turgenev such as *'Ušš al-nubalā'* (Gentlefolk's Nest) and *Rūdīn* (Rudin), together with his collection of short stories *Muḏakkirāt ṣayyād* (Memoirs of a Hunter). She also wrote some essays on Russian literature, including *Ta'ammulāt fī l-ši'r al-rūsī* (Reflections on Russian Poetry), *Madḫal ilà l-adab al-rūsī* (Introduction to Russian Literature) and *Dīwān al-ši'r al-rūsī* (A Collection of Russian Poetry)[38].

Meanwhile, daily life for the Iraqi people kept going from bad to worse because the country had just emerged from the conflict with Iran with an extremely high number of casualties and a very heavy foreign debt[39]. Despite this, in 1990 Saddam Hussein launched a second attack: the invasion of Kuwait. This operation led to the immediate condemnation on the part of the UN, which imposed an embargo on Iraq. As Balqīs Šarārah writes, the blocking of all economic, financial, and commercial relations proved to be disastrous, especially for civilians, with serious humanitarian consequences. It must be borne in mind that the economic sanctions imposed were among the most extensive and severe ever applied. Balqīs also recalls that the embargo completely isolated the Iraqi intellectual class, depriving it of all information and culture from abroad, such as books, magazines, cassettes, videos[40]. As further poignant proof of the

37. Ḥ. Šarārah 1994.
38. In 2011, the Lebanese publishing house Dār al-Madà republished most of these works, with the aim of rediscovering this brilliant scholar who had been unjustly forgotten.
39. The Iraq-Iran War claimed about 400,000 lives – 100,000 Iraqis and 300,000 Iranians – and about 750,000 wounded, while the external debt amounted to about 80 billion dollars. See Galletti 2011, p. 74.
40. B. Šarārah 2011, p. 80.

dire situation in which Iraqis were forced to live during the embargo, we have the words of the writer Inʿām Kağah Ğī (1952) who, in addition to denouncing the difficulties in finding basic necessities, stresses how difficult it was "to write":

> But today, writing in Iraq becomes a real undertaking when one takes into account the innumerable difficulties, material and ethical, caused by the war – the wars – and above all by the embargo. After all, the publisher's job is an almost impossible mission in a country where there is a lack of paper, ink, spare parts for printers. Most of all, that beautiful rose with shining petals, coveted everywhere, is missing: freedom of expression. [...] Iraqis write on dark sheets of paper, scraps, used sheets, old school notebooks. They write a verse or a passage from a novel on anything that is usable: an old receipt, an unpaid bill, a crumpled paper bag that once was used to carry fruit (for those who could afford it then). They even write on the back of medical prescriptions [...][41].

Therefore, it should come as no surprise that a great number of Iraqi writers, both male and female, put their artistic talent at the service of social commitment during those years. Through narration, they denounced the desperation, pain, and violence inflicted on the Iraqi people, at times drawing from their personal situation, at other times from the collective experience. This way, they become witnesses of the trauma left by the regime in the consciousness of entire generations[42].

From what has been said so far it is clear that, during the years of Saddam Hussein's regime, Ḥayāt had to put up with abuse and injustice

41. Kachachi 2003, p. 15. In those years, worthy initiatives by Iraqi writers residing abroad stood out. For example, Buṯaynah al-Nāṣirī (1947) conducted a campaign from Cairo to collect second-hand books and magazines to send to Iraq. In addition, also in Cairo, she founded Ishtar Publishing House with which she launched a book series to help the publication of works by writers residing in Iraq. Ibid., p. 53.
42. For further information on female Iraqi writers who wrote about war and exile during those years, see Kashou 2013. Among the many male Iraqi writers who wrote novels or short stories on the aftermath of last century's Iraqi conflicts, including exile, we will simply mention the names of Samūʾīl Šimʿūn (1956), Salīm Maṭar (1956), Muḥsin al-Ramlī (1967), Sinān Anṭūn (1967), Raḍwān al-Ḫālidī (1971), Aḥmad Saʿdāwī (1973), Ḥasan Balāsim (1973), ʿAlī Badr (1979). Many of their works have been translated into European languages. For further details, see *A Journey in Iraqi Fiction* 2018, pp. 21–135; Masmoudi 2015; Mustafa 2008.

as an academic, a woman, a wife and a mother. Not even her daughters were spared: in 1994, after graduating, her daughter Mahā applied for a job at the Oil Ministry. She passed the interview but was not hired for two reasons: she was not a member of the Baʿath Party, and her mother was Ḥayāt Šarārah[43]. Thus, day after day, life became more and more oppressive and dangerous. According to Balqīs Šarārah, Ḥayāt felt she was under surveillance at work and spied upon wherever she went and whatever she did. For this reason, she asked her family to stop sending her correspondence to her workplace. She realised that some of her letters had been opened by the university security apparatus because "she was considered a suspect because of her acquaintances and because she was not a party member"[44]. At that point, Ḥayāt simply stopped going to work, with the result that her absence was classified as an official resignation and she lost all the benefits that she had accumulated in 26 years of service[45].

2. The Silent Rebel

On 1 August 1997, a gas pipe exploded in her home in Baghdad, in the historic *Madīnat al-salām* (City of Peace), killing her and her daughter Mahā, while her other daughter Zaynab was wounded. Although this "last event of her life is still shrouded in mystery, for political, social and religious reasons, it is plausible that mother and daughters went into the kitchen, closed all doors and windows, plugged every crack and then, turned on the gas"[46]. With regard to this, the Iraqi scholar Fāḍil al-Ǧalabī, in his article entitled *Ḥayāt Šarārah al-kātibah al-muntaḥirah fī Baġdād wa-riwāyatuhā: al-Šahādat* Iḏā al-ayyām aġsaqat (The Suicide Writer in Baghdad and Her Novel: The Testimony of *When the Days Grow Dark*), wrote:

> All Iraqi intellectuals, especially those who were forced to flee and live in exile to escape the Iraqi hell, were saddened by the news of Ḥayāt Šarārah's suicide: a writer from a Lebanese family, the

43. B. Šarārah 2011, p. 75.
44. Ibid., pp. 78–79.
45. Ibid.
46. Kachachi 2003, p. 24.

> bearer of virtue and science, highly cultured and educated, which had made Iraq its home. And Iraq welcomed this family which, in turn, returned the welcome by working hard to enrich thinking and consolidate education in the country[47].

Another testimonial is that by Ḫālid Ḥusayn Sulṭān, editor of the volume *Ḥayāt Šarārah al-ṯāʾirah al-ṣāmitah* (Ḥayāt Šarārah: The Silent Rebel)[48]. As Sulṭān states in his *Muqaddimah* written in 2009, the volume was conceived out of respect for *al-nubl al-insānī* (nobility of the human soul) that distinguished the deceased and her husband, despite the fact that he had never actually met them[49]. According to him, the two women's violent death:

> was a shock to all those who knew the deceased or had heard of her or had read some of her publications. It was the same for literary, didactic, and student circles when they learned of her death from the obituary posted on the university walls. That tragic episode caused a great uproar and raised many questions: Was it an actual suicide or was the secret hand of the regime behind it? Whatever actually happened, the conclusion is that the regime was responsible, directly or indirectly[50].

Sulṭān adds that, in her *Muqaddimah*[51], Balqīs Šarārah tried to silence everyone by referring to the event as a case of suicide, without however going into detail. Because of this, doubts still linger, and Sulṭān also writes:

47. al-Ǧalabī 2019. This article was written originally on 18 September 2000 and published anew in 2019 in "al-Nāqid al-ʿirāqī". Some passages of this long article have been translated into English by the magazine "Banipal", 63, 2018. See Chalabi 2018, pp. 26–28.
48. Sulṭān 2016. The volume includes some essays on the author, on her role as a scholar, and as a political militant.
49. Sulṭān adds that Ḥayāt and her husband had been his father's companions. In particular, he states that her husband was a respected and well-liked doctor, always available to provide both medical and personal advice, especially during his work in the emergency room at Baghdad Hospital. Ibid., p. 8.
50. Ibid., p. 7.
51. Balqīs Šarārah's *Muqaddimah* is also included in Sulṭān (2016), under the title *Sīrat ḥayāt al-faqīdah "Ḥayāt Šarārah"*(The Biography of the Late "Ḥayāt Šarārah"). Ibid., pp. 10–73.

> A number of articles on the deceased, especially those published after the occupation and the fall of the former regime, indicated that the regime's security services were responsible for her death. Others considered it an outright execution and included the names of the deceased and her husband, Doctor Muḥammad Ṣāliḥ Sumaysim, in the lists of those condemned to martyrdom by the regime. Others, finally, wondered who were behind the explosion in the home of the scholar and her two daughters. The inhalation of toxic gases has even been attested in some documents. Therefore, it would have been more appropriate for Ms Balqīs to go into some detail about the incident, also because Zaynab, the late writer's second daughter, has survived. She could certainly provide accurate information on what really happened in spite of the pain that recalling the event would cause her[52].

If it was indeed a suicide, however, al-Ğalabī tries to offer a sociological explanation for the reasons behind it. According to him, although suicide rates were low in Iraq before the economic and social collapse that hit the country with the advent of Saddam Hussein's dictatorship, they eventually increased, especially among the middle class. Actually, in al-Ğalabī's opinion, the real reasons for that dramatic event are to be found between the lines of the novel *Iḏā al-ayyām aġsaqat*. Ḥayāt was a brilliant academic at the peak of her intellectual production, and if she had been seized by despair because of deprivation and indigence, she would have done what many other professors did to continue teaching at the university, that is, join the regime's party. Similarly, if she had been overwhelmed by discouragement because, among the many injustices she suffered, there was also the interdiction against travelling with her daughters[53], she could have overcome this ban by asking the authorities for an exemption. According to al-Ğalabī, Ḥayāt did none of this because she

52. Ibid., pp. 7–8.
53. This ban was based on "a strange rule contrary to Islamic law according to which women under 45 were not authorised to travel without a man acting as their *maḥram* (guardian), father, brother or uncle"; al-Ğalabī 2019. He alludes to an episode mentioned by Balqīs Šarārah in her *Muqaddimah*: in 1991: in a letter to her sister, Ḥayāt talks about this new law enacted to prevent girls from leaving the country. In reality, the economic crisis was forcing many of them into prostitution as a means of earning enough money to emigrate. Elsewhere, "See" is used. See B. Šarārah 2011, pp. 63–64.

wanted to defend her dignity and freedom and not submit to principles she did not believe in. Regarding the travel ban, "she was convinced that travel was a basic human right and not a favour allowed by the government"[54]. Therefore, for him, Ḥayāt's suicide was a form of protest against the subversion experienced by the country under the regime. This was both an economic and cultural upheaval that

> targeted Iraqi intellectuals for their work and also harassed them in their personal lives, [...] crushing their human and cultural personality. And so, the university professor became a deformed individual who applauded like everybody else, repeated slogans that went against his convictions, took part in marches and military exercises, and went to war. The professor put up with all this to avoid unpleasant consequences, such as deprivation of the ration card, dismissal or forced retirement, or fearing that the intelligence services would push him towards an unknown fate[55].

Also, according to Sulṭān, "this tragic epilogue, although contrary to divine law, is not unusual among intellectuals, scholars, or people with a high degree of sensitivity. This mostly happens when they live under a dictatorship and are convinced that they are no longer able to make their cultural contribution, because of the adverse circumstances around them"[56]. He then presents an additional interpretation of the alleged suicide, hypothesising that, through her studies and research on Russian literature, Ḥayāt had been struck by the violent death of the Russian poet and writer Majakovskij, cantor of the October Revolution. He had decided to end his life by shooting himself in the heart and left a farewell letter which began with these words: "To all! I am dying; do not accuse anyone and not gossip […]"[57]. Thus, the tragic end of the Russian poet "would have imprinted itself in Ḥayāt's memory as a page to be used if the need ever arose. And, in fact, she took refuge in that page to announce

54. al-Ǧalabī 2019.
55. Ibid.
56. Sulṭān 2016, p. 8.
57. Ibid.

her silent revolution and end her life so that her death would be a slap in the tyrant's face"[58]. In addition, according to Sulṭān,

> if the deceased were still alive, she would have committed suicide over and over again in seeing her comrades of yesteryear sitting at the same table with the enemies of humanity and their country's occupiers. Seeing those who had waved the red flags – under whose banner she had long fought – celebrate and acclaim that occupation with everything it entailed and sealing a humiliating agreement with them passed off as the lesser evil[59].

Therefore, this "darkening" of Iraq's social and cultural life under Saddam Hussein is the main reason for the novel *Iḏā al-ayyām aġsaqat*[60], published three years after the author's death. The title alludes to that dark period lived between wars and embargo, which transformed Iraq "in a short time, from the land of plenty, with human and intellectual capital as well as natural resources such as oil and water, perpetually coveted by foreign powers, into a needy country. A country whose GNP per capita is even lower than that of countries bordering the Sahara Desert, which are the poorest in the world"[61].

Set in a Baghdadi university, the novel denounces the difficulties of academics and intellectuals at a time when culture was institutionalised and imbued with political ideology. The educational institution described in the novel is a place poisoned by political corruption and psychological pressures in which values have been turned upside down: study and scientific rigour have been subjected to power and dominant political groups; teachers' voices, expressions of culture and free circulation of thoughts and ideas, seem to be stifled by fear and intimidation. The university thus becomes a microcosm which, reflecting the social and intellectual

58. Ibid. Fāḍil al-Ǧalabī also grasps the influence of Russian literature on Ḥayāt Šarārah's literary production. According to him, the novel *Iḏā al-ayyām aġsaqat* recalls some of Turgenev's works due to its style and rich enthralling plot. See al-Ǧalabī 2019.
59. Sulṭān 2009. On the complex transformation of the Iraqi Communist Party from its formation in 1934 as vanguard actor under Iraqi conservative monarchy to the flatterer of the 2003 American occupation, see Ismael 2012.
60. An excerpt from this novel has been translated into English by "Banipal", 63, 2018. See Sharara 2018.
61. al-Ǧalabī 2019.

degradation of the country, appears haunted by the government intelligence services. Under the pretext of defending national security from enemies who oppose the philosophy of the ruling party, informants are recruited among students and even professors. Wiretapping devices are so widespread that professors have to speak in a low voice, for fear of being intercepted, while students associated with the security services or ruling party manage their education without the teachers having a say, role, or any authority in this regard since "the ignorant are favoured with promotions and publications. All this, even though they are unable to correctly write a standard article for a simple but important reason: they lack talent, and writing requires talent and has nothing to do with an abundance of information"[62].

The human and scientific decline of learning institutions is represented by the novel's protagonist, Professor Nuʿmān. After a life spent between research and teaching, he considers the established procedure for evaluating students, judged by political affiliation and not by academic merit, an insult to his dignity, both as a man and an academic. His conscience and his moral integrity force him to turn in his resignation. A number of additional characters are outlined around him: some are symbols of authority and power, such as the dean of the faculty, who always welcomes professors and students at the university entrance in a military uniform and with intimidating and vexatious words and attitude. With the regime's censorious eye, he monitors everybody's movements and conduct. Many other voices represent those who agree to collaborate with the security apparatuses to guarantee safety and security for themselves and their families – only to resort to alcohol in an attempt to calm their conscience and their inner lacerations. Addiction to bottles of *ʿaraq* is a reality that is repeated in the novel as an outlet for frustrations and humiliations. This is the case of Professor Badrī and Professor Akram. The latter, a distinguished researcher, is fired one day because of his alleged betrayal of institutions and whose real nature is not clearly understood. As an immediate consequence, his colleagues avoid him for fear of suffering repercussions. His complete human and professional isolation pushes him towards alcohol. Only Professor Nuʿmān goes to visit him every now and then and to him Professor Akram confides his humiliation as a man and an intellectual:

62. Kāẓim 2017.

> Since my dismissal from the faculty a month ago, no one has come to see me. Not even my children have asked about me! I miss many things that I imagined were normal and unimportant: the fleeting morning greetings with colleagues, tea before going to class, students' faces, their questions, my discussions about religion, history, morality, law, philosophy, our brief laughter [...]. All those manifestations that embodied my university life seem to me bittersweet, beautiful, and dear[63].

Regarding his intellectual activity, to Professor Nuʿmān's question as to whether he still writes, he replies:

> Would you be surprised if I told you that writing seems like stagnant swamp water? What is the point of writing if writing does not have a purpose? What if you cannot publish what you write nor reach the readers? What is the purpose of writing something if it stays in the drawers of your desk or on the shelf? Imagine a skilled musician composing wonderful musical pieces in his home, playing them on the piano or violin, but he cannot give concerts! [...] I have not published anything for many years and my old books are read as part of history, not the present, while I am still alive! My blood still pulses with vitality. All I can hope for is that my production will be published after my death, if I am lucky. [...] I am over seventy, so what am I waiting for? How many years do I have left and what will change? Everything is getting worse; we are standing on a sloping, slippery ground that always brings us down[64].

Iḏā al-ayyām aġsaqat has been defined as a novel of social criticism, "delimited in space, time, and characters"[65]: the space is the university campus and classrooms, while the protagonists are students, professors, and employees at a university in the Iraqi capital. The events, while referring to the 1990s, actually take place in the space of a year, which represents the last year of Professor Nuʿmān's work. The novel, in fact, opens with the professor preparing for the beginning of the academic year and ends with him walking away from the university, after having given students their final exams, leaving behind the pressures and harassment

63. Šarārah, Ḥ. 2011, pp. 156–157.
64. Ibid., pp. 258–259.
65. Kāẓim 2017.

suffered as an academic: from censorship to intimidation, from meagre salaries to long queues to get food with ration cards. In the novel, however, one of the most absurd acts of psychological violence imposed on professors is having their body weight checked:

> The greatest humiliation is represented by the submission to body weight control and the related administrative punishments for those who exceed the weight limit. To avoid punishment, they reluctantly submit to cruel fasts, despite the hunger caused by the embargo. Professor Nuʿmān thus transmits the painful image of human frailty, showing us a university professor waiting in line to be weighed, exhausted by the heat and the humid and suffocating air. Exasperated, he runs away but then comes back through the weighing room window, thus losing his academic and social dignity, as if he were a child[66].

And so, among professors, conversations on cultural topics give way to discussions about calories and calculations between height and body weight. These passages of the novel are inspired by what really happened in those years: after the invasion of Kuwait, orders from the highest levels of the regime imposed on state officials of all administrations, including universities, the obligation to maintain a weight compatible with age and height, under threat of having their salaries reduced[67].

Therefore, the novel chronicles the misery of living in Iraq under Saddam Hussein and the Baʿath party, but as the Saudi writer Turkī al-Ḥamad (1952) writes:

> [I]n *Iḏā al-ayyām aġsaqat*, the real misery is not the search for a meagre bite to eat nor the misery coming from the fact that this search has become everyone's obsession in a country blessed with two important rivers and oil wells from north to south. A country that gets black gold from the earth and rain from the sky. Everyone in Iraq, from university professors to the garbage men who sweep the streets of al-Rašīd, Abū Nuwās, and al-Mutanabbī, is constantly preoccupied with finding the next meal, a morsel that will temporarily alleviate the hunger pangs that assail them from dawn to dusk. Only a restricted group of privileged individuals is able to escape

66. Ibid.
67. Kachachi 2003, p. 26.

> this cruel destiny. Yet this all, as cruel as it might be, is not the real misery. The real misery in Iraq is that souls have become soulless and life has become lifeless. It is the fear that envelops everything with its cloak when the angel of death controls one's breath, until he makes sure that the only breath is that of the Leader and that there is no heartbeat except the one that praises his name[68].

Consequently, the novel is also an act of denunciation of the silence generated precisely by fear and terror "which oppress the breast and suffocate the breath"[69]. As the Saudi writer reminds us, silence is the acceptance of slavery and "whoever accepts slavery as his destiny cannot blame anyone but himself. We are all responsible when we remain silent in the face of a crime or before an insult to human dignity carried out in the name of the nation and its pride. But, in the end, it is the nation that loses out"[70]. Al-Turkī concludes that every Arab country risks becoming another Iraq if that silence is not broken. Therefore, *Iḏā al-ayyām aġsaqat* is a deafening cry breaking that silence, which is the direct consequence of fear and terror.

Ḥayāt Šarārah was certainly an inconvenient figure for academic and government institutions, as evidenced by the difficulty in finding her novel in Iraq where there were only a few copies in circulation, often clandestinely. Furthermore, for years it was not available in libraries[71]. She has represented the Arab intellectual who, while remaining in his own country, must relate to the regime in power and survive it:

> It is well known that, in totalitarian societies, the intellectual class is usually the first group to be subjected to pressures by the regime. What matters for a dictator is to subjugate the consciences of that class or threaten their livelihood by paralysing their thinking. A regime does not fear for its legitimacy any more than it fears free intellectuals with independent thinking because they are a threat to its authority. History is full of similar testimonials[72].

68. al-Ḥamad 2002.
69. Ibid.
70. Ibid.
71. Sulṭān 2016, p. 9.
72. *Ḥayāt Šarārah... ʿirāqiyyah min zaman al-tawahhuǧ* 2010.

This way, her story poses once again the dilemma that affects the intellectuals in the Arab world: What tools or escape route, apart from emigration or exile, do they have to express themselves freely in their own country[73]? Unfortunately, Ḥayāt Šarārah did not find any or rather did not want to find any, preferring to remain firm in her position, at the cost of her life. She chose not to bow and scrape to the regime that at that time was forging the university community and transforming it into tools in its hands. Although the regime deprived Ḥayāt of her rights and eventually of her life, she believed to the very end in the university as a centre for the democratic spread of free knowledge, a promoter of a peaceful society based on the rule of law that guarantees justice and equal opportunity for all. It is precisely with these words that sum up the identity of this illustrious Iraqi colleague that I would like to conclude my contribution, in the hope that her cultural battle may one day be won in all the universities of the world, within and outside the Arab World.

References

A Journey in Iraqi Fiction (2018), in "Banipal", 61, pp. 21–135.

Barbaro, A. (2019), *"Message in a Bottle": tra realismo magico e memoria, una metafora di appropriazione dell'universo femminile in un romanzo iracheno,* in Avino, M., Barbaro, A., Ruocco, M. (eds.), *QAMARIYYĀT: Oltre ogni frontiera tra letteratura e traduzione: Studi in onore di I. Camera D'Afflitto*, Istituto per l'Oriente "C. A. Nallino", Rome, pp. 39–60.

Bishop, E. (2013), *Democracy and Monarchy as Antithetical Terms? Iraq's Elections of September 1954*, in "Studia Politica: Romanian Political Science Review", 13, 2, pp. 313–326, available at https://nbn-resolving.org/urn:nbn:de:0168-ssoar-447205 (last accessed 23 November 2021).

Caiani, F., Cobham, C. (2013), *The Iraqi Novel: Key Writers, Key Texts*, Edinburgh University Press, Edinburgh.

Camera d'Afflitto, I. (2007), *Letteratura araba contemporanea dalla* nahḍah *a oggi*, Carocci, Rome.

Campanini, M. (2008), *Storia del Medio Oriente 1798–2006*, Il Mulino, Bologna.

Chalabi, F. (2018), *Heroic outcry against injustice*, trans. Adil Babikir, in "Banipal", 63, pp. 26–28.

73. On the figure of the Arab intellectual and his relation to power in social and public life, see Said 1996.

Diana, E. (2019), *Letteratura irachena d'esilio: la scrittura di Muḥsin al-Ramlī*, in Avino, M., Barbaro, A., Ruocco, M. (eds.), *QAMARIYYĀT: Oltre ogni frontiera tra letteratura e traduzione. Studi in onore di I. Camera D'Afflitto*, Istituto per l'Oriente "C. A. Nallino", Rome, pp. 181–206.

al-Ǧalabī, F. (2019), *Ḥayāt Šarārah al-kātibah al-muntaḥirah fī Baġdād wa-riwāyatuhā: al-Šahādat* Iḏā al-ayyām aġsaqat, in "al-Nāqid al-ʿirāqī", 2 May, available at: فاضل الجلبي : حياة شرارة الكاتبة المنتحرة في بغداد وروايتها - الشهادة "إذا الايام اغسقت" (ملف/7) - الناقد العراقي (last accessed 23 November 2021).

Galletti, M. (2011), *Iraq: Il cuore del mondo*, Tipolitografia Lamberti Domenico, Tarquinia.

Ḥamad, M. (2007), *Wa-"Iḏā al-ayyām aġsaqat". Lā tansaw Ḥayāt Šarārah*, in "Dīwān al-ʿarab", 28 kānūn al-ṯānī, available at: و"إذا الايامُ أغسَقَتْ" فَلا تَنسوا "حياة شرارة"! - ديوان العرب (diwanalarab.com) (last accessed 23 November 2021).

al-Ḥamad, T. (2002), *Iḏā al-ayyām aġsaqat wa-iḏā al-aḥlām tabaʿṯarat...*, in "Šarq al-Awsaṭ", 8741, 3 nūfimbir, available at: إذا الأيام أغسقت وإذا الأحلام تبعثرت.. - تركي الحمد (aawsat.com) (last accessed 23 November 2021).

Ḥayāt Šarārah... ʿirāqiyyah min zaman al-tawahhuğ (2010), in "Rābiṭat al-marʾah al-ʿirāqiyyah", 30 April, available at: https://iraqiwomensleague.com/mod.php?mod=news&modfile=item&itemid=3974#.X_R59TSg-Gw (last accessed 23 November 2021).

Husin, J. Y. et al. (2006), *Costruire lo Stato moderno e la futura memoria dell'Iraq*, trans. Amelia Mariano, in "'da Qui'. Sull'orlo della civiltà", 8, pp. 49–73.

Ismael, T. Y. (2012), *The Rise and Fall of the Communist Party of Iraq*, Cambridge University Press, Cambridge.

Kachachi, I. (2003), *Parole di donne irachene: Il dramma di un Paese scritto al femminile*, trans. A. Costa, B. Lupoli, M. Al Saadi, Baldini & Castoldi, Milan.

Kashou, H. H. (2013), *War and Exile in Contemporary Iraqi Women's Novels*, PhD thesis, Ohio State University.

Kāẓim, Š. (2017), *Ḥayāt Šarārah wa-riwāyatuhā* Iḏā al-ayyām aġsaqat, in "al-Zamān", 10 māyū, available at: https://www.azzaman.com/%D8%AD%D9%8A%D8%A7%D8%A9-%D8%B4%D8%B1%D8%A7%D8%B1%D8%A9-%D9%81%D9%8A-%D8%B1%D9%88%D8%A7%D9%8A%D8%AA%D9%87%D8%A7-%D8%A5%D8%B0%D8%A7-%D8%A7%D9%84%D8%A3%D9%8A%D8%A7%D9%85-%D8%A3%D8%BA%D8%B3%D9%82%D8%AA/ (last accessed 23 March 2021).

Masmoudi, I. (2015), *War and Occupation in Iraqi Fiction*, Edinburgh University Press, Edinburgh.

Mustafa, S. (ed. and trans.) (2008), *Contemporary Iraqi Fiction. An Anthology*, Syracuse University Press, New York.

Ruocco, M. (1999), *L'intellettuale arabo tra impegno e dissenso*, Carocci, Rome.

Ruocco, M. (2014–2015), *Finzione, caffè e filosofia nel romanzo* Bābā Sārtr *di ʻAlī Badr*, in "Studi Maġrebini", 12–13, 2, pp. 509–528.

Saeed, H. (2021), *"When Darkness Falls": On the Shortened, Brilliant Life of Iraqi Author Hayat Sharara*, in "ArabLit Quarterly", 21 January, available at: https://arablit.org/2021/01/21/when-darkness-falls-on-the-shortened-brilliant-life-of-iraqi-author-hayat-sharara/ (last accessed 23 November 2021).

Said, E. W. (1996), *Representations of the Intellectual*, Vintage Books, New York.

Šarārah, B. (2011), *al-Muqaddimah*, in Šarārah, Ḥayāt, *Iḏā al-ayyām aġsaqat*, Dār al-Madà, Beirut, pp. 9–84.

Šarārah, Ḥ. (1994), *Ṣafaḥāt min sīrat Nāzik al-Malāʾikah*, Dār Riyāḍ al-Rayyis, London.

Šarārah, Ḥ. (2011), *Iḏā al-ayyām aġsaqat*, Dār al-Madà, Beirut.

Šarārah, M. (1981), *al-Mutanabbī bayna l-buṭūlah wa-l-iġtirāb*, al-Muʾassasah al-ʿarabiyyah li-l-dirāsāt wa-l-našr, Beirut.

Šarārah, M. (1982), *Naẓarāt fī turāṯinā al-qawmī,* al-Muʾassasah al-ʿarabiyyah li-l-dirāsāt wa-l-našr, Beirut.

Sharara, B. (2018), *She Felt She Was under Surveillance at the University*, trans. Adil Babikir, in "Banipal", 63, pp. 14–25.

Sharara, H. (2018), *When the Days Grow Dark*, trans. Jonathan Wright, in "Banipal", 63, pp. 29–48.

Sulṭān, Ḫ. Ḥ. (2009), *Ḥayāt Šarārah al-ṯā'irah al-ṣāmitah*, in "al-Ḥiwār al-mutamaddin", 2624, 22 April, available at: https://www.ahewar.org/debat/show.art.asp?aid=169607 (last accessed 23 November 2021).

Sulṭān, Ḫ. Ḥ. (ed.) (2016²), *Ḥayāt Šarārah al-ṯāʾirah al-ṣāmitah*, Dār al-ḫālidī li-l-tibāʿah wa-l-našr, Baghdad.

Transforming our World: The 2030 Agenda for Sustainable Development, available at: https://sdgs.un.org/2030agenda#:~:text=Transforming%20our%20world%3A%20the%202030%20Agenda%20for%20Sustainable,Prosperity.%20...%205%20Peace.%20...%206%20Partnership.%20 (last accessed 23 November 2021).

Tripp, C. (2007), *A History of Iraq*, Cambridge University Press, Cambridge.

Elvira Diana is Associate Professor of Arabic Language and Literature at Università degli Studi "G. D'Annunzio" di Chieti-Pescara (Italy). Her line of research focuses on the Arabic literary production from the 19th century to present with particular attention paid to the modern Arabic literatures of dissidence, exile and prison. She has published many academic essays and has been studying Libyan literature for years to which she has dedicated two monographs: *L'immagine degli italiani nella letteratura libica dall'epoca coloniale alla caduta di Gheddafi* (Istituto per l'Oriente C.A. Nallino, Rome 2011) e *La letteratura della Libia. Dall'epoca coloniale ai nostri giorni* (Carocci, Rome 2008).

Chapter 5

Pluralism and Ethnoreligious Identities in Iraqi Fiction: ʿAbdullāh Ṣaḫī's Trilogy on Thawra City

Antonio Pacifico

Abstract

Since the fall of the Baʿathist regime, the question of pluralism and ethnoreligious identities has become crucial for the actors in the Iraqi literary field. Ethno-religious elements were gradually (re)introduced in the works of many writers who tried to counteract the mainstream narrative on the country's identity through fiction. Drawing on Bourdieu's field theory, this chapter thus focuses on the case study of the trilogy written between 2008 and 2017 by the Iraqi writer ʿAbdullāh Ṣaḫī. It considers the "trajectory" and current "position" of this writer in the literary field and explores, from an "internal" perspective, the representations of the Shia contained in his texts. Finally, in the concluding remarks, it highlights further possibilities of research in the field of Arabic literary studies regarding this subject.

Keywords: Iraqi fiction; pluralism; ethnoreligious identities; Shia; Thawra City.

1. Introduction

Ethnoreligious identities, along with their cultural, political, and social manifestations, have been taboo subjects for most of modern Iraqi history.

To quote Fanar Haddad, they have been its "proverbial skeleton-in-the-closet [...]: an undeniable fact known to all but one which was seldom discussed beyond the confines of the single sect"[1]. Thus, throughout the 20th century, the official narrative of the state – as well as that of other political actors, such as the Iraqi Communist Party – has always been opposed to forms of ethnoreligious expression, and words such as "Sunni" or "Shia" were seldom used in Iraqi public discourse before the 1990s[2]. This situation started to change after the March 1991 political uprisings and, more importantly, after a series of crucial events, such as the long sanctions era that followed the first Gulf War (1990–1991), the US invasion, and the fall of the Baʿathist regime in 2003. From this moment onwards, Iraqi society has seen the emergence of more salient ethnoreligious identities, and their manifestations have done nothing but increase since then.

This radical change in the expression of ethnoreligious identities has led to well-known historical consequences, including the fierce civil conflict that took place in Iraq between 2006 and 2007. But this change has also pushed an increasing number of scholars to deepen their understanding of such a thorny issue, with the result that, in recent times, many of them have started questioning the inherent negativity of ethnoreligious identities and their manifestations. Some Western and Iraqi scholars, for instance, have noticed that the issue of peacebuilding in Iraq is intimately connected to its ethnoreligious divides, while some others have gone further, contesting the very notion of ethnoreligious identities as elements intrinsically opposed to the construction of a single and unified nation[3]. In this perspective, the latter have argued that it is primarily the failure of the state in absorbing and transcending divisions which has determined the rise of these "secondary identities" and that there are a variety of ways to display them, which sometimes are far from representing a threat to the nation, as in the case of the "passive" or "banal" attitude adopted by the majority of Iraqis most of the times[4].

Nevertheless, the main objective of this chapter is not to focus on the current academic debates existing on ethnoreligious identities, nor is it

1. Haddad 2011, p. 1.
2. Bengio 1985; Haddad 2011.
3. Haddad 2011, 2013; Sallūm 2013, 2017.
4. Haddad 2011, pp. 25–32.

to elaborate on the concrete consequences of their expressions in Iraqi society. Rather, the chapter addresses the phenomenon of their retrieval within the Iraqi literary output produced in recent decades. Indeed, since the fall of Saddam Hussein's dictatorship – but to a lesser extent also during the 1990s – a certain idea of "Iraqiness" and "national identity" that was propagandised by the former regime and other political actors has begun to implode in literature as well. Ethnoreligious elements were gradually (re)introduced in the works of many writers who tried to counteract the mainstream narrative on the country's identity through fiction. Returning to the object of this chapter, it must be stressed that I concentrate here on a specific case study, i.e., the literary trilogy written between 2008 and 2017 by the Iraqi writer ʿAbdullāh Ṣaḫī[5]. This trilogy not only deals with one of the most relevant ethnoreligious divides of modern Iraq, namely, the Sunni-Shia divide but also revolves around a highly meaningful place for the Shia community of Baghdad, Thawra, or Sadr City. Hence, in my analysis, I first look at the academic literature available on the retrieval of ethnoreligious identities in Iraqi fiction. Drawing on Pierre Bourdieu's field theory, I subsequently consider the "trajectory" and current "position" occupied by Ṣaḫī in the literary field and explore the firsthand representations of the Shia contained in his texts[6]. Finally, in my concluding remarks, I reflect on the meaning of such literary practices for the process of peacebuilding in Iraq and highlight further possibilities of research in the field of Arabic literary studies on the representation of ethno-religious identities.

2. Contemporary Iraqi Fiction and Ethnoreligious Identities: A Short Overview of the Literature

In one of the few academic works devoted entirely to the topic of this chapter, Ronen Zeidel argues that the retrieval of ethnoreligious identities

5. Ṣaḫī 2008, 2013, 2017.
6. Bourdieu distinguishes between the "position" and "position-takings" of a writer in the field of literature. According to his theoretical approach, both elements need to be taken into account while investigating literary texts. On this, see Bourdieu 1992.

first emerged in the works of writers with a Shia background[7]. In 1988, the writer and intellectual ʿAzīz al-Sayyid Ǧāsim published *al-Zahr al-šaqī* (The Miserable Flower), a novel in which one could clearly detect "motifs of Shia religiosity"[8]. Before that time, according to Zeidel, the topic of ethnoreligious identities was either totally avoided or addressed in pejorative ways by the actors in Iraqi literature. This was the case, for instance, with writers close to the regime and its political elite – in other words, those writers who represented the most "heteronomous" part of the field. However, this was also the case with prominent Iraqi writers of different origins and religious denominations, who represented its most autonomous part, such as Ḏū l-Nūn Ayyūb, Ġāʾib Ṭuʿmah Farmān, Fuʾād al-Takarlī or Fāḍil al-ʿAzzāwī[9].

During the 1990s, ethnoreligious identities started gaining more ground in the field of literature as in the field of politics, and the main signs in this respect came once again from writers with a Shia background. As pointed out by Zeidel, this radical change was first implemented by writers living abroad in the Iraqi diaspora, such as Ǧinān Ǧāsim al-Ḥillāwī, Hadiyyah Ḥusayn, Naǧm Wālī, Salīm Maṭar or Ḥamīd al-ʿIqābī. Their works contained elements that dealt not only with their own ethnoreligious community but also with other groups. Moreover, according to Zeidel, these writers often expressed a Shia identity "that was both cultural and political, traditional and secular"[10].

After the fall of the Baʿathist regime and the political change brought by the US invasion, this trend was also imported into the Iraqi field of the "inside"[11] for reasons that can significantly vary according to the position occupied by the writers in the literary field[12]. The Shia literati who

7. Zeidel 2020, pp. 26–27. It is worth noting that I am using adjectives like "Shia" or "Sunni" here only in relation to the origin, the background, of these authors, and not about their actual feelings of belonging to a specific ethnoreligious community.
8. Ibid.
9. On the literary output of some of these writers, see Caiani, Cobham 2013.
10. Zeidel 2020, p. 47
11. On the internal split of the Iraqi literary field that opposes the literati of the "inside" to the literati of the "outside", see Hanoosh 2012; Mohsen 2012.
12. In producing a first categorisation of these novels, Zeidel looks only at their content and not at their aesthetic and symbolic features. Moreover, Zeidel does not include significant texts such as the one I am investigating in this chapter. On this first categorisation, see Zeidel 2020, pp. 35–36.

(re)introduced ethnoreligious elements in their works include Šawqī Karīm, Murtaḍà Kzār, Naṣīf Falak, Aḥmad Saʿdāwī, or other writers of the so-called "generation of the 1990s"[13]. In their literary texts, these writers continued to refer to specific ethnoreligious identities and explored topics such as interreligious and interethnic dialogue or other motifs of the country's historical and cultural narratives. In the same phase, even the writers of the most heteronomous part of the field of the "inside" started including some ethnoreligious elements in their works. Unfortunately, however, only the works of a few of these writers have been investigated from a "qualitative" perspective[14]. While scholars have written multiple articles on the retrieval of ethnoreligious identities in the works of famous Iraqi writers, such as Aḥmad Saʿdāwī for instance[15], the texts of other authors still remain largely understudied in the field of Arabic literary studies.

In the aftermath of the US invasion, even the Sunnis started developing their own means of addressing the topic of ethnoreligious identities in the novel. For Zeidel, while some authors with a Sunni background who belonged to the most autonomous part of the field, such as Muḥsin al-Ramlī or ʿAbd al-Sattār Nāṣir, employed references to their ethnoreligious communities to criticise their own group or some of its members who were widely implicated in the political system of the Baʿath, others applied the same logic to develop a "Sunni narrative" that was mostly based on a post-2003 feeling of "victimhood and marginalization", a "feeling of inferiority" and resentment towards "the Shīʿa threat"[16]. Also in this case, however, the production of some of these actors still remains largely understudied, at least from a "literary" perspective.

As for other ethnoreligious communities, it should be noted that, in the same phase, the Iraqi field has witnessed significant growth also in

13. This label of the "generation of the 1990s" may represent an arbitrary definition for the actors of the Iraqi field. For this reason, I am using it for illustrative purposes only.
14. Zeidel affirms that he adopted only a "quantitative" perspective in his work, that is, a perspective that does not take the specific features of literature into account. See Zeidel 2020, p. 15.
15. On the references contained in Aḥmad Saʿdāwī's literary works to multiple of ethno-religious communities, see also Bahoora 2015; Shuiskaja 2018; Campbell 2020.
16. Zeidel 2020, pp. 75–76.

the literary representations of the Christian and Kurdish communities. Yasmeen Hanoosh, for instance, has explored the representations of the Christian minority in the works of two of the most prominent writers of the "generation of the 1990s", who are also living abroad: Sinān Anṭūn and Inʿām Kağahğī. Looking at their literary texts, Hanoosh has argued that it was the diasporic background of these writers that pushed them to deconstruct the mainstream narratives on Iraq's national identity and to employ marginal elements in a nonviolent struggle against the symbolic violence of the state[17]. Zeidel, for his part, has given us a preliminary account of the presence of the Kurds in the novels of writers with different ethnoreligious backgrounds, although he barely considers the texts produced in Arabic by the Kurds themselves. From his brief analysis, we learn that the Kurds were "only rare guests in Iraqi novels prior to the 1990s" and that, even after 1991, only a handful of novels refer to them[18]. Moreover, we learn from his analysis that the presence of the Kurds in the Iraqi novel has been increasing a lot over the last several years, as shown by the works of authors such as Šākir al-Anbārī, Šākir Nūrī, Hayfāʾ Zankanah or Ḥawrāʾ al-Nadāwī.

A final element that needs to be highlighted here concerns the general approach of Arabic literary studies on the topic of ethnoreligious identities. As I have also shown in this short overview of the literature, the researchers who have dealt with this topic have been more interested in the production of the "first actors" in the literary field than in the work and texts of other writers, maybe less renowned on an international level[19]. It is this preliminary remark in particular that pushed me to pay close attention to the texts of a writer like Ṣaḫī. Indeed, as far as these texts are concerned, I must stress that they, too, like many other literary texts, have been much sidelined by the previous research literature on the topic. Zeidel, for instance, dedicated only a few lines to the texts of Ṣaḫī's

17. Hanoosh 2019.
18. Zeidel 2020, p. 104.
19. Here, I am referring once again to a writer such as Aḥmad Saʿdāwī, but also to other writers of the so-called "generation of the 1990s", who at present enjoy a high level of international recognition, such as Sinān Anṭūn, ʿAlī Badr, Ḥasan Balāsim, or Inʿām Kağahğī.

literary trilogy and reported several inaccurate data also in relation to his personal trajectory[20].

3. Between a Hobby and a Profession: Ṣaḫī's Literary Trajectory as an Iraqi Writer in Exile

ʿAbdullāh Ṣaḫī is an Iraqi writer, journalist, and translator living in London. He was born in Iraq in 1951 and, during his youth, studied at Mustansiriya University. After spending the first part of his life in Iraq and more specifically in Thawra City, Ṣaḫī left his country at the beginning of 1979, when Iraq experienced a severe deterioration of its sociopolitical situation and the collapse of the alliance existing at that time between its two most prominent parties, the Baʿath and the Communists[21]. Since then, Ṣaḫī lived first in Beirut and then moved to England, where he arrived as an asylum seeker after leaving the Middle East.

As for his literary trajectory, Ṣaḫī started writing when he was only 16 years old, even though it was only much later that he would start writing on a more regular and solid basis. It was during this period and, more precisely, while he was attending secondary school, that he became familiar not only with the "popular" and oral stories "recounted by the old women who were visiting his Baghdadi house at nighttime"[22] but also with written and "legitimate" literature from both Western and other Arab countries. In this phase, moreover, Ṣaḫī engaged profoundly with the reading of a number of authors who would mark his writings, such as Yūsuf Idrīs, Naǧīb Maḥfūẓ, Iḥsān ʿAbd al-Quddūs, Muḥammad ʿAbd al-Ḥalīm ʿAbd Allāh, and Ṭāhā Ḥusayn[23]. During the 1970s, Ṣaḫī published a few short stories in several Iraqi journals and cultural magazines, such as "al-Fikr

20. Zeidel 2020, p. 111.
21. This is one of the most striking differences to Zeidel's version of Ṣaḫī's personal trajectory. Zeidel states that ʿAbdullāh Ṣaḫī "lived in Iraq his all life", even though the latter left Iraq in 1979. On this, see Zeidel 2020, p. 111.
22. Personal interview with the author, 23 December 2020 (unpublished).
23. Ibid. It is interesting to note, in this regard, that all these authors evoked by Ṣaḫī are different from the authors evoked by the "first actors" of the Iraqi field. The latter commonly refer to previous generations of Arab and Western writers who are associated with literary traditions that differ quite a bit from old-fashioned Egyptian realism.

al-ğadīd", "al-Ṯaqāfah al-ğadīdah", and "Ṭarīq al-šaʿb"[24], while his first book, *Ḥuqūl dāʾimat al-ḫuḍrah* (The Evergreen Fields), was published in Lebanon in 1983[25]. During the 1980s, Ṣaḫī also started devoting himself to translation, another crucial activity of his career. As a result, he published, in 1984, his Arabic version of *Strange News from Another Star* (1919) by the German-Swiss writer Herman Hesse first and then, in 1988, his translation of *The River Between* (1965) by the prolific Kenyan author Ngũgĩ wa Thiong'o[26]. In other words, in the first part of his trajectory, writing was more of a "hobby", a "passion" for Ṣaḫī than a profession[27].

The following phase of his literary trajectory was inaugurated in 2008 with the publication of his second book which is also the first part of his trilogy, *Ḫalf al-saddah* (Behind the Dam). In this work, he includes a number of elements that relate not only to his personal life but also to the life experiences of his parents. This book represented his first literary success and was followed, after five years, by the second novel of his trilogy, *Durūb al-fuqdān* (The Pathways of Loss, 2013). In this novel, the author recalled more directly his personal trajectory as well as that of the whole community in which he grew up in Iraq. His fourth book, or third part of his trilogy, *al-Lāğiʾ al-ʿirāqī* (The Iraqi Refugee), was published in 2017. This novel deals with the migration story of many young people from the Baghdadi suburb district of Thawra City to Europe. This migration was motivated by the terrible sociopolitical conditions experienced by the Iraqi people during the previous decades, precisely as in the case of the author himself.

Concerning Ṣaḫī's position in this latter phase, it can be noted that all the novels that form his literary trilogy were published after the fall of the Baʿathist regime (2003), although this does not necessarily mean that the author shares the same beliefs and ideas as those movements that have

24. Personal interview with the author, 24 March 2021 (unpublished). Significantly, these are all journals that were close to the leftist forces of the country. Moreover, during the 1970s, the editor-in-chief of two of these journals quoted above was the same Faḫrī Karīm, who also is the publisher of Ṣaḫī's trilogy. On Karīm, see below.
25. Ṣaḫī 1983.
26. Hīssīh 1983; Nġūġī 1988.
27. The word *hiwāyyah*, which means "hobby" or "passion" in Arabic, is a recurring word in my personal interview with ʿAbdullāh Ṣaḫī. Cf. my personal interview with the author, 23 December 2020.

repeatedly instrumentalised their Shia identity in the field of politics since then[28]. Moreover, regarding Ṣaḫī's position in this phase, it should be stressed that he has continued to define himself as a writer who "practices writing in a way that combines hobby and professionalism" as can be seen in the presentation he gives of himself on the website of the prestigious *Katara Prize for Arabic Novel*[29]. In this sense, Ṣaḫī has also stated that he does not cultivate any solid relation either with the other writers living in the Iraqi diaspora or with the writers who remained in the country[30], despite his participation in some literary events in Iraq and his close relationship with Faḫrī Karīm, the owner of the notorious *Mu'assasat al-Madà li-l-i'lām wa-l-ṯaqāfah wa-l-funūn* (Al Mada Foundation in Media, Culture and the Arts), also known as the *Al Mada group*[31]. This publishing house, which published all the works of Ṣaḫī's trilogy, clearly represents one of the strongest institutions of the Iraqi literary field of the "inside" but also publishes the works of several up-and-coming writers who don't have any symbolic capital.

Furthermore, looking at Ṣaḫī's literary trajectory, one cannot avoid considering another element that is also crucial for any author coming from a "dominated" and "peripheral" field like the Iraqi one, i.e., the translation of his literary works[32]. Unlike the works of many other writers living in the Iraqi diaspora, Ṣaḫī's books have not yet been translated into any major language of the Western cultural fields. Only an excerpt from the second book of the trilogy has been translated into English and published by the British literary magazine specialising in modern Arab literature, "Banipal"[33]. Ṣaḫī is therefore barely known in Western literary

28. Ṣaḫī, moreover, does not see himself as a Shia writer, and this is the reason why I prefer to use the word background, instead of the word identity, when discussing him (personal interview with the author, 23 December 2020). On these political movements in Iraq, see Jabar 2003; Haddad 2017, 2020.
29. https://www.kataranovels.com/novelist/عبد-الله-صخي/ (last accessed 23 March 2021).
30. Personal interview with the author, 23 December 2020.
31. Faḫrī Karīm, the owner of this publishing house, was a militant member of the Iraqi Communist Party and the editor-in-chief of its journals and cultural magazines, as discussed above. On the relation between Ṣaḫī and Karīm, see https://www.youtube.com/watch?v=8qTxXMyb_18 (last accessed 26 April 2021).
32. On the opposition between "dominant" and "dominated" literary fields, see Casanova 1999.
33. Sakhi 2018.

circles and seems to enjoy a low level of recognition within them. From this point of view, everything suggests that Ṣaḫī occupies a very marginal position in his literary field as well, which is very different, of course, from the position of many other Iraqi writers, such as those of the aforementioned "generation of the 1990s".

4. The Narrative Plot of Ṣaḫī's Trilogy on Thawra City

The narrative plot of Ṣaḫī's trilogy opens with the inclusion of some historical events that happened in the Iraqi South at the beginning of the 20th century. Although they are seldom mentioned in the texts, these events mostly concern the well-known "Iraqi revolution of the 1920s", which is (re)narrated here through the stories of Salmān al-Yūnus and his wife, Makiyyah al-Ḥasan. Shortly after the "revolution", the farmers who participated in this historical event were harassed by the government and were obliged to migrate from the southern part of the country to the Iraqi capital city, precisely as Salmān al-Yūnus and his wife do at the beginning of the first book.

In the subsequent scenes of *Ḥalf al-saddah*, we follow the two protagonists of the novel, together with other farmers fleeing the Iraqi South, in their settlement experience on the outskirts of Baghdad. Under the spiritual leadership of al-Sayyid Ǧār Allāh, they decide to settle down in two areas that will become, just like Thawra, two of the most meaningful places of the present-day city[34]. The first, known as al-ʿĀṣimah, corresponds to the area located behind the dam built by the Ottoman governor al-Wālī Nāẓim Bāšā in 1910. The second, known as al-Šākiriyyah, corresponds to the notorious "Green Zone" that first became the centre of the *Coalition Provisional Authority* during the US occupation and later the centre of the international forces in the city. It is within this framework, thus, that the reader finds himself confronted for the first time with the individual and collective stories of the protagonists of the trilogy.

In the central and final parts of the novel, Salmān al-Yūnus, his family and the other migrants are able to find some peace, despite the extreme poverty that afflicts them. This apparent peace, however, is not meant

34. Ṣaḫī 2008, p. 9.

to last since, in the middle of the first book, an enormous fire spreading from the oil wells located close to these two settlements threatens to kill them[35]. The protagonists are thus obliged to leave their houses again and live through a second experience of displacement. Their second displacement, moreover, is followed by a third one at the end of the book, when all the inhabitants of al-ʿĀṣimah and al-Šākiriyyah resettle in the place that had been built for them by the government of ʿAbd al-Karīm Qāsim (1958–1963)[36], which will be called Thawra City[37].

In *Durūb al-fuqdān*, the second book of the trilogy, the scene is finally set in this crucial place of the Iraqi cultural and historical imagination, although here the main character is not the old Salmān nor his wife but their second child, ʿAlī. At the beginning of the book, we read about his first experiences with love, his artistic dreams as a singer and a musician, and his sociopolitical concerns. Interestingly, all these narratives come to intersect with those of all the other inhabitants of Thawra City who, exactly like ʿAlī, live in a time of abuse and brutality. The narration is now clearly set during the 1970s, a choice that gives the narrator the opportunity to describe not only the oppressive system established by the Baʿathist regime but also the social effects of its abusive conduct.

After the death of Salmān al-Yūnus, the second book continues to recall some other historical events of the Iraqi recent past and delves into several folkloric and cultural aspects concerning the community of this Baghdadi district. In this respect, it is interesting to note that this is the part of the trilogy in which the most references to the cultural, social and political reality of contemporary Iraq can be found, a point that will be discussed in greater detail in the next section of this chapter. For the moment, we may observe that here the narrator starts recalling such significant events as the Baʿathist coup of 1963[38] or the failed countercoup carried out by the Director of Nationality Security Nāẓim Kzār in 1973[39], as well as a variety of elements that could be seen as part of the Iraqi "popular culture" of the time, such as the songs of Salmān al-Mankūb[40],

35. Ṣaḫī 2008, pp. 46–56.
36. Ibid., pp. 106–112.
37. Ibid., p. 141.
38. Ṣaḫī 2013, p. 159.
39. Ibid., pp. 175–177.
40. Ibid., p. 118.

ʿAbd al-Ḥalīm Ḥāfiẓ[41], Muḥammad ʿAbd al-Wahhāb[42], Nāẓim al-Ġazālī or Farīd al-Aṭraš[43].

In the last part of *Durūb al-fuqdān*, the narrative plot revolves again around Salmān al-Yūnus' second child, ʿAlī. This time, the young man is arrested by the Iraqi security forces and put into jail for reasons unknown to the reader. This event is followed by a period of great apprehension and suffering on the part of his friends and relatives, which culminates in the death of the mother of the protagonist, Makiyyah al-Ḥasan, after losing her mind through grief.

The third book of the trilogy, *al-Lāǧiʾ al- irāqī*, opens with ʿAlī's release and the story of another displacement, that is, his migration from Iraq to Europe. Here, the reader comes to know that ʿAlī is not dead, as was the case with many others jailed by the regime. Through a narrative that does not follow a chronological order and seems much more fragmented than the previous ones, we find him first of all in London, in the act of remembering his past life experiences in Iraq and then in Damascus during his displacement to Beirut. We start following the protagonist of the novel through all his vicissitudes outside of Iraq, and we are led by the author to experience, through the protagonist's eyes, all the difficulties that the migrants who moved from the Middle East to Europe at the end of the 1970s faced[44].

At the end of the third book, we find ʿAlī again in the act of remembering his past. However, here ʿAlī recalls his love experiences with Ḫawlah, the woman whom he married, and Nisrīn, the woman with whom he had a love affair until the last days of his life. In the final part of the trilogy, moreover, there is a lengthy description of the sentiment of longing and nostalgia that characterises ʿAlī's life in the English capital city. The trilogy then closes with its main character, now an old man, dying from an unknown disease that affected his psyche, precisely like his mother[45].

41. Ibid., p. 120.
42. Ibid., p. 130.
43. Ibid., p. 163.
44. Ṣaḫī 2017, pp. 129–142.
45. Ibid., p. 189.

5. The Representations of the Iraqi Shia Contained in his Trilogy

Reading these few lines, one could also view Ṣaḫī's trilogy as a literary fiction that focuses above all on the topic of displacement. This is a recurring theme in Ṣaḫī's texts, and the author himself has not hesitated to state on multiple occasions that his trilogy could have also been entitled *Ṯulāṯiyyat al-hiğrah*, "The Trilogy of Migration" or, more generally, "The Trilogy of Displacement"[46]. Nonetheless, as noted by several critics, another element that is also crucial in his literary texts is the space Ṣaḫī gives to the representations of the Iraqi Shia[47]. The latter are the ethnoreligious community that experienced the most tense and difficult relations with the former regime, in addition to being the one in which the March 1991 political uprisings originated[48]. Moreover, as brilliantly highlighted by scholars such as Fanar Haddad, the divide that opposes the Shia to the Sunnis, for instance, has been one of the most relevant divides in modern Iraq. It has shaped and continues to shape the social, cultural, and political mechanisms of Iraqi nation-building[49].

Thus, on a first and more manifest level, we may note a variety of motifs in Ṣaḫī's trilogy that are specific to the myth-symbol complexes of the Shia, which mainly appear in the first two books. Here, one can find numerous references to Ḥusayn, ʿAlī ibn Abī Ṭālib's son, and to the 7th-century Battle of Karbalāʾ (680 CE), i.e., two symbolic elements that encapsulate all the sense of victimhood that is so crucial to the Shia identity[50]. These elements, moreover, are often (re)narrated by Ṣaḫī through the representations of ʿĀšūrāʾ, the annual Shia celebration for the commemoration of Ḥusayn's death. Its description occupies a consistent

46. Personal interview with the author, 23 December 2020. On this, see also the interview published by ʿAbdullāh Ṣaḫī on the occasion of the 12th edition of the *Maʿraḍ Arbīl al-duwalī li-l-kitāb* (The International Book Fair of Erbil), available at: https://www.youtube.com/watch?v=8qTxXMyb_18 (last accessed 24 March 2021). All translations from Arabic to English are mine.
47. On this, see, for instance, Saeed 2021.
48. Haddad 2011, pp. 65–86.
49. Ibid., pp. 32–50.
50. Ibid., p. 18.

number of pages in the first two books of the trilogy and is a recurring theme within them.

The first time we read of such a celebration in *Ḫalf al-saddah* is in its second chapter. This chapter opens with a scene in which Makiyyah al-Ḥasan takes her son ʿAlī to see the reenactement of the Battle of Karbalāʾ in the biggest square of their settlement, while Salmān al-Yūnus goes to the café to listen to its oral account. Significantly, this first reference to ʿĀšūrāʾ is associated here with a first presentation of the main features and habits of the protagonists of the trilogy[51]. In the second chapter, we then find the first description of this celebration, along with the feeling experienced by Makiyyah al-Ḥasan to be part of the same community with the other men and women who have gathered to attend:

> اقتربت من الضفة الأخرى للميدان وهي تهتف في أعماقها: "أسنده يا مولاي". واستمرت في سيرها لتجتاز السور البشري إلى البرية الواسعة الخالية الموحشة التي تشبه أرض الغاضرية كما تخيلتها من الحكايات والأقوال المنقولة. هناك جلست تسمع إيقاعات الطبول وخفق الرايات ورنين الشراريب النحاسية المتدلية من خوذ المحاربين. تنهدت بعمق والتفتت إلى السور البشري وخيل إليها أنهم جميعا مثلها، رجالا ونساء، جاءوا ليغمروا أجسادهم بدون النذور الغزير كأنهم بذلك يخرجون لأول مرة إلى الشعاع المضيء، شعاع الإطمئنان والأمنيات الرحبة.
>
> She approached the other side of the square, muttering to herself: "Support him, my lord", and continued walking to overcome the human wall that separated her from the vast, empty, and desolate space that resembled the land of al-Ġāḍiriyyah[52], at least as she had imagined it from the stories and sayings she heard. There she sat, listening to the beat of the drums, the shaking of the banners, and the ringing of the coppery ornaments dangling from the warriors' helmets. She sighed deeply and turned towards the human wall. It seemed to her that they were all like her, men and women. They had come to immerse their bodies in an abundant blessing, as if they were thus exposing themselves for the first time to a ray of bright light, a ray of peacefulness and copious wishes[53].

51. Ṣaḫī 2008, p. 25.
52. al-Ġāḍiriyyah is another name for the city of Karbalāʾ generally employed by the Shia.
53. Ṣaḫī 2008, p. 29.

In the sixth chapter of the book, we also read a long account of how this community usually prepared for such an important event of Shia religiosity, as in the following passage:

> أغلقت الدكاكين مبكرا، ورفع المزيد من الرايات الخضر السود فوق سقائف السوق والأكواخ والغرف الطينية الخفيضة. وسحبت البسطات إلى داخل الدكاكين لتوفير متسع أكبر للمشاركين في الموكب والمتفرجين. في نهاية السوق عند الجهة الأقرب إلى بيت مكية الحسن رشت الساحة بالماء و كنستها الأيادي الصغيرة للمتطوعين من الصبايا والأولاد. [...] تسلق عبد الحسين أعمدة الكهرباء المتباعدة لسحب الطاقة لإيصالها في سلك طويل على امتداد الطريق الذي سيسلكه الموكب الضيف. سرقة الكهرباء أمر مقبول في مثل هذه الأيام عمل يكرسه العرف وتقبله السلطات الحكومية. وبعد أن تنتهي مراسم إحياء ذكرى حادثة مقتل الحسين بن علي يتوقف سحب الكهرباء تماما، تجمع الأسلاك وتحفظ لاستخدامات العام المقبل.
>
> The shops closed early, and more green and black flags were raised over the market sheds, the shacks, and the small rooms made of mud. The stalls were pulled into the shops to provide more space for the participants and spectators of the procession. At the end of the market, on the side closest to Makiyyah al-Ḥasan's house, the square was sprinkled with water and swept up by the little hands of the girls and boys who had volunteered. […] ʿAbd al-Ḥusayn fixed the supports for electricity distant from each other in order to let the energy pass through a long wire placed along the path that the procession of their guests would take. Electricity theft was acceptable in those days, an act enshrined in customs and tolerated by the ruling authorities. After the end of the memorial ceremony for the killing of Ḥusayn b.ʿAlī, the electricity withdrawal was stopped and the wires were collected and stored to be used the following year[54].

Or in this further passage of the same chapter:

> أوقدت نيران تحت قدور نحاسية ضخمة لإعداد الرز والقيمة لتوزيعه على المشاركين في الموكب بالدرجة الأولى ثم المتفرجين الذين سيشهدون العرض الطقوسي الاستذكاري، فإعداد الطعام جزء من تقليد قديم يتبرع فيه المقتدرون طلبا للثواب. قبل المساء بقليل خرج الناس من بيوتهم بملابسهم السود، وانتشروا في السوق والأزقة والشوارع القريبة. وحول القدور النحاسية تجمعت النسوة للمساعدة في غسل الصحون وتنظيف الحمص المجروش بأطباق كبيرة.

54. Ibid., pp. 91–92.

> Fires were lit under the huge copper pots for the preparation of the rice and the *qīmah*[55]. These were distributed above all to the participants of the procession and, after that, to the spectators who had come to attend the ritual performance for the commemoration. Food preparation is part of an ancient tradition in which the rich donate to get a divine reward. Shortly before the evening, people left their homes in their black clothes and spread out into the market, the alleys and the nearby streets. Around the copper pots, the women gathered to help wash dishes and clean the crushed chickpeas in the large plates[56].

In addition, in the sixth chapter, one may observe one of the most accurate and longest descriptions of the religious procession performed by this community during the celebration of ʿĀšūrāʾ. This time, however, this Shia element is recounted through the eyes of the young ʿAlī and his first love, Badriyyah, who take advantage of the celebration to meet away from the prying eyes of their parents. Here, great prominence is also given to the folkloric aspects of the procession:

> إشارة الانطلاق بدأت من قارعي الطبول الذين بدؤا إيقاعا جنائزيا بعصي من الخيزران ذات رؤوس مدورة تهبط برتابة موزونة على النقارات التي علقت برقابهم، يتبعهم ضاربو الصناجات الصفر النحاسية. وإذ تحركت الفرقة الأولى من الموكب لحقتها الفرق التالية ليبدأ ضرب السلاسل على الظهور وإطلاق الردات الشعرية بين مجموعة الشباب لاطمي الصدور. [...] من حين لآخر كان حاملو اللوكسات يتبدلون، ويقوم حامل المشعل بعدة دورات حتى تقترب النار من رؤوس المشاركين والمتفرجين، فتنسحب رؤوس النسوة والأطفال إلى الخلف لتفادي اللهب، فيما يواصل لاطمو الصدور الضرب على إيقاع الردات التي يساهم فيها المحتشدون على الطريق، أمام البيوت والمحال والدكاكين. حتى إذا اقتربوا من الموقع المقرر للوقوف في نهاية السوق المطلة على الساحة ارتفع حماس ضاربي السلاسل ولاطمي الصدور، وازدادت حدة ايقاعات الطبول والصناجات.

> The starting signal came from the drummers. They produced a funeral rhythm with their rounded head bamboo sticks that were coming down in a monotonous and balanced way on the drums hanging from their necks. They were followed by the cymbalists with their yellow and coppery instruments. Since the first unit of the procession started to move, this was followed by other units and even the rattling of the

55. This is an Iraqi sauce very common in the region of Naǧaf as well as in other Iraqi areas. It is generally prepared by the Shia community of the country when celebrating ʿĀšūrāʾ and is made of beef, tomato paste, oil, chickpeas, salt, pepper, and other spices.
56. Ṣaḫī 2008, p. 92.

> chains and the melodic echoes began to resonate amongst a group of young men who were beating their breasts. […] From time to time, those holding the lanterns were taking turns and the torchbearer was making multiple rounds to let the fire approach the heads of the participants and the spectators. The women and children's heads were being drawn back to avoid the flame. At the same time, the young men were continuing to beat their chests to the rhythm of the echoes produced also by the crowd, who were standing outside, in front of the houses, the stores, and the shops. The moment they got closer to the place where they were supposed to stop, at the edge of the market at the square, the enthusiasm of those who were beating their breasts as well as the intensity of the beats of the drums and the cymbals increased[57].

An interesting representation of Shia religiosity and, more particularly, of the celebration of ʿĀšūrāʾ is then (re)narrated by Ṣaḥī in the eighth chapter of the second book, *Durūb al-fuqdān*. Telling the story of Madīḥah, one of ʿAlī's twin sisters, the author recounts here a feminine version of the latter, one that includes a reference to another prominent figure of Shia religiosity, Zaynab as well as the songs and performances carried out by the women of the community on this occasion:

> نامت فتيات المدينة فترة ما بعد الظهر كلها. استيقظن عصرا. اغتسلن ومشطن شعورهن بالمحلب والقرنفل والمسك. وحين احتشد الظلام خلعن فوطهن وكشفن عن شعور نظيفة معطرة مرسلة عازمات على السهر حتى الصباح اعتقادا منهن بأنهن يرافقن السيدة زينب التي لم يغمض لها جفن تلك الليلة بحسب الروايات التي تحدثت عن واقعة كربلاء. في جلستها في باحة الدار كانت مكية الحسن ترى السيدة زينب وحيدة بين الخيام تستعيد ذكرياتها وأيام دلالها وهنائها في كنف والديها وأخوتها، وتفكر في ما آلت إليه بعد أن فقدتهم جميعا ولم يبق معها في غربتها من يعيدها إلى مدينة جدها إلا رجل عليل ضعيف لا يستطيع حمل جسده النحيل. وسمعت صوتا قريبا ينشد عبر مكبر للصوت: «هاي آخر ليله يدري من العمر/ والفراق يصير لو صار الفجر / ما مثلها ليله بالدنيا تمر / على حسين وعيلته وأطفاله». ويرد جوق متنافر: «حسين للتوديع لم عياله». [...] كن ينثرن شعورهن في الهواء فينهمر العبير ليستدل به العشاق على حبيباتهم اللواتي يضربن أضلعهن بسواعدهن والأرض بأقدامهن، وكان الشباب يقتربون منهن باحتراس خشية أن يعترض عليهم آباء أو أخوة أو أزواج.

> The girls of the city slept the whole afternoon and woke up in the evening. They washed themselves and combed their hair with

57. Ibid., pp. 93–94.

> *maḥlab*[58], cloves and musk. When the night fell, they took off their towels and their hair was clean, flowing, and scented. It was their intention to stay awake the whole night since they were convinced that they would thus act like Zaynab who, according to the accounts of the disgraceful event of Karbalā', never closed her eyes on that night. Sitting in the courtyard of her house, Makiyyah al-Ḥasan saw her alone amongst the tents. She was remembering the days of her comfort and joy in the care of her parents and brothers. [Zaynab] was thinking of what she had come through after she lost all of them and that there was no one left with her, in her loneliness, to bring her back to her grandfather's city. There was only a weak, sick man who could not even bear his own slender body. Makiyyah heard the sound of a chant coming from a loudspeaker: "Ḥusayn knows it is the last night of his life / His departure will occur with the advent of the dawn / There will be no other night like that in this world / Not for Ḥusayn, not for his family, not for his children". But another one as well from a different chorus: "Ḥusayn gathered his family to tell them goodbye". [...] [The girls'] hair was blowing in the wind and their fragrance was pouring down, so that the lovers could be guided to their beloved ones. They hit their ribs with their forearms and the ground with their feet. The young men approached them cautiously, fearing a reaction from their fathers, brothers, or husbands[59].

As can be seen from these short quotes, Ṣaḫī usually refers to Shia religiosity from a complex and multifaceted perspective and thus he does not limit himself to considering its ritualistic or theological aspects but also its social and folkloric dimensions. Moreover, all these references to Shia religiosity intersect here with the cultural and political reality of modern Iraq, as in the case of my third quote, where the writer mentions the government's attitude during Shia celebrations like ʿĀšūrā', or with other secular aspects of the life of this community – as in my last quote, where ʿĀšūrā' also becomes an occasion to give way to sentiment and love experiences.

Nonetheless, while considering the inclusion of Shia elements in Ṣaḫī's trilogy, one should take into account another aspect in addition to the most direct and evident references to Shia religiosity described

58. This is an aromatic spice made from the seeds of a species of cherry found in the Middle East.

59. Ṣaḫī 2013, pp. 149–150.

above, that is, the specific context in which most of Ṣaḫī's narrative takes place. On a deeper level, indeed, we may observe that these ethnoreligious references are intimately connected with a highly meaningful place for the Shia community of Baghdad, Thawra or Sadr City. At present, this Baghdadi district is an area inhabited by more than one million Shia, but it is also one of the most contested places of the country's cultural and historical narratives for reasons that go beyond and, at the same time, merge with the ethnoreligious divides of Iraqi society[60]. Thawra City was built as a public housing project by the then-Prime Minister of Iraq ʿAbd al-Karīm Qāsim in 1959[61]. Shortly after its foundation, it became one of the symbols of his political revolution and, at the end of the 1970s, Thawra was already one of the main strongholds of the Iraqi Communist Party. During the 1980s, this Communist district was renamed after Ṣaddam and began hosting entire families that left the Iraqi South due to the Iran-Iraq War (1980–1988). Also known for its high poverty rate, Thawra City saw its latest change of name after the US invasion in 2003, when it was unofficially renamed Sadr City in memory of the deceased Shia leader Muḥammad Sādiq al-Ṣadr.

Concerning the presence of this city in Ṣaḫī's trilogy, one might notice that this element appears explicitly for the first time at the end of the first book, when all the inhabitants of the first two settlements, al-ʿĀṣimah and al-Šākiriyyah, are invited by the Iraqi government to resettle there after a fire had destroyed all their homes. However, the story of this Shia community/district is also narrated by Ṣaḫī in a more implicit way in the first part of the same book and well before this specific event. It is (re)narrated by the writer through the stories of its future inhabitants, their existential problems, and material contingencies, which, ironically, are the same they end up experiencing in Thawra. At the same time, this element is also included in other parts of the trilogy, such as its third book, where the author tells the story of ʿAlī's displacement. Indeed, his story clearly represents the story of many other young people who were also born in this place and were obliged to leave their country for the same reasons.

60. On the presence of Thawra City in contemporary Iraqi literature, see Zeidel and Melamed 2017. However, even in this article, the two authors dedicate only a few lines to Ṣaḫī's texts and do not produce a detailed analysis of this trilogy.

61. On the foundation of this Baghdadi district, see Nooraddin 2010, pp. 66–67.

In other words, in his trilogy, Ṣaḫī recounts even the "(hi)stories" that lay behind the foundation of this Shia community/district, along with its most striking contingencies and most recent vicissitudes[62]. Incidentally, as also stated by the prominent Iraqi writer Aḥmad Saʿdāwī with regard to one of the settlements in which the protagonists of *Ḫalf al-saddah* settle down at the beginning of the first book:

> Shākiriyya itself (or Mayzara, etc.) as a settlement was a temporary construct for immigrants. It was relocated elsewhere but remained the same. It moved northeast of the capital yet nothing in it changed: tin, mud, frond, and pipe houses were dismantled in Shākiriyya only to be rebuilt in Thawra City. These building materials disappeared as the new building materials took over and the city was transformed into brick, iron, paved streets, squares and filled-in vertical streams that used to serve as external conduits for transporting sewage water. Still, Shākiriyya did not seem to disappear. [...] The contingent, uncertain presence of Shākiriyya is what continued in Thawra, and consistently so[63].

And Saʿdāwī repeatedly expressed himself also about the shared destiny of many young women and men born in Thawra City, as in the following passage:

> On the benches of the tea vendor in the workers' waiting area in the district of ʿAlāwī Jamīla in the mid-1990s, a group of friends gathered on a wintery night and decided to migrate. This is what subsequently each of them did in his own special way. Those who stayed preserved the obsession with the unaccomplished migration. The option of leaving the country was considered by all, to the point that, during the 1990s, an entire tribe that used to live in Thawra City gradually moved to Montreal, Canada, according to rumors that circulated at the time[64].

Furthermore, in (re)narrating the (hi)stories of this Shia community/district on the margins of Baghdad, Ṣaḫī also refers to its connections with the social and political reality of the rest of the country. He often

62. On the notion of (hi)story, see Mehrez 1994, pp. 8–9.
63. Saʿdāwī 2012, p. 239.
64. Ibid.

refers, for instance, to the abuses and violence carried out by the well-known *Ḥaras qawmī* (National Guard) and other security forces of the Baʿathist regime in Thawra[65]; to the collapse of *al-Ǧabhah al-waṭaniyyah al-taqaddumiyyah* (The National Progressive Front) and its impact upon the inhabitants of this community/district[66]; or to several historical figures of modern Iraqi history, such as the then Prime Minister ʿAbd al-Karīm Qāsim, who was "the only twentieth-century Iraqi leader to seriously struggle against sectarianism in public life"[67]. An enthusiastic representation of the latter is provided by Ṣaḫī when he explicitly mentions the first visit of Qāsim to the future inhabitants of his district while they were still living in al-ʿĀṣimah and al-Šākiriyyah:

> ذلك اليوم بدا رئيس الوزراء أنيقا وسيما عازما على قول شيء يمس حياتهم وتاريخهم. ألقى خطابا طويلا فيما كانت تقاطعه الهتفات والأهازيج. استقبلوا كلماته بدهشة وحب إذ أحسوا بعمقها وصفائها. لقد كان يوما ما قريبا منهم عندما رأس اللواء الذي أسهم في درء خطر آخر فيضان وأنقذ البلدة من الهلاك. لذلك تحدث في خطابه عن أهمية إنجاز مشاريع السدود في حماية البلاد من الفيضانات. تحدث عن أسلافهم عبر القرون، عن وعود الحكومات السابقة، عن شركات النفط الأجنبية، وعن ثروات الشعب المهدورة. وقبل أن يختتم حديثه قال إنه سوف يشكل لجنة مختصة لوضع مشروع إنشاء دور سكنية حديثة لهم فيها الماء الصافي والكهرباء والمدارس والمستشفيات.

> On that day, the prime minister looked elegant, handsome, and determined in saying things that would change their lives and history. He gave a long speech that was interrupted by chants and songs. They welcomed his speech with astonishment and love since they felt its depth and purity. He was with them on the day he led the brigade that warded off the danger of another flood, saving their town from destruction. In his speech, therefore, he spoke about the importance of implementing the dam project in order to protect the country from floods. He talked about their ancestors over the centuries; about the promises of the former governments; about the foreign oil companies; and the nation's squandered fortunes. Before concluding his speech, he said that he would form a specialised committee which would develop a project for a modern residential settlement for them, equipped with pure water, electricity, schools, and hospitals[68].

65. Ṣaḫī 2008, p. 119.
66. Ṣaḫī 2013, p. 218.
67. On this, see Davis 2005, pp. 118–119, which sees ʿAbd al-Karīm Qāsim as "the only twentieth-century Iraqi leader to seriously combat sectarianism in public life".
68. Ṣaḫī 2008, p. 63.

Another historical figure of the country mentioned by Ṣaḫī while (re) narrating the (hi)story of Thawra or Sadr City is that of the Iraqi lance corporal Ḥasan Sarīʿ[69], a figure who is strongly connected not only to the (hi)story of this particular community/district, but also to that of the entire country. Here, the (hi)story of this political figure is (re)narrated through the story of a fictional inhabitant of Thawra City, Ḥamdān ʿAbd al-Wāḥid:

> كان حمدان عبد الواحد يسكن قريبا من علوان عزيز في منطقة خلف السدة، وكان معجبا بشخصيته وولعه بالقراءة [...]. ولطالما تمنى أن يواصل دراسته ويدخل معهد إعداد المعلمين مثله تماما لكن فقر عائلته دفعه إلى التطوع في الجيش فالتحق بمدرسة قطع المعادن في معسكر الرشيد حيث التقى لأول مرة بالعريف الشيوعي حسن سريع. تحدر حسن سريع من عائلة فلاحية من مدينة السماوة. أكمل دراسته الابتدائية في منطقة عين التمر بكربلاء. ولكي يساعد عائلته المعدمة تطوع في الجيش وانضم إلى مدرسة قطع المعادن بمعسكر الرشيد فانتقل للإقامة في منطقة الشاكرية بجانب الكرخ من بغداد. ونتيجة لذكائه وقدراته أصبح عريفا وعين معلما في المدرسة نفسها. في الثالث من تموز عام ٣٦٩١ قاد العريف حسن سريع حركة للإطاحة بسلطة البعثيين والقوميين الذين أسقطوا حكومة الزعيم عبد الكريم قاسم وأعدموه، من دون محاكمة، في دار الإذاعة بالصالحية، وشنوا حملة إبادة ضد الشيوعيين وأنصارهم في عموم البلاد.
>
> Ḥamdān ʿAbd al-Wāḥid was living near ʿAlwān ʿAzīz, in the area of Ḫalf al-Saddah, and was admiring him for his personality and passion for reading [...]. He had always wished to continue his studies and, just like [ʿAzīz], enter the Institute for the Teachers' Education, but his family's poverty pushed him to enlist in the army. For this reason, he enrolled in the "Qaṭʿ al-Maʿādin" school of the al-Rašīd military camp, where he met the communist corporal Ḥasan Sarīʿ for the first time. Ḥasan Sarīʿ came from a peasant family from the city of al-Samāwah. He completed his primary education in ʿAyn al-Tamr, in the district of Karbalāʾ. To help his poor family, he enlisted in the army and joined the "Qaṭʿ al-Maʿādin" school of al-Rašīd military camp. He moved to the area of al-Šākiriyyah, near al-Karḫ, in Baghdad. As a result of his intelligence and abilities, he became a corporal and was appointed a teacher in the same school. On 3 July, 1963, the corporal Ḥasan Sarīʿ led a movement to remove the authority of the Baʿathists and the nationalists who had overthrown the government of ʿAbd al-Karīm Qāsim and had him executed, without trial, in the radio station located in al-Ṣāliḥiyyah. This

69. This historical figure is barely considered in the academic works available on Iraqi modern history. For an exception to this, see al-Ṭāʾī 2019.

> launched a campaign of extermination against the communists and their supporters in every part the country[70].

Additionally, one must consider that Ṣaḫī paid close attention to the folkloric and cultural dimensions of this Baghdadi community/district in a way that, once again, goes beyond and intersects with the representations of Shia religiosity mentioned above. In this sense, we may find references to the magical rituals and nonconventional medicine coexisting in this community/district of Baghdad with "official" religion[71]. But we will also find references to the so-called "pop culture" of the time, such as the music that was performed and listened to by its inhabitants; or some of its most prominent figures that are recalled by Ṣaḫī with the purpose of linking the reality of Thawra to that of the rest of the country[72]. Among these, we read of the famous Iraqi football player of the 1970s, Bašār Rašīd, also born in Thawra. The narration of his detention and death, described by the author as a "collective death"[73], occupies a consistent part of the second book of the trilogy and is employed by Ṣaḫī to (re)narrate the abuses of the Iraqi political regime of the time:

> في ذلك اليوم، وعقب مباراة فريقه مع فريق الجامعة بملعب الشعب، فوجئ الرياضيون بدخول عناصر من الاستخبارات العسكرية غرفة اللاعبين. طوقوا بشار رشيد واعتقلوه وانطلقوا به إلى مكان مجهول. وبعد سنتين ونصف السنة ويومين أمضاها خلف القبضان نفذ فيه حكم الإعدام بتهمة الانتماء للحزب الشيوعي وممارسة نشاط سياسي في مؤسسة عسكرية. روت أم بشار قائلة إنها تسلمت جثة ابنها لكن المسؤولين أرسلوا معها سيارة تغص برجال الأمن، مشترطين ألا تصل الجثة مدينة الثورة بل تقف عند معبر قناة الجيش خوفا من رد فعل السكان. لكن الخبر انتقل من بيت إلى بيت فخرج الآلاف من عشاق اللاعب الشهير لوداعه. وحين وصلت السيارة التي تقل جثته إلى معبر قناة الجيش أحاطوها بالنشيج والقبلات.

> On that day, after the match between his team and the university team at al-Šaʿb stadium, the athletes were surprised to see that members of military intelligence entered the players' room. They surrounded Bašār Rašīd, arrested him, and drove him to an unknown location. After spending two and a half years and two days in prison, he was executed on charges of belonging to the Communist Party and

70. Ṣaḫī 2013, p. 238.
71. On these magical rituals and nonconventional medicine practised by the inhabitants of this district/community, see, for instance, Ṣaḫī 2013, pp. 96–98.
72. On this, see also the previous section of this chapter.
73. Ṣaḫī 2013, pp. 218 and 233.

> engaging in political activity in a military institution. Umm Bašār recounted that she received her son's body, but she also said that the officials sent a car full of security men along with it. They wanted to prevent the body from reaching Thawra City and stopped at the Qanāt al-Ǧayš crossing, fearing the residents' reaction. But the news spread from house to house, and thousands of fans of the famous player came out to say goodbye to him. When the car carrying his body arrived at the Qanāt al-Ǧayš crossing, they surrounded it with wails and kisses[74].

Finally, in this same regard, the last element that should be stressed here is the space left by Ṣaḫī for the description of the internal diversity that characterised this Shia community/district. It is in this perspective, for instance, that one could better grasp the meaning of a character such as that of the Fayli Kurd, Ḫānzād[75]. The writer barely develops this character in his literary trilogy. Yet, it appears in both the first and second book and, more particularly, in some of the most crucial passages of the entire narrative, such as in the scene of the visit of the then Prime Minister of Iraq, ʿAbd al-Karīm Qāsim, quoted above[76].

6. Concluding Remarks

This analysis has shown that Ṣaḫī includes his ethnoreligious background in his fictional texts through multiple devices. On a first level, such retrieval is implemented through specific motifs of Shia religiosity, which are (re)narrated by the writer from a multifaceted and secular perspective. On a second level, Ṣaḫī's ethnoreligious background is recalled through the explicit reference to Thawra or Sadr City, a significant place for the Iraqi Shia. Moreover, the expression of the writer's background is intimately connected here to a major (re)writing of history, which Ṣaḫī carries out not only about this particular place located on the outskirts of Baghdad but also in regard to other elements of the social, cultural,

74. Ibid., p. 214.
75. Fayli Kurds are also Shia and generally represent an internal minority of this latter community. On them, but also their relationship with the former Iraqi regime, see Eskander 2006.
76. Ṣaḫī, 2008, pp. 61–62 and 152–153.

and political imagination of modern Iraq, as in the quote above regarding ʿAbd al-Karīm Qāsim who is still one of the most popular political leaders amongst the Iraqi Shia precisely because of his commitment to fighting against sectarianism and ethnoreligious divisions.

Against this background, the present analysis also seems to confirm some of the observations already expressed by Ronen Zeidel (2020) and other researchers who argued against the inherent negativity of ethnoreligious identities in Iraqi fiction. Indeed, Ṣaḫī's literary representations may also fit into the category of "banal" ethnoreligious expressions suggested by Fanar Haddad about Iraqi "popular" culture. These forms of ethnoreligious expressions do not necessarily constitute a threat or danger to the Iraqi state and peacebuilding process. On the contrary, they could help build a national narrative where ethnoreligious identities are asserted in a harmless and inoffensive way and their "aggressive" or "assertive" expressions may be eradicated[77].

Nevertheless, drawing on these preliminary remarks, one cannot avoid considering another element that also involves Ṣaḫī and his literary production. As shown at the beginning of this chapter, Ṣaḫī does not occupy a "dominant position" in the literary field but a rather marginal one. In addition, his literary references and aesthetics differ quite a lot from those of the "first actors" of the field I mentioned above who are currently endowed with a greater "symbolic capital"[78]. From this point of view, several further questions may come to mind. One might wonder, for instance, about the similarities and differences existing on the question of ethnoreligious identities between the works of these authors and those of marginal authors such as Ṣaḫī. Moreover, one could ask oneself the same question about the major (re)writing of history, which in the case of Ṣaḫī strongly intersects with the issue of ethnoreligious expression. Another interesting question may also involve the effects of the "refraction" of the field itself on Iraqi literary production and, more specifically, on the relation between this literary production and the multiple ethnoreligious divisions existing today in Iraq. All these questions are much more than rhetorical questions for the field of Arabic literary studies. They are crucial

77. Haddad 2011, pp. 25–32.
78. Bourdieu 1992.

research questions that we hope to answer in the next future, thanks to a more systematic analysis of the Iraqi literary output.

References

Bahoora, H. (2015), *Writing the Dismembered Nation: The Aesthetics of Horror in Iraqi Narratives of War*, in "Arab Studies Journal", 23, 1, pp. 184–208.

Bengio, O. (1985), *Shi'is and Politics in Ba'thi Iraq*, in "Middle Eastern Studies", 21, 1, pp. 1–14. https://doi.org/10.1080/00263208508700610

Bourdieu, P. (1992), *Les règles de l'art: genèse et structure du champ littéraire*, Seuil, Paris.

Caiani, F., Cobham, C. (2013), *The Iraqi Novel: Key Writers, Key Texts*, Edinburgh University Press, Edinburgh.

Campbell, I. (2020), *Double Estrangement and Development in Arabic Science Fiction: Aḥmad Saʿdāwī's* Frankenstein in Baghdad, in "Mashriq & Mahjar", 7, 2, pp. 1–26, available at: https://lebanesestudies.ojs.chass.ncsu.edu/index.php/mashriq/article/view/255/298 (last accessed 25 march 2021). https://doi.org/10.24847/77i2020.255

Casanova, P. (1999), *La République mondiale des lettres*, Seuil, Paris.

Davis, E. (2005), *Memories of State: Politics, History, and Collective Identity in Modern Iraq*, University of California Press, Berkley, London, and Los Angeles.

Eskander, S. B. (2006), *Fayli Kurds of Baghdad and the Ba'ath Regime*, in F. A. Jabar and H. Dawood (eds), *The Kurds: Nationalism and Politics*, Saqi, London, pp. 180–202.

Haddad, F. (2011), *Sectarianism in Iraq: Antagonistic Visions of Unity*, Oxford University Press, Oxford and New York.

Haddad, F. (2013), *Sectarian Relations in Arab Iraq: Contextualizing the Civil War of 2006–2007*, in "British Journal of Middle East Studies", 40, 2, pp. 115–138. https://doi.org/10.1080/13530194.2013.790289

Haddad, F. (2017), *Shia-centric State-Building and Sunni Rejection in Post-2003 Iraq*, in F. Wehrey (ed), *Beyond Sunni and Shia: Sectarianism in a Changing Middle East*, Hurst, London, pp. 115–135.

Haddad, F. (2020), *From Existential Struggle to Political Banality: The Politics of Sect in Post-2003 Iraq*, in "The Review of Faith & International Affairs", 18, 1, pp. 70–86. https://doi.org/10.1080/15570274.2020.1729588

Hanoosh, Y. (2012), *Contempt: State Literati vs. Street Literati in Modern Iraq*, in "Journal of Arabic Literature", 43, 2–3, pp. 372–408. https://doi.org/10.1163/1570064x-12341237

Hanoosh, Y. (2019), *In Search of the Iraqi Other: Iraqi Fiction in Diaspora and the Discursive Reenactement of Ethno-Religious Identities*, in "Humanities", 8(4), 157, available at: https://www.mdpi.com/2076-0787/8/4/157/htm (last accessed 23 March 2021). https://doi.org/10.3390/h8040157

Hīssīh, H. (1983), *Anbāʾ ġarībah min kawkab aḫar*, al-Muʾassasah al-Ǧāmiʿiyyah li-l-Dirāsāt wa-l-Našr wa-l-Tawzīʿ, Beirut.

Jabar, F. A. (2003), *The Shi'ite Movement in Iraq*, Saqi, London.

Mehrez, S. (1994), *Egyptian Writers between History and Fiction: Essays on Naguib Mahfouz, Sonallah Ibrahim, and Gamal al-Ghitani*, The AUC Press, Cairo and New York.

Mohsen, F. (2012), *Debating Iraqi culture: Intellectuals between the Inside and the Outside*, in S. Milich et al. (eds), *Conflicting Narratives: War, Trauma and Memory in Iraqi Culture*, Reichert, Wiesbaden, pp. 5–23.

Nġūġī, W. T. (1988), *al-Nahr al-Fāṣil*, Manšūrāt Wizārah al-Ṯaqāfah al-Sūriyyah, Damascus.

Nooraddin, H. (2004), *Globalization and the Search for Modern Local Architecture: Learning from Baghdad*, in Yasser Elsheshtawy (ed.), *Planning Middle Eastern Cities: An Urban Kaleidoscope in a Globalizing World*, Routledge, Oxford and New York, pp. 59–84.

Saʿdāwī, A. (2012), *Thawra City: Native Dust in the Wind*, in S. Milich et al. (eds), *Conflicting Narratives: War, Trauma and Memory in Iraqi Culture*, Reichert, Wiesbaden, pp. 237–244.

Saeed, H. (2021), *Abdullah al-Sakhi on Writing his Multigenerational Iraqi Trilogy*, in "Arablit Quarterly", 14 January, available at: https://bit.ly/3u7107W (last accessed 24 March 2021).

Ṣaḫī, ʿA. (1983), *Ḥuqūl dāʾimat al-ḫuḍrah*, Dār al-Farābī, Beirut.

Ṣaḫī, ʿA. (2008), *Ḫalf al-saddah*, Dār al-Madà, Baghdad and Damascus.

Ṣaḫī, ʿA. (2013), *Durūb al-fuqdān*, Dār al-Madà, Baghdad and Damascus.

Ṣaḫī, ʿA. (2017), *al-Lāǧiʾ al-ʿirāqī*, Dār al-Madà, Baghdad, Beirut, and Damascus.

Sakhi, A. (2018), *Execution in the Stadium: Chapters from the Novel* Duroob al-Fuqdan *(Paths of Loss)*, trans. by P. Starkey, in "Banipal", 61, pp. 38–58.

Sallūm, S. (2013), *al-Tanawwuʿ al-ḫallāq: ḫarīṭat al-ṭarīq li-taʿzīz al-taʿaddudiyyah fī l-ʿIrāq*, Masārāt, Baghdad.

Sallūm, S. (2017), *al-Waḥdah fī l-tanawwuʿ: al-taʿaddudiyyah wa-taʿzīz al-muwāṭanah al-ḥāḍinah li-l-tanawwuʿ al-ṯaqāfī fī l-ʿIrāq*, Masārāt, Baghdad.

Shuiskaja, N. M. (2018), *Sectarian Conflicts in the 21st Century Novel Literature of Iraq*, in "Vestnik of Saint Petersburg University. Asian and African Studies", 10, 2, pp. 246–253. https://doi.org/10.21638/11701/spbu13.2018.208

al-Ṭāʾī, Ṣ. (2019), *Ḥasan Sarīʿ wa-inqilābuhu al-fāšil fī l-ʿIrāq ʿām 1963*, in “Ahl al-bayt”, 24, 1, pp. 224–243, available at: https://www.iasj.net/iasj/download/d0c960abe53f70ca (last accessed 24 March 2021).

Zeidel, R. (2020), *Pluralism in the Iraqi Novel after 2003: Literature and the Recovery of National Identity*, Lexington Books, Lanham.

Zeidel, R., Melamed, U. (2017), *Madinat al-Thawra: The Development of a Poor Quarter in Baghdad and the Literary Texts about It*, in “HaMizrah HaHadash”, 56, pp. 58–82 (in Hebrew).

Antonio Pacifico is a PhD candidate at the Jean Moulin University of Lyon 3. He obtained his Master’s in Comparative Literature from the University of Naples ‘L’Orientale’. With his project, which he conducts under the joint supervision of Prof. Elizabeth Vauthier and Prof. Monica Ruocco, he explores the main cleavages and symbolic struggles that have emerged in the Iraqi literary field since the 1990s. His academic interests include contemporary Iraqi literature and theatre, the relationship between literary and historical narratives and Arab intellectual history. He has also published several articles in Alif: Journal of Comparative Poetics, La rivista di Arablit and LiCArC. He is currently a member of the Bureau des jeunes chercheur·e·s of the Groupement d’Intérêt Scientifique Moyen-Orient et mondes musulmans (GIS MOMM).

Chapter 6

In Search of the Virtuous City: Coexistence and (In)Hospitality in ‘Alī Badr’s *ʿĀzif al-ġuyūm*[1]

Annamaria Bianco

Abstract

This chapter analyses Ali Bader’s novel *ʿĀzif al-ġuyūm* (Musician in the Clouds, 2016) in the light of the current “refugee crisis” and situates the novel in the global debate on in-/hospitality. In this pseudo-fictional work, the author takes stock of his life in the West and portrays the image of a cosmopolitan artist aspiring to universal recognition against the identity blackmail imposed on him by asylum. The story of the writer’s alter ego Nabīl and his resettlement in Belgium thus becomes a pretext for rethinking exile and displacement in the age of globalisation. Here, Bader scrutinises the very idea of Europe, suggesting new possible scenarios of coexistence and solidarity in our transnational societies through the fictional

1. This chapter stems from some preliminary reflections developed during two study days for French junior scholars in which I participated between 2019 and 2020. Respectively, the titles of the papers presented are: *L’identité artistique face à la diaspora : « Réfugiés », « écrivains réfugiés » ou simplement « écrivains » ?*, VII rencontres de la Halqa – Association des doctorants en sciences sociales sur les mondes musulmans modernes et contemporains, 6–7 June 2019 MMSH, Aix-en-Provence; and *À la recherche de la Cité Vertueuse : le voyage utopique d’un réfugié irakien vers l’Europe dans* Le Joueur de nuages *d’Ali Bader*, Géographies de l’imaginaire: Journée d’étude jeunes chercheurs, 23–24 September 2020, MMSH, Aix-en-Provence (as part of the Imaginary Geographies CRISIS Research Programme: “Le voyage-prétexte comme machine à penser”).

tools of humour and utopia. From this perspective, he makes several meta-textual references to *Mabādi' ārā' ahl al-madīnah al-fāḍilah* (Principles of the Opinions of the Inhabitants of the Virtuous City) by the medieval Persian thinker Abū Naṣr al-Fārābī are which I consider to be vital to the development of the plot as well as to the speculative interpretations of the Harmonious Society suggested by the open ending of the novel.

Keywords: Ali Bader, hospitality, literary utopias, refugees, al-Farabi

1. Introduction: The "Refugee Crisis" and the New East-West Literary Encounters

East-West relationships have always been complex, subjected to several and often sudden changes over history. Both counterparts' attitudes have been cyclically shifting from mutual enchantment to mutual aversion, while keeping a precarious balance of interdependence[2]. The 2015 "refugee crisis"[3] complicated things further. The European media coverage spread a climate of socioeconomic uncertainty and suspicion regarding migrants, with special concern about their integration. At the same time, a process of victimisation of the asylum seekers started, nourished by a narrative of pity addressing their desperate background[4].

This Manichean representation of the refugee – either a potential criminal or a poor wretch – was quickly dismantled by contemporary Arabic literature on forced migration (*adab al-tahğīr*), which foregrounds the perspectives of undocumented migrants and asylum seekers on flight, border crossing, and life in Europe since the beginning of the post-Cold War era[5]. Such issues demanded new creative approaches to writing about exile and diaspora, forging what we might call an "aesthetics of

2. See El-Enany 2006, Said 1991.
3. In 2015, more than one million refugees arrived at the southern borders of the European Union. Another 3,771 people died in the same attempt. UNHCR data: https://data2.unhcr.org/en/situations/mediterranean (last accessed 26 January 2021). Before the Russian invasion of Ukraine in 2022, this vast increase, mostly due to the Syrian situation, was the highest amount ever reached since World War II.
4. Greussing, Boomgaarden 2017, p. 1749.
5. Sellman 2013, pp. 2–3.

refugeedom", fitted with its own tropes and themes[6]. These latter turn around a crucial quest for shelter and security, embedded in the largest demand from many Arab authors for equal recognition of people's sufferings and their rights to mobility and self-determination. Nowadays, this renewed cultural engagement[7] contributes to the multidisciplinary debate about the practices of (in)hospitality and biopower[8] in Western society, revealing the disparities between receiving populations and newcomers in the same way as other literary productions dealing with forced migration worldwide[9].

Iraqi refugee writers, who came to fill the ranks of the previous generations of expatriate intellectuals[10], occupy a special position in this scene as part of a community affected by the second longest Arab diaspora[11]: their history of mass displacement started with the disaster of the 1980–1988 Iran-Iraq war and eventually worsened with the two Gulf Wars

6. For a comprehensive approach to refugeedom, refugeehood, and refugeeism, see Cox et al. 2020.
7. Stephan Milich underlines the emergence of a new Arabic trauma literature, "which carries forward reflections on the possibility of literary writing during and after human disasters (and the difficulty in adequately representing and narrating them) in a new way […] challenging the discursive, epistemological, and power-political privileged position of the 'West'. […] In contrast to the often strongly ideologized 'committed literature' of earlier decades, its aim is to shed light on the politically – and socially-motivated roots and entwined causality of injustice, violence, and disenfranchisement without propagating a single, solely valid view of reality" (Milich 2015, p. 286).
8. As is widely known, the term was first coined by Michel Foucault, who referred to "[the new form of] power [embodied by Modern Nation States] that exerts a *positive* influence on life, that endeavors to administer, optimize, and multiply it, subjecting it to precise controls and comprehensive regulations" (Foucault 1976, 140 [italics mine]). More recently, however, several philosophers and anthropologists started relating this concept to the practices of exclusion and domination exerted by contemporary Western governments on migrants (Agamben 1998; Farrier 2013). It is with this specific meaning that we will use this term in our chapter.
9. August 2020; Gallien 2018.
10. Mostly Marxist intellectuals who had been in diaspora since the early Baʿathification campaigns started in the 1970s, and who used to focus their writings on the socio-political situation of their country of origin. Their circles include the revolutionary poets Muḥammad Mahdī al-Ǧawāhirī (1899–1997), ʿAbd al-Wahhāb al-Bayātī (1926–1999), Saʿdī Yūsuf (1934–2021) and the prolific writer Fāḍil al-ʿAzzāwī (b. 1940). See Hanoosh 2012.
11. Notably, after the Palestinians. See Sassoon 2009, p. 6.

(1990–1991, 2003–2011) and the rise of ISIS (2014)[12]. The protracted exile and consequent resettlement led to the configuration of a whole literary corpus which problematises the migration policies and the East-West discourses, inaugurated by Ibrāhīm Aḥmad's 1994 short story *The Arctic Refugee*[13]. In these works, migration to Europe is often described as an encounter with "wilderness" (*waḥšah*), a kind of trope transforming European spaces into "empty forests, barren snowy landscapes, and fantastic arctic vistas, or into spaces where humans are hunted, cannibalised, and subject to unmediated bodily violence"[14]; a form of "nightmare realism" whose major example lies in the production of the award-winning author Hassan Blasim (Ḥasan Balāsim, b. 1973)[15].

Nevertheless, not all this "refugee literature"[16] depicts the experience of displacement in such terms. Ali Bader (ʿAlī Badr), another successful Iraqi writer[17] who relocated abroad in 2012, shows a much more cosmopolitan attitude, arguing that "every time he faces the West, he finds himself facing his own self"[18]. Since the very beginning of his literary

12. After 2003, about 2.7 million people were internally displaced, and more than two million left the country in search of refuge. More than three million Iraqis have been scattered across the country since 2014 and over 260,000 have sought refuge abroad. UNHCR Iraq: https://www.unhcr.org/iraq-emergency.html (last accessed 26 January 2021).
13. The story was originally published as *Lāǧīʾ ʿinda l-iskīmū* (A refugee among the Eskimos) in the collection *Baʿda maǧīʾ al- ṭāʾir: qiṣaṣ min al-manfà* (After the Bird's Arrival: Exile Stories). Sellman 2013, pp. 23–24.
14. Ibid, pp. 6–7.
15. Sakr 2018.
16. The expression has to be taken with a pinch of salt because the debate about the definition of this literary genre is still wide open in the fields of Post-Colonial Studies and World Literature. Scholars and critics are divided on the appropriateness of the expression and its eventual split from the category of Migration Literature(s), as it emerged during the panel "Refugee Literature Workshop" organised during the 2nd GIS-MOM congress in Paris in 2017. The programme is available online at: https://redila.hypotheses.org/files/2017/06/Prog_Refugee_Literature_Workshop_july_6_2017.pdf (last accessed 26 January 2021).
17. Ali Bader is the spelling the author has chosen to adopt in the Western world for its Arabic pen name, while his true identity still remains uncertain. We will use it throughout the entire contribution. He is the author of fifteen works of fiction and several works of non-fiction. Many of his books received prizes both in the Arab and the Western world and were translated into European languages.
18. Bader 2008, p. 28.

career in 2001, he has in fact been increasingly exploring the embroilment of East-West relationships, particularly through his heterogenous cultural background: he was a hungry reader of *Weltliteratur* masterpieces and managed to study philosophy and French literature at Baghdad University. Once he had arrived in Belgium, where he had to adapt to his new condition of stranger, he deepened his reflections about history and society in the age of globalisation by publishing three novels in a row whose main characters leave Iraq for Europe: *al-Kāfirah* (The Infidel Woman, 2014)[19], *ʿĀzif al-ġuyūm* (Musician in the Clouds, 2016)[20], and the latest *al-Kaḏḏābūn yaḥṣulūn ʿalà kull šayʾ* (The Liars Get Everything, 2017)[21]. They are all set in Brussels, the city where Bader currently lives, and explore the issues of identity, belonging, and integration to different degrees.

Still, the matter of coexistence, confronted to the diehard rhetoric of the "Clash of Civilizations"[22], is at the very heart of *ʿĀzif al-ġuyūm*, mostly inspired by Bader's own biographical experiences and his understanding of extremism as a widespread plague, "also present in the European nation-state model"[23]. In this pseudo-fictional work[24], the author takes stock of his life in the West and portrays the image of a naive young artist aspiring to a universal recognition of his talent, despite the many stereotypes tied to his refugee condition. The traumatic story of Nabīl's flight and resettlement in Belgium – who flees Islamic fundamentalists just to end up confronting them again in Europe – is then turned into a pretext to rethink forced displacement and to restore the stolen agency of the migrants.

19. The book, preceded in 2013 by a play called *Fāṭima allātī ismuhā Sūfī* (Fatima, Whose Name is Sophie), was translated into Italian as *L'infedele*. See Bader 2019. An English excerpt was also published in *Banipal 53 – The Short Stories of Zakaria Tamer*, available on the website at: https://www.banipal.co.uk/selections/91/311/ali-bader/ (last accessed 28 January 2021).
20. The book has been translated in Dutch, Italian and English. See Bader 2017, 2018, 2024.
21. Not translated into a Western language yet.
22. Huntington 1997.
23. Bader 2008, p. 30.
24. For more information on this literary trend in the Arab context, see Anishchenkova 2014, pp. 107–143.

The aim of this chapter is to show how the author carries out, through the tool of fiction, a proper philosophical exercise intended to postulate the making of a truly harmonious society that goes beyond the archetypal East-West opposition. As Theodor W. Adorno concluded after the tragedy of the Holocaust, the only true and everlasting conflict lies between art and destruction, and when it comes to beauty, the latter must prevail over the horror of violence[25]. Thereupon, Bader's main theoretical reference appears to be a classic of ancient Arabic literature, *Mabādi' ārā' ahl al-madīnah al-fāḍilah* (Principles of the Opinions of the Inhabitants of the Virtuous City) by the mediaeval Persian thinker Abū Naṣr al-Fārābī (872–950)[26], whose excerpts shape the metatextual frame of the novel.

As we shall see, such a transcultural approach allows the writer to offer an original contribution to the contemporary debate about asylum in neoliberal society, marked by the rise of xenophobia and the multiplication of borders. Thanks to his unorthodox narrative of the "refugee crisis", Bader reconfirms himself as a true critical author – as many scholars have already detected[27] – constantly committed to dismantling taboos and preconceived ideas.

2. Ali Bader and his Poetics: A Journey Against the Tide

Ali Bader is an eclectic intellectual: poet, novelist, playwright, journalist and essayist all at once. The limits between literary categories and genres seem to be too tight for him, just like the borders between countries and cultures. Born in Baghdad in 1964, his literary talent was both encouraged and influenced by his family of aristocratic origins and yet openly

25. "Auschwitz irrefutably demonstrated the failure of culture. That it could happen in the midst of all the traditions of philosophy, art and the enlightening sciences, says more than merely that these, the Spirit, was not capable of seizing and changing human beings. […] Whoever pleads for the preservation of a radically culpable and shabby culture turns into its accomplice, while those who renounce culture altogether immediately promote the barbarism, which culture reveals itself to be" (Adorno 2005a, p. 358). "The sole adequate praxis after Auschwitz is to put all energies toward working our way out of barbarism" (Adorno 2005b, p. 268).
26. For the English version with a commentary, see al-Fārābī 1985.
27. Hanoosh 2012, Masmoudi 2015, Pacifico 2019, Ruocco 2012, 2014, and 2017; Sciortino 2018.

communist. The same goes for his critical thinking, inherited from his father and his grandfather, which brands Bader's attitude towards life and writing. According to Monica Ruocco, his style could be defined as that of the "documentary novel", since he makes free use of historical sources and facts to practise an alternative reading of the past[28]. Moreover, the propensity for such a technique is a special popular trend amongst the new generation of Iraqi writers, as Yasmeen Hanoosh points out[29]. But Bader's peculiar contribution is to combine it with an extensive use of humour and sarcasm[30]. And indeed, in the eyes of the author, irony is a political tool meant to dismantle the authority of power and its official propaganda[31].

The very beginning of Bader's career was marked by the publication of a truly controversial novel, *Bābā Sārtr* (Papa Sartre, 2001), critically acclaimed[32] but unwelcomed by the endogenous literary *milieu* who nearly ostracised him. The plot is structured as a fictional investigation of the life of the first alleged Iraqi existentialist philosopher – a character inspired by his own father – which results in a parody of the pseudo-intellectuals of the Sixties Generation[33] in Baghdad. The hostile environment generated by the book launch pushed him to leave the country for the first time. He came back in 2003 to work as a war correspondent after the American invasion and the subsequent fall of Saddam Hussein. His stay did not last long: his second novel *Ḥāris al-tabġ* (The Tobacco Keeper, 2009) generated a much worse scandal due to its recalling of the bloody Farhoud (1941), a pogrom of the Iraqi Jews of Baghdad[34]. Some threatening posters

28. Ruocco 2012, p. 209.
29. Hanoosh 2012, pp. 405–406.
30. Pacifico 2019.
31. Ali Bader explicitly made this statement on the occasion of a private interview conducted on Zoom on 16 January 2021.
32. For this work he was awarded the State Prize for Literature in Baghdad in 2002 and the Tunisian Abu Al-Qassem Al-Shabi Award in 2003. The novel has recently been translated into English (2009) and French (2014).
33. It was a retrospectively self-designated generation of Iraqi intellectuals who espoused Sartrian philosophy as an alternative to political propaganda. Yet most of those who read Sartre were accused of not fully understanding him, which gave rise to mutual mockeries and accusations. See Hanoosh 2012, p. 383.
34. For further discussion on this violent episode see Méir-Glitzenstein 2016.

appeared in the capital, showing a gun pointed at the cover of the book[35]. This time, the author decided to leave for good.

After a restless stay in Amman, where one of his articles about the issue of Palestinian identity in Jordan drew allegations that he had been bribed by Zionists[36], he started wandering between the Middle East and Europe. The travel account *Ḫarā'iṭ muntaṣaf al-layl* (Midnight's Maps, 2009) dates back to this period. The book, which describes his journey through Tehran, Istanbul, Algiers, Athens, Cyprus, Paris, and Marseille emphasising its literary and intercultural dimension, won the Ibn Battuta Prize for Contemporary Travel Literature (*Ǧā'izat Ibn Baṭṭuṭa li-adab al-riḥlah*), established by the Emirati Arabic Center for Geographic Literature "Irtiyad al-Afaq" (*al-Markaz al-ʿarabī li-l-adab al-ǧuġrāfī – Irtiyād al-āfāq*).

Charmed by the beauty of these multiple and different discoveries, Bader eventually made his way to Belgium in 2009, where he was granted political refugee status. This allowed him to find the serenity to rebuild his life in Brussels but also elicited a categorisation process on the part of the local literary community which considered him a mere refugee and was not willing to accept him in its cultural circles[37]. His disappointment at that rejection was deep, but Bader did not recede from his previous cosmopolitan beliefs about art because he was persuaded that the Iraqi and Western intellectuals are alike because they both "feel that culture has a crucial role to play"[38] in society.

After lengthy efforts, Bader has finally achieved his goal of being integrated into Belgian literary circles[39], gaining legitimation through its

35. This detail of the posters was mentioned by the author himself during the above-mentioned interview. Cf. note 30.
36. The event was reported in Lançon 2016.
37. To properly understand these dynamics of inclusion/exclusion, proper to every artistic field, as theorised by sociologist Pierre Bourdieu, we should not forget that "the majority of notions which artists and critics employ to define themselves or to define their adversaries are weapons and stakes in struggles" (Bourdieu 1996, p. 297). The labels (*categories*) "which art historians [and not only they] deploy to treat their topic are nothing more than classificatory schemes issuing from these struggles, and then more or less skilfully disguised or transfigured" (Ibid.).
38. Bader 2008, p. 32.
39. Nonetheless, Belgium is not unfamiliar with multicultural production, especially the Arab one. In this respect no. 35 of the "Banipal Magazine for Arabic Literature

institutions and acquiring Belgian nationality in 2012. During the fifth edition of the Brussels Book Fair, in February 2019, the author was invited to participate in a literary meeting with Annelies Verbeke, the *grande dame* of the Flemish novel, as an "Iraqi author who recently became *Brusseleir*"[40]. In May, with the sponsorship of the Belgian Embassy and the support of Wallonia-Bruxelles International, he flew to Athens to give a talk about his poetics. The description of the event introduced him to the audience as a "Belgian author of Iraqi origins"[41]. In 2020, he further expanded his ambitions for universal artistic recognition by founding "an interdisciplinary and European literary journal"[42], *Eurolitkrant*, which he currently runs as editor-in-chief.

Ali Bader's positioning in the international literary scene moves on the assumption that he does not want to be considered either a writer in exile or, even worse, a refugee author but just as an intellectual[43]. According to him, this kind of labelling is indeed "an absurd game, which marginalises people by using the idea of place and temporality"[44]. To free himself from these dynamics and assert his independence, the writer even went so far as to establish his own publishing house in Brussels, Alca Books (*Dār*

in English Translation, Writing in Dutch", presented ten authors from Morocco, Palestine and Iraq who live both in the Netherlands and Belgium and have been writing in the language of their countries of adoption since the 1990s. They have been described as "new and energetic voices" in the field, "taking up themes that had never been explored before" (Schiferli 2009, p. 92).

40. See the press pack of the Brussels Bookfair, 2016 edition, p. 9, available at: https://flb.be/wp-content/uploads/2019/01/DPFLB2019.pdf (last accessed 29 January 2021).
41. See the description on the official website of the Wallonia-Bruxelles International, available at: https://wbi.be/fr/events/event/conference-lecrivain-belgo-irakien-ali-bader-librairie-lexipoleio-athenes (last accessed 29 January 2021).
42. It is a website combining "distinctive voices" in poetry, fiction, and nonfiction as well as works in translation, available at: https://eurolitkrant.com/About.aspx (last accessed 29 January 2021).
43. As the professor of Comparative Literature, Alexis Nouselovici underlines in his essay dedicated to the shifts in the literary representations of the *exilé* figure, the notion of *exiliance* (exilehood) has declined in condition and consciousness, and the two do not necessarily coincide: "one can feel in exile without concretely being in exile (consciousness); one can concretely be in exile, without feeling it (condition)" (Nouss 2015, p. 126).
44. Bader 2013, p. 104.

Alkā li-l-Našr), whose acronym stands for "Free Association of Culture and Arts" (*Association libre de la culture et des arts*)[45].

ʿĀzif al-ġuyūm is nothing more than the fictional account of this long process of awareness, as narrated by the voice of Nabīl. Indeed, just like the young Bader, Nabīl's literary alter ego embarks upon an almost utopic quest for a peaceful and dignified life "somewhere beyond the Seas" (*fī-mā warāʾ al-biḥār*)[46], towards a halfway point between reality and imagination. A romantic idea of travelling that the bohemian hero likes better than any other scenario conjured up by words such as "emigration" (*al-hiğrah*), "asylum" (*al-luğūʾ*) or "exile" (*al-manfà*)[47], when thinking about his experience of displacement in search of personal fulfilment.

3. *ʿĀzif al-ġuyūm*, Between Coexistence and In-/Hospitality

The novel has a simple two-part structure: the first narrates Nabīl's flight from Iraq to Belgium, while the second is centred on the adaptation to his new life in the West. The caesura is exclusively thematic, since the form, structure and language of the book remain essentially the same, accompanying the evolution of the protagonist's thoughts, just as in a *Bildungsroman*. In fact, as we will see from the following analysis, the two parts are almost mirrors of each other.

The story opens with a phone call between the hero and his father. The former informs the latter of his decision to leave the country the same night: some fundamentalists destroyed his cello when he refused to give them the money they wanted to fund the construction of a new mosque. The elder tries to convince his son to change his mind and warns him that he will not be happy in exile, like many other people who made the same choice and regretted it afterwards. However, the protagonist does not

45. To be more precise, ALCA was founded in 1967 as an organisation for the defence of culture and art by a group of Arab students living in Marseille. It then became a literary café in the same city before moving to Paris in 1984 as a French-language publishing house. After a break of more than 20 years, it reemerged as an Arabic language publishing house, directed by Bader. For further details, see the description on the official site, available at http://www.daralca.com/SubPage.aspx?PageId=1 (last accessed 5 September 2021).
46. Badr 2016, p. 37.
47. Ibid, p. 40.

listen to the prophetic words of his father and sticks to his plan: instead of sailing with a zodiac from Izmir to Greece and ending up like "fish food" (*ṭaʿām al-asmāk*)[48], he entrusts all his savings to a series of smugglers who bring him to Belgium by truck, like "a VIP refugee" (*lāǧiʾ VIP*)[49]. The picaresque framework of the journey and the sarcasm employed by the author in describing the naivety of his hero emphasise the first gaps between Nabīl's expectations and reality, while denouncing the abuses endured by the asylum seekers heading to Europe:

> لقد اعتقد نبيل أول الرحلة أنه بواسطة هذه الشاحنة سيصل إلى بلجيكا، سيصل، وهو جالس إلى جوار السائق، يدخّن السجائر، ويقرّ البرتقال، ويأكل! إلا أن السائق فاجأه أن الأمر لا يتعدى أن يوصله إلى الحدود من جهة أوربا، ومن هناك، سيقطع كل أوربا للوصول إلى الطرف الآخر؛ حيث تقع بلجيكا. وكان من المفترض أن المبلغ قد وصل المهرّب من طرف ثالث كاملاً، إلا أنه أصرّ على أن يحصل من نبيل على مائتي دولار إضافية، لا سيما بعد أن رأى ملابس نبيل الأنيقة، فقد بدا على نبيل من ملابسه أنه ذاهب إلى موعد «ديت غرل فريند» أكثر مما بدا عليه أنه لاجئ بائس، ذاهب إلى أوربا، طلباً للحماية.[50]

> At the beginning of his journey, Nabīl was convinced that he would go all the way to Belgium with that truck, sitting next to the driver, while smoking cigarettes, peeling oranges, and eating. Instead, the driver suddenly informs him that his task is limited to bringing him to the border of the European Union, which he will cross with another smuggler until their arrival in Belgium. The driver had already been paid, for sure, but demanded another two hundred dollars because of Nabīl's fancy clothes: he looked like someone going on a date with his girlfriend, certainly not a poor refugee travelling to Europe in search of international protection[51].

Nabīl is so scared of the idea of not reaching the West that, once the driver drops him off in Schaerbeek, the ancient birthplace of Jacques Brel[52], now turned into a multiethnic district, he believes he is the victim of a scam: the idea of Europe he had in mind when leaving was based on a

48. Ibid, p. 41.
49. Ibid.
50. Ibid, p. 42.
51. All the English translations of the excerpts are by me.
52. Jacques Romain Georges Brel (1929–1978) was a famous Belgian singer-songwriter, considered to be a master of the modern *chanson*. He was the reason why Bader chose to live in this district, just like Nabīl.

completely different imaginary, one that stemmed from the books he had read and brought there[53].

He buys a kebab but is immediately reprimanded by a Salafist. The latter reproaches him for not observing the fasting of the holy month of Ramadan and offers him an occasion of redemption by asking him to make contribution to the construction of a mosque, exactly as it had occurred in Baghdad. This game of repetition – "*tikrār*, a technique" etc. that Bader considerably employs in his novels[54] – provokes laughter in the reader and foretells the absurdity of the situation that will soon arise. Even if Nabīl manages to obtain refugee status, is offered a new cello, and finds love in the arms of a young Belgian named Fanny, it does not take long for the problems with the fundamentalists to recur. The sexual disinhibition shown by the couple draws the hatred of the neighbourhood upon him, and history repeats itself: the hero is attacked by a new group of Muslim fanatics who destroy his musical instrument.

Nabīl falls then into a sort of depression, linked to the failure of his expectations about the West, where he believed he would "live in perfect harmony with the society", without feeling like the "stranger" (*ġarīb*) he used to be in his homeland[55]. Moreover, in the tradition of Islamic thought of his country, discussions on hospitality (*ḍiyāfah*) focus largely on the host/guest and host/traveller relationships, rather than on the dichotomy host/foreigner so widespread in the Western world[56]. There, the young man thought he had found a society ready to welcome his artistic spirit, but, in the end, he was unable to freely express his identity or to integrate with the local population, which kept looking at him with a mixture of condescension and mistrust.

As in other Arab literary productions about asylum seekers[57], Europe turns out to be a space of contradiction, offering supposed shelter from violence and oppression while depriving the migrant of his agency by

53. According to Bernard Westphal, in literature the writer becomes the author of the space. Cities like London, Rome, Venice, and Paris are filtered by the books, according to a brand-new geography. See Westphal 2007, p. 156.
54. For Bader's learning of Bergson's critical theories on humour, see Pacifico 2019, p. 95.
55. Badr 2016, pp. 95–96.
56. Siddiqui 2015, p. 10.
57. Especially the Syrian one, as in al-Sallūm 2018.

forbidding him to exercise his right to citizenship[58]. The city in particular, understood by Jacques Derrida as a privileged site of refuge and reflections on solidarity, eventually emerges as a pole of rejection where forms of conditional and inauthentic hospitality are enacted[59]. In fact, the philosopher argues that the question of hospitality, which should represent a consistent part of the human condition in his eyes, has too often been cynically employed by Western states and media to promote the inclusion of those sole migrants seen as "worthy" of protection; namely, "the good refugees", who match the profiles determined by the politics[60]. Unconditional hospitality requires instead that one opens up one's home and gives "not only to the foreigner (provided with a family name, with the social status of being a foreigner, etc.), but to the absolute, unknown, anonymous other", letting them come, arrive, and take place, "without asking of them either reciprocity (entering into a pact) or even their names"[61]. In other words, offering true hospitality is more than mere tolerance: it is about taking risks and becoming vulnerable, rather than being in power and exerting it.

Derrida's notions find their echo in the following excerpt, which shows the patronising attitude of the host society towards Nabīl, whom they would like to reduce to a state of mute gratitude, ignoring his individuality and opinions, as he is basically an alien in their community:

> أما ملاحظته عن بلجيكا؛ هذا أمر غير ممكن، هم ليسوا بحاجة لها على الأقل. حتى في الموسيقى العرض الوحيد الذي تلقّاه هو أن يعزف مع فرقة من الهواة في يوم اللاجئ. أنت لاجئ؟ أنا عازف تشيللو. ولكنّك لاجئ في بلجيكا. قد غضب إلى الدرجة التي أراد أن يقول لمحدّثته: إن تكلّمنا عن الموسيقى، فإن بلجيكا هي اللاجئة عندي! كان يحب أن يقول هذه الجملة بغضب، ولكنّه كتم أنفاسه، شعر نبيل ألا تكون من أوربا، فأنت لاجئ! عليك ألا تكون مثلهم، وعليك ألا تجاهر بأيّ رأي. إنهم سيحبّونك إن مدحت بلدهم. ولكنْ؛ لو أردت أن تفعل ما يفعله البلجيكيون بكراهيتهم لبلدهم، وقلت مثلاً: ما هذا البلد الزبالة! فإن لحظة صمت مرعبة ستحول بينك وبينهم. سيقولون لك: عليك أن تسعد في حياتك هنا، لو كنتَ في بلد آخر؛ لأعادوك للجحيم الذي هربتَ منه. أو سيقولون لك: عليك أن تشكرنا، أليس كذلك؟! لا نعرف ما هو مصيرك، لو لم نأوك عندنا.[62]

58. Agier 2004, p. 122.
59. Darling 2020, p. 556.
60. Derrida 2001.
61. Derrida and Dufourmantelle 2000, p. 25.
62. Badr 2016, pp. 92–93.

> His remarks on Belgium weren't allowed; or, at least, they didn't need them. Even for music, the only offer he received was to play in an amateur band on Refugee Day. "Are you a refugee?" "I am a cello player". "But you are a refugee in Belgium". He became angry to the point that he wanted to say: if they were talking about music, it was Belgium then that had taken refuge in him! He would have liked to shout this angrily, but he held his tongue. Nabīl felt that, if you are not European, you are nothing but a refugee! You cannot be like them, and you cannot express any opinion. They love you if you praise Belgium, but if you want to do what the Belgians do and say, for example, "What a junk country!", then a terrifying moment of silence would tear you apart. They would tell you: "You should be happy with your life here. If you were in another country, they would have sent you back to the hell you escaped from". Or they would say: "You should thank us, shouldn't you?! Who knows what fate you would have if we hadn't hosted you?!"

In this new continent affected by the "refugee crisis", Nabīl's illusions of coexistence quickly dissipate in the face of the dominant xenophobic culture, the do-goodism of open-minded people, and the superficiality of human relations; the latter is symbolised by the failure of his love affair with Fanny. As a matter of fact, the young woman, who simply aspires to lead an ordinary life with her partner, cannot really understand his troubles nor, consequently, his sorrow. The crucial issue lies in the detail that the musician does not only see himself as a target of racism but also as the victim of a social downgrading since his dislocation has absolutely nothing to do with the lyrical and ennobling experiences of 19th century intellectuals, whether Arab or Westerner[63]. His identity seems to disappear

63. In his *Reflections on Exile*, Edward Said already sensed that "the refugee" and "the exiled" are two antithetical figures in the common imaginary: "The word 'refugee' has become a political one, suggesting large herds of innocent and bewildered people requiring urgent international assistance, whereas 'exile' carries with it, I think, a touch of solitude and spirituality" (Said 2012, p. 178). Nouselovici took up this notion by affirming that, today, the exiled has lost his place in the world, without knowing if he would really find another one because the world itself has changed, as well as the migration phenomenon, by the numbers of displaced people becoming too high: "Exilic consciousness is an unhappy consciousness, revealing a mismatch between the self and the world. This is evident at a psychological level as the exile is cut off from the mental and cultural frameworks that offered him or her reference

in the eyes of others who associate him with the anonymous mass of migrants gathering in the streets, reduced to a "ghost-like presence"[64].

Just as in Iraq, Nabīl starts feeling out of place and becomes addicted to alcohol, pointed at as "the poor refugee who drains his girlfriend's wallet"[65]. Then, one day, he sees a far-right racist demonstration in the street and has a sort of epiphany: the reason for his misery in Belgium is the presence of other immigrants, always "getting in trouble amongst themselves"[66]. Therefore, he tries to infiltrate the march so he can convince the participants that he is one of them and that he stands by them. The result is catastrophic and grotesque at once: the musician almost gets lynched by the crowd and is saved by another group of Muslim fundamentalists who nurse his wounds in the days following this event. The reversal pushes Nabīl into a double shock, which shakes and dismantles his undifferentiated view of the world once again, by making him understand that extremism is proper to all civilisations.

The trauma helps him reconcile himself with his life in the West, whose contradictions are finally accepted and even valued. In the last scene of the novel, the musician comes back home and decides to take a cathartic shower, leaving the reader with an open ending full of questions about the meaning of peace and coexistence in a true multicultural society:

> ما معنى الحياة، بالنسبة له؟ شيء لم يتحدّد بعد! لكنْ؛ عبر الموسيقى يمكن أن يصل إلى بعض التآلف الكائن خلف التناقض الحي في المظهر العام للوجود. هكذا إذنْ؛ فالأماكن الحيوية والفنية في المدينة، وبعض المقاهي والمطاعم، تكشف له عن معنى آخر للحياة. إن التعدّد والاختلاف بين البر تمحوه الأضواء الخافتة، والخمرة، تقريباً! ويصبح الجميع في ثقافة واحدة!
>
> مناظر كثيرة متناقضة تتحول إلى مناظر متآلفة. وقد قابل بداية هذا التآلف بإحساس من الحذر. لكنْ؛ بعد فترة، تفهّمه. فَتَحْتَ مظهر تعدّد ألوان المدينة وتناقضاتها واختلافاتها، هنالك الإشارات الداخلية للحياة تطلّ بصورة أكثر حميمية، وهي أكثر تآلفاً، لكنّها لا تظهر إلا خلف مجموعة من التناقضات الماديّة.[67]

What does life mean to him? He does not know yet. But only through music will he be able to find a certain harmony in the seeming

points and comfort, a bruising that the exilic experience shares with any traumatic phenomenon" (Nouss 2015, p. 157; translation mine).

64. Bauman 2007, p. 37.
65. Badr 2016, p. 89.
66. Ibid, p. 93.
67. Ibid, pp. 108–109.

> contradictions of existence. So then, the lively and artistic spaces of the city, as well as some cafes and restaurants, reveal to him another meaning of life. "Alcohol and soft lights attenuate the differences between people, and diversity merges into a single culture!" Many contradictory aspects end up converging. Nabīl is at first cautious about this concept of uniformity; then he has an intuition. The many shades, differences, and contradictions of the city reveal the deepest traces of existence. And the latter manifests itself in its most intimate and familiar way through its many contradictions.

Hence, as for other migrant writing incorporating the element of music into their plots, this latter proves to be the ultimate way "of understanding the multifaceted experience of diasporic travel and global mobility"[68]. To recognise this complexity is vital for the reconstruction of Nabīl's personal identity and agency in the aftermath of the border crossing.

4. The Harmonious Society beyond Utopia and Disappointment

If Nabīl's migratory project seems to evoke at the very beginning of the novel the image of many other asylum seekers escaping from wars and devastation, it is soon understood that the real driving force behind his journey is not really the same. His destination is not physical Europe in itself but a "Virtuous City" (*al-madīnah al-fāḍilah*) "where artists spend their lifetime playing in the clouds"[69].

The hero is not just willing to seek shelter from the death threats received by the fundamentalists because of his interest in Western classical music; he wants to flee a decadent society where "people despise anything beautiful and elegant"[70] and where he feels he is "the only dissonant note" (*al-naġmah al-wahīdah al-šāḏḏah*)[71]. And, in fact, according to his vision of the world – reflecting the writer's – the real existing conflict is between two polarised cultures that goes far beyond the East-West dichotomy: the society of arts and beauty on one side and the mass society

68. Nyman 2017, p. 189.
69. Badr 2016, p. 37.
70. Ibid, p. 21.
71. Ibid, p. 95.

shaped by brutality and ugliness on the other, forcing all different people "to fit their rules and behaviours"[72]. Nabīl's goal is to flee the cultural decline in which his country plunged since the time of Saddam Hussein[73], to eventually find harmony, the only sustainable solution for coexistence and mutual understanding, just as it is for music and its paradigms:

> الموسيقى هي سيدة الأشياء. قال في نفسه! يمكنه من خلال أصواتها تسمية أي شيء يخطر في باله. بل يمكنه - من خال تناغمها - أن يمضي مباشرة إلى الحياة المحيطة به، أن يهبط إلى قعر الحياة، إلى نسغها الأول، وأن يرى ما يكمن في أسفلها. لا توجد أشياء لا يمكن تسميتها عبر الموسيقى، بينما شعر بالعجز - تماماً عبر اللغة العربية التي يتكلّمها – من أن يفهم الأشياء الكثيرة التي أخذت تتوالد من الفوضى، أشياء كثيرة أخذت تنمو دون أن يملك أية كلمات كافية للدلالة عليها.[74]
>
> Music was the Master of All Things! Through its sounds, he could name anything he could think of. Even more, through its harmony, he could join the life around him; get to its essence, to its first sap, and discover its remotest depths. There was nothing that could not be named through Music, while he felt powerless – through the Arabic language he spoke – to understand the many elements that started sprouting out of chaos. Just as for the other [new] things that had begun to appear while he wasn't able to find a way to define the [previous] ones.

It is precisely on this pattern of music, linking *ʿĀzif al-ġuyūm* to the previous *Ḥāris al-tabġ*[75], that the ideal city sought by the cellist is to be built. The model he has in mind is clear: it is the one postulated by the 10th-century Muslim philosopher, Abū Naṣr al-Fārābī, in *Mabādiʾ ārāʾ ahl al-madīnah al-fāḍilah*[76]. This thinker, inspired in turn by Plato's *Republic* (c. 375 BC), devotes his work to the description of a true political utopia, which sees the basis of social justice, culture and civilisation in musical harmony and its regulatory aspect, and serves as a constant reference for Nabīl during his journey through Europe and his process of resettlement:

72. Ibid, p. 21.
73. Ibid, p. 37.
74. Ibid, p. 28.
75. If *Ḥāris al-tabġ* was genuinely "built like a musical experience", as Monica Ruocco has already detected (Ruocco 2012, p. 206), *ʿĀzif al-ġuyūm* provides a musical metaphor for contemporary society.
76. Badr 2016, p. 53.

«ما يبحث عنه في أوربا هو الأساس الهارمني الداخلي، لنقل إنها فكرة النظام التي تأخذ معناها الدقيق من الكلاسيكية، وهذه الأخيرة هي التي ستوصلنا إلى المدينة الفاضلة». «لم أفهم»، قالت فاني مبتسمة. «اسمعي، سأشرحها بطريقة عملية»، وعبّ نصف قدح الموخيتو في جوفه. «يصبح المجتمع مثل أوركسترا، الوتريات هم الغربيون الشقر، يمثلون العمود الفقري في الأوركسترا مثل: الكان، والفيولا، والكونترباص، والتشيللو. ثم اللاتينيون، ويمثلون الآلات النفخية، مثل: الأبوا، والفلوت، والكلارينيت، والباصون. ثم الشرقيون، عرب، أتراك، فرس، أكراد، فهم مثل الآلات النحاسية: ترومبيت، هورن، ترومبون، وتيوبا. وهنالك الأفارقة مثل الطبول، والدرامز. وهنالك الآسيويون، مثل: بعض أنواع السيمبالات».[77]

"What I am looking for in Europe is the internal harmonic base or, rather, that idea of order developed by the classicism that will lead us to the Virtuous City." "I do not understand," Fanny replies, smiling. "Wait, I will explain it to you with a concrete example." In the meantime, she pours herself a mojito, filling up her glass halfway. "Imagine society as an orchestra. Stringed instruments are blonde Westerners, representing the spine of the orchestra: violins, violas, double basses and cellos. Next, Latinos are the wind instruments: oboes, flutes, clarinets, bassoons. Then, the Middle Eastern peoples: Arabs, Turks, Persians and Kurds are brasses, trumpets, horns, trombones and tubas. Africans are drums and percussion. Asians are some kinds of cymbals".

The novel is strewn with metatextual references to *The Virtuous City*, which turns from a dreamed lifeline into the highest source of disappointment, once the hero finally discovers that the West – at the core of his ideal society/orchestra – is not the cradle of progress he assumed it was and that the world is much more complex than he thought on the basis of his logical-mathematical point of view. At first, and as we have already explained in the previous section, he blames the other immigrants for having made a hell out of his imaginary heaven:

ألم يقل الفارابي إذا وجد الشخص الفاضل نفسه، في مدينة فاسدة، عليه أن يهجرها إلى مدينة فاضلة؟! إن لم تكن موجودة في زمانه، فإنه سيعيش غريباً، وفي حياة رديئة، الموت فيها أفضل من الحياة! وهكذا جاء هنا إلى أوربا... مدينة فاضلة! لكنّ المشكلة أن المهاجرين هم الذي يدمّرون فضائلها! هؤلاء سيحوّلونها إلى أرض فساد وفوضى.[78]

Had al-Fārābī perhaps not said that, if a worthwhile person is found in a corrupt environment, he has a right to leave it to look for the

77. Ibid., p. 65.
78. Ibid, p. 102.

> Virtuous City? And if the ideal city has not yet materialised at this time, then he would be forced to lead a miserable life, as an alien, and that it would be preferable to die. This is why he came to Europe, to find his Virtuous City! The problem is that immigrants there are corrupting and turning it into a place of decay and chaos.

According to Nabīl, the presence of immigrants in Brussels is the cause of the loss of harmony in that society:

> لأنهم من ثقافة مختلفة. هم يشكّلون نوعاً من الهارموني في مجتمعاتهم، حين كان بينهم؛ أي حينما كان في بلده، كان يشكّل صوتاً نشازاً، كان يهدم التناغم في مجتمعاتهم.[79]

> because they come from a different culture and they manage to create harmony only within their own community, while he, when he was in his native country, represented the dissonance destroying the harmony of that society.

This is why he decides to join the far-right extremists asking for the repatriation of all migrants. He has no bad intentions. In his mind, he does it to create a "better, harmonious world, free from any dissonance" (*ʿālam ǧamīl, ʿālam mutanāġim ḫālin min al-aṣwāt al-našāz*)[80]. But, in reality, he has never discussed with those neo-Nazis before and, thus, he does not have any idea about the true nature of their ideology. Unaware of the risk represented by his Eastern traits, he approaches them, willing to share his readings of al-Fārābī. They do not listen at all and immediately attack him. He feels misunderstood, lonely, and helpless to change society for the better:

> هو وحده الذي يعتقد أن الإيمان هو الذي يوحّد الناس لا ميثولوجيا الأعراق، ولا ميتافيزيقيا الألوان، ولا الملامح.[81]

> He is the only one who is convinced that it is beliefs that unite people, not the mythology of race, the metaphysics of [skin] colour, or facial features.

Ironically, Nabīl is cast aside by both communities, the immigrants and the hosts, but this liminal condition helps him accomplish his process of becoming: it is exactly in this grey zone between utopia and

79. Ibid., p. 95.
80. Ibid, p. 103.
81. Ibid.

disillusionment, which Homi Bhabha calls the "third space"[82], that the hero starts to renegotiate meanings and identities, managing to complete the whole picture of harmony. Such hybrid contexts, where refugees often find themselves, serve precisely as sites of differentiated encounters between hegemonic and non-hegemonic forces or ideologies which eventually collide, creating new readings of reality[83]. Utopian visions, along with alternative perceptions of space and time, occur indeed as frequent elements in immigration literature, undergoing key changes in the adaptation of the individual to his new country[84].

Nabīl's journey results then in an ongoing journey across both national and mental borders, leading him to understand that there are no unbridgeable differences between people, just as it had occurred to Bader during his wanderings through Europe, Africa, and the Middle East[85]. Being rejected by that part of the world into which he was trying to integrate and being saved instead by those same individuals who had tried to kill him earlier makes the musician realise that the contradictions of life constitute its own unavoidable essence:

> فالصوت الواحد لا ينتج موسيقى، إنما الموسيقى تتشكّل من خيال الاختلاف بين الأصوات، لكنّ هذا الاختلاف بحاجة إلى هارموني، إلى تناغم كامل، وإلا يتحوّل الاختلاف إلى نشاز، يُبطل الفكرة الأساسية التي تتخلق الموسيقى أصالً من أجلها. هذا غير مهمّ، ذلك أن المدينة الفاضلة لم تتحقّق بعد، على لأرض، منذ أفلاطون إلى اليوم، أليس كذلك؟[86]

> To make music, one sound is not enough. It takes different sounds, and these different sounds must be combined to achieve Absolute Harmony. Otherwise, we find ourselves mixing dissonant sounds that will not give birth to any harmony. [...] It does not matter that the Virtuous City does not exist yet on earth. [After all, we have just been waiting for it] since the time of Plato, haven't we?

Nabīl's quest for the Ideal Society ends exactly when he understands that it does not really exist. Harmony, on the contrary, is already part of existence and the rediscovery of its mechanisms helps him embrace the world with a reborn trust in humankind as well as a renewed optimism for his

82. Bhabha 2006.
83. Nyman 2017, p. 79.
84. Al-Saadi 2011.
85. Cf. the above-mentioned *Ḥarā'iṭ muntaṣaf al-layl* and Ruocco 2014.
86. Badr 2016, pp. 63–64.

future in the West. The artist regains his true nature, while the refugee finally finds his place, getting out from his condition of in-betweenness and becoming a citizen.

Conclusion

The aim of this chapter was to investigate the role played by Ali Bader in the Arabic literary representation of the contemporary "refugee crises" by analysing one of his latest novels, *'Āzif al-ġuyūm*. Although Bader does not want to be considered a writer in exile, he deeply explores the experience of forced displacement and its consequences among both migrant and host communities by letting stereotypes and paradoxes proper to the Western welcoming system emerge from a pseudo-fictional work based on his own biographical experience.

The novel, centred on the quest of an Iraqi young cellist for an "Ideal City beyond the Seas", scrutinised the very idea of Europe and contributes to the debate about (in)hospitality and coexistence within our globalised societies, suggesting new possible scenarios of solidarity through the fictional tool of tuopia. The naive and elitist Nabīl does indeed have his personal idea of the Perfect Society, based on the same regulatory mechanisms of music where there is no room for any jarring note or dissonant element, as suggested in al-Fārābī's *al-madīnah al-fāḍilah.*

But when the hero finally leaves Baghdad in search of Ultimate Harmony, he only discovers that the West is not the Gracious Heaven he had previously imagined by experiencing old forms of persecution and new practices of racism. Religious and political extremism then brings to light the complexities of the East-West relationship, as well as the difficulties of today's intercultural coexistence, through the series of tragicomic situations in which the protagonist finds himself. Eventually, his thinking comes to maturity, and he ends up understanding that the real world is much more complex than his fantasies: in other words, the musician learns that he must accept all dissonances and contradictions of the universe to leave the rest of his life in peace, both as an artist and a man, transplanted into a new place to call home.

Thus, in this critical work, built both in Arab intellectual tradition and European philosophy, Ali Bader manages to prove that there is no irreparable fracture between East and West[87]. As Adorno taught us, the only real conflict is found between the Culture of Love and the Culture of Hate, whose "soldiers" have engaged in an endless, ancient fight across the world. In doing so, the author finally restores the primordial role of art as a bridge between society and the agent of peace, presenting himself to the reader as the bearer of a message of beauty and civilisation against universal barbarism, through the voice of his literary persona.

References

Adorno, T. W. (2005a), *Negative Dialectics*, trans. E. B. Ashton, Continuum International Publishing Group, London and New York.

Adorno, T. W. (2005b), *Minima Moralia: Reflections on a Damaged Life*, trans. E. F. N. Jephcott, Verso, London-New York.

Agier, M. (2004), *Le camp des vulnérables: les réfugiés face à leur citoyenneté niée*, in "Les Temps Modernes", 627, 2, pp. 120–137. https://doi.org/10.3917/ltm.627.0120

Agamben, G. (1998), *Homo Sacer: Sovereign Power and Bare Life,* trans. D. Heller Roazen, Stanford University Press, Stanford.

Anishchenkova, V. (2014), *Autobiographical Identities in Contemporary Arab Culture*, Edinburgh University Press, Edinburgh.

August, T. (2020), *The Refugee Aesthetic: Reimagining Southeast Asian America*, Temple University Press, Philadelphia (PA).

Bader, A. (2008), *From Extinction to Formation Story*, in Mendez, S. A. (ed.), *MNSG: Navigating the Space Between Home and Exile*, Heinrich-Böll-Stiftung, pp. 28–33, available at: https://www.boell.de/en/2009/01/27/iraqi-refugees-navigating-space-between-home-and-exile (last accessed 29 January 2021).

Bader, A. (2013), *Iraq: A Long Phantasmagorical Dream for Those Who Are Not Part of the New Capitalism or Retired Communism*, in Al-Ali, N., Al-Najjar, D. (ed.), *We Are Iraqis: Aesthetics and Politics in a Time of War*, Syracuse University Press, Syracuse (NY), pp. 103–126.

Bader, A. (2017), *De wolkenmuzikant: roman*, trans. Richard van Leeuwen, Uitgeverij Jurgen Maas, Amsterdam.

Bader, A. (2018), *Il suonatore di nuvole*, trans. Monica Ruocco, Argo, Lecce.

Bader, A. (2019), *L'infedele*, trans. Maria Grazia Sciortino, Argo, Lecce.

Badr, 'A. (2016), *'Āzif al-ġuyūm*, Manšūrāt al-Mutawassiṭ, Milan.

87. Corm 2012.

Bader, A. (2024), *Musician in the Clouds*, trans. Ikram Masmoudi, Georgetown University Press, Washington (forthcoming).

Bauman, Z. (2007), *Liquid Times: Living in an Age of Uncertainty*, Polity Press, Cambridge.

Bhabha, H. K., Rutherford, J. (2006), *Le tiers-espace*, in "Multitudes", 26, 3, pp. 95–107, available online at https://doi.org/10.3917/mult.026.0095 (last accessed 5 September 2021).

Bourdieu, P. (1991), *Le champ littéraire*, in "Actes de la recherche en sciences sociales", 89, September, pp. 3–46. https://doi.org/10.3406/arss.1991.2986

Bourdieu, P. (1996), *The Rules of Art: Genesis and Structure of the Literary Field*, trans. Susan Emanuel, Stanford University Press, Stanford.

Corm, G. (2002), *Orient-Occident, la fracture imaginaire*, La Découverte, Paris.

Cox, E. et al. (eds) (2020), *Refugee Imaginaries: Research Across the Humanities*, Edinburgh University Press Ltd, Edinburgh, pp. 18–35.

Darling, J. (2020), *"Another Politics of the City": Urban Practices of Refuge, Advocacy and Activism*, in Cox E. et al., (eds), *Refugee Imaginaries: Research Across the Humanitie*s, Edinburgh University Press Ltd, Edinburgh, pp. 554–570.

Derrida, J., Dufourmantelle, A. (2000), *Of Hospitality: Anne Dufourmantelle Invites Jacques Derrida to Respond*, trans. R. Bowlby, Stanford University Press, Stanford.

Derrida, J. (2001), *On Cosmopolitanism and Forgiveness*, trans. M. Dooley and M. Hughes, Routledge, London.

Farrier, D. (2013), *Postcolonial Asylum: Seeking Sanctuary Before the Law*, Liverpool University Press, Liverpool.

Foucault, M. (1998), *The History of Sexuality, Vol. 1: The Will to Knowledge*, Penguin Modern Classics, London.

Gallien, C. (2018), *"Refugee Literature": What Postcolonial Theory Has to Say*, in "Journal of Postcolonial Writing: Special Issue on Refugee Literature", 54, 6, pp. 721–726. https://doi.org/10.1080/17449855.2018.1555206

Greussing, E., Boomgaarden, H. (2017), *Shifting the Refugee Narrative? An Automated Frame Analysis of Europe's 2015 Refugee Crisis*, in "Journal of Ethnic and Migration Studies", 43(11), pp. 1749–1774. https://doi.org/10.1080/1369183X.2017.1282813

Huntington, S. P. (1997), *The Clash of Civilizations and the Remaking of World Order*, Penguin Modern Classics, London.

El-Enany, R. (2006), *Arab Representations of the Occident. East-West Encounters in Arabic Fiction*, Routledge, New York.

al-Fārābī, A. N. (1985), *On the Perfect State (Mabādi' ārā' ahl al-madīnah al-fāḍilah). A Revised Text with Introduction, Translation and Commentary by Richard Walzer*, Clarendon Press, Oxford.

Hanoosh, Y. (2012), *Contempt: State Literati vs. Street Literati in Modern Iraq*, in "Journal of Arabic Literature", 43, 2–3, pp. 372–408. https://doi.org/10.1163/1570064x-12341237

Méir-Glitzenstein, E. (2016), *Le Farhoud: pogrom à Bagdad*, trans. C. Drevon, in "Revue d'Histoire de la Shoah", 205, 2, pp. 511–533. https://doi.org/10.3917/rhsho.205.0511

Lançon, P. (2016), *Le « loup » du tigre: rencontre avec Ali Bader*, in "Libération", 3 June, available at: https://next.liberation.fr/livres/2016/06/03/le-loup-du-tigre-rencontre-avec-ali-bader_1457156 (last accessed 29 January 2021).

Masmoudi, I. (2015), *War and Occupation in Iraqi Fiction*, Edinburgh University Press, Edinburgh.

Milich, S. (2015), *Narrating, Metaphorizing or Performing the Unforgettable? The Politics of Trauma in Contemporary Arabic Literature*, in Pannewick, F., Khalil, G. (eds), *Commitment and Beyond: Reflections on / of the Political in Arabic Literature since the 1940s*, Verlag Reichert, Wiesbaden, pp. 285–301.

Nouss, A. (2015), *La condition de l'exilé: Penser les migrations contemporaines*, Maison des Sciences de l'Homme, Paris.

Nyman, J. (2017), *Displacement, Memory, and Travel in Contemporary Migrant Writing*, Brill, Leiden.

Pacifico, A. (2019), *Entre humour et (ré)écriture de l'histoire: la (les) communauté(s) imaginée(s) transculturelle(s) de 'Alī Badr*, in "LiCArC Littérature et culture arabes contemporaines", 7, pp. 87–102.

Ruocco, M. (2012), *Between Symphony and Novel: 'Alī Badr's Ḥāris Al-Tabġ (The Tobacco Keeper)*, in "Quaderni di Studi Arabi", 7, pp. 205–224.

Ruocco, M. (2014), *Ḫarā'iṭ muntaṣaf al-layl (Mappe della mezzanotte, 2009) di 'Alī Badr e la ridefinizione dell'immaginario geografico e culturale mediterraneo*, in "La rivista di Arablit", 4, 7–8, pp. 7–17.

Ruocco, M. (2017), *Finzione, caffè e filosofia nel romanzo Baba Sartr di 'Ali Badr*, in De Angelo, C., Manzo, A., Straface, A. (eds), *Labor limae: Atti in onore di Carmela Baffioni*, 2, Università degli studi di Napoli " L'Orientale", Naples, pp. 509–528.

al-Saadi, T. (2011), *Utopia / Dystopia through the Theme of Immigration in Two Arabic Short Stories*, in Eksell, K., Guth, S. (eds), *Borders and Beyond. Crossings and Transitions in Modern Arabic Literature*, Harrassowitz, Copenhagen, pp. 83–102.

Said, E. (1991), *Orientalism*, Penguin Books, London.

Said, E. (2012), *Reflections on Exile and Other Literary and Cultural Essays*, Granta Books, London.

al-Sallūm, M. (2018), *Adab al-luǧū' al-sūrī: al- šatāt wa-l-ta'bīr al-adabī*, Harmoon Center for Contemporary Studies, Doha, available at: https://harmoon.org/wp-content/uploads/2018/01/Literature-of-Syrian-asylum-diaspora-and-literary-expression.pdf (last accessed 7 February 2021).

Sakr, R. (2018), *The More-than-Human Refugee Journey: Hassan Blasim's Short Stories*, in "Journal of Postcolonial Writing: Special Issue on Refugee Literature", 54, 6, pp. 766–780. https://doi.org/10.1080/17449855.2018.1551269

Sassoon, J. (2009), *The Iraqi Refugees: The New Crisis in the Middle East*, I.B. Tauris, London.

Schiferli, V. (2009), *Walking in a Slipper and a Clog*, in "Banipal Magazine of Modern Arabic Literature: Writing in Dutch", 35, pp. 92–96.

Sciortino, M. (2018), *Waiting for Fatima to Become Sophie: The Time of Waiting in Al-kāfira* by 'Alī Badr, in "LiCArC Littérature et culture arabes contemporaines", 6, pp. 25–37.

Sellman, J. (2013), *The Bio-Politics of Belonging: Europe in Post-Cold War Arabic Literature of Migration*, PhD thesis, The University of Texas, Austin, available at: http://repositories.lib.utexas.edu/bitstream/handle/2152/21155/SELLMAN-DISSERTATION-2013.pdf?sequence=1 (last accessed 29 January 2021).

Siddiqui, M. (2015), *Hospitality and Islam: Welcoming in God's Name*, Yale University Press, New Haven and London.

Westphal, B. (2007), *Geocriticism: Real and Fictional Spaces*, trans. Robert T. Tally Jr., Palgrave Macmillan, New York.

Annamaria Bianco holds a double PhD in modern and contemporary Arabic literature from the University of Naples "L'Orientale" (DAAM) and the University of Aix-Marseille (IREMAM), where she is currently teaching and working as a research assistant. Her research focuses on the cultural productions of migrants, refugees and exiles as well as on the circulation of Arabic literature and publishing industry. She is an editor of the junior scholars journal *Maydan* and works as a translator for cinema, theater, and the press. Her thesis, *« Adab al-malǧa' »: Représenter le refuge dans le roman arabe du XXIe siècle*, has received a special mention in the General Prizes for the Middle East and Muslim Worlds and the Institute for the Study of Islam and Societies of the Muslim World in 2023.

Chapter 7

Literature as a Mirror: The Search for Peace and Pacification in Moroccan Society as Depicted in *Banāt al-ṣubbār* (2018) by Karīmah Aḥdād

Paola Viviani

Abstract

Various periods of war and peace – or, better, pacification – have characterised the history of Morocco during the 20th century and up to the present. In turn, pacification was achieved in the country by means of both violent and non-violent strategies, depending on the actors involved, and the glocal context. Recently, Morocco has been going through major changes in many fields that have been affecting the lives of some of its most marginalised members. Literature has always served as a mirror, reflecting and registering events and their outcomes on individual and collective levels. This chapter investigates whether and to what extent a renewed approach to pacification in Moroccan society can still be possible in light of the considerations and proposals present in the novel *Banāt al-ṣubbār* (Cactus Girls, 2018) by Karīmah Aḥdād.

Keywords: peace; pacification; Morocco; Riffian women; *Banāt al-ṣubbār*

1. Introductory Remarks

Peace and pacification as concepts and practices have meant much in Moroccan history. Discourse about them has been going on in Moroccan society for decades, before and after 1956, the year of the country's independence from France and Spain. The negative connotations related to the country's so-called "pacification" process *par excellence*, i.e., the French conquest of Morocco (1907–1934)[1], are well known. The Rif War and the creation of the Confederal Republic of the Tribes of the Rif (1921–1926)[2] occurred in the same period, and were named after the mountainous region mainly inhabited by Amazigh communities that had always felt marginalised by the central authorities. The leader and champion of both the war and the Republic was Muḥammad b. ʿAbd al-Karīm al-Ḫaṭṭābī (Morocco, 1882/3-Egypt, 1963)[3], whose memory was revived during the 2011 protests that reached their peak with the *Ḥarakat 20 fibrāyir* (20 February Movement)[4]. This happened in many Riffian towns during the manifestations organised in the wake of 20 February:

> Grande manifestation rassemblant près de 30 000 personnes (Daum, 2012) […] dans la ville d'Al Hoceïma : des milliers de citoyens entament une marche pacifique pour réclamer plus de justice sociale et de libertés individuelles. […]
> Les manifestations dans le Rif sont nombreuses en 2011 : Aït Bouayach, Imzouren, Ajdir, Boukidan, Al Hoceima, Nador, Taza, etc. Elles comptent parmi les plus violentes et surtout les plus

1. Dulucq et al. 2008, p. 87: "Le mot [pacification], attesté en français depuis le 16e siècle, a pris tout son importance à la fin du 19e siècle quand les militaires français de l'armée coloniale, au premier rang desquel Lyautey et Gallien, ont élaboré une doctrine soucieuse de concilier l'expansion armée avec les exigences des principes humanistes mis en avant par la République. Selon cette doctrine, la conquête d'un territoire doit être menée dans le souci de réduire au maximum l'action de la force, de façon à établir le plus rapidement possible une situation de paix et de prospérité. […] Cette doctrine est mise en œuvre au Tankin, puis à Madagascar. Lors de l'occupation du Maroc, le terme de *pacification* finit par se substituer totalement à celui de *conquête*". For more details on this topic, see Simon 1934; Bernard et al. 1936.
2. On the Spanish Protectorate, see M. Aragón Reyes (ed.) 2013.
3. See, for instance, Courcelle-Labrousse, and, Marmié 2008; Pennell 2017; Mouna 2018.
4. See, for instance, Desrues 2012; Slyomovics 2016; Radi 2017.

> symboliques : on peut voir une partie des manifestants brandir le drapeau de la République rifaine, d'autres le portrait d'Abdelkrim al-Khattabi[5].

The 2011 manifestations and revolts led to the enactment of a new Constitution that was hailed by some observers as a highly revolutionary document, a path to a real and concrete achievement of freedom and rights for all the citizens of Morocco, regardless of their living conditions, gender, language, ethnicity, social class, and opinions. It was also a means to *pacify* those Moroccans who were involved in the protests[6]. It might thus be stated that Morocco had entered a new phase of "pacification", and "peace". But those promises were not kept, and that resulted in a sort of martial situation whose effects became patently clear later. Despite not having anything to do with a war situation in the strict sense, the socio-political conditions resembled such a situation in some ways because many people did feel that a good many of the promises made by the 2011 Constitution had been disregarded, which implied that the pacification process initiated by the King through the above-mentioned document was coming to a possibly dangerous end. Moreover, they also felt that their life continued to be menaced by *hogra*[7], as further revolts testify. The revolts by the would-be *Ḥirāk al-Rīf* (Hirak Movement) that began after the tragic death of the young fishmonger Mouhcine Fikri (Muḥsin Fikrī) in the Riffian port town of Al Hoceima in November 2016[8], where the connection with ʿAbd al-Karīm al-Ḫaṭṭābī is clear, are an instance of this:

> De alguna manera, la muerte del pescador despertó al Rif de un sueño profundo apelando al pasado anticolonial. Así, una de las principales estrategias empleadas por los líderes del movimiento fue la recuperación de la memoria del líder del Rif Abd Al-Krim Al-Khattabi (el líder nacionalista contra el colonialismo español) junto a un líder [Nasser Zefzaf] que también desafiaba al neocolonialismo del *mahzen*. Esta recreación del pasado y su vinculación con el presente alimentó la energía necesaria para que los activistas se unieran al *Hirak*. [...] El *Hirak* del Rif personificó un momento de

5. Abourabi 2015, p. 216.
6. Cf., for instance, El Rhazy 2011, p. 139; Bendourou et al. (eds) 2014.
7. On the Constitution, see n. 31; on the concept of *hogra*, see no. 41.
8. Cf., e.g., Wolf 2019; Rhani et al. 2020; Diouani 2021.

> confrontación entre el Estado central y la región del Rif, utilizando elementos del momento colonial y de las tradiciones culturales propias de la disidencia que dieron origen a la efímera República del Rif[9].

Again, there is a strong link between the Riffians' claim and the work of the Equity and Reconciliation Commission (*Hay'at al-inṣāf wa-l-muṣālaḥah*/Instance Equité et Réconciliation – IER) established in 2004[10], whose action did not lead to any reconciliation (or pacification) at all between the region and the centre of Moroccan power, according to the signatories of *La déclaration du Rif* (2005)[11].

Firmly convinced that literature is a mirror reflecting and registering events and their outcomes on both an individual and a collective level, I want to analyse *Banāt al-ṣubbār* (Cactus Girls, 2018), the debut novel by the young journalist, activist, feminist, and short story writer, Karīmah Aḥdād[12] since the story mainly takes place in the Rif and deals with issues that are strongly linked to its history as well as to the various steps of the Moroccan peace/pacification process, in both its negative and positive facets. These topics are very clearly perceptible, despite the various degrees of vagueness used to refer to them. For example, the verbal root at the basis of the term *muṣālaḥah*, which means both pacification and reconciliation, occurs only once, to refer to a seemingly neutral context. More precisely, when Ṣūniyā, one of the novel's main characters, remembers that, as a little girl, she was watching a football match the boys in her neighbourhood were playing one day in June 2002. She was at home because she was not allowed to go out: her mother was afraid that Ṣūniyā could be in danger if she was walking in the street, since she had been

9. Sánchez-García, Touhtou 2021 (online edition). On the special status of the Amazigh people and the "barrier" created between them and the Arabs by the French colonial power in the Maghreb as a whole, cf., for instance, Hannoum 2021.
10. Among others, cf. Mohsen-Finan 2007.
11. Ibid. (page not clearly defined in the online edition). See also Slyomovics 2016; El Guabli 2020; Maddy-Weitzman, Zisenwine 2013.
12. Van de Vate 2020. The novel was awarded the *Prix Mohamed Zefzaf du roman arabe* in 2020 for being "un roman empreint de fraîcheur, novateur et une plume d'une grande modernité. Le style est épuré et sans fioritures. La polyphonie du texte est originale. Un roman contemporain et audacieux". Ouiddar 2020. See also Zakariasalhi 2020.

accidentally injured some time before by a stone thrown by a boy to one of his friends. Ṣūniyā comments: “Boys here hit their friends hard, and only after an hour do they make peace (*yuṣāliḥūna)*”[13].

Other events are instead directly recalled and discussed, such as those of November 2016 and their consequences. They are dealt with by an upper-middle class married couple, Aḥmad and Sārah, in a short but interesting scene. The two have controversial views on the topic: Sārah reveals her disgust of politics, but she also discloses good knowledge of Moroccan society’s main problems that led to the protests of the *Ḥirāk al-Rīf*. Before she was married, she was a committed journalist and cannot overlook the palpable difficulties that her unfortunate fellow citizens have to cope with. Aḥmad, in his turn, is highly critical of the activists and takes an ironic tone towards his wife, a rich and educated woman who, in his opinion, has only a superficial understanding of and support for the poorest in the country while simultaneously exploiting them[14]. Moreover, the fact that this conversation takes place in an expensive restaurant in Al Hoceima, where the couple is trying to talk about their personal marriage crisis, debases the other crisis – that of all the poor and humiliated people in the Rif who are losers in their confrontation with Morocco’s peripheral and central power.

I will try to show, then, to what extent this novel can be intended as a lucid analysis not only of the state of things but also of the strategies of negotiation practised – or perhaps suggested or dreamed of, in some cases – in Moroccan society as a whole in hopes of achieving a new peace/pacification in the broadest sense of these terms. On the basis of these premises, this chapter intends to investigate the world depicted in *Banāt al-ṣubbār*, where the major agents of peace and pacification may be detected in some of those members of Moroccan society who have been “traditionally” marginalised, such as women, and ethnic and linguistic minorities, the weakest and least powerful strata of the population, i.e., people from the middle class to the lower class.

13. Aḥdād 2018, p. 119.
14. Ibid., pp. 60–65.

2. *Banāt al-ṣubbār*: The Multilayered Significance of a Semitic Verbal Root and its Relevance in Today's Morocco

The title of *Banāt al-ṣubbār* raises at least two major questions: 1) What does the highly evocative word *ṣubbār* hint at in this context? 2) Who are the *banāt*?

Ṣubbār is the Arabic term for the English word "cactus", the family of succulents distinguished not only by their stiffness but also by their beautiful flowers, and their harmful spines and glochidia. Among the species of this plant, the *Opuntia ficus-indica,* which is just one of the many cacti widespread in the Arab world. It is greatly appreciated for its very sweet and palatable fruits. It is known under different names, the most common of which is "prickly pear". The word *ṣubbār* derives from the Semitic verbal root *ṣ-b-r* that originally meant "to restrain or bind"[15]. Many different definitions and concepts are connected to it; one of the most usual ones is related to semantic fields comprising the signifiers "endurance, tenacity", and "resignation"[16]; moreover, the latter are linked to the lemma "patience" and its adjacent notions. *Ṣabr* can be used in Arabic to translate all the aforementioned signifiers – and their signifieds – while *ṣabīr* means "patient" and both *ṣabūr* and *ṣabbār* mean "very patient". The concept of *ṣabr* is of utmost importance in the religious (and legal) field, as proven by reading Quranic suras. Among the verses where the root *ṣ-b-r* is to be found, the following pericope is especially meaningful in this context:

> It is not piety, that you turn your faces to the East and to the West. True piety is this: to believe in God, and the Last Day, the angels, the Book, and the Prophets, to give of one's substance, however cherished, to kinsmen, and orphans, the needy, the traveller, beggars, and to ransom the slave, to perform the prayer, to pay the alms. And they who fulfil their covenant when they have engaged in a covenant, and endure with fortitude misfortune, hardship and peril, these are they who are true in their faith, these are the truly godfearing[17].

15. Wensinck 2012.
16. Ibid.
17. Qur. II:177. From Arberry's translation.

In this passage, where the essence of *true piety* is being explained to believers, the root *ṣ-b-r* is used in *al-ṣabirīn*: "[...] *and endure*[18] with fortitude misfortune, hardship and peril [...]". The whole passage provides an appropriate background to read the experience of the main characters in *Banāt al-ṣubbār* who are, first, the "girls" described by Karīmah Aḥdād and, second, all the Riffian people. In fact, apart from dealing with the aforementioned issues in Riffian (and Moroccan as such) past and present, the story narrated in this novel also explores how some authentic Islamic teachings are being disregarded today and how "kinsmen, and orphans, the needy" are being left to their destiny based on other Islamic norms, namely, some of those contained in the 2004 Family Code, as I argue below. Besides, according to this code – and in spite of many positive changes brought about by this document – a woman can be viewed as an adult only after she is married. Thus, a single woman will always be treated as a girl, whatever her education and professional or social position may be[19]. Nonetheless, the girls/*banāt* Karīmah Aḥdād describes in the novel include married women. This implies that the writer feels, knows, and wants to show that all women, whatever their marital status, are still discriminated in both Riffian and non-Riffian Moroccan society, despite all the reforms that were approved to bridge the gap in gender issues. Consequently, the reason I chose to use the term "girls" every time to refer to the female characters in this novel, regardless of their age, is my intention to adhere to the writer's solution that, in turn, originates from the *status quo* of women's situation in Morocco.

Thus, the verbal root *ṣ-b-r* is used extensively in this novel in all its forms. It refers first to Aḥdād's "girls" and, second, to their male counterparts, who are thorny and sweet at the same time: they have an ineffable tenderness within them, as the events of the novel clearly show, and have to endure many difficult situations.

The novel revolves around the vicissitudes of a lower-class family and some of their relatives and friends (or acquaintances). Nearly all characters are from the Rif, and most of them are either from or live in the port town of Al Hoceima, where the novel is mainly set, except for some scenes that take place in Rabat and Casablanca. The novel's focus is on the

18. Italics mine.
19. Žvan Elliott 2015, p. 3.

members of the family composed by Ḥamīd al-Ziyyānī, his wife Luwīzah and their four daughters Ṣūniyā, Šādiyā, Šaymāʾ, and Ṣafāʾ. Ḥamīd is a fishseller who suddenly dies of a heart attack in his sleep after quarrelling with his wife while he is watching his favourite religious TV show. Suddenly, the life of Luwīzah and her daughters becomes more difficult, poorer, and sadder than it was before the death of the family's patriarch, whose personality had undergone a deep change over the years. Ḥamīd has turned from a gentle and loving husband and father to a stubborn and sombre man who, in the wake of obscurantist Islamist teachings and proselytising, began to victimise his "girls" in several ways, to the point that, for example, he would not allow them to watch Egyptian films on TV. The *niqāb* had been imposed on the family, and Ḥamīd himself had changed his own dress code as well as almost all his old habits. The fundamental change took place in June 2002, the same day that Ṣūniyā was watching the aforementioned football match from home. Ḥamīd, who was in his 30s and was used to wearing jeans and listening to music, began to listen to religious preachers, marking the beginning of an absolutely new phase in his family's life[20].

When the narrative starts, Ḥamīd al-Ziyyānī is still alive or, rather, his elder daughter Ṣūniyā is unaware that he is about to die, as Luwīzah, the mother, narrates in the second chapter. In the first chapter, the 26-year-old Ṣūniyā is recalling her old life – she does so all the time during her daily routine, perhaps because of her deep unhappiness. Thus, the initial chapter is devoted to the thoughts of Ṣūniyā, who reveals to the readership "the misfortune, hardship and peril" that she, her mother, and her younger sisters must endure with fortitude. In particular, she complains about the rules imposed on the five of them by her father, influenced by ultra-traditionalist sheikhs and Islamic jurists. In the opening scene, Ṣūniyā is on her way to work, which is two kilometres from her home. This distance usually takes her twenty minutes, but this time she is walking faster than ever to avoid not only the daily harassment (*taḥarruš*), but also the tremendous rain and mud. Indeed, she seems to be almost floating in water and mire, and her long *ǧilbāb*, the robe that should protect her from dirt coming from the natural and social environment, is a hindrance to her safety. In fact, her black *ǧilbāb* attracts and retains what it should deflect,

20. Aḥdād 2018, pp. 119–124 (Chapter *al-Ab al-Qadīm* [The Former Father]).

i.e., male attention, dirt, cold. Ṣūniyā usually compares her running in the street every day to a mouse; on this day, however, she compares herself to a beetle, i.e., a filthier animal than a mouse in the collective imagination[21]. Moreover, she remembers that she learnt to move very quickly and to hide from people's eyes because having a job goes contrary to her father's rules. Ṣūniyā had to abandon her studies when her father discovered her talking to her schoolmates in front of the school. From that moment on, she had to stay at home, without any hope of resuming her studies, earning a diploma, or looking for a job. However, she secretly found work at a hairdresser's, a place absolutely forbidden to her even as a customer. Hers is a dishonourable occupation in the eyes of her father and Al Hoceima's communitarian ethos. Despite her fear of accepted values and codes, Ṣūniyā is not simply a girl who submissively practices patience (*ṣabr*). On the contrary, she is a defiant and resilient person. In fact, in this chapter, the first of the entire novel and of a long series where this character makes her own voice heard, Karīmah Aḥdād immediately discloses Ṣūniyā's – and, ultimately, her mother's – innermost character for the readers:

> To win over life, we have to fight it to the death. This is what my mother has been teaching me since I began to learn to use reason and to understand. For this, I patiently endure rain, mud, harassment, and also a long day's stressful work for 800 *dirhams* a month. I patiently endure both the boredom of waiting for customers by helping myself to handfuls of grain until I have a stomach ache and the chitchat of the workers in the haircutting room, which makes me feel sick, as well as the hairdressers who just share the fact of their womanhood with me[22].

This "girl" is indeed a surprising mixture of dejection and disappointment on the one hand and firmness and determination on the other. At the beginning of the novel, Ṣūniyā is not optimistic about her future, but she decides to fight so that she does not meet the same cruel fate as her mother; and against all odds, she will succeed in resuming her studies and buying, thanks to her job, some land to build a new home for her family.

21. Ibid., p. 11.
22. Ibid. All the translations from the novel are mine.

Still in the first chapter, however, she ponders her situation at a certain point:

> Eight years have passed since then. Eight long years, and the sadness for having left school has not abandoned my heart, nor has my feeling of suffocation. Here I am, today, at 26 years of age: a poor girl with no dreams, no ambitions, no hopes, and a prisoner in the town of despair. I secretly work at a hairdresser's to get money to buy myself underwear at the end of the month. Above all, (I am) a failure in love and with regard to marriage, since until now no one has come forward to propose to me, apart from long-bearded men who have my father's same mindset. I refused all of them because I do not intend to live as unhappily as my mother does[23].

Just like Ṣūniyā, the suffering people, and especially the "girls" described in *Banāt al-ṣubbār* are endowed with very deep resilience, endurance, and patience, all qualities due to a plurality of causes. They share many peculiarities with the prickly pear cactus, one of the Riffian natural elements, to the extent that this plant can be used as a symbol and a metaphor for this region and the individuals who inhabit it or are originally from it and have been obliged by circumstances to migrate to other places in Morocco or elsewhere. They strongly feel that they belong to their land and nation but are confused. What and which is their land? And what about their nation? They are the offspring – in the dual sense of children and the direct consequence of something – of both Riffian and non-Riffian Morocco, two entities often perceived as separate from one another over the centuries and also currently. They cannot deny or give up their motherland and mother tongue, but they feel compelled to leave them behind if they want to be part of the bigger country, even though it may be painful[24]. Choosing to do so in the hope of finding opportunities for a better life frequently leads to complete disappointment when an individual realises that nothing is waiting for her/him, apart from poverty and subjugation in various forms.

Karīmah Aḥdād's character Šādiyā experiences that. She is a clever university student in Arabic language and literature in Rabat who decides

23. Ibid, p. 16.
24. See, for instance, n. 9.

to specialise in this field because it is the easiest way for her to find a job due to her talent in writing. Nonetheless, she feels uneasy about this solution because of her "betrayal" of Amazigh culture. Šādiyā is interested in activism and attracted by a young university leader, Anīr, who is of Amazigh origins himself and is also disappointed by everything in his life – from the Moroccan social system (starting with its educational system) to his own inability to cope with love and with the idea of becoming a father. Anīr shifts the blame for this to society and the central power[25]. Šādiyā and Anīr are thus bewildered and confused, but she abandons her intention to abort Anīr's child and chooses instead to be a single mother. Thus, she finally makes up her mind to live her life fully. Unfortunately, she eventually dies in childbirth[26]. Likewise, her sister Ṣūniyā decides not to be overwhelmed by her own fears and demonstrates her ability to hold on to the good side of life hidden under its harshness and pain. I also argue that this is the way *Banāt al-ṣubbār* presents to try at least to achieve pacification in Morocco. Once again, in this context, Ṣūniyā turns out indeed to be the most emblematic figure: in the married couple of Aḥmad and Sārah – this latter is an old schoolmate of Ṣūniyā whom she has not seen for many years – she unexpectedly finds two persons who prove to be fundamental for her path to independence. Aḥmad and Sārah belong to well-to-do families, and their own nuclear family is this as well. They live in a villa surrounded by a garden; they have a car and can go to expensive restaurants; and they can easily spend large sums of money[27]. These details and many others are given throughout the novel, especially in the chapters where the narrators are Aḥmad, Sārah, and Ṣūniyā, who works for some time as their maid, and Šaymā', who contacts unknown men through social media to make money and finally discovers that her "benefactor" is Aḥmad[28].

While Ṣūniyā describes her gloomy existence and environment in Chapter I, her father is being given a place in paradise – or, at least, that is what he thinks. From this moment on, the family's problems and tribulations grow exponentially, and these five "girls" have to learn how to

25. Aḥdād 2018, *passim*.
26. Ibid.
27. Regarding Moroccan middle class, cf., for instance, Arbouch and Dadush 2019, pp. 12–16.
28. Aḥdād 2018, *passim*.

endure – with more fortitude than ever before – all sorts of challenges coming from several directions, especially from Ḥamīd's brothers and sisters. Based on the 2004 Moroccan Family Code and particularly *al-Kitāb al-sādis: al-mīrāṯ* (Book VI, On Successions), that incorporates Quranic norms, if a man who has daughters and no sons dies, the female heirs/his daughters do not have the right to inherit the property of the deceased without sharing it with the deceased's male and other female heirs. This often means that their uncles and aunts precede them in the inheritance[29]. This is what happens in *Banāt al-ṣubbār*: Ḥamīd's wife and daughters are deprived of their only property, their home, which goes to his brothers and sisters. His sister Suʿdiyyah – who is also one of the first-person narrators in the novel – spurs her brothers and sisters to claim their rights, even though they do so reluctantly. As a result, Luwīzah and her daughters are forced to move away from their home and rent a squalid place in the town centre. This leads to mental breakdowns: losing one's home is extremely humiliating for anyone, especially when it has required many sacrifices. Aḥdād describes this as a very frequent occurrence in Morocco, something that throws (poor) people into despair too often, and she seems to wonder why this norm still works today, given its nefarious conseuqences The crucial issue pointed out by the Family Code's articles on inheritance is the red line that runs through the entire novel, but it is only one of the several issues discussed in *Banāt al-ṣubbār*. In fact, through the experiences faced by its characters, this novel could also be seen as a thorough debate on some of the thorniest issues that have been shocking Moroccan civil society and activism. Karīmah Aḥdād refers to more than one text produced by the Moroccan legislative system during King Muḥammad VI's reign without naming them. Particular reference is made, as we have seen, to the Family Code and similarly to the 2011 Constitution, a document considered to be a turning point in the pacification process carried out by the Moroccan establishment. At the same time, however, the enactment of the Constitution has been seen as a way to demobilise the revolts that led to it[30]. Nonetheless, it seemed to be trying to provide a firm categorisation and systematisation for several age-old

29. Bouarek 2019.
30. Badran 2020, pp. 628–629.

issues[31], including gender equality before the law in every field. Article 19 is the milestone statement in this sense since it enshrines that "[t]he State works for the realisation of parity between men and women"[32].

Banāt al-ṣubbār investigates gender inequality and gender relationships within the framework of a patriarchal and misogynist society in depth. Actually, these subjects are not new in Moroccan fiction. What is new here is that, in her novel, Aḥdād provides a very detailed account of the results achieved by the reforms brought about from 2004 and especially from 2011 onwards. She reviews a good number of these reforms, the validity of which is being questioned. Notoriously, the Family Code and the Constitution had, among their multifarious goals, that of reducing gender disparity, with women becoming the "intended and strategic" target because of their objectively difficult conditions both within the family and in society since time immemorial. Despite all the various relevant improvements achieved in their situation by means of these urgently needed reforms, Moroccan women in general have not experienced concrete advancement in some fields.

Actually, topics related to gender disparity are displayed in full in *Banāt al-ṣubbār*, with dexterity and a sympathetic attitude that is not, however, devoid of a critical and scientific-like approach. In fact, Aḥdād observes her characters' actions and listens to their words almost without intervening. First-person narrative allows the opportunity for the reader

31. Contributors to *The 2011 Moroccan Constitution: A Critical Analysis* (2012) admit that this Constitutional Charter includes "many human rights that were not previously recognized in the country", while underlining the presence of a good deal of ambiguity and contradiction in both its form (especially regarding some divergences between the original Arabic and its French version) and content. In particular, they state: "The 2011 constitution sets out a list of new rights that were not included in the 1996 constitutional text [...]: the right to life; the right to security of the person; the right to physical or moral integrity; the right to protection of privacy; the presumption of innocence and the right to a fair trial; the right of access to justice; the right of access to information; the right to health care; the right to social welfare; the right to decent housing; and the right to present petitions, among other rights. However, several items are simple statements without precise normative content and refer to ordinary or organic laws. The rights to life and physical integrity have not been accompanied by a clear abolition of the death penalty. Other rights and freedoms are written in a contradictory way". *The 2011 Moroccan Constitution: A Critical Analysis* 2012, pp. 6, 8, 16–17, and 49ff. See also Viviani 2019, pp. 269ff.

32. *Morocco's Constitution of 2011* 2012, p. 8.

to enter directly into the inner reality of the people introduced who can thus express themselves freely. This way, they are able to deal with sensitive matters like extramarital sexual intercourse, abortion, and being a single mother[33], prostitution, patriarchy, unemployment, social indifference, politics, poverty, education, etc. When they do so, they are able to dissect their own self as well as the reality around them, providing a firsthand analysis and knowledge of their inner and outer world and of the real injustices and perils they have to cope with in everyday life. The novel's characters are of various ages and belong to various social classes and express different views of the world. Consequently, the readers are allowed to come into direct touch with the problems and questions inherent to a good number of "sociological samples". These concern pre-adolescents' and adolescents' responses to socioreligious rules and/or poverty; their obsessive search for money to help their family; and their coping with risks stemming from a misuse of social media; young women's and young men's reaction to love in general and to loveless marriage dictated by social conventions; university students' considerations on their study choices, the state of education in Morocco, and their future; their sometimes excessive drug, alcohol and tobacco use[34]; the widows' situation in a traditional society; people's search for work and the difficulties they meet; the scopes and limits of the patriarchal society in contemporary Morocco; and women's strategies to overcome their often miserable status.

Aḥdād traces the process of "redemption" and "liberation" of some of the Riffian people introduced in her novel, who strive to get rid of a tormented former life under various standpoints and manage to find their own way in a society that, despite all the reforms put in place, continues to be indifferent to a good number of its members' sufferings and concerns. This is the case with Ṣūniyā and her sisters, and also with Sārah,

33. Ranieri 2020, pp. 85ff.

34. Legalisation of cannabis, traditionally cultivated in the Rif, where it is the sustainment of thousands of households, for therapeutic use was voted on 26 May 2021 by the Moroccan Parliament. This decision was mainly due to economic reasons and might lead to further problems between centre and periphery, between the Rif and central government. Kadiri 2021. The anthropologist Khalid Mouna devoted a large part of his works to the Rif, its youth and the movements originating in it, and the cannabis issue. See, for instance, Mouna 2018, Chap. V.

who leaves Aḥmad, and Suʿdiyyah, who finds relief in faith. She does not consider it a mere stopgap; actually, it gives her the necessary strength to prevent her disrespectful husband from endangering her and their children's life[35]. Other characters in *Banāt al-ṣubbār* do not free themselves from their thorny present in this life, but in the afterlife, which is the case for Šādiyā.

The last chapter of this novel is narrated by Ḥamīd al-Ziyyānī in his grave. Like all the other narrators, Ḥamīd also reveals his inner feelings and thoughts to those who wish to pay attention to the individual as well as the collective story told by *Banāt al-ṣubbār*'s many characters. Now that he is dead, Ḥamīd has discovered the truth, which is completely different from the one instilled in him by TV preachers. While he is in what is known as *barzaḫ*, "either the space between the worlds of the living and the dead as the time between death and resurrection"[36], he says:

> I am dead now. I am the father, Ḥamīd al-Ziyyānī, speaking from my grave. There is no bald-headed or hairy snake, neither Munkar nor Nakīr[37]. Here there is only a huge monitor that somehow found room in a narrow grave like mine. A huge monitor through which I can watch all the details of the life I left behind. A monitor on which all the consequences of my mistakes are being displayed. […]
> My favourite sheikh, whom I watched on TV for years, did not inform me. He lied to me. He told me that there would be a bald-headed snake, and two men called Munkar and Nakīr who would ask me four questions: Who is your Lord? What is your religion? Who is your Prophet? Do you believe in the predestination of the good and the bad[38]?

He can watch Ṣūniyā crying about her situation and her longing for Aḥmad; Šādiyā's suffering during pregnancy and childbirth; Šaymāʾ's desperate search for money to help her mother; and Ṣafāʾ's happiness because his death allowed her to reject the *niqāb*[39]. In short, he can see

35. Aḥdād 2018, pp. 313 ff.
36. Tesei 2016, p. 32.
37. In Islamic eschatology, the two angels are in charge of testing the deceased's faith by asking him some specific questions, as it becomes clear in the quotation further on.
38. Aḥdād 2018, pp. 331–332.
39. Ibid., p. 331. It is very interesting how Karīmah Aḥdād affords an in-depth analysis of the status of religion/religiosity in today's Morocco and primarily in the Rif

and feel their pain, but only the pain caused by his behaviour. He also comments:

> Here there is only a frightening silence, and images of the life I left behind continuously shown on the monitor, and a feeling of regret. A regret as thick and strong as suffocating smoke. There is a violent feeling of shame, and a desire for change, without any possibility of doing that.
> There is no punishment in the grave, no paradise, no hell, no afterlife. [...]
> The only punishment here is what my hands have committed. [...]
> Then I hear a voice resembling all those I know:
> What did your hands do?
> I tremble and am afraid. [...]
> If only I were a stern prickly pear that lives and dies and then hides and turns into nothingness.
> If only I were anything else... but not a human being.
> If only. If only. If only[40].

Ḥamīd is so sad and upset about the bad things he did that he is not able to realise to what extent, and despite how much pain and difficulty, his "girls" have started to see the light, thanks to their determination and sacrifice. Ḥamīd is deeply disillusioned with religion as he learnt it from his TV sheikh, which means he is also disillusioned by sociopolitical and juridical norms that are seen as unshakeable. Therefore, we can consider his words to be a hope for the assumption of responsibility by a patriarch towards his own family and its female members particularly. This happens because he finally decides to watch his loved ones striving simply to have a "normal" life. What is more, Ḥamīd has always been sincere in his faith and absolutely confident in the words uttered by men of religion. This means that he himself was deceived by his own society at large. In the grave, he questions his own role as a family patriarch and the institution of patriarchy. Moreover, challenging the credibility of patriarchy also means challenging *al-hogra*[41] and those who exercise and perpetrate it. In

region, while showing how it affects gender and generational relationships.

40. Ibid., p. 332.
41. "The word *Al-hogra* comes from the Arabic *ihtiqaar*, meaning disdain, contempt, humiliation, and deprivation. In Morocco, *Al-hogra* is an overloaded term when used in Moroccan Darija (Moroccan colloquial Arabic) as it expresses a number of

other words, it means giving credibility to all the people at the margins and primarily to women.

The strategies of negotiation with the central power described in *Banāt al-ṣubbār* stem from the margins themselves: they come directly from the *banāt* who, on the basis of engrained patriarchal ethos, are viewed as not having reached adulthood; hence, no independence, autonomy, or maturity. Such strategies imply these female characters' voluntary and conscious liberation from social and religious norms if they are used to the detriment of the least powerful. Some scabrous situations are portrayed in this novel, but I argue that they are intended as a sociological analysis of the different situations that an innocent and poor girl/woman may stumble in, in her journey towards freedom and self-confidence.

Both Sārah and Aḥmad say they are in love with Ṣūniyā and have sexual intercourse with her, but they do not hesitate to treat her coldly because she is different from them – at least, this is what Ṣūniyā feels. She truly loves Aḥmad but surrenders to Sārah because she reminds her of her happy days at school where they had met in childhood and also because Ṣūniyā needs Sārah's friendship and to work in her villa. Once she decides to resume her studies, after having asked for Aḥmad's support and suggestions, she perceives that she needs to leave them and her job: she can no longer be afraid of Sārah and put Aḥmad at risk. Moreover, Ṣūniyā cannot tolerate being a possible tool in their hands: she has to avoid even the slightest suspicion of having to face up to *al-hogra*, intended here as "injustice, outrage inequality, inferiority, disempowerment, frustration, feelings of contempt"[42] in the private sphere that reflects what happens in the public sphere.

---

negative feelings and moods (injustice, outrage inequality, inferiority, disempowerment, frustration, feelings of contempt). In this paper, the word is used mainly to express the feeling associated with exclusion and the feeling of the loss of dignity one experiences after being treated inequitably or unfairly in the provision of public services or in the protection of his/her civil or human rights. This is usually manifested in different situations such as excessive use of force by the police, inability and denial to benefit from a public service, confiscation of one's goods and the contempt shown by some local government authorities in various administrative institutions because of one's poverty or social background. In Morocco, the word *Al-hogra* gained popularity and 'acceptance in framing public discontent and anger which sparked the uprisings of the February 20 Movement (Feb20Mvt) in 2011, and the ongoing protests in the country' (Ilahiane, 2019)". Yachoulti, Lachhab 2018, p. 22.

42. Ibid.

3. Conclusion: Is Pacification Still Possible?

Banāt al-ṣubbār portrays Riffian and all Moroccan "girls" in their quest for a "pacific coexistence," which might be achieved through their fight against all sorts of inequalities present in their own society. The story is told from different standpoints, by female and male voices that intertwine with increasing originality and subtlety, thanks to the novelist's effective use of language, rhetorical devices, and narrative techniques. Not to speak of her ostensible nonchalance, sympathy, and a perceptible need to understand the psychological reasons that lead (or led) to a specific result in her characters' lives. This occurs when sensitive issues, such as vexing feelings and situations, are described in full. Actually, in the case of this work, vexatiousness applies to all fields of one's private and public life, whenever it implies a deviation from normally accepted codified behaviours – in the sexual, family, social, political, and religious sphere – or a visceral need to analyse every situation, feeling, person, not to mention a correspondingly visceral need to concretely act, even against a certain ethos. In this case, this means a fight against patriarchal society as it is in Rif today and in Morocco as a whole.

While giving a gruesome overall image of her nation's conditions, Aḥdād seeks to demonstrate that escape from such a terrible situation is possible only if men and women make up their minds and assume responsibility for their own lives and community. More importantly, such an assumption of responsibility would be likely to take non-violent and non-tragic forms and, at the same time, could be the way to achieve a new pacification process, perhaps more stable than ever. These are the deepest and most innovative messages conveyed by the novel *Banāt al-ṣubbār.* Choosing life against all odds and facing the various hindrances that a person, and primarily a woman, can meet in the Rif today (and Morocco as a whole) where *al-hogra* is continuously perpetrated is the only opportunity left for this country to develop. When imagining and reporting solutions, Aḥdād evidently behaves as the spokesperson for some parties of the Moroccan civil society that work on behalf of their undervalued fellow countrymen. Moreover, because of her belonging to two of the most marginalised categories of people, i.e., women and the Amazigh inhabitants of the Rif region, Aḥdād is most likely not just an activist fighting in favour of some people from the outside but also from within.

As a Riffian woman, she knows the local women's situation very well. And she also knows how relationships of all kinds dramatically work in that microcosm, as opposed to the country's macrocosm. Aḥdād perfectly understands this territory, its history, its people and their daily routine, the forces at work in the local society, and its relation to those at play on governmental and national levels. The inhabitants of this area have rooted fierceness and resilience that come, perhaps, from the harshness of both the natural environment, to which they had to adapt since time immemorial, and the harshness of the events that they have been coping with for centuries. As history teaches us, and without attempting to idealise them, the Riffians can be said to have a long and steadfast tradition of struggle for independence, which originated from and resulted in the achievement of local nationalism against all forms of colonialism and imposed power. On the other hand, the Riffian experience taught all Moroccans, and still does, as recent events show, what nationalism – and especially Moroccan nationalism – ought to be. This is so thanks to the example given by the Confederal Republic of the Tribes of the Rif and Muḥammad b. ʻAbd al-Karīm al-Ḫaṭṭābī, whose spirit clearly becomes manifest in *Banāt al-ṣubbār*. Two sentences by this leader were used as the epigraph to the third and fourth parts of the novel. "Naḥnu fī ʿaṣr yuḍīʿu fī-hi al-ḥaqq iḏā lam tasnudhu quwwah" (We are in an epoch where truth, if not supported by strength, fades away)[43] introduces the section *al-Ġazālah al-mağrūḥah* (The Hurt Gazelle), while "Laysa fī qaḍiyyat al-ḥurriyyah ḥall waṣaṭ" (There is no compromise in matters of freedom)[44] introduces *Taḥarrur* (Liberation)[45]. Truth and rights must be defended with and by means of strength; freedom cannot be achieved through easy solutions. These teachings are always valid, especially in the time of turmoil caused by the everlasting preoccupation in the most marginalised strata of the population or in all those who feel this way, whatever their status is.

Hopefully, *Banāt al-ṣubbār*'s message of faith, confidence, and shift of perspective within Riffian/Moroccan patriarchal society will leave its mark on all the actors involved in the process of change and novel

43. Aḥdād 2018, p. 183.
44. Ibid., p. 253.
45. The other two parts of this novel have as their epigraphs, respectively, a Riffian saying and a sentence by the famous writer Muḥammad Šukrī, who was also from the Rif region.

pacification within the country, and marginalised individuals and communities will have their voices heard without being obliged to resort to violence, self-inflicted or not. This is what Yachoulti and Lachhab stress in their interesting essay on some of the actions put in place by women in their personal fight against *al-hogra*[46]. Lastly, may Abdellatif Laâbi's (ʿAbd al-Laṭīf al-Laʿābī) and other committed Moroccans' wondering about a *possible* return to the "Years of Lead" – given the Casablanca Court of Appeal's confirmation on 5 April 2019 of the verdicts declared against many detainees involved in the 2016–2017 Riffian protests – remain nothing more than an idea[47].

References

Abourabi, Y. (2015), *La réapparition du drapeau de la République du Rif lors du printemps arabe au Maroc*, in Rhani, Z. et al., *Le Maroc au présent: D'une époque à l'autre, une société en mutation*, Centre Jacques-Berque, Fondation du Roi Abdul-Aziz Al Saoud pour les Études Islamiques et les Sciences Humaines, Casablanca, pp. 617–626, available at: https://books.openedition.org/cjb/1092 (last accessed 31 July 2021).

Aḥdād, K. (2018), *Banāt al-ṣubbār*, Editions Le Fennec/Dār al-Fannāk li-l-našr, Casablanca.

Aragón Reyes, M. (ed.) (2013), *El Protectorado español en Marruecos: La historia trascendida*, 3 vols., Iberdrola, D.L., Bilbao, available at: https://dialnet.unirioja.es/servlet/libro?codigo=562926 (last accessed 10 April 2022).

Arbouch, M., Dadush, U. (2019), *Measuring the Middle Class in the World and in Morocco*, Policy Center for the New South, Rabat, available at: https://www.policycenter.ma/ (last accessed 11 August 2021).

Badran, S. Z. (2020), *Demobilising the February 20 Movement in Morocco: Regime Strategies during the Arab Spring*, in "The Journal of North African Studies", 25, 4, pp. 616–640, available at: https://doi.org/10.1080/13629387.2019.1634558 (last accessed 8 August 2021).

Bendourou, O. et al. (eds) (2014), *La nouvelle Constitution marocaine à l'épreuve de la pratique. Actes du colloque organisé les 18 et 19 avril 2013*, L'Equipe de recherche Droit constitutionnel et science politique Faculté de droit de Souissi-Rabat, La Croisée des Chemins, Casablanca.

46. Yachoulti, Lachhab 2018, p. 22.
47. Rhani et al. 2020, p. 25.

Bernard, M. et al. (1936), *La pacification du Maroc*, Publications du Comité de l'Afrique du Nord, Paris.

Bouarek, T. (2019), *Moudawana: dix ans de lacunes juridiques en dix points*, in "Telquel", 31 octobre, available at: https://telquel.ma/2015/10/31/moudawana-dix-ans-lacunes-juridiques-en-dix-points_1468449 (last accessed 08 August 2021).

Courcelle-Labrousse, V., Marmié, N. (2008), *La guerre du Rif: Maroc 1921–1926*, Tallandier, Paris.

Desrues, Th. (2012), *Le Mouvement du 20 février et le régime marocain: contestation, révision constitutionnelle et élections*, in "L'Année du Maghreb [En ligne]", VIII. https://doi.org/10.4000/anneemaghreb.1537 (last accessed 18 May 2021).

Diouani, A. E. (2021), *Exploring the Voices of the Rif Hirak activism: The struggle for democracy in Morocco*, in "Mediterranean Politics", 28, 1, pp. 98–123. https://doi.org/10.1080/13629395.2021.1915448 (last accessed 9 August 2021).

Dulucq, S. et al. (eds) (2008), *Les mots de la colonisation*, Presses Universitaires Mirail, Toulouse.

El Guabli, B. (2020), *The Absent Perpetrators: Morocco's Failed Accountability; Tazmamart Literature and the Survivors' Testimony for their Jailers (1973–1991)*, in "Violence: An International Journal", 1, 1, pp. 80–101. https://doi.org/10.1177/2633002420904672

El Rhazy, S. (2011), *Le Maroc, un cas à part*, in "Outre terre", 3, 29, pp. 137–140. https://doi.org/10.3917/oute.029.0137 (last accessed 11 April 2022).

Hannoum, A. (2021), *The Invention of the Maghreb: Between Africa and the Middle East*, Cambridge University Press, Cambridge.

Kadiri, Gh. (2021), *Au Maroc, les petits cultivateurs de marijuana craignent d'être les perdants de la légalisation*, in "Le Monde", 2 août, available at: https://www.lemonde.fr/afrique/article/2021/08/02/au-maroc-les-petits-cultivateurs-de-kif-craignent-d-etre-les-perdants-de-la-legalisation_6090254_3212.html (last accessed 13 August 2021).

Maddy-Weitzman, B., Zisenwine, D. (eds) (2013), *Contemporary Morocco: state, politics and society under Mohammed VI*, Routledge, Abingdon.

Mohsen-Finan, Kh. (2007), *Mémoire et réconciliation nationale au Maroc*, in "Politique étrangère", 2 Été, pp. 327–338, available at: https://www.cairn.info/revue-politique-etrangere-2007-2-page-327.htm (last accessed 9 August 2021).

Morocco's Constitution of 2011 (2012), English Translation, trans. Jefri J. Rucht, William S. Hein & Co., Inc., available at: https://www.constituteproject.org/constitution/Morocco_2011.pdf (last accessed 12 August 2021).

Mouna, Kh. (2018), *Identité de la marge: Approche anthropologique du Rif*, Peter Lang, Bruxelles.

Ouiddar, N. (2020), *Les lauréats des Prix de la région Casablanca-Settat*, 14/02, available at: https://lematin.ma/journal/2020/laureats-prix-region-casablanca-settat/331683.html (last accessed 10 August 2021).

Pennell, C. R. (2017), *How and Why to Remember the Rif War (1921–2021)*, in "The Journal of North African Studies", 22, 5, pp. 798–820. https://doi.org/10.1080/13629387.2017.1361826 (last accessed 9 August 2021).

Radi, A. (2017), *Protest Movements and Social Media: Morocco's February 20 Movement*, in "Africa Development / Afrique et Développement", 42, 2, Special Issue on Study on Oblique Identity Dynamics / Numéro spécial sur l'Étude des dynamiques identitaires obliques, pp. 31–55, available at: https://www.jstor.org/stable/10.2307/90018190 (last accessed 25 March 2021).

Ranieri, E. (2020), *Maternità proibita e infanzia negata: essere madre nubile in Marocco*, in Ferrara, M., Karami, L. (a cura di), *Madri d'Oriente fra tradizione e dissenso*, Introduzione di A. Vanzan, Jouvence, Milan, pp. 85–111.

Rhani, Z. et al. (2020), *'The Rif again!' Ppopular Uprisings and Resurgent Violence in Post-Transitional Morocco*, in "The Journal of North African Studies", 27, 2, pp. 326–362. https://doi.org/10.1080/13629387.2020.1780921 (last accessed 1 August 2021).

Sánchez-García, J., Touhtou, R. (2021), *De la* Hogra *al* Hirak*: Neocolonialismo, memoria y disidencia política juvenil en el Rif*, in "Revista Latinoamericana de Ciencias Sociales, Niñez y Juventud", 19, 1, pp. 204–223. https://doi.org/10.11600/rlcsnj.19.1.4591 (last accessed 10 August 2021).

Simon, H. (1934), *La pacification du Maroc*, in "Journal of the Royal African Society", 33, 133, pp. 329–337. https://doi.org/10.1093/oxfordjournals.afraf.a100790 (last accessed 7 June 2021).

Slyomovics, S. (2016), *The Moroccan Equity and Reconciliation Commission: the promises of a human rights archive*, in "The Arab Studies Journal", 24, 1 (Spring 2016), pp. 10–41, available at: https://www.jstor.org/stable/44746844 (last accessed 25 March 2021).

Tesei, T. (2016), *The Barzakh and the Intermediate State of the Dead in the Quran*, in Ch. Lange (ed.), *Locating Hell in Islamic Traditions*, Brill, Leiden-Boston, pp. 31–55, available online at: https://library.oapen.org/bitstream/id/ddd3c16c-ce86-496e-bcf8-84aca404e1b9/612691.pdf (last accessed 13 August 2021).

The Koran Interpreted (1996), A Translation by A. J. Arberry, Simon & Schuster, New York, 1st ed. 1955, George Allen & Unwin Ltd.)

The 2011 Moroccan Constitution: A Critical Analysis (2012), Contributors: Mohamed Madani, Driss Maghraoui, Saloua Zerhouni, International Institute for Democracy and Electoral Assistance, Stockholm, available at:

https://www.idea.int/sites/default/files/publications/the-2011-moroccan-constitution-critical-analysis.pdf (last accessed 12 August 2021).

Van de Vate, K. (2020), *WiTMonth conversations: Karima Ahdad on 'Cactus Girls'*, 4 August, available at: https://arablit.org/2020/08/04/witmonth-conversations-karima-ahdad-on-cactus-girls (last accessed 12 August 2021).

Viviani, P. (2019), *What Does Fiction Tell us about Morocco Today? Shortlisted Moroccan Novels at IPAF*, in *Arabic Literature in a Posthuman World. Proceedings of the 12th Conference of the European Association for Modern Arabic Literature (EURAMAL), May 2016, Oslo*. Edited by S. Guth and T. Pepe, Harrassowitz, Wiesbaden, pp. 269–285.

Wensinck, A. J. (2012 online), s.v. «Ṣabr», in *Encyclopaedia of Islam*, 1st ed., available at: http://dx.doi.org/10.1163/2214-871X_ei1_SIM_5010 (last accessed 17 June 2021).

Wolf, A. (2019), *Morocco's Hirak Movement and Legacies of Contention in the Rif*, in "The Journal of North African Studies", 24, 1, pp. 1–6. https://doi.org/10.1080/13629387.2018.1538188 (last accessed 10 August 2021).

Yachoulti, M., Lachhab, M. (2018), *Moroccan Women's Resistance to* Al-Hogra *in the Aftermath of Arab Spring: Patterns and Outcomes*, in "Feminist Research", 2, 1, pp. 22–28. https://doi.org/10.21523/gcj2.18020105 (last accessed 13 August 2021).

Zakariasalhi (2020), Banât al-sabbâr, *les quatre filles du pêcheur de Karima Ahdad*, in "Telquel", 05/06, available at: https://telquel.ma/2020/06/05/banat-al-sabbar-les-quatre-filles-du-pecheur-de-karima-ahdad_1686400 (last accessed 10 August 2021).

Žvan Elliott, K. (2015), *(Dis)Empowering Education: The Case of Morocco*, in "Urban Anthropology and Studies of Cultural Systems and World Economic Development", Spring-Summer, 44, 1/2, Special Issue: *Muslim Women in the Middle East*, pp. 1–42, available at: https://www.jstor.org/stable/24643135 (last accessed 10 August 2021).

Paola Viviani is Senior Lecturer at the Dipartimento di Scienze Politiche, Università degli Studi della Campania *Luigi Vanvitelli* Caserta, Italy. Her research focuses on modern Arabic literature, especially the *Nahḍah* press and prose, and the contemporary novel. She has translated short stories and novels from Morocco, Egypt, Yemen, Palestine, Saudi Arabia, UAE from Arabic into Italian. She also edited the Italian translation of Ṭāhā Ḥusayn's *Fi-l-ši'r al-ğāhilī* as *La poesia araba preislamica* (2020).

Chapter 8

Youssef Fadel's Trilogy: Testifying Violence to Negotiate Peace in Moroccan Literature

Cristina Dozio

Abstract

This chapter examines Youssef Fadel's trilogy on the recent history of Morocco to understand how the fictional representation of the pairing of violence/peace intertwines with the ongoing reconciliation process in the country. This process aims at coming to terms with the brutal experience of the Years of Lead (*sanawāt al-raṣāṣ*), a period of political crackdown under the rule of King Hassan II. Fadel's novels *Qiṭṭ abyaḍ ǧamīl yasīru maʿī* (2011), *Ṭāʾir azraq nādir yuḥalliqu maʿī* (2013), and *Faraḥ* (2016) shed light on contested memories, such as political imprisonment, the Western Sahara conflict, and the construction of King Hassan II Mosque. These novels contribute to the collective memorialisation of this historical period by re-elaborating testimonial literature, developing the collective dimension through multiple narrators and fragmented time, and depicting the private resistance of female characters. In doing so, they expose several forms of violence across society and conceive of peace as something that must never be taken for granted but rather as something to be achieved through negotiation.

Keywords: contemporary Moroccan literature, testimonial literature, Youssef Fadel, Years of Lead, reconciliation process, violence

1. Introduction

إلى شهداء معتقلات الإبادة في تزمامارت، أكدز، قلعة مكونة، سكورة، مولاي الشريف، الكوربيس، الكومبليكس، دار المقري، الأحياء منهم والأموات.

To the martyrs of the extermination prison camps in Tazmamart, Agdz, Kalaat M'Gouna, Skoura, Moulay Chérif, Kourbis, the Complex, and Dar Moqri; those among them who are living and those who are dead[1].

The novel *Ṭā'ir azraq nādir yuḥalliqu ma'ī (A Rare Blue Bird Flies with Me)* by Youssef Fadel (Yūsuf Fāḍil) opens with the above dedication which condenses the complexity of dealing with the so-called Years of Lead (*sanawāt al-raṣāṣ*) in Moroccan public discourse to a few words. The terms *šuhadā'* (martyrs) and *mu'taqalāt al-ibādah* (extermination prison camps) are very precise but at the same time evoke inconceivable violence. The mention of several torture centres across the country indicates a collective dimension, whereas referring to both the victims and the survivors projects an act of memorialisation from the past to the future, thus involving civil society. In 1974–1975, Fadel himself was detained in Derb Moulay Chérif for eight months because of his writings, especially the collective play *Lguirra* (The War). His detention exemplifies the arbitrariness of state repression and the attempt to silence critical voices. Nevertheless, after this conflictual phase, Fadel pursued his literary career and is now an established novelist, playwright, and screenwriter.

Born in Casablanca in 1949, he devoted the first part of his career to drama. His play in the Moroccan dialect, *Ḥallāq darb al-fuqarā'* (The Barber of the Poor People's Neighbourhood, 1978) enjoyed great success in the theatre and was turned into a film by Mohamed Reggab in 1982[2]. Besides his collaboration with Reggab and other film directors, Fadel published several novels and achieved international recognition at the beginning of the 2000s. His novel *Ḥašīš* (Hashish[3]) won the Grand

1. Fāḍil 2011, p. 5; Fadel 2016b, Kindle position 20. The names of characters are provided in a simplified transliteration as they appear in the English translation; the names of places and public figures are spelt in accordance with their most common English rendition.
2. Jay 2005, pp. 185–188.
3. Fāḍil 2000.

Atlas Prize in 2001, and his loose trilogy on Morocco's recent history was translated into English, French, and partly into Italian. The first volume of this trilogy *Qiṭṭ abyaḍ ǧamīl yasīru maʿī* was translated into English as *A Beautiful White Cat Walks with Me*[4]. The story is told by two alternating first-person narrators: Hassan, an aspiring comedian from Marrakesh, and his father Balloute, the official king's jester. When Hassan is drafted into the army because of his sketches and fights in the Western Sahara conflict, his father does not try to save him but falls into disgrace as well. The second novel covers the same period by looking at forced disappearances during the Years of Lead: *Ṭāʾir azraq nādir yuḥalliqu maʿī*, translated into English as *A Rare Blue Bird Flies with Me*[5], was shortlisted for the International Prize of Arabic Fiction (IPAF) and awarded the Prix du Maroc du Livre in 2014. It follows Zina's odyssey in search of her husband Aziz who disappeared on their wedding night, never to come back; he is thrown into a dark prison cell from which he emerges after 18 years. Moving a decade forward, the last novel of the trilogy tackles a lesser-known issue, i.e., the building of King Hassan II Mosque in Casablanca, which was inaugurated in 1993. *Faraḥ* (literally, Joy), translated into English as *A Shimmering Red Fish Swims with Me*[6], follows the story of an entire neighbourhood that is repositioned on the city's outskirts to leave space for the construction of the grand mosque. The mosque's beauty clashes with the destroyed aspirations of ordinary people, such as Outhmane who works with his father as a woodcarver and Farah who dreams of becoming a singer. The novel also deals with migration to Europe and the Gulf, a topic that had already been tackled in *Ḥašīš*. The author's latest novel, *Ḥayāt al-farāšāt* (The Life of Butterflies), longlisted for the IPAF in 2021, further delves into contemporary Moroccan history with its account of the 1972 coup[7].

In his writings, Fadel portrays everyday life in the city and the countryside with realistic details while exploring the characters' inner world through an extensive use of interior monologue. This results in a poetic language that is interspersed with references to the local culture and

4. Fāḍil 2011; Fadel 2016a.
5. Fāḍil 2013; Fadel 2016b. This novel is the only one that has been translated into Italian as *Ogni volta che prendo il volo* (Fadel 2019b).
6. Fāḍil 2016; Fadel 2019a.
7. Fāḍil 2020.

experimentation with Moroccan Arabic as a literary language, especially in the dialogues[8]. As emerges from the novels' summaries, violence permeates these narratives: this trilogy deals with war, mass conscription, political detention, terror inflicted upon prisoners' families, forced extraction of contributions to build the mosque, domestic violence, and prostitution. Violence cuts across the private and the public sphere, leading to a violation of human integrity, even when it seems authorised by the state. As Guabli and Jarvis remark about the notion of violence, "The English (and French) word is linked etymologically to violation and rape, and its use in philosophical literature and political discourse [is] marked by an equivocation between violence that is authorised (state force, legitimated by rule of law, often called 'war') and violence that is not (that which threatens or moves outside the law, often called 'terror')[9]".

While there is much violence, it is worth exploring whether there is space for political and inner peace in this trilogy. This chapter examines Fadel's fictionalisation of the recent past to understand how fiction engages with the Moroccan reconciliation process and the collective memory of contested events. Besides exploring the interplay of testimonial literature and fictionalisation of the Years of Lead, which has already been investigated by recent scholarship, this contribution also tackles the literary memorialisation of the Western Sahara conflict and the mosque's construction within the broader reconciliation discourse. In particular, it examines how the trilogy's thematic and stylistic features shape peaceful coexistence as an ongoing process that is achieved through negotiation. It also identifies common narrative strategies and cross-references across the three novels.

The Years of Lead was a period of social and political repression that began at the same time as the country's independence in 1956 and intensified under King Hassan II (1961–1999). It was characterised by the violation of human rights, arbitrary detentions, and the disappearance of political opponents, especially during the 1960s and 1970s. While state repression affected the lives of many Moroccan families, the monarchy began to admit the truth only in the 1990s due to internal and international pressure. A reconciliation process thus started, including programs of

8. Aguadé 2013; Moestrup 2012.
9. El Guabli and Jarvis 2018, p. 3.

transitional justice, the publication of testimonial prison literature, public debates, and collective initiatives to keep the memory of this historical phase alive. The Years of Lead were not confined to political imprisonment in the notorious detention centres but rather were a collective experience affecting Moroccan society through a web of fear, authoritarian rule, and institutionalised corruption. El Guabli places Fadel's writings within the second wave of testimonial literature because of his ability to re-elaborate this collective experience:

> This second wave is characterised by creative writers' ownership of this collective past by using it to creatively address the wider and more ordinary aspects of the "years of lead". This second wave tasks itself with the daunting and risky mission of re-imagining a collective experience to speak to a history and a collective memory that are still institutionally unwelcome. The cruciality of this work of re-imagination lies in bringing into social memory the experience of state repression, disintegrated homes, and shattered lives due to disappearance. Many of the foundational testimonial books of the first wave of memoirs are out of print. Many more have not had a chance to be read widely, which limited their circulation in social memory. *Les Archives du Maroc*, the official institution created to organise archives as per the recommendation of the Equity and Reconciliation Commission, does not consider testimonial literature as something that should be saved for future generations. Consequently, literary re-imagination of "the years of lead" remains decisive for the circulation of these stories in society. Ultimately, creative writing is now using the most powerful aspects of lived experiences recounted in memoirs and media to craft fictional works that speak to the nation and not just to the direct survivors[10].

The next sections illustrate how Fadel belongs to this second wave by reimagining several layers of this collective experience and by exposing the violence of those years beyond prison. After giving an overview of the systematic use of political imprisonment and the subsequent reconciliation process in section 2, each of the next sections looks at one dimension

10. El Guabli 2018, p. 287. It is possible to classify Fadel's trilogy as a historical novel, but I prefer to place it under the second wave of testimonial literature because the historical references remain in the background while the private (hi)stories of the characters cover and testify about what happened to many people.

of this historical period (prison, war, the mosque) to explore the fictional representation of the pairing of violence/peace.

2. Testifying about the Past to Reconcile the Future

During the Years of Lead, arbitrary detention and forced disappearance were directed against several opponents of the monarchy such as leftists, members of students' and workers' unions, Sahrawis, Amazigh/Berber activists, feminists, and Islamists. Besides being subjected to the arbitrary administration of justice, the prisoners were inhumanly tortured. Among the demonstrations and strikes that were silenced with an excessive use of force, the public protests in Casablanca in March 1965 and 1981, student demonstrations and hunger strikes in prison are crystallised in the collective memory. The unsolved case of Mehdi Ben Barka, leader of the leftist opposition party who was exiled in France and disappeared in 1965, exemplifies the files that still cannot be closed[11].

In the 1970s, state repression intensified because of two failed coups aimed at overthrowing King Hassan II. On 10 July 1971, the military barged into Skhirat Palace, where the king was celebrating his birthday with local and international guests. The attack resulted in a bloodbath causing several casualties, but the king survived. On 16 August 1972, pilots from the Moroccan air force attacked the royal plane, which managed to land safely in Rabat. The suspected mastermind of the coup, General Oufkir, reportedly committed suicide. Until then, he had been the king's right hand and responsible for administering state repression. The fate of his widow and children remained unknown until 1991, when they were liberated because of international pressure after living in inhuman conditions for 18 years. The convicted soldiers from both coups were put on trial and initially jailed in civil prison, until 1973, when they were transferred to Tazmamart, a secret prison built in South-East Morocco where they were intended to die. There were 58 prisoners who entered Tazmamart and only 28 of them survived after 18 years.

Their liberation was made possible by Moroccan and international human rights institutions, who often leveraged the prisoners' messages

11. Pepicelli 2017, pp. 131–138; Soudi 2004.

that miraculously reached their families. Moreover, the international political scenario was changing, and the monarchy needed to renegotiate its authority in the national context. In 1990, Hassan II established the *Conseil consultatif des droits de l'homme* (CCDH, *al-Mağlis al-istišārī li-ḥuqūq al-insān*), later reformed as the *Conseil national des droits de l'homme* (CNDH, *al-Mağlis al-waṭanī li-ḥuqūq al-insān*)[12]. While the council was harshly criticised for its composition and dependence on the government, it launched some initiatives that included pecuniary compensation for the victims. Another attempt to enact a reconciliation process was made by King Muhammad VI as soon as he succeeded his father by establishing the *Instance d'arbitrage indépendante* (IAI, *Hay'at al-ta'wīḍ*) in 1999. This institution collected the claims of human rights violations and investigated them for four years, hearing 8,000 testimonies. Nevertheless, its work was met with criticism because pecuniary reparations were often perceived as blood money and granted the perpetrators blanket amnesty.

The limits of the IAI led to the establishment of an independent truth commission that operated from 2004 to 2005, known as the *Instance équité et réconciliation* (IER, *Hay'at al-inṣāf wa-l-muṣālaḥah*). Its role was to investigate claims of human rights violations and to provide recommendations to the government to implement these rights in the future. According to the final report, the commission examined 16,861 files granting financial compensation to 9,779 victims and their families (58% of the applicants) and provided additional reparations to those who had benefited from the earlier 1999 IAI[13]. Recent scholarship has praised this commission as a valid attempt to overcome this dark page in Moroccan history but does not deny its limits[14]. On the positive side, Morocco was the first Arab country to establish a truth commission, even without a change in regime, covering a period of 43 years (1956–1999). Besides written testimonies, public auditions were broadcast live on television. The final report was published in 2005 and is available online in Arabic, French, and English. On the negative side, torturers were granted impunity since their names are listed in the files but remain unspoken in public;

12. He also created the Ministry of Human Rights in 1993.
13. Slyomovics 2016, p. 15.
14. Menin 2016; Pepicelli 2017; Slyomovics 2016.

the monarchy's responsibility is not addressed; and several forms of pressures were exerted to silence further claims for justice, especially in unsolved cases of disappearance.

What remains untold in the national archives has been voiced through a collective process of memorialisation, including testimonial writings, interviews, documentaries, and marches called caravans. The first testimonies were published soon after the prisoners' liberation in the 1990s, starting with those who lived abroad, but it was only after Hassan II's death that many survivors enjoyed enough freedom to write about their experience. Slyomovic remarks that the IER chose the term *ifādah* (statement) to refer to indemnification petitions. After perusing the archives with the activist and former detainee Fatna El Bouih, Slyomovic notes that the files are hard to access, whereas El Bouih's published memoir still resonates in Morocco and abroad thanks to translation[15]. In this respect, official attempts to record the past (*ifādah*) are compared to the collective recalling of memories to fight imposed silence (*šahādah*):

> Indeed, the post-1999, post-Hassan II period became an era of research, public debates and testimonies, and publications in mass-circulation newspapers about the contingent truths about past histories of repression. The stories of past opposition to human rights violations were transformed and became transformative when narratives surrounding years of repression came to light. Such testimonies by surviving actors supported the quest for knowledge by the current generation of Moroccans about the dark periods of the past that live on in the present. Between any scholarly historical reconstruction of that past and the history of its retelling in the context of current Moroccan politics, it is *shahada* that embodies its two meanings of "to testify" as well as "to witness". *Shahada* narrates personal witness and puts it in a situation specific register. It calls out aloud and clearly the names of torturers and perpetrators. This is radically opposed to the act of giving testimony in the form of the *ifada*/statement that Morocco's commissioners sought[16].

15. El Bouih 2001; Dransfeldt Christensen 2018; Menin 2014; Orlando 2010. This memoir was translated into English as *Talk of Darkness* (El Bouih 2008) and into Italian as *Narrare il buio* (El Bouih 2004).
16. Slyomovics 2016, p. 18.

Fadel weaves these prison testimonies together and contributes to collective memorialisation through his fiction.

3. Weaving Testimonies from Prison Together

The characters and events of *Ṭāʾir azraq* are easily recognisable by the Moroccan reader, although no real name is mentioned and historical references are blurred in the stories of ordinary people. The author, who read prison memoirs and whose legitimacy as a political detainee cannot be doubted, weaves together many details taken from several accounts of his own generation.

This combination of recognisability and indeterminacy may be found in Aziz, the male protagonist and pilot stationed in the Kénitra aviation military base who takes part in the failed coup. One reason for his decision to participate in the military action lies in his love for flying, which can be read as a metaphor for freedom and the aspiration of improving one's social condition. Moreover, he sees his colonel as a new father figure. As further proof of how history and ordinary stories are intertwined in the novel, the coup is planned for the dawn after Aziz and Zina's wedding, thus turning the couple's big day into "our big day" and bonding the pilot and his colonel in a project for the whole nation.

Due to this reference to the coup, the reader should expect Aziz to be sent to Tazmamart. However, he is imprisoned in an undefined place, one of the *kasbahs* of Pasha El Glaoui in the Moroccan South whose kitchens were turned into prison cells. This undefined setting combines several elements taken from prison memoirs and fictionalised testimonies that can be traced through a genealogical reading. The references to the Tazmamart prison camp include the time span (18 years), the violence in the death factory from which prisoners are not expected to emerge alive, and the guards' brutality, which is exemplified by the practice of burying the dead in the courtyard without any religious burial rites[17]. Unlike other

17. El Guabli 2014; Elinson 2009; Hachad 2018; Moukhlis 2008; Sellman 2006. The study of prison memoirs and fictionalised accounts requires looking at the interplay of several languages in the Moroccan cultural field, an issue that is addressed in theoretical terms and with a focus on the Moroccan novel in Fernández Parrilla 2016 and Laachir 2016.

testimonial accounts describing collective survival strategies, such as storytelling and Quran recital, Aziz is the only survivor, and everything is seen from his individual perspective: his physical and psychological pain, cold, darkness, and the tricks he uses to keep track of the passing of time. Since there is no one else, the protagonist describes whatever surrounds him, focusing on the tiny animals that keep him company but are also very aggressive:

> Aziz – 10 p.m.
> 1
> TIME PASSED WHILE I WAS having a lot of fun watching life in the corridor. When I was in good health, I could move to the door. Life's moving from side to side a few steps from me. Cockroaches play. They move behind each other like a drunken train. Their long wings move in every direction like finely made radars. Near them are scorpions with tails erect, waiting to ambush them. The cockroaches dance around them, indifferent to their threatening weapons. Rats surprise them and they flee. Some are saved in the cracks while others spread their wings to land on the highest point on the wall. The rats that think they're playing, they too attack them, pouncing on them, biting, sinking their teeth into the flesh of some, producing horrible noises, and eating others. Then the snakes appear, so the rats surviving the massacre are now forced to flee. After a while, you don't know who's running after who. Who's hunting who and who's eating who[18].

This passage recalls Abdellatif Zrikem's testimony about Derb Moulay Chérif, which employs military metaphors to describe the torture inflicted by lice:

> I left her there and I went back to the Derb, getting used again and starting again the battle against the black hate spewing out of the guards' mouths… And the fire unleashed by their whips… And also the pain caused by armies of lice.
> In our intimate relation with lice, we learnt how to recognise the different species according to the degree of pain caused by their bites. Each species had its own pain intensity and speed. Each species had its way of attacking, its way of camouflaging among the hordes that

18. Fadel 2016b, Kindle position 167–173.

> slowly moved all together. They grazed without remission in our hair. The black fat ones advanced in neat rows like columns of tanks. Isolated units, greyish and solid, like heavy artillery, lurked around under the pubic hair. A light and fast division, with its specialised vehicles, was conducting a guerrilla war, moving in open fields: chest, belly, back, arms[19].

While the setting is unidentified, many details taken from other accounts are woven together to create the main character[20]. His first name links him to Aziz Binebine, the son of Hassan II's personal jester, who spent 18 years in Tazmamart. His experience was fictionalised in Tahar Ben Jelloun's novel *Cette aveuglante absence de lumière* (This Blinding Absence of Light) – causing a controversy about the legitimacy of this appropriation – and was told by the victim himself in his memoir *Tazmamort*[21]. Other references are very specific:

> The parallels between Fadel's character Aziz and Boujmâa Azendour in *Tazmamort* are crucial in knowing that there was a real person who defied his grandfather to go to school. The fact that Aziz was a victim of his love for airplanes also recalls the story of Allal Mouhage, a real Tazmamart victim who was passionate about his job and just happened to be on base while on vacation the day of the coup, which cost him his life in Tazmamart[22].

In this web of cross references, the animals of the prison camps become fully developed characters with human feelings who contribute to memorialising the inhuman experience of detention. Some prison memoirs mention that the convicts captured some birds until they realised that they were depriving other creatures of their freedom[23]. In particular, Tazmamart survivor Ahmed Marzouki mentions Faraj, the bird who talks to Aziz and accompanies him in his liberation in *Ṭāʾir azraq*. Besides Faraj, Fadel's novels are full of birds that are compared to the characters

19. Zrikem 2002, p. 20. Translation is mine.
20. El Guabli 2018, pp. 285–290.
21. Ben Jelloun 2001; Binebine 2009. For a comparison of memoirs and fiction about Tazmamart, see Hachad 2018, which provides further bibliographic references on the controversy over Ben Jelloun's novel.
22. El Guabli 2018, p. 289.
23. Marzouki 2001; Zrikem 2002.

(doves and seagulls in *Faraḥ*) or crushed, because of their fragility, in the flashbacks recalling some youthful memories.

Another emblematic character is the female dog Hinda. As reported in testimonial narratives, Hinda arrived in Tazmamart in 1982 when a wealthy French resident gave her to the prison director. She lived in bad conditions, like the prisoners, until she was taken away by a hunter. In addition to memoirs, the short story *La chienne de Tazmamart* by Abdelhak Serhane places Hinda in France and going to an analyst to face the trauma of her incarceration[24]. While the dog cannot come to terms with her past, the analyst starts barking and walking on all fours. As Hachad notes, "With its unexpected dialogue and reversal, *La Chienne* raises the question about the possibility of testimony in the face of extreme and abject violence, in part residing in the inability of the reader/listener – anyone on the outside – to fully comprehend the survivor's suffering. It is also an allegory of the impossibility to interpret testimonial narratives"[25]. A decade later, Fadel gives Hinda a voice in *Ṭāʾir azraq*: she is one of the seven narrators who saves Aziz and dreams of a better life like the other female characters.

Another dog with human thoughts and feelings is presented in *Faraḥ*. It is the pit bull Rihane, who follows the narrator Outhmane, reminding him of not having paid his share for the mosque. Through aggressiveness and later persuasion, the dog imposes his presence on the narrator's life until he achieves total identification with him[26]. Despite a certain bond between the two characters, Rihane is also vicious because he was a guard dog in a secret prison:

> One time, he takes me to an odd place – a tall, black, three-story building hidden among some high eucalyptus trees. He tells me, "There are hundreds of secret prisoners crammed inside these walls". I look up at the windows. Small open windows covered with steel bars that are hung with drying underwear. There isn't a window that doesn't have a woman's blouse or pants, or children's clothes. What strikes me about it is that entire families, including children, have been thrown behind these bars. Then he says, "These are the apartments

24. Serhane 2001.
25. Hachad 2016, p. 214.
26. Fadel 2019a, p. 98.

> for the guards' families. The cells are in the basement. The guards' families live above them. They can't get away from them, like birds that are unable to live far from the swamp. The prisoners are thrown into subterranean vaults. Dark halls that are dank from humidity and crawling with rats. They remain lying down day and night. Hands bound, blindfolded, forbidden to stand, sit, or speak". I wonder if they were imprisoned because they hadn't contributed their share to the building of the mosque. Rihane says, "Pretty much," and adds that he had guarded the gate in front of us for six months, before they transferred him following this depressing and disturbing visit[27].

Fadel's fictionalisation of political detention weaves together details that were taken from various accounts, thus giving a voice to those who were silenced and imagining alternative forms of communication. For instance, while animals were already mentioned in memoirs, Fadel gives them a personality of their own and uses them to insert a magical dimension into the narrative. Thus, the brutality of the detention is blurred by the poetic language and the magical atmosphere. Moreover, in this and the other novels of the trilogy, the collective dimension of violence is rendered through multiple narrators and fragmented time. The next section explores these narrative techniques in Fadel's memorialisation of the Western Sahara war in relation to patriarchal violence.

4. (Un)authorised violence: the Western Sahara conflict

While *Ṭā'ir azraq* focuses on political imprisonment, *Qiṭṭ abyaḍ* is one of the few fictional discussions on the Western Sahara conflict, a protracted confrontation for sovereignty between Morocco and the Polisario Front[28]. The latter was established in 1973 when Spain, having occupied this territory since 1884, started a decolonisation process under international pressure. In an attempt to recover the territories of Greater Morocco and regain unity after the failed coups, the monarchy decided to pressure Spain to withdraw: after deploying troops, on 31 October 1975, it launched the Green March, with 350,000 Moroccans crossing the southern border on 6 November 1975. When Spain withdrew on 14 November

27. Ibid., p. 99.
28. Correale et al. (eds) 2018; Ojeda Garcia et al. (eds) 2017; Mohsen-Finan 2008.

1975, the Madrid Accords divided the territory between Morocco and Mauritania, while Algeria was excluded. The Polisario Front established the Sahrawi Arab Democratic Republic (RASD) in February 1976, which was recognised by some countries but not admitted to the United Nations. When Mauritania withdrew in August 1979, the conflict with Morocco escalated: the guerrilla war conducted by the nationalist movement was countered by building security walls and sending troops, with a dramatic increase from 56,000 soldiers in 1974 to 141,000 in 1982. Meanwhile, much of the Western Sahara's local population left the region and tens of thousands settled in Polisario-administered camps in Tindouf, Algeria. Although the number of battle-related deaths decreased to the point of not qualifying this confrontation as a war or armed conflict, no solution has been found. In 1991, the UN announced a ceasefire and promised a referendum for or against independence that has never taken place.

The difficulty of defining this conflict and the current situation highlights the porous boundaries between authorised and unauthorised violence, especially when military intervention violates civil rights. Among the long-term consequences of this war, the internal crisis caused by high military expenditures and mass conscription, combined with economic stagnation in the 1980s, the economic exploitation of the Western Sahara's natural resources, and human rights violations on both sides of the border should be noted.

The impact of the war on society emerges in Fadel's fictional reconstruction in *Qiṭṭ abyaḍ*. An effective technique to represent this conflict consists in alternating multiple narrators who provide an account from the front line and from inside the palace[29]. The story is narrated in the first person alternatively by Hassan, an aspiring comedian from Marrakesh, and his father Balloute, the king's jester. When he was a street performer in Djemaa El-Fna, Balloute was sent to jail for a petty crime and was

29. The same technique is employed in the other two novels under scrutiny. In *Ṭā'ir azraq*, seven narrators alternate: Aziz, Zina, her sister Khatima, the prison's guards Baba Ali and Benghazi, Hinda, and the child Aziz. *Faraḥ* employs a recurrent pattern in each of the seven parts: the opening chapter is told in the third person from the perspective of Outhmane, a lonely man remembering the past, the central chapters are told in the first person by young Outhmane, and the last chapter is told in the first person by one of the other characters (Farah, Naima, Our Neighbor Kenza, Father, Mother, Suleiman, and Farah again).

saved by the king who was visiting the prison and laughed at his jokes[30]. As two professional entertainers, the narrators embody the conflict between comedy and power, freedom of expression and censorship. In fact, Hassan's sketches cause him to be drafted for military service, while his father is involved in a palace conspiracy planned by the hunchback Zerwal. These characters in this novel recall real individuals since they evoke the above-mentioned jester Mohammed Binebine (d. 2008) and his son who was sent to Tazmamart. The buffoon's delicate position was also fictionalised in *Le fou du roi* by his other son, Mahi Binebine[31].

Violence, emerging in the private and public spheres, allows Fadel to address the Western Sahara conflict, which is still a taboo topic in Moroccan society. "In addition to the volatile father-son relationship, the novel is probably the first to critically delve into the human and economic cost of the war in the Western Sahara. Mentally disturbed youth, low-spirited officers and unqualified personnel are both the cause and the consequence of a protracted war situation whose many victims have not yet told their stories"[32]. Hassan tells the story of his conscripts Brahim, Mohamed Ali, and Naafi to contrast the sacrifice of innocent young men with the ongoing struggle for power and widespread corruption: while they are sent to the front poorly equipped to fight an invisible enemy, the general exploits the war to elude the king's orders and increase his wealth. Moreover, he has absolute power over their lives, as demonstrated by the additional torture inflicted upon them by his whimsical daughter. The next passage summarises all these elements by narrating the absurd destiny of Naafi, who is shot in the leg while pissing on the wall of the fort:

> Naafi had not yet begun his state of delirium. The lights were still on in many parts of his brain, but his leg was shattered, and the pain had reached an intolerable level. No one was bold enough to remove the rag it was wrapped in. And what would be the use of removing it? We would find a leg like any of the other legs pierced by the bullets of an enemy whose whereabouts we didn't know, and whose distance from us we were unable to measure.

30. Djemaa El-Fna is the main square in the medina of Marrakesh. Traditional forms of entertainment take place there for the local people and tourists.
31. Binebine 2017.
32. El Guabli 2018, p. 285.

> When he's around, the general sometimes gives us the impression that he knows who the enemy is, but at other times he gives us an entirely different impression. In any case, he's now busy at his farm pressing olives. The general loves to see the oil flow between his fingers, but at times like this, when the enemy opens fire on us, we don't know how to respond to it because the general hasn't yet told us what to do.
> The enemy wears the same clothes as we do, they speak the same language, they sing the same songs, and they dream the same dreams that inspire all of us, but they aren't visible to us as we are to them[33].

The invisible enemy has more in common with the soldiers than what the rhetoric of war claims. This recognition of the Other is highlighted by the poetic description of the vast desert and its colours. While this humanising vision is an attempt to end an unfair war, the impact of militarisation on society is clearly visible throughout the trilogy. For example, Farah's father does not sleep well after returning from the Western Sahara with a missing leg[34]. He still believes that the only way to gain people's respect is by working in the army or having a connection with it. Nevertheless, this is not true for his eldest daughter: she married a low-ranking soldier who left her only after one year, sending her back to her paternal home with twins[35]. Instead, in *Ṭāʾir azraq*, the intimidating power of the army is a legacy of the French occupation that penetrated private spaces. In one scene, the sound of military boots scares the prostitutes[36]. In another, Aziz remembers that, when he was a child, they could not turn the light on in the evening unless his father was at home because he wore a uniform similar to the ones the French soldiers wore[37].

Since violence is legitimised in the public arena, it is also exerted by patriarchal authorities: all three novels stage conflictual father-son relations that are never peacefully resolved. In *Qiṭṭ abyaḍ*, after rejecting his son, the jester does not meet him until he is dying; in *Ṭāʾir azraq*, both Zina and Aziz come from a harsh background, with the latter sent to live with his uncle who forbids him to go to school; in *Faraḥ*, the father would

33. Fadel 2016a, p. 135.
34. Fadel 2019, p. 354.
35. Ibid., pp. 63–64.
36. Fadel 2016b, Kindle position 697.
37. Ibid., Kindle position 1658–1675.

like his two sons to continue his profession as a woodcarver and is disappointed when his elder son Suleiman migrates to the Gulf. Sometimes, fathers and sons communicate in a dreamlike dimension when one of them is dying or already dead but speaks as if he were alive. Moreover, the two generations have a different vision of love: while sons believe in romantic love, fathers think that women are created for their own pleasure and do not attribute any sanctity to marriage since they leave their families. Female characters are also victims of patriarchal oppression, but their fight for inner peace is depicted through fragmented time and poetic images, as is illustrated in the next section.

5. From the Time of Waiting to Joy

In the conflictual world portrayed by Fadel, female characters share the sufferings caused by the repressive regime with their male counterparts, but they also experience gender-based oppression. Among the victims of the dominant ideology is Zineb, Hassan's lover in *Qiṭṭ abyaḍ*, an aspiring singer who is manipulated by two married doctors supporting the Marxist ideology first and the Islamist one later. Although the doctors are represented as grotesque characters, they prevail and change her life. The resurgence of religious zeal is also criticised in *Faraḥ*, whose female characters pay the price for Abdullah, a male family member taking an extremist approach to religion[38]. Another form of oppression is caused by the precarious socioeconomic conditions in which female characters live, often because of their absent fathers: some are prostitutes and others suffer from mental instability. Nevertheless, not all female characters are innocent victims because they contribute to a system of widespread corruption[39].

38. Abdullah is the narrator's brother-in-law. When he becomes more religious, he stops working and providing for his family; he probably informs the police of the presence of Uncle Mustafa in the family house, which leads to his arrest; he is indirectly accused of sacrificing his children as a sort of compensation for building the mosque and takes his mentally ill sister-in-law as his second wife.
39. Interesting characters in this respect include the jester's second wife and his mother-in-law in *Qiṭṭ abyaḍ*, Aziz's sister in *Ṭā'ir azraq*, and Kenza in *Faraḥ*.

The realistic details on these women's conditions are combined with two techniques disrupting the mimetic approach, i.e., fragmented time and poetic images. Although these techniques are used repeatedly throughout the trilogy, it is worth exploring them in relation to female characters to examine how they negotiate a positive (possibly peaceful) resolution of public and private conflicts.

As regards time, the trilogy provides some precise references, such as the date of the coup in *Ṭāʾir azraq* and the passing of hours or days at the beginning of each chapter. Time is fragmented, however, through the accounts of multiple narrators and flashbacks evoking a dreamlike atmosphere. This is the case of Zina, who recalls her first attempts to find Aziz by combining realistic and magical details. In one of these attempts, she approaches the king during a street parade to submit her petition and is taken away by the security forces, but one might wonder if the account as such is plausible. While the king's presence in *Qiṭṭ abyaḍ* is very concrete due to the novel's setting at court, he features in dreamlike episodes in the other two novels: in *Ṭāʾir azraq*, an old sick king visits Aziz in his prison cell, and in *Faraḥ* the father dreams he meets the monarch in the forest and talks to him about their power to determine the children's future. Another strategy disrupting temporal linearity through dreamlike accounts consists in letting the dead speak. In all three novels there are characters making their voice heard from an implausible temporal point, thus partly confounding the reader about their destiny.

Besides fragmented time, *Ṭāʾir azraq* develops the temporal dimension to represent those who had to wait, especially women. In her article on forced disappearance, Menin defines waiting as an imposed temporality reiterating traumatic memories, which was a pervasive and subtle form of state violence during the Years of Lead. This kind of violence targeted the families of those who disappeared and the detainees, thus causing fear, silence, and lack of agency. Through individual and collective acts of resistance, the time of waiting was appropriated to break the imposed silence and claim justice[40].

In Fadel's novel, Zina goes through all the experiences described by Menin: she often receives false news, but still hopes to obtain a tiny piece of reliable information that might lead her to Aziz; she is monitored and

40. Menin 2016, especially pp. 82–83 and 97.

threatened by the security system; she only receives solidarity from her sister Khatima and feels isolated from her own family; she cannot move on because there is no corpse or death certificate. While mothers waiting for their children who have disappeared are usually praised as powerless victims and authoritative accusers of the system, this novel confirms that the whole family is involved in this personal and political trauma[41]. It is the liminal condition of waiting that makes Zina a complex character, since she becomes a full-grown woman despite her young age as soon as she loses her husband. While she fails to obtain official answers about Aziz, her resolve remains unshaken. She is an independent woman who travels across the country and develops a strong connection with other female characters who are bound by their maternal feelings. Zina, who had a miscarriage soon after her husband's disappearance, helps the wife of the prison guard give birth to her eighth daughter and takes the baby with her to save her from patriarchal violence. When Aziz comes home, the couple is reunited by a kiss they had promised each other 18 years before and by the little girl named Aziz, who was raised as their child although she was the child of one of the oppressors. In this scene of reconciliation, the little girl sees people running in the streets and asks her mother what is happening: the king has died.

While *Ṭāʾir azraq*'s epilogue is positive, *Farah*'s denouement is more ambiguous, and women's voices are heard through poetic images. This novel depicts the harsh socioeconomic conditions that many families were experiencing at the time of the grand mosque's construction. The main narrator, Outhmane, describes urban change and is haunted by the financial burden imposed on the citizens[42]. Though he expresses his disappointment, he is unable to take action against the governmental projects. These projects are embodied by the employee supervising the mosque's construction who manages the residents' displacement to the

41. Ibid., p. 89.
42. The site where the mosque is built used to be a swimming pool: Outhmane recalls his personal memories of swimming with his uncle and compares the drowned children to work-related fatalities on the construction site. The people were encouraged to make a financial contribution through ads in the newspapers and attested by a certificate on which the words: "His throne was on the water" were written in golden ink. For other contemporary Moroccan novels tackling urban change, see Viviani 2019.

new residential buildings in the periphery. Almost a grotesque figure, this employee is the spokesman of the authorities:

> The voice of the National Department of Electricity employee waxed almost poetic. "Electricity changes life. With electricity comes the refrigerator, then the radio, then television. Once you get used to electricity, your mentalities might change too, and your children's sensitive eyes won't strain in the candlelight as they study their nationally mandated lessons. The light will illuminate their young minds because electricity, as I explained before, changes lives…"[43]. This discourse is challenged by Outhmane's mother, who works hard to provide for her family (as evidenced by the sound of her sewing machine) and accepts displacement hoping for a better future. Nevertheless, she is aware of what she is losing in the city centre and expresses it through a popular song: "There's no city like Casablanca. 'The blanca, mon amour, I'll marry her without any magic allure…' I already miss it even though I've just left"[44].

Singing is also what pushed Farah from her small town to Casablanca to pursue a career. Although she encounters several obstacles on her way, the young protagonist is described in a poetic way by Outhmane, who falls in love with her: she wears colourful dresses and is compared to a bird with respect to her voice and fragility. However, her sensuality and passion for singing (especially singing in the mosque at night) leads to a disproportionate reaction when somebody throws acid in her face. After she dies and is floating on the ocean in a wooden box made by Outhmane, she praises singing as a way of overcoming the hardship of life and poetically becomes a cricket, hence confirming the magical representation of nature throughout the trilogy:

> Life is what it is. Neither short nor long. Tears of joy come to my eyes. […] Dawn. It's time to go. Slowly I rise up. A second soul takes the place of the first. A small, happy cricket's soul. That's right. Humans will turn into crickets when they die. Their lives dedicated to singing. The only pleasure that will remain. They'll sing all the time. With their legs and their wings and everything inside them.

43. Fadel 2019a, p. 144.
44. Ibid., p. 255.

> They will realize how much singing they have missed. Singing is life[45].

After several years, Outhmane also reconciles with his past and calls his newborn child Farah, even before he knows whether it is a boy or a girl.

6. Conclusion

Fadel's trilogy about Morocco's recent history does not feature recurring characters but employs similar narrative techniques, such as multiple narrators, interior monologues, fragmented time, dreamlike episodes, and the magical representation of nature. Besides these similarities, each novel develops its own different style: *Qiṭṭ abyaḍ* portrays the tragicomic unpredictability of life and targets the sociopolitical scenario by using sarcasm; *Ṭāʾir azraq* ties love and pain together while exploring the several meanings of the metaphor of flying viewed as freedom, social amelioration, and sexual desire; finally, *Faraḥ* depicts a young singer who is unable to fulfil her dreams but still sends a message of hope even in the face of tragedy.

Regarding the themes, each novel delves into one aspect of King Hassan II's reign to bring collective memories and remaining unwelcome truths to the surface: the Western Sahara conflict, political imprisonment during the Years of Lead, and the forced extraction of contributions to build the grand mosque in Casablanca. These events are explored in relation to their consequences on the lives of the ordinary people, thus shedding light on the subtle forms of violence that cause repeated trauma and impose silence. In this respect, Fadel's ouvre is a *šahādah* (testimony) to those accounts that did not surface in the course of the official reconciliation process, while fictionalisation allows Fadel to speak about painful memories and forms of oppression that would otherwise be harder to communicate. The analysis conducted in this chapter confirms that this trilogy belongs to the second wave of testimonial literature, since it appropriates the collective past and creatively elaborates it, focusing on the more ordinary and pervasive aspects of the Years of Lead. This appropriation is clear in Fadel's fictionalisation of political imprisonment, which

45. Fadel 2019a, p. 356.

combines recognisability and indeterminacy to shape the characters and the setting, merges many details about survival strategies and symbolic animals taken from the memoirs, and explores the time of waiting.

Although the Western Sahara conflict and the mosque's construction did not produce a similar amount of testimonial literature, they also belong to the reconciliation process. As is evident from the analysis, war fuels power struggles and corruption, while wearing out the conscripts. The representation of this kind of authorised violence is compared, through multiple narrators and the father-son relation, to patriarchal violence characterising society at large. The economic and emotional sacrifices required from the families seem to crush women who respond by becoming independent selves fighting for their dreams that are expressed through dreamlike narratives and poetic images. To sum up, the trilogy does not conceive of peace as something to be taken for granted but as a collective confrontation with the authorities in which individual characters also try to find inner peace and fulfil their endeavours. This introspective dimension turns individual stories into collective claims for justice.

While prison literature has been extensively examined, the memorialisation of the Western Sahara conflict and the mosque's construction in cultural productions should be further explored. Moreover, Fadel's latest novel goes back to the 1972 coup and might provide further insight about the reconciliation process. The study of Fadel's literary output could enrich some current research trends, such as the fictional representation of urban change and the resurgence of the historical novel in Moroccan fiction. In more general terms, literature written after the Years of Lead could be related to the post-civil war period in Lebanon and hopefully other contexts[46], such as that of Tunisia, which has recently started a process of transitional justice.

References

Aguadé, J. (2013), *Des romans diglossiques: le cas de Youssef Fadel*, in M. Benítez Fernández et al. (eds), *Évolution des pratiques et représentations langagières dans le Maroc du XXIe siècle*, 2 vols, L'Harmattan, Paris, vol. 1, pp. 207–220.

46. Hegasy et al. (eds) 2018.

Bartuli, E. (ed.) (2004), *Sole nero: Anni di piombo in Marocco*, Mesogea, Messina.
Ben Jelloun, T. (2001), *Cette aveuglante absence de lumière*, Seuil, Paris.
Binebine, A. (2009), *Tazmamort: Dix-huit ans dans le bagne de Hassan II*, Denoël, Paris.
Binebine, M. (2017), *Le fou du roi*, Stock, Paris.
Correale, F., Boulay, S. (eds) (2018), *Sahara Occidental: Conflit oublié, population en mouvement*, Presse Universitaires François-Rabelais, Tours.
Dransfeldt Christensen, T. (2018), *Narrating the Unnarratable: The Role of Literary Memory in Moroccan Testimonial Writing. Ḥadīth al-ʿatmah by Fāṭnah al-Bīh*, in Allen, R. et al. (eds), *New Geographies: Texts and Contexts in Modern Arabic Literature*, Ediciones Universidad Autónoma de Madrid, Madrid, pp. 237–250.
El Bouih, F. (2001), *Ḥadīṯ al-ʿatamah*, Dār al-Finnik li-l-Našr, al-Dār al-Bayḍāʾ.
El Bouih, F. (2004), *Narrare il buio*, trans. Paola Gandolfi, in E. Bartuli (ed.), *Sole nero: Anni di piombo in Marocco*, Mesogea, Messina, pp. 27–140.
El Bouih, F. (2008), *Talk of Darkness*, trans. Mustapha Kamal and Susan Slyomovics, University of Texas Press, Austin.
El Guabli, B. (2014), *The 'Hidden Transcript' of Resistance in Moroccan Tazmamart Prison Writings*, in "Arab Studies Journal", 22, 1 (Spring), pp. 170–207.
El Guabli, B. (2018), *Youssef Fadel's Re-Imagination(s) of Moroccan Testimonial Literature: A Book Review Essay*, in "The Journal of North African Studies", 23, 1–2 Special Issue: Violence and the Politics of Aesthetics: A Postcolonial Maghreb Without Borders, pp. 282–291. https://doi.org/10.1080/13629387.2017.1366290
El Guabli, B., Jarvis, J. (2018), *Violence and the Politics of Aesthetics: A Postcolonial Maghreb without Borders*, in "The Journal of North African Studies", 23, 1–2 Special Issue: Violence and the Politics of Aesthetics: A Postcolonial Maghreb Without Borders, pp. 1–12. https://doi.org/10.1080/13629387.2018.1400233
Elinson, A. (2009), *Opening the Circle: Storyteller and Audience in Moroccan Prison Literature*, in "Middle Eastern Literatures", 12, 3, pp. 289–303. https://doi.org/10.1080/14752620903302376
Fadel, Y. (2016a), *A Beautiful White Cat Walks with Me*, trans. Alexander Elinson, Hoopoe, Cairo and New York.
Fadel, Y. (2016b), *A Rare Blue Bird Flies with Me*, trans. Jonathan Smolin, Hoopoe, Cairo and New York. Kindle edition.
Fadel, Y. (2019a), *A Shimmering Red Fish Swims with Me*, trans. Alexander Elinson, Hoopoe, Cairo and New York. Kindle edition.
Fadel, Y. (2019b), *Ogni volta che prendo il volo*, trans. Cristina Dozio, Francesco Brioschi Editore, Milan.

Fādil, Y. (2000), *Ḥašīš*, Dār al-Finnik li-l-Našr, Casablanca.
Fādil, Y. (2011), *Qiṭṭ abyaḍ ğamīl yasīru maʿī*, Dār al-Ādāb, Beirut.
Fādil, Y. (2013), *Ṭāʾir azraq nādir yuḥalliqu maʿī*, Dār al-Ādāb, Beirut.
Fādil, Y. (2016), *Faraḥ*, Dār al-Ādāb, Beirut.
Fādil, Y. (2020), *Ḥayāt al-farāšāt*, Manšūrāt al-Mutawassiṭ, Milan.
Fernández Parrilla, G. (2016), *The Novel in Morocco as Mirror of a Changing Society*, in "Contemporary French and Francophone Studies", 20, 1, pp. 18–26. https://doi.org/10.1080/17409292.2016.1120547
Hachad, N. (2018), *Narrating Tazmamart: Visceral Contestations of Morocco's Transitional Justice and Democracy*, in "The Journal of North African Studies", 23, 1–2 Special Issue: Violence and the Politics of Aesthetics: A Postcolonial Maghreb Without Borders, pp. 208–224. https://doi.org/10.1080/13629387.2018.1400775
Hegasy, S., Nikro, S. (2018) (eds), *The Social Life of Memory: Violence, Trauma and Testimony in Lebanon and Morocco*, Palgrave Macmillan, New York.
Jay, S. (2005), *Dictionnaire des écrivains marocains*, Éditions Paris-Méditerranée, Paris.
Laachir, K. (2016), *The Aesthetics and Politics of "Reading Together" Moroccan Novels in Arabic and French*, in "The Journal of North African Studies", 21, 1 The Aesthetics and Politics of Contemporary Cultural Production in Morocco, pp. 22–36. https://doi.org/10.1080/13629387.2015.1084098
Marzouki, A. (2001), *Tazmamart: cellule 10*, Editions Paris-Méditerranée, Paris.
Menin, L. (2014), *Rewriting the World: Gendered Violence, the Political Imagination and Memoirs from the "Years of Lead" in Morocco*, in "International Journal of Conflict and Violence", 8, 1, pp. 45–60, available at: https://www.ijcv.org/index.php/ijcv/article/view/3044 (last accessed 01 March 2021).
Menin, L. (2016), *'Scomparsi (mkhtafyin)': violenza, attesa e letteratura di testimonianza nelle sparizioni forzate nel Marocco degli 'anni di piombo'*, in "Antropologia", 3, 2, pp. 81–100, available at: https://www.ledijournals.com/ojs/index.php/antropologia/article/view/753/718 (last accessed 01 March 2021).
Moestrup, E. (2012), *Diglossia and the Ideology of Language: The Use of the Vernacular in a Work by Youssef Fadel*, in "Orientalia Suecana", 61 (Supplement), pp. 139–151.
Mohsen-Finan, Kh. (2008), *Trente ans de conflit au Sahara occidental*, in P. Gandolfi (ed.), *Le Maroc aujourd'hui*, Quaderni Merifor, Casa Editrice Il Ponte, Bologna, pp. 62–74.
Moukhlis, S. (2008), *The Forgotten Face of Postcoloniality: Moroccan Prison Narratives, Human Rights, and the Politics of Resistance*, in "Journal of Arabic Literature", 39, 3, pp. 347–376. https://doi.org/10.1163/157006408X377174

Ojeda Garcia, R., Fernández-Molina, I., Veguilla, V. (eds) (2017), *Global, Regional and Local Dimensions of Western Sahara's Protracted Decolonization: When a Conflict Gets Old*, Palgrave Macmillan, New York.
Orlando, V. (2010), *Feminine Spaces and Places in the Dark Recesses of Morocco's Past: The Prison Testimonials in Poetry and Prose of Saïda Menebhi and Fatna El Bouih*, in "Journal of North African Studies", 15, 3, pp. 273–288. https://doi.org/10.1080/13629380902745884
Pepicelli, R. (2017), *Memorie degli 'anni di piombo' e percorsi della giustizia transizionale in Marocco*: Storia dell'Instance équité et réconciliation (Hay'at al-Inṣāf wa'l-Muṣālaḥa), in A. M. Di Tolla (ed.), *Percorsi di transizione democratica e politiche di riconciliazione in Nord Africa*, Editoriale Scientifica, Naples, pp. 134–178.
Saoudi, N. (2004), *Il Marocco degli anni di piombo*, in E. Bartuli (ed.), *Sole nero: Anni di piombo in Marocco*, Mesogea, Messina, pp. 261–289.
Sellman, J. (2006), *Memoirs from Tazmamart: Writing Strategies and Alternative Frameworks of Judgment*, in "The Journal of the Midwest Modern Language Association", 39, 2 (Fall), pp. 71–92. https://doi.org/10.2307/20464188
Serhane, A. (2001), *La chienne de Tazmamart*, Editions Paris-Méditerranée, Paris.
Synthèse du rapport final (2006), Royaume du Maroc, Instance Equité et Réconciliation, Rabat.
Slyomovics, S. (2016), *The Moroccan Equity and Reconciliation Commission: The Promises of a Human Rights Archive*, in "Arab Studies Journal", XXIV, 1, pp. 10–41.
Viviani, P. (2019), *What Does Fiction Tell us about Morocco Today? Moroccan Novels Shortlisted at IPAF*, in S. Guth, T. Pepe (eds), *Arabic Literature in a Posthuman World: Proceedings of the 12th Conference of the European Association for Modern Arabic Literature (EURAMAL), May 2016, Oslo*, Harrassowitz Verlag, Wiesbaden, pp. 269–285.
Zrikem, A. (2002), *Riqqat al-ṣaḫr*, self-published, Rabat.
Zrikem, A. (2004), *Com'è dolce la roccia*, trans. Letizia Osti, in E. Bartuli (ed.), *Sole nero: Anni di piombo in Marocco*, Mesogea, Messina, pp. 141–213.

Cristina Dozio is Assistant Professor of Arabic Language and Literature at Università degli Studi di Milano, Italy. Her research interests are modern and contemporary Arabic literature, satire, urban representation, and literary translation. Her book on literary humour in Egyptian fiction is *Laugh like an Egyptian* (De Gruyter Mouton 2021). She translates Arabic fiction into Italian.

Part 3

Practices of Mediation

Chapter 9

Lā tuṣāliḥ in the *Sīrat al-Zīr Sālim*: A Hymn to a Long-Term Peace

Daniela Potenza

Abstract

The slogan "*lā tuṣāliḥ*" (do not reconcile!) that has spread throughout various town squares during the Arab revolts in the last decade is derived from the epic legend of *Sīrat al-Zīr Sālim al-Muhalhil*. Its protagonist is a determined pre-Islamic warrior who waged a forty-year war against his cousins. Following the fatal wounding of his brother King Kulayb by a cousin, Zīr received a poem written by Kulayb imploring him to refrain from reconciling with his cousin. While it may appear that war and vengeance are the dominant themes of the narrative (referred to as *ḥarb al-Basūs*, War of al-Basūs), this chapter concentrates on the distant reasons for the conflict, depictions of peaceful life and multiple efforts for mediation, emphasising how Zīr's story promotes the importance of peace even while acknowledging that, at times, the only way to secure long-term peace is by not reconciling.

Keywords: *Sīrat al-Zīr Sālim al-Muhalhil*, mediation, reconciliation, street art, popular culture

1. Introduction

In 1970, when the journalist Richard Carleton asked Ġassān Kanafānī (1936–1972) in an interview why his organisation did not engage in peace talks with the Israelis, the writer and spokesman of the Popular Front for the Liberation of Palestine replied: "Talking with whom? [...] This is a kind of conversation between the sword and the neck, you mean"[1]. With this metaphor, Kanafānī highlighted that, under certain circumstances, the possibility of (re)conciliation between two parties simply cannot exist. By saying that, it does not mean that Kanafānī wanted war. Instead, he aimed for a stable peace that, according to him, could not be realised between Palestinians and Israelis, the occupied and the occupiers, so that conflict was compulsory[2].

Similarly, the slogan *lā tuṣāliḥ* (do not reconcile), which spread in the last ten years through many town squares of the Arab revolts and is often written under the pictures of Palestinian martyrs shown during demonstrations, invites people not to reconcile and to look instead for a rebalancing of powers that can be attained only through combat[3]. Despite its local and contemporary agency, the command *lā tuṣāliḥ* originates from the legend of *al-Zīr Sālim al-Muhalhil*[4] and became famous during the 1970s thanks to Amal Dunqul's poem bearing the same title[5]. The

1. The interview is available on YouTube: https://www.youtube.com/watch?v=3h_drCmG2iM, minutes 4'-4'30" (last accessed 10/08/2022).
2. Ibid., until the end of the video.
3. I want to express my gratitude to Atef Botros who kindly read this article and engaged with me in a discussion that improved this analysis of the *Sīrat al-Zīr Sālim al-Muhalhil* from the perspective of the dialectics of peace.
4. The epic legend on the War of al-Basūs is known for its resolute pre-Islamic warrior, Zīr, who led a forty-year war against his cousins. His brother, King Kulayb, had been run through with a spear by a cousin. Before dying, however, he wrote a poem to Zīr , using his blood as ink, repeatedly asking him not to reconcile. Only in recent years has the *Sīrat al-Zīr Sālim al-Muhalhil* received proper attention from scholars. Among the first who studied the *Sīrat al-Zīr Sālim* are Giovanni Canova and Jaroslav Oliverius (see the References list). Marguerite Gavillet Matar has largely contributed to the study of the *Sīrat al-Zīr Sālim* by editing a manuscript, translating it into French, and classifying the different manuscripts of the *Sīrah* according to the region of their origin and the tradition they belong to (poetic, storytellers' or mixed) (Gavillet Matar 2005, but also 1997 and 2003). Further studies and perspectives are suggested in Potenza 2020a. Weipert (2021) briefly explains the differences between the poet al-Muhalhil, often considered the first Arab poet, and the protagonist of the *Sīrah*. Heath (1984) suggests approaching the *Sīrah* through literary criticism or folklore methodology, as Canova (1985) does.
5. *Lā tuṣāliḥ* (1976) is drawn from Dunqul's first anthology *al-Bukāʾ bayna yaday Zarqāʾ al-Yamāmah* (An Elegy to Zarqāʾ al-Yamāmah), published by Dār al-Adāb in Beirut in 1969. Yamāmah is the name of Kulayb's daughter.

poem was a critique of the Egyptian regime, occasioned, as the date of its composition (13 June 1967) confirms, by the military defeat of 5 June 1967[6].

Al-Zīr Sālim's adventures were originally part of the oral tradition and, indeed, several versions of this story exist in the Middle East, presenting different plots. Variations in the story can be more or less evident in epic literature, as well as variations in length, style, means of transmission (oral, written or mixed), region of transmission, and proportions of poetry and prose[7].

The text I analyse here was published in 1950 in Egypt as *Qiṣṣat al-Zīr Sālim Abū Laylà al-Muhalhil* (al-Ǧumhūriyyah edition)[8]. Together with al-Ḫuṣūṣī edition from the same period and only slightly different, this text largely reflects the pan-Arab ideology of the 1950s, especially in the language that was modified to meet the standards of Modern Standard Arabic, but it also respects the *Sīrah* as a part of the Arab *turāṯ* (heritage) that must be promoted to affirm a pan-Arab identity. This edition was thus printed to spread the *Sīrah* in a time when it was no longer commonly recited[9]. I have chosen to study this specific version of the *Sīrah* for many reasons. The first reason is that it was intended to be a popular version and to maintain the memory of the *Sīrah*. Therefore, this version does not drastically modify the plot. In other words, like the other printed editions emerging over several manuscripts, it is "the tip of the iceberg"

6. Radwan 2014, p. 218.
7. Gavillet Matar (2005) provides the plot of the text she translated and also classifies the existing recensions. Lyons (1995) gives an account of the main recensions, highlighting common features and differences in the story. In his accounts, there is no mention of mediation processes.
8. *Qiṣṣah* means "story", while a *sīrah* here meant as a *sīrah ša'biyyah* ("popular *sīrah*"), is the modern Arabic designation for Arabic heroic narratives. It was not considered a literary genre until the 1930s, when scholars began to define it. See Potenza 2020b, pp. 151–158.
9. According to Marguerite Gavillet Matar's classification, this text can be included in a "semi-savant" tradition as it draws from a list of narrative sayings common to all popular epics. At the same time, it includes some episodes known only from classical sources that do not exist in other popular versions. The language of the prose is close to literary language and contains some words from dialect (2005, p. 46). The language of this edition is the result of a compromise between the original language of the oral tradition and some "corrective" adjustments made by the editors.

of the *Sīrat al-Zīr Sālim*[10]. As a consequence, it was a point of reference for many readers and artists who were inspired by it. And thus it can also be considered the final stage of the *Sīrat al-Zīr Sālim*[11].

As a matter of fact, over the past century, al-Zīr Sālim's adventures have been rewritten, adapted, and reshaped in genres other than the *Sīrah*, such as novels, short stories, poems, theatrical plays, and a famous television series. All of them reinterpret the *Sīrah* and in many cases they are even more popular than the *Sīrah* itself. I can mention, for instance, the success of the television series *al-Zīr Sālim Abū Laylà al-Muhalhil* (2000) produced by Syrian Art Production International. On YouTube alone, its episodes have been viewed millions of times and in 1998 its author, Mamdūḥ ʿAdwān (1941–2004), wrote a critical commentary on the work which was reprinted in 2015. In 1967, the Egyptian playwright Alfred Farağ (1929–2005) wrote *al-Zīr Sālim*, a play in three acts about justice, power, and governance that was produced in the same year by the National Theatre in Cairo (and again in 1991). More recent plays are *al-Zīr Sālim wa-l-duktūr Fāwst* (al-Zīr Sālim and Dr. Faust, 2009) by Šakīb Ḫūrī (b. 1932), and *al-Zīr Hāmlit* (al-Zīr Hamlet), in French, text and direction by Ramzī Šuqayr (b. 1971), staged at Le Théâtre de Belleville (Paris) in March 2016.

The rewritings of the *Sīrah*, instead of the *Sīrah* itself, are often the source of inspiration for further uses of the story of al-Zīr Sālim. For instance, in one of the first stencil graffiti works in Cairo, dating presumably to the beginning of June 2011, a verse from Dunqul's poem *Lā tuṣāliḥ* was written on the front of the Egyptian Ministry of the Interior, under the portrait of the activist and blogger Ḫālid Saʿīd, who was tortured and murdered in 2010 by the police in Alexandria:

10. Gavillet Matar 1997, p. 165. Gavillet Matar well demonstrates how the manuscripts, especially those from a mixed oral and written traditions, reveal themselves to be richer than printed editions in content and style. Indeed, a study of the piece in a broader perspective that considers different versions of the *Sīrat al-Zīr Sālim* would doubtlessly be fruitful, as each version of the *Sīrah* mirrors some aspects of the society in which it was fixed. But this is not the aim of this chapter.
11. The practice of having professionals recite the *Sīrah* to a public audience is certainly less common today than in the past, but it still exists. In Luxor, for instance, at least until the 1980s, storytellers would chant their own versions of the *Sīrah*, as Canova's transcriptions show. These are non-published documents indicated as Māzin, S. (1980) and Māzin, Y. (1980) in the References list.

هل يصير دمي بين عينيك ماءً؟ / أتنسى ردائي الملطَّخ بالدماء...[12]

Would my blood turn into water between your eyes? / Would you forget my clothes stained with blood...[13]

Focusing on the first part of the *Sīrat al-Zīr Salim*, and especially on some episodes of it that critics have disregarded, this chapter provides some reflections on the topic of peace, highlighting how remote the causes of the war are, how happy life is in peacetime, as opposed to the suffering during war, how many mediation efforts are made to avoid war, and how Kulayb reaches a critical moment when he can no longer tolerate any conciliation. In other terms, this chapter explores the context of Kulayb's command in the printed version of the *Sīrat al-Zīr Salim* to highlight, that, in this text peace is a precious gift and the refusal of conciliation comes as the extreme solution aiming at long-term peace.

Bearing in mind Gérard Genette's studies on intertextuality as well as Umberto Eco's idea of the reader's encyclopaedia, namely, his or her possibilities of filling in the gaps in a text through their knowledge, including that of other texts[14], I attempt to link the message of the printed version of the *Sīrah* to a manuscript of the *Sīrah*[15] and its revivals in Dunqul's poem and recent slogans and graffiti. Using Genette's terms, I refer to al-Ǧumhūriyyah edition as the "hypertext", while the manuscript studied by Gavillet Matar (2005) will be referred to as the "hypotext"[16]. Indeed, as Canova and Gavillet Matar suggest, the printed version can be considered a transformed version of the manuscript[17]. Final remarks will show whether, in their brevity, the recent uses of Kulayb's command retain any traces of the importance of peace and whether the impossibility of conciliation is the extreme solution or not.

12. Dunqul 1987, p. 325. The last two words are added in the graffiti text, but they do not exist in the original poem where it is clear from the previous verses that the clothes are stained "with blood".
13. All translations from Arabic are mine.
14. Eco 1979.
15. The manuscript studied here is the text that Gavillet Matar 2005 edited, translated, and annotated. She called it "We 822-6", from the Wetzstein collection.
16. Genette 1982, p. 13.
17. Canova 1985, p. 115; Gavillet Matar 2005, vol. 1, p. 132.

2. Remote Causes of the War: A Necessary Murder

According to the *Sīrat al-Zīr Sālim* (al-Ǧumhūriyyah edition), the reasons for Ǧassās' murder of Kulayb are to be found twenty years earlier, when the Yemeni King Tubbaʿ invades the territories of the Banū Qays, ruled by King Rabīʿah together with his brother, Murrah. Tubbaʿ kills Rabīʿah and expects to marry Ǧalīlah, Murrah's daughter, who is betrothed to Rabīʿah's son, Kulayb. Helped by Ǧalīlah, his brothers and cousins – including Ǧassās – Kulayb kills Tubbaʿ and thus avenges his father. Once the usurper is killed, peace returns for twenty years, until old Suʿād, Tubbaʿ's sister, comes to avenge her brother. Pushed by Suʿād, Ǧassās – Ǧalīlah's brother – kills Kulayb. Before dying, Kulayb invokes his brother Sālim's vengeance, repeating the famous *lā tuṣāliḥ*.

If Suʿād's fabrications can be justified by the law of vengeance – and indeed, as we will see, she is not punished for her misleading behaviour – Tubbaʿ has no defence because he acts only for his own benefit. First, he is moved by jealousy since he asks his vizier if there are any kings more powerful than him, and when the vizier answers that Rabīʿah is stronger, he becomes angry, gathers his huge army, and invades Rabīʿah's kingdom just to prove that he can do that. When Rabīʿah and Murrah try to curry favour with Tubbaʿ by offering him some gifts, the latter refuses because he wants Rabīʿah killed. Indeed, he orders his soldiers to capture Rabīʿah and slaughter him. Thus, because Tubbaʿ defeats the valiant king of the Qays not in a duel but with the help of his soldiers, he proves himself to be a coward.

In the printed version of the *Sīrah*, Tubbaʿ's arrogance is measureless. He demands that Ǧalīlah, Murrah's daughter, be married to him even if she is betrothed to her cousin Kulayb. Because of that, her father does not agree to his demand. Tubbaʿ is not even able to understand that Ǧalīlah only pretends to seduce him so that Kulayb can kill him. Indeed, he is often drunk, a condition that is seen as generally negative in the printed edition of the *Sīrah*. When Tubbaʿ recognises Kulayb, he is terrified ("his heart stopped for fear")[18]. In a face-to-face confrontation, Tubbaʿ cannot succeed, and he begs Kulayb not to kill him. He asks for mercy, but Kulayb answers that he must kill him because he needs to avenge his

18. *Qiṣṣat al-Zīr Sālim* 1950, p. 28.

father. Tubbaʿ asks for mercy again in a poem in which he predicts Qays' end. Kulayb answers that he cannot abstain from cutting off his head as he is a usurper and repeats that he must decapitate him (*la budda min qaṭʿ rāʾsika*[19]). Facing the brave hero, Tubbaʿ appears to be even more despicable. While Kulayb explains to him why he must kill him and in turn asks Tubbaʿ why he killed his father, Tubbaʿ does not answer but asks for mercy for a third time. Once again, Kulayb's reply is neat. In a moment of climactic clarity, he answers "I have to kill you (*la budda min qatlika*) with the edge of the knife so that people can rest from your evil"[20] and then cuts off his head.

The printed version of the *Sīrah* underscores that Tubbaʿ is an antihero. He is jealous, a coward, ruthless, arrogant, and a drunk. Even those who came with him are happy that he is dead and that they can now serve Kulayb instead[21]. Kulayb explains to one of Tubbaʿ's cousins who comes to avenge him that he killed Tubbaʿ because it was necessary given his behaviour[22], as he had warned Tubbaʿ himself many times before killing him. As we will see, the negative image of Tubbaʿ develops in opposition to Kulayb, who appears as an absolute hero. In some manuscript versions, the characters from Yemen are treated positively, according to the historical conditions and geographical positions where these versions developed[23]. In such versions, Tubbaʿ is not a drunk and wants to marry Ǧalīlah because she fascinates him to the point that he is not fully rational when he speaks to her (he admits repeatedly that he is drunk because of her and not because of wine)[24]. In these versions, only once does Kulayb say that he has to kill Tubbaʿ, but his reason is that he needs to take revenge[25].

This aspect of Tubbaʿ's murder helps us frame Kulayb's order. At this point of the story, in the hypotext, Kulayb's reaction fits the practice of retaliation, which is not extraordinary in the context in which the *Sīrah* is set. The innovations introduced in the hypertext, however, insist that Kulayb is killing a person who deserves it because of his bad actions

19. Ibid., pp. 21–22.
20. Ibid., p. 22.
21. Ibid., p. 23.
22. Ibid., p. 24.
23. Gavillet Matar 2005, vol. 1, pp. 37–38.
24. Gavillet Matar 2005, vol. 2, pp. 53–58.
25. Ibid., p. 64.

and intentions, not just because he has killed and so he must be killed in turn. The hypertext reflects new ideas of justice, of bad and good, where vengeance loses its importance. In the new emended version of the *Sīrah*, Tubbaʿ's murder is even more necessary.

3. Happy Life in Peace

The consequences of Tubbaʿ's necessary murder will become manifest twenty years later. With the usurper's death, peace returns with happiness as a result. First, Ǧalīlah and Kulayb can finally marry each other[26]. This wedding is not described in detail. Right after the opening of the *Sīrah*, however, marriage is celebrated and is depicted as the epitome of good living. In the first poem of the *Sīrah*, Murrah asks his brother Rabīʿah to have Ḍibāʿ – the latter's daughter – marry his son Hammām. Rabīʿah is happy to accept. The wedding brings great joy: for ten days, music, food and beverages abound amongst the numerous guests, then the bridal procession joins Hammām, and that was "a great night, nobody had ever heard of such a night in ancient times"[27].

Regarding the marriage between Kulayb and Ǧalīlah, the *Sīrah* emphasises the rich palace that Kulayb constructed for his wife at her request. The palace is one of the most magnificent structures, embellished with a garden that accommodates a variety of plant species. The palace's builder had been purposely invited for this task because his specialty was beautiful palaces[28]. A bit further on, the *Sīrah* insists on this garden, which was especially beautiful, describing it as a paradise (*firdaws*), with all kinds of trees, fruits, flowers, and flowing water[29], remarking that it was a source of joy for Kulayb. The storyteller adds that the garden was paradisiac, one of the greatest parks (*muntazah*) on earth and that Kulayb did not let anybody in, apart from himself and his sons[30]. The focus on the beautiful garden highlights the splendour of the Qays in peacetime, but it also points out how much Kulayb cared for it. Not only does this

26. *Qiṣṣat al-Zīr Sālim* 1950, p. 23.
27. Ibid., p. 3.
28. Ibid., p. 23.
29. Ibid., p. 26.
30. Ibid., p. 42.

detailed description in the manuscript versions lead critics to see Kulayb as a symbol of the Bedouins living a settled life[31], but it is also important for understanding Kulayb's reaction when he sees a camel destroying it, as related in the next section of this chapter.

The *Sīrah* also highlights that Murrah's and Rabīʿah's sons constitute a cohesive union. Seeing Kulayb's force, Murrah asks him if he can move with his people to his land and Kulayb replies that the country belongs to them all (*al-bilād bilādunā*)[32]. Marriages between cousins are described as blessed unions: more than once the storyteller says that Hammām loved Ḍibāʿ and Kulayb loved Ǧalīlah out of a great love. Before the war, the couples lived happily and had children. Even deeper is the love between brothers. Kulayb has many brothers; they are all handsome and strong and love one another, but his relationship with his younger brother Zīr is special. Even if Zīr drinks day and night and Kulayb disapproves of that, when Zīr tells Kulayb that he is happy with his life, his brother smiles and leaves him to his affairs[33]. In time of war, such relationships start assuming a tragic dimension, as when Ḍibāʿ risks her life to save Zīr. Likewise, descriptions of killings take the place of marriages and pleasant life. Intimate situations of suffering because of the loss of a close relative give voice to the pain of the war and its sacrifices reach a climax in Ḍibāʿ's cry at the death of her two sons killed by her brother – in contrast to their happy life in peacetime. The hypertext agrees with the hypotext in the suffering due to the war. The moments of joy occur only during peacetime and are merely pauses in the narration of war and conflict that pervades the tale.

4. Mediation: Reason versus Impulse

Peace lasts for twenty years until Tubbaʿ's sister Suʿād comes to avenge her brother. Suʿād is a complex character. Heartbroken, she devises a sophisticated ruse to deceive the Qays tribe, aimed at creating a division among them. Despite the ambitious nature of her plan, she will succeed[34].

31. Gavillet Matar 2005, vol. 1, p. 137.
32. *Qiṣṣat al-Zīr Sālim* 1950, p. 25.
33. Ibid., pp. 25–27.
34. Oliverius 1971, p. 135.

Often considered the villain of the *Sīrah*[35], Su'ād embodies the character of the old woman who operates outside of male control as she has no sexual or reproductive role: her power comes from her independence from these obligations[36]. But she has also a glorious past as a warrior woman that the *Sīrah* recounts to us through a large digression[37].

Disguised as a poet, Su'ād approaches Ǧassās and asks him to protect her special camel, which releases sweet perfumes – she says. Ǧassās believes her and wants to have that animal, so he tells the woman that her camel can pasture freely wherever it wants. Su'ād's servants enter Kulayb's beloved garden with the camel and let it damage trees and flowers. The guard tries to chase it and the servants tending it away, but they refuse to leave, so he calls Kulayb. Kulayb arrives with four servants and finds the camel and Su'ād's servants destroying his garden. As the servants run away, he orders the camel to be slaughtered. Su'ād asks a servant to bring her the camel's skin, then calls Ǧassās, shows him the skin, and tells him that Kulayb had killed her camel although he (Ǧassās) had promised her protection, and now he must defend her rights against Kulayb.

The story continues:

> And when the old woman finished talking, Ǧassās considered the matter important (*ista'ẓama*) and his mind was overwhelmed by the Ǧāhiliyyah's pride, so he said to the old woman: "Go in safety, I know what to do". Proud of her achievement, she went to her tent. So, Prince Ǧassās turned to those princes who were around him and said, "Look what our cousin and brother-in-law did to us, he offended us with this act, and I have to fight him this same day. Either I kill him, or I cause a scandal". "Prince", said the noblest men of the clan, "slow down! Maybe he did not recognise the camel; it is wise to send him a message to reproach him and ask him the blood money for the camel, then wait for his answer because if he sends the amount and apologises, it is fine. If he refuses, then you do what you want". Ǧassās considered this view to be right[38].

35. See, for instance, 'Adwān 2015, pp. 69–75.
36. Steinberg 2018, p. 48.
37. On warrior women in the siyar, see Kruk 1993. On the power of women and their words in the *Sīrat al-Zīr Sālim*, see Potenza 2022.
38. *Qiṣṣat al-Zīr Sālim* 1950, p. 43.

The comments and judgement by the narrator in the hypertext are clear: Ǧassās amplifies the affair, namely, he does not judge wisely and reacts impulsively. The "Ǧāhiliyyah's pride" that overwhelms him is an expression that recurs in the printed version of the *Sīrah* every time a character acts by impulse, and this behaviour leads always to bad consequences. Indeed, the older princes contradict Ǧassās' intentions and have him reflect: first, they hypothesise that Kulayb might not have recognised the camel, giving him the benefit of the doubt. Then they suggest retaliation as the last resort. If Kulayb apologises and offers reparation, Ǧassās cannot ask for more. Only if Kulayb does not follow the common rules, can Ǧassās take a different approach. Reason – a quality Ǧassās does not have, but others do – plays a pivotal role in this short text, since mediation can avoid conflict. The same facts are reported in the hypotext, but the narration is more condensed, and the narrator does not mention any of the bad consequences of the "the Ǧāhiliyyah's pride"[39].

In both the hypotext and the hypertext, despite the wise instructions from the council, Suʿād finds a way to interfere and to ruin their plans. She intercepts the servant carrying the message Ǧassās has written, gets him drunk and unable to think clearly (*sakkara wa-ġāba ʿan al-ṣawāb*). She then takes the message and replaces it with a message in which Ǧassās declares his desire to kill Kulayb. The first attempt at keeping the peace seems to have failed. At this point, Kulayb's wisdom is remarkable. Reading Ǧassās' message, Kulayb is initially very upset and wants to kill the servant, "but he was a wise man, patient and responsible", so he stops to think a bit and realises that Ǧassās might have been drunk and not in his right mind (*ġāʾib min al-ṣawāb*) when he wrote the message[40]. A second attempt at giving someone the benefit of the doubt means another attempt at avoiding conflict. Kulayb tears up the message, orders the servant to be beaten, and tells him to go to his master in peace *(bi-salām)*. When the servant joins Ǧassās, he tells him that Kulayb tore up the message, had him beaten, and adds that he insulted Ǧassās.

After Ǧassās hears these words, he becomes angry and immediately puts on his battle gear. He gathers an army from amongst the men of his tribe, giving them words of encouragement. In both versions of the tale,

39. Gavillet Matar 2005, vol. 2, p. 117.
40. *Qiṣṣat al-Zīr Sālim* 1950, pp. 43–44.

these men categorically refuse to join the fight because they recognise Kulayb's valour, which cannot be compared to a stupid (*ḥaqīrah*) camel[41]. Once again, people close to Ǧassās do not comply with his arrogance and try to avoid conflict. Both the hypotext and the hypertext highlight the mediation among the members of the same family. Only in the hypotext, however, does Ǧassās – strangely enough – act wisely. He goes to Su'ād and proposes that he pay the price of the camel, whatever it is, because he wants to avoid evil (*al-šarr*) spreading in his country[42]. According to this version, Ǧassās seems to be trying to redeem himself because he understands that it is better to avoid conflict with his cousins. In the hypertext, he simply asks Su'ād what she wants to compensate for her loss, and when she answers that she will not accept any money, he simply obeys.

In this episode, the hypertext takes the motif of mediation from the hypotext, but exaggerates it, insisting first on the fact that Ǧassās acts by instinct, while wise men, such as the council and Kulayb, reflect before acting. Eventually, even Ǧassās admits the importance of avoiding the war. In the light of that, in the hypertext, his future actions can be seen as an obligation he reluctantly has to fulfil to keep his word.

5. Words Written in Blood

In both the hypertext and the hypotext, the cunning Su'ād declares she will accept one of three things: having her bag filled with stars, having the hide of her camel put on its corpse and that it walks again (i.e., she wants her dead camel restored to), or Kulayb's head. Ǧassās answers that he cannot satisfy the first two requests, so he will bring her Kulayb's head. And he goes straight to Kulayb's palace. Ǧalīlah informs Ǧassās that Kulayb is in the valley training his colt. Ǧassās joins Kulayb, who is alone and unarmed. Seeing Ǧassās, Kulayb asks him why he is fully armed. Ǧassās lies, saying that he was going to go hunting, but since he saw him, he wanted to ask him something: Why did he kill the camel of the old poet who was under his protection?

41. Ibid., p. 45.
42. Ibid.

What follows is the last attempt by Kulayb to avoid the conflict:

> Kulayb clapped Ǧassās on the shoulder to show his sorrow and said, "Oh my God, my cousin, I didn't know that this camel belonged to your guest", then Kulayb reminded Ǧassās of the two shepherds' lack of manners and the damage they did to the garden, but despite all that, I will repay her giving her four hundred camels and if she wants more, I will give her more, this cannot be a cause of conflict between us because we are cousins[43].

Ǧassās replies that he will repay her, and so he invites Kulayb to fight. Kulayb hits Ǧassās softly with a palm branch and tells Ǧassās to hit him back to end the conflict, but Ǧassās suffers too much from the pain and cannot even stand up. Kulayb gets down from the colt, Suʿād's servant – who was ordered to finish Kulayb and come back with a piece of cloth soaked in Kulayb's blood – arrives and encourages Ǧassās to fight back, helping him to mount his horse.

Then Ǧassās goes back to Kulayb and calls him; Kulayb thinks that Ǧassās is going to hit him with the palm branch, so he does not even turn around, but Ǧassās strikes him with his spear instead. Kulayb falls to the ground with the spear struck right through his body. Now Ǧassās regrets what he has done, hugs his cousin, tells him that he acted without thinking (*bi-dūn ʿaql*) and asks for forgiveness[44]. Once again, the motif of instinct emerges as a negative force. At first, Kulayb says that this was his destiny, and he recites a poem in which he says to Ǧassās that he has been killed by his cousin for a camel. Ǧassās is frightened and runs away. Suʿād's servant approaches Kulayb to kill him, but he fears Kulayb's strength, so Kulayb asks him the truth about his murder, and the servant tells him about Suʿād. Kulayb requests him to bring a nearby flat stone and uses his blood to inscribe the well-known poem commanding his brother Zīr not to reconcile. Following this, Kulayb instructs his servant to end his lifeThen Kulayb passes away.

As for Suʿād, once her servant brings her the cloth with Kulayb's blood, she disappears in the night without any punishment, which is an anomaly for a woman causing *fitnah* (conflict, temptation, trial) in the

43. Ibid.
44. Ibid., p. 46.

Sīrah[45]. After all, despite everything, Suʿād is a brave woman who has been able to accomplish her vengeance alone. And Ǧassās is her perfect victim because she can manipulate him. Indeed, she chooses him because Ǧassās is jealous (he wants to own the "magic" camel and envies his cousin's power) but also because he is instinctive, and we have seen the consequences of that: after killing Kulayb he regrets his actions. And then, of course, she chooses him because he is Murrah's son, related to Kulayb by a double family link: they are both cousins and brothers-in-law. In sum, Ǧassās is one of the most prestigious men in the family, but he is weak. His character does not develop in the following part of the *Sīrah*,. While Kulayb is dying, a scared Ǧassās goes to his family and tells them what he did. His father, King Murrah, scolds him and proposes to give Ǧassās to Zīr so that he can kill him to compensate for Kulayb's death and avoid the *fitnah*[46], but his brothers refuse because they do not want Zīr to be their king.

Ǧassās' inability to do anything right contrasts with his ambition and makes him a ridiculous character. Suffice it to say that when he asks a Christian king for help in fighting Zīr, the way he talks and the words he uses only irritate the king who decides instead to kill him. Ǧassās is saved by his sister Ǧalīlah, who manages to calm the king. A coward, an instinctive and jealous man who involves his family in a long-lasting war, Ǧassās is the archetype of the antihero and is eventually punished with death. The hypertext is also neat in the way it depicts Ǧassās negatively.

In contrast, though he dies and appears only in a short portion of the *Sīrah*, in the printed version, Kulayb is shown as the positive hero of the *Sīrah* and his behaviour is considered more respectful than that of the protagonist, Zīr, who is certainly loyal, strong and brave, but drinks too much, lives with the beasts, is not married, and is said to have sexual relationships with many women. But Kulayb is a good husband, a good king, and a good brother. He acts wisely and cares for his family and tribe. He does everything possible to avoid the war, but he must face Ǧassās' instinct and jealousy that Suʿād's ruse fomented and exacerbated. And so, when Kulayb is going to die at the hands of his cousin and brother-in-law,

45. See Steinberg 2018, p. 87. In Gavillet Matar (2005), Suʿād is not punished. In other versions she is killed by Zīr (Lyons 1995, p. 656).

46. *Qiṣṣat al-Zīr Sālim* 1950, p. 50.

who has let a stranger manipulate him and break the family's union, Kulayb clearly sees the necessity to fight back. His call to his brother to not reconcile, written in a poem with his own blood, is the correct, ultimate response of the hero who uses his last resources to triumph after his death.

In this pivotal moment of the story, Kulayb's words are roughly the same in the hypertext and the hypotext. But in the hypotext, Kulayb does not emerge as the unrivalled hero. In the hypotext, Zīr is considered a hero who possesses the Bedouin values of force, courage and honour[47], and, thanks to them, his tribe can triumph over the cousins. Such values are mitigated in the hypertext, where Kulayb's anti-Bedouin features are exalted and enhanced. Pronounced in a different context and by a Kulayb with different characteristics, his words have different meanings in the hypotext than in the hypertext[48]. On the plan of the message, we notice that the actions in the hypotext are rooted in vengeance and retaliation, while the hypertext insists on a new set of values exalting the need to kill because an innocent, wise king has been treacherously killed by his weak cousin and because of antiquated reasons that are extraneous to the family. Therefore, the text resorts to intrinsic reasons to motivate Kulayb's order and its consequent war.

The transformation from the manuscripts to the printed version we are analysing has a serious tone and, in Genettian terms, it would be called a transposition that mainly aims at formal changes. But the printed edition also involves transformations of the content that are aimed at deleting what the editors must have believed to be "bad" or "out of fashion", thus providing an emended version of the hypotext. As for the transformations of the content, it is difficult to trace a precise ideology in the printed version of the *Sīrah*. Indeed, only a few passages vary from the hypotext. We can assume that in the modern printed adaptation, many Bedouin values are rejected and substituted by causes that are deemed morally acceptable in motivating a war. For instance, in both cases, Kulayb's order, tragically written with his own blood before his death, is the result of the serious fault of an individual that must be expiated by a community. Its radical elimination can occur only through an extreme solution, namely, war.

47. Gavillet Matar, 2005, vol. 1, p. 138.
48. In pre-Islamic poetry, Kulayb is characterised differently: he is a despot who forbids anybody to enter his lands to pasture their herds and flocks (Canova 1985, p. 119).

6. Kulayb's Words Today

As mentioned above, adaptations of the *Sīrah*, instead of the *Sīrah* itself, often lie behind recent uses of Kulayb's message. For instance, the poem *Lā tuṣāliḥ* – which Amal Dunqul derives from the *Sīrat al-Zīr Sālim* in 1967 – was used in graffiti during the 2011 revolts in Cairo[49]. *Lā tuṣāliḥ* has been heavily circulated on electronic media, especially in the context of the queries about the ethical course of action in the aftermath of the killing of hundreds of protesters during the events of 2011 and after[50]. Since then, this poem has become famous among younger generations.

Within a broader discussion on commitment regarding the poet and dramatist Nağīb Surūr (1932–1978) and the poet Aḥmad Fu'ād Nağm (1929–2013), Botros argues that Dunqul is not only part of the tradition of cultural resistance in his period of activity but also in his reception and "afterlife", particularly following the 25 January 2011 uprising. Thus, we can see a link across motifs and forms within a tradition of dissent and resistance in modern Arabic literature and art spanning more than a century[51]. But how does the poem *Lā tuṣāliḥ* relate to the *Sīrah* and its idea of a dialectics of peace? Does it retain the idea that words of non-reconciliation come as the ultimate reaction of the hero? And also: Do its recent uses repeat the same idea?

Dunqul tightly links his poems – more than one are inspired by the *Sīrah* – to the hypotext, which in this case is most probably the printed version of the *Sīrah*. Claiming to provide a modern version of the *Sīrat al-Zīr Sālim*, Dunqul inserts some "historical notes", namely, short descriptions of each of the main characters[52] and a quote from the *Sīrah* that almost corresponds to the text of the al-Ğumhūriyyah edition to introduce his poems. This introduction shows he is willing to engage with his source[53].

The poem *Lā tuṣāliḥ* has ten stanzas, matching the number of verses in which Kulayb repeats the order not to reconcile:

49. Botros 2015, p. 48.
50. Radwan 2014, p. 239.
51. Botros 2015, pp. 45–67. On popular poetry and graffiti in the Egyptian revolution, see also Canova 2012 and Casini 2014.
52. Dunqul 1987, pp. 345; 349–353.
53. *Qiṣṣat al-Zīr Sālim* 1950, p. 47; Dunqul 1987, p. 323.

فأول شرط أخوي لا تصالح / ولو أعطوك زينات النهود
وثاني شرط أخوي لا تصالح / ولو أعطوك مالاً مع عقود
وثالث شرط أخوي لا تصالح / ولو أعطوك نوقًا مع نقود
ورابع شرط أخوي لا تصالح / واحفظ لي ذمامي مع عهودي
وخامس شرط أخوي لا تصالح / فإن صالحت لست أخي أكيد
وسادس شرط أخوي لا تصالح / وقد زادت نيران الوقود
وسابع شرط أخوي لا تصالح / واسفق دمهم في وسط بيد
وثامن شرط أخوي لا تصالح / واحصد جمعهم مثل الحصيد
وتاسع شرط أخوي لا تصالح / فإني اليوم في ألم شديد
وعاشر شرط أخوي لا تصالح / وقد شكوتك للودود[54]

The first condition, my brother, is that you do not reconcile / even if they give you jewels;
The second condition, my brother, is that you do not reconcile / even if they give you properties with contracts;
The third condition, my brother, is that you do not reconcile / even if they give you a camel with money;
The fourth condition, my brother, is that you do not reconcile / and you observe my rights with my vows;
The fifth condition, my brother, is that you do not reconcile / because if you do, you are certainly not my brother;
The sixth condition, my brother, is that you do not reconcile / and the flames became more ardent;
The seventh condition, my brother, is that you do not reconcile / and pour their blood in the middle of the deserts;
The eighth condition, my brother, is that you do not reconcile / and cut them all down like the harvest;
The ninth condition, my brother, is that you do not reconcile / because today I am in a great pain;
The tenth condition, my brother, is that you do not reconcile / as I told you to refrain from benevolence.

The reasons why one should not reconcile are different but, as in the *Sīrah*, we can still find desperation, blood, tears, and death, as the first stanza from Dunqul's poem shows:

لا تصالحْ !
.. ولو ملكوك الذهب
أترى حين أفقأ عينيك،
ثم أثبت جوهرتين مكانهما..

54. *Qiṣṣat al-Zīr Sālim* 1950, pp. 47–48

هل ترى..؟
هي أشياء لا تشترى..
ذكريات الطفولة بين أخيك وبينك ،
حسُّكما - فجأةً - بالرجولةِ ،
هذا الحياء الذي يكبت الشوق.. حين تعانقُهُ،
الصمتُ - مبتسمين - لتأنيب أمكما..
وكأنكما
ما تزالان طفلين!
تلك الطمأنينة الأبدية بينكما:
أنَّ سيفانِ سيفَكَ..
صوتانِ صوتَكَ
أنك إن متَّ:
للبيت ربٌّ
وللطفل أبْ.
هل يصير دمي - بين عينيك - ماءً؟
أتنسى ردائي الملطَّخَ..
تلبس - فوق دمائي - ثيابًا مطرَّزَةً بالقصب؟
إنها الحربُ !
قد تثقل القلبَ ..
لكن خلفك عار العرب.
لا تصالحْ ..
ولا تتوخَّ الهرب![55]

Do not reconcile!
Even if they give you gold.
I wonder, if I were to gouge out your eyes
and replace them with two gems …
Would you see?
These things are priceless …
Childhood memories between your brother and you,
when you – suddenly – felt like men.
Bashfulness suppresses your yearning … when you embrace him,
the silence with a smile, while your mother blames you
as if you're
still two kids!
Eternal comfort between the two of you:
such that two swords are your sword …
two voices are your voice,
such that if you were to die:
there is a guardian for the house

55. Dunqul 1987, p. 323.

and a father for the child.
Would my blood turn into water between your eyes?
would you forget my stained clothes ...
Would you wear – over my blood – clothes embroidered with gold?
This is war!
It may wear heavy on the heart ...
but behind you will be the shame of all the Arabs.
Do not reconcile.
Do not try to escape.

Dunqul's poem maintains the same insistence on the "do not reconcile" motif. And thus we can see the confirmation of the idea of Kulayb as a hero and the refusal to reconcile as an extreme solution. But the reasons for not reconciling become more complex and insist on the uniqueness of each human being and his irreplaceable value in his family. The poem also affirms that the murder was an act of treachery against an innocent man[56].

According to Genette's classification, Dunqul's poem falls into the category of transposition, implying a serious transformation of the hypotext. As for the audience's reception of this transformation, we can infer that it was not perceived. In fact, Dunqul accompanies his poems with commentaries, through notes he inserts into the introduction. These notes provide information about al-Zīr Sālim's story. They are aimed then at filling in the meaning of his poems, namely, at completing the "reader's encyclopaedia", a complex system of shared knowledge that governs the production and interpretation of signs withiin communicative contexts[57]. If Dunqul believed that he needed to present information about the *Sīrah* to his reader, we can assume that, in the 1970s in Egypt, the *Sīrat al-Zīr Sālim* was not commonly known. In 1967, the playwright Alfred Farağ also introduced the story of al-Zīr Sālim in the preface to his play bearing the same title[58]. The two Egyptian editions from the 1950s – al-Ǧumhūriyyah and al-Ḫuṣūṣī – also show an interest in printing a story that would otherwise perhaps be forgotten.

56. Radwan 2014, pp. 241–242.
57. Eco 1985, pp. 95–106.
58. Farağ (1988), pp. 164–167.

Dunqul's "new sayings about the War of al-Basūs"[59] give new life and contemporary significance to the *Sīrat al-Zīr Sālim* because, through them, the poet expresses radical opposition to President Sādāt's politics and the peace agreement with Israel[60]. In this new context, the respect of human life and human rights triggers the fight, and Kulayb's death appears as a heroic act, which is not the case in the hypotext. Referring to Kulayb's last words, Dunqul could simultaneously both "criticize Arab governments and confirm his attachment to an Arab history and culture of honor, defiance, and love of human freedom and dignity"[61]. It is perhaps worth remembering that, a year after the poem was printed, in November 1977, Sādāt outlined his plans for peace in a speech to the Israeli Knesset (Parliament). This unilateral peace offer that led to the 1978 Camp David Accords did not solve the situation of the Palestinian refugees and the status of Jerusalem and the Occupied Territories. In short, Sādāt's reconciliation led to a deviation from a comprehensive and coherent solution to the Israel-Palestine conflict.

In the wake of January 2011, despite the distance between the immediate context of the poem and that of the recent events, Kulayb's words assume new significance. In the context of the Egyptian uprisings, the political struggle once again faces the challenge of deciding when it is best to reconcile, and when reconciliation is itself an act of betrayal[62]. In this new context, Kulayb's words serve, again, as a command to keep fighting, this time against state repression.

It might be interesting now to briefly consider whether the message delivered by Dunqul's poem today still reflects the *Sīrah*'s concern regarding the importance of peace. First, we can assume that most of the readers of graffiti might know Dunqul's entire poem (which also circulates online on YouTube), while the text of the *Sīrah* is probably not part of their knowledge, i.e., it is not part of the "reader's encyclopaedia". That means that the verses from the graffiti are not identified as quotations/comments from the *Sīrah*. In other words, it is unlikely that the spectators think about the context of the *Sīrah* in which Kulayb acts and where, as

59. Dunqul 1987, pp. 321 and 345. Dunqul revisits narratives of other popular characters, such as Spartacus and ʿAntar (see Radwan 2014).
60. Radwan 2014, p. 239.
61. Ibid., p. 243.
62. Ibid., pp. 242–243.

we have seen, the command not to reconcile comes as an extreme solution. Accordingly, understanding the graffiti is not mediated by the idea of peace and war found in the *Sīrah*. Indeed, the character of Kulayb takes another shift: closely resembling the images (pictures or graffiti) of the martyrs, a new set of values is attached to him.

> Through the imaginary formation of the idealized martyr figure, societies emphasize crucial moments in their common history and integrate them into their collective memory. Broadly speaking, in this process the communities shaping these literary visions of the martyr perceive themselves to be a community of victims, and their readiness to offer one of their own members for the sake of a higher cause then transforms it into a community of sacrifice[63].

In 2011 graffiti, Kulayb's words advocate for the causes of the Egyptian uprisings. Approximating the image of Ḫālid Saʿīd, a young man who has sacrificed his life for the sake of a laudable cause, they rely on the Arab legend to challenge the spectator's courage in spite of the possibility of dying. The tragic context in which Kulayb's words appear still suggest that refusing peace is an extreme solution aiming at a more ambitious target, that is, a long-term peace[64].

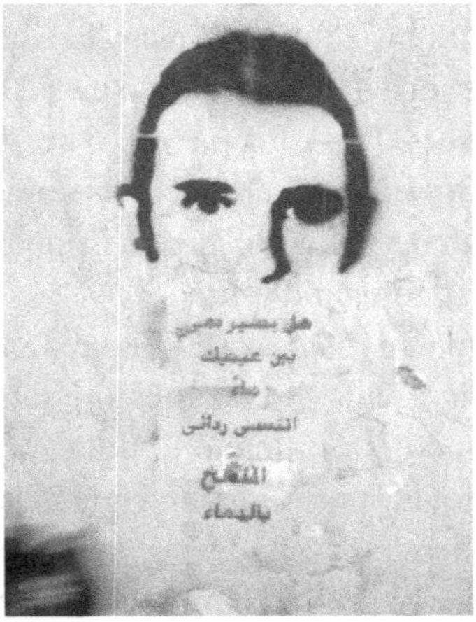

Figure 1. https://creativecommons.org/licenses/by-nc-sa/2.0/
Source: https://www.flickr.com/photos/wild_atheart/5805320193

63. Pannewick 2004, p. 1.
64. See the graffiti at https://gate.ahram.org.eg/News/79531.aspx.

Conclusion

The various adaptations of the *Sīrat al-Zīr Sālim* respond to historically shifting social-moral criteria which each community establishes for itself. Though at first glance the main motif of the *Sīrat al-Zīr Sālim* seems to be war (al-Basūs War), and this is generally the main point critics highlight from the *Sīrah*, the context of Kulayb's order of not reconciling reveals instead that a main topic of the story is peace. Living in peace means a pleasant life, with love, family, hobbies, and even caring for plants and flowers. Because no peace means ruin, the positive characters of the *Sīrah* do whatever is in their power to avoid war. For that reason, mediation is reiterated throughout the story, especially when Ǧassās is about to kill Kulayb. The hero of the story, Kulayb, is a master of mediation both in the printed version of the *Sīrah* and in the manuscripts: he even blocks his impulses to avoid conflict. Conversely, the one who promotes war for his personal satisfaction, namely Ǧassās, is the antihero. The printed version underlines this aspect even more than the manuscripts.

The reasons for the war are rooted in a far-away past and Suʿād is heart-broken for the loss of her brother: she alone follows her plan incessantly until she succeeds. Despite the two tribes' unity, she finds the weak link, Ǧassās, and manipulates him until the rupture in the family is accomplished. Confronted with his cousin's cowardice, having let Suʿād manipulate him, and having tried so many times to avoid the conflict, Kulayb on the verge of death cannot but ask for justice to be done, and so he asks his valiant brother Zīr not to reconcile. Read in its context, Kulayb's message appears to be the ultimate solution, the only one possible in a context where, otherwise, injustice would reign.

In Amal Dunqul's poem *Lā tuṣāliḥ*, Kulayb's words are adapted to his contemporary reality. Kulayb becomes the innocent man whose life has been taken away and his command to fight sounds like a moral duty, a necessary action to retain one's human rights. Twenty-five years later, Kulayb's words, mediated by Dunqul's interpretation, appear in the streets of Cairo, together with the picture of a martyr, in the same place where the uprisings were going on. Within the paradigm of martyrdom, *lā tuṣāliḥ* becomes both the fruit of a community's need and an incitement to the community. As in the *Sīrat al-Zīr Sālim al-Muhalhil*, the story of Zīr still propagates its message that *lā tuṣāliḥ* is the extreme solution in a context where a still cherished and yearned for peace is simply not possible, as the picture of the martyr Ḫālid Sa'īd shows.

References

'Adwān, M. (2015), *al-Zīr Sālim, al-baṭal bayna l-sīrah wa-l-tārīḫ wa-l-binā' al-drāmī*, Dār Mamdūḥ 'Adwān li-l-Našr wa-l-Tawzī', Damascus [first edition 1998].

Botros, A. (2015), *Rewriting Resistance: The Revival of Poetry of dissent in Egypt after 2011 (Surūr, Najm and Dunqul)*, in F. Pannewick, G. Khalil, Y. Albers (eds.), *Commitment and Beyond: Reflections on/of the Political in Arabic Literature since the 1940s*, Reichert, Wiesbaden, pp. 45–62.

Canova, G. (1977), *Gli studi sull'epica popolare araba*, in "Oriente Moderno", 57, pp. 211–226. https://doi.org/10.1163/22138617-0570506003

Canova, G. (1984), *La funzione del sogno nella poesia epica hilaliana*, in "Quaderni di Studi Arabi", 2, pp. 107–125.

Canova, G. (1985), *Osservazioni a margine della storia di Zīr Sālim*, in "Quaderni di Studi Arabi", 3, pp. 115–136.

Canova, G. (1998), *s.v.* «*Sīra* Literature», in J. Scott Meisami, P. Starkey (eds.), *Encyclopedia of Arabic Literature*, Vol. III, Routledge, London and New York, pp. 726–27.

Canova, G. (2003), *Hilāli Narratives from Southern Arabia*, in "Oriente Moderno", 83, pp. 361–375. https://doi.org/10.1163/22138617-08302007

Canova, G. (2012), *Piazza Tahrīr: graffiti e poesia*, in "Quaderni di Studi Arabi. Nuova serie", 7, pp. 261–264.

Canova, G. (2016), *Considerazioni sulla definizione di 'epica' nella letteratura araba*, in "Quaderni di Studi Arabi. Nuova serie", 11, pp. 165–183.

Casini, L. (2014), *Verses (in a) Changing Discursive Order: Egyptian Poetry in Colloquial Arabic and the Unaccomplished Revolution*, in "Quaderni di Studi Arabi. Nuova serie", 9, pp. 239–256.

Dunqul, A. (1987), *al-a'māl al-ši'riyyah al-kāmilah*, Maktabat Madbūlī, al-Qāhirah [first edition 1969].

Eco, U. (1985), *Lector in fabula: Le rôle du lecteur*, Grasset, Paris.

Farağ, A. (1988), *al-Zīr Sālim*: *Mu'allafāt* 2, al-Hay'ah al-Miṣriyyah al-'Āmma li-l-Kitāb, al-Qāhirah [first edition 1967].

Gavillet Matar, M. (1997), *A propos de quelques manuscrits et éditions de la geste de Zīr*, in "Quaderni di Studi Arabi", 15, pp. 165–182.

Gavillet Matar, M. (2003), *Situation narrative et fonctions de l'extra-narratif dans les manuscrits des conteurs. L'exemple de la geste de Zīr Sālim*, in "Oriente Moderno", 15, 2, pp. 377–397. https://doi.org/10.1163/22138617-08302008

Gavillet Matar, M. (2005), *La geste du Zīr Sālim: d'après un manuscrit syrien*, Institut français du Proche-Orient, Damascus, 2 vol.

Genette, G. (1982), *Palimpsestes. La littérature au second degré*, Seuil, Paris.

Heath, P. (1984), *A Critical Review of Modern Scholarship on "Sīrat ʿAntar ibn Shaddad" and the Popular Sīra*, in "Journal of Arabic Literature", 15, pp. 19–44. https://doi.org/10.1163/157006484X00032

Kruk, R. (2013), *The Warrior Women of Islam: Female Empowerment in Arabic Popular Literature*, Tauris, London.

Lyons, M. C. (1995), *The Arabian Epic: Heroic and Oral Storytelling*, Cambridge University Press, Cambridge.

Māzin, S. (al-rāwī) (1980), *Qiṣṣat al-Zīr Sālim: Nusḫah ḫaṭṭiyyah li-Ǧūfānnī Kānūfā* (Giovanni Canova), al-Aqṣar.

Māzin, Y. (al-rāwī) (1980), *Qiṣṣat al-Zīr Sālim: Nusḫah ḫaṭṭiyyah li-Ǧūfānnī Kānūfā* (Giovanni Canova), al-Aqṣar.

Oliverius, J. (1965), *Aufzeichnungen über den Basūs-Krieg in der Kunstliteratur und deren Weiterentwicklung im arabischen Volksbuch über Zīr Sālim*, in "Archiv Orientalni", 33, pp. 44–64.

Oliverius, J. (1971), *Themen und Motive im arabischen Volksbuch über Zīr Sālim*, in "Archiv Orientalni", 39, pp. 129–145.

Oliverius, J. (1975), *The Epic and Genealogical Cyclization in the Arabic Folk Book about Zīr Sālim*, in "Acta Universitatis Carolinae Philologica", 5, pp. 27–44.

Oliverius, J. (1977), *Der Reflex der sozialen Verhältnisse und historischen Begebenheiten im arabischen Volksbuch von Zīr Sālim*, in "Acta Universitatis Carolinae Philologica", 4, pp. 49–60.

Oliverius, J. (1996a), *Erzähltechnik, Stilmittel und Sprache im arabischen Volksbuch von Zīr Sālim*, in P. Zemanek (ed.), *Studies in Near Eastern Languages and Literatures*, Academy of Sciences of the Czech Republic Oriental Institut, Prague, pp. 481–497.

Oliverius, J. (1996b), *Das Heroische und Romantische im arabischen Volksbuch über Zīr Sālim*, in Veseli, R., Gombar, E. (eds), *Ẓafar Nāme, Memorial Volume of Felix Tauer*, Enigma corporation Ldt, Prague, pp. 231–241.

Pannewick, F. (2004), *Introduction*, in F. Pannewick (ed.), *Martyrdom in Literature*, Reichert Verlag, Wiesbaden, pp. 1–26.

Potenza, D. (2020a), *Le avventure di al-Zīr Sālim al-Muhalhil: studi e prospettive*, in "Illuminazioni", 53, pp. 115–141.

Potenza, D. (2020b), *The Kaleidoscope Effect: Rewriting in Alfred Farağ's Plays as a Multifunctional Strategy for a Multi-Layered Creation*, Istituto per l'Oriente Carlo Alfonso Nallino, Rome.

Potenza, D. (2022), *Il potere delle donne e della loro parola nella* Sīrat al-Zīr Sālim, in "Quaderni di Studi Arabi", 17, pp. 1–22, Advance article. https://doi.org/10.1163/2667016x-17010005

Qiṣṣat al-Zīr Sālim (1950), Maktabat al-Ǧumhūriyyah al-Miṣriyyah, al-Qāhirah.

Qiṣṣat al-Zīr Sālim al-kubrà [s.d.], al-Ḫuṣūṣī, Cairo.

Radwan, N. (2014), *Amal Dunqul: The Prince of Protest Poets*, in "Journal of Arabic Literature", 45, 2/3, pp. 218–243. https://doi.org/10.1163/1570064x-12341285

Steinberg, A. H. (2018), *Wives, Witches, and Warriors: Women in Arabic Popular Epic*, PhD thesis, University of Pennsylvania.

Weipert, R. (2021), *s.v.* «al-Muhalhil», in *The Encyclopaedia of Islam*, 3rd ed. online, Brill, Leiden, available at http://dx.doi.org/10.1163/1573-3912_ei3_COM_36596 (last accessed 18 March 2021).

Daniela Potenza is a temporary researcher (RtdA) in Arabic Language and Literature at Università degli Studi di Messina (Italy), where she also teaches. She holds a PhD in Arabic Literature from INALCO (Paris) and UNIOR (Naples). Her book, *The Kaleidoscope Effect. Rewriting in Alfred Farag's Plays*, has been published by IPOCAN (Rome, 2020). Her research focuses on Modern and Contemporary Egyptian literature, Arabic theatre, popular culture and intertextuality.

Chapter 10

Twofold Slavery: Slave in Malta, Slave to Love of his Beloved Master. The Peaceful Letter a Muslim Sent to Baldassarre Loyola Mandes SJ (1631–1667)[1]

Federico Stella

Abstract

This chapter conducts a historical-textual analysis of a passionate letter a Muslim slave in Malta sent to Baldassarre Loyola Mandes (1631–1667), a seventeenth-century Moroccan ruler who converted to Christianity and became a Jesuit. The author of the letter reacts to Baldassarre's conversion to Christianity by expressing love and nostalgia for him, while almost completely avoiding religious polemics. I will therefore trace the historical roots of the homoerotic poetics of missed love and nostalgia for the beloved, as it was conceived in much Islamic culture, in the letter by the Muslim slave. Furthermore, I will analyse the Italian translation made by Baldassarre himself in order to understand how Islamic cultural and religious elements were made intelligible to an early modern Christian audience. In the conclusion, I will express some reflections about translation as a practice and about the asymmetrical position of sender and addressee.

1. I would like to thank Prof Martin M. Morales, Dr Irene Pedretti, and Dr Lorenzo Mancini for their help in researching the Historical Archives of the Pontifical Gregorian University in Rome. I would also like to thank Prof Leonardo Capezzone and Prof Iman Mansub Basiri for their suggestions.

Keywords: Baldassarre Loyola Mandes; Christian-Muslim relations; Society of Jesus; Mediterranean Sea; Malta.

1. Introduction

This chapter deals with the context, the style, and the content of a letter a Muslim slave in Malta sent to Baldassarre Loyola Mandes SJ on an unspecified date in 1659. The situation is as follows: a Muslim slave in Malta sends a letter to a Muslim convert to Christianity who is going to become a Catholic priest in the Society of Jesus. The surviving versions of the letter are the original Arabic text and the Italian translation carried out by Baldassarre himself. The style of the letter is that of classic homoerotic Islamic courtly love poems. The letter contains several Islamic religious references and was translated into Italian. Rather than engaging in polemics, it deals with the theme of undertaking a religious conversion using the language of love and friendship. This interreligious encounter is played out with the Mediterranean Sea and the phenomenon of slavery in the early modern age as a constant backdrop.

In particular, the fact that both the Arabic letter written by the anonymous slave and Baldassarre's translation have been preserved allows the text to be read from a dual perspective. On the one hand, I deal with the courtly love language the anonymous Muslim employed in his letter; I will present the topoi he used as well as the possible references and meanings between the lines. On the other hand, I will consider how Baldassarre translated the text, often providing a quite literary translation from Arabic into Italian – a faithful translation, according to Baldassarre (*voltata fedelmente dall'Arabico*) – while sometimes changing or deleting words and sentences.

2. The Recipient and Sender of the Letter

One day in 1659, right before his departure from the Jesuit College in Messina (Sicily) to go to Rome, Baldassarre Loyola Mandes SJ (1631–1667) received a letter from someone who identified himself as al-Ṭālib

Imḥamad Ibn ʿAbd al-Salām al-ʿUlayǧ[2] (*Il Dottore Mahmed figlio di Aabd el slam el hulieg*). As Nabil Matar stated, he was a shop owner and perhaps a member of a Sufi brotherhood[3]. The sender is well aware of the conversion, real name, and previous life of the addressee: born Muley Muḥammad al-Tāzī, Baldassarre was a Moroccan Muslim ruler[4] captured by the Knights of St. John while making the pilgrimage to Mecca in 1651. After five years of imprisonment in Malta, during which he became a renowned anti-Christian preacher among the Muslim slaves as well as a tireless writer of Islamic religious books and copyist of the Qurʾān, he converted to Christianity in 1656. This unexpected conversion happened after the payment of the ransom which would free him just prior to his scheduled departure from Malta[5].

According to his autobiography, visions and dreams were the precise reasons for his astonishing conversion; in particular, a vision of the personification of Holy Baptism which appeared to him in his sleep was decisive for his conversion to Christianity[6]. Sometimes, however, Baldassarre felt nostalgia and was stirred by memories from his previous life and of

2. I am following Nabil Matar's transliteration of "Imḥamad Ibn ʿAbd al-Salām", as it appears in his article concerned with the Arabic version of this letter: Matar 2021a, p. 256.
3. Ibid., pp. 256–257.
4. Both De Castries and Bono suggest that Baldassarre was related to a Moroccan Sufi brotherhood called the Zāwiyah of Dilāʾ, which increased its political influence after the death of Aḥmad al-Mansūr: De Castries 1922, pp. 203–240; De Castries 1928, pp. 151–154; Bono, p. 440. Goldáraz and Colombo agree on considering Baldassarre a member of the Saʿadi dynasty (the great-grandson of Aḥmad al-Mansūr, according to Colombo): García Goldáraz 1944, pp. 19–59; Colombo 2013, p. 481; Colombo 2011, pp. 165–166. More recently, Matar has stated that Baldassarre did not belong to any royal family: Matar 2021, p. 178. On Aḥmad al-Mansur and Saʿdi dynasty see García-Arenal 2009. On intellectual life during the Saʿadi dynasty see Hajji 1976–1977.
5. The summary of Baldassarre's life within the first paragraph of this article is mainly based on Colombo 2013, pp. 479–486. See also Colombo 2011; Lebessou 1910, pp. 488–498; Ledóchowski 1937, pp. 784–792; Pouzet 1983, pp. 157–169. On the role played by Malta as a border zone in Christian-Muslim relations in the early modern age, see Brogini 2006. Regarding slavery in the Mediterranean Sea, see G. Fiume 2009, (on Baldassarre: pp. 274–280).
6. APUG, Ms. 1060–02, fols. 24v–25v; Colombo 2013, pp. 486–487.

his family, but he fought these emotions, which he saw as nothing more than temptations sent to him by the devil.

After being educated and baptised by the Jesuits in Malta, Baldassarre travelled to Sicily (Messina) and eventually became a novitiate of the Society of Jesus at St. Andrea al Quirinale in Rome in 1661. Ordained a priest in 1663, he devoted the last few years of his life (1664–1667) to convert Muslims in Italian cities like Naples, Livorno, and Genoa. According to the letters he sent to his spiritual director Domenico Brunacci SJ (1616–1695), as well as to other Jesuits, he converted more than three hundred Muslims, who listened to him preaching in hospitals, port areas or close to churches. His missionary zeal led him to ask his superiors (two *indipetae* letters are housed in the Archive of the Society of Jesus – ARSI) to send him to India amongst the Muslims. However, his dream of travelling to the Mughal Empire to convert Muslims remained unfulfilled since he died in Madrid on 15 September 1667. More than two hundred letters and other documents belonging to Baldassarre or related to the case of his conversion are now housed mainly in the Historical Archives of Pontifical Gregorian University (APUG)[7].

Therefore, the letter I am going to discuss in the following pages was sent to Baldassarre before he was intensely involved as a Catholic preacher among the Muslim slaves in Italian cities (Genoa, Naples etc.). According to both this letter and Baldassarre's autobiography, however, the news of his radical change of life and faith was already a well-known fact among the Muslim slaves.

7. After his death, several Jesuit literary writings including the sacred drama written by the dramatist Pedro Calderón de la Barca called *El Gran Principe de Fez* (1669) made Baldassarre's story renowned. He was then forgotten from the 18th century up until the studies of Louis Lebessou, Wlodimir Ledóchowski and Louis Pouzet in the 20th century. Before Emanuele Colombo's recent studies, however, the only study which was based on and relied on the documents housed in APUG was García Goldáraz 1944. See Colombo 2020, pp. 49–79. See the section on Baldassare on the web-platform GATE of Historical Archives of Pontifical Gregorian University (APUG): https://gate.unigre.it/mediawiki/index.php/Balthasar_Loyola_Mandes_Collection

3. The Versions of the Letter

The letter survived in three versions. Two of them are in the APUG: an Arabic one written in jumbled handwriting[8], and an Italian translation[9]. This Italian version appears to have been translated by Baldassarre himself – most likely to make it readable to a non-Arabic speaking priest who was following his spiritual journey. But it was far from being as readable and grammatically correct as Baldassarre's later writings would be. In fact, here it looks as if Baldassarre was still learning Italian and Western handwriting, while in his following writings – especially those between 1664 and 1667 – he proves to have acquired mastery both in Italian and in Latin, as well as in handwriting and theological argumentation. The third version is a copy of the Italian letter included by Domenico Brunacci SJ (Baldassarre's spiritual director) in his biography of Baldassarre (1692)[10].

But why did Baldassarre undertake an Italian translation? The answer may that, in just the same way as Baldassarre used to report his spiritual experiences to Domenico Brunacci in Rome[11], he did the same with his spiritual director in Messina, Francesco Navantieri, as he wrote in the autobiography. According to Baldassarre's autobiography, he used to report his spiritual experiences to him:

> Dopo che sparì tal visione [when Jesus appeared to Baldassarre in the Holy Sacrament during mass], ritornai a casa Professa, subito andai alla camera di mio Padre Spirituale Francesco Navantiericominciai a raccontargli la storia né potevo però spiegarla perchè m'impedivano le lacrime di tenerezza. Vedendo il detto Padre tal cosa, mi accompagnò anche lui con le sue lacrime (considerando io quello che era, cioè poco tempo fa, era nemico di Dio, e vedendomi con tal tenerezza, et alegrezza tanto maravigliosa senz'alcun mio merito ristai tutto confuso fra me stesso) all'hora il Padre Francesco mi

8. APUG, Ms. 1060–1, fols. 123r–124v. I owe my understanding the Arabic handwriting to the transcription made by Prof. Nabil Matar on the web-platform of the Archive of Pontifical Gregorian University GATE.
9. APUG, Ms. 1060–01, fols. 101r–103v.
10. Brunacci 1692, 103, 138r–141v.
11. It should also be recalled that, as the centre of Catholic missionary activity, Rome had been an important place for Oriental and Arabic studies since the end of the 16th century. See Pizzorusso 2004, pp. 471–498; Fani, Farina 2012; Girard 2017, pp. 189–212.

> comandò, che io notassi queste cose, e perché non sapevo né scrivere né leggere con lingua Italiana ne latina, non dimeno le notai con il mio carattere, e lingua nativa, però secondo la mia ignoranza non aveva notato né il mese, né l'anno nel quale successero queste cose a me ma tuttavia andavo considerando la cosa fra me stesso mi pare che fu nell'anno 1658 che fu dopo il mio Battesimo un anno e qualche mesi. Le notai in Roma con la mia mano dalla lingua Arabica in Italiana nel tempo del mio noviziato (oggi di 20 di giugno 1662) per una certa causa del mio Padre Spirituale e Maestro dei Novitii Domenico Brunacci, il quale mi comandò, che la voltasse in lingua italiana[12].

Similarly, just as Baldassarre translated the polemical letter sent to him by Muḥammad Abū l-Ġayṯ al-Darawī[13] – a Muslim jurist who was a slave in Livorno – in 1664, so that Domenico Brunacci could read it, he may have done the same with Francesco Navantieri while he was in Messina. This means that the Italian translation of the Arabic letter that the Muslim slave sent him may be a readable version created for his spiritual director in Messina, who also referred to the event in a short writing[14].

4. The Poetics of the Letter and its Historical Background

This letter presents us with an incredible account of a peaceful dialogue between a Muslim and a former Muslim who has renounced his faith. The peaceful approach the Muslim slave employed to deal with Baldassarre's case should not be taken for granted. According to Baldassarre's autobiography, due to his renowned position as an Islamic preacher and an author among the slaves in Malta, Muslims did not gladly welcome or accept his conversion. Such a radical change was abhorred by the Muslims slaves on the island, who harassed Baldassarre by telling him fake news about his family and even made an attempt on his life[15].

12. APUG, Ms. 1060–02, fol. 51r.
13. On Muḥammad Abū l-Ġayṯ al-Darāwī, see Tommasino 2018a, pp. 94–120; Santus 2019, pp. 141–145.
14. This writing is included in the documents after the autobiography: APUG, Ms. 1060–02, fols. 130r-v.
15. APUG, Ms. 1060–02, fols. 26v–27r.

In contrast to what Baldassarre had to endure in Malta after his conversion, the letter from the Muslim sender was of a completely different tone and subject matter from speeches and actions by other believers: instead of using hate or a polemical approach, he focused on the nostalgia he felt for his beloved master, his misery and sadness during Baldassarre's absence, and reminiscing on the good old days when they were together. Even though some polemical remarks have been implied, the fundamental tone of the whole letter was by far the language of love[16], which was already an established literary topos.

In terms of poetic style, the letter alternates between sentences in prose and others which can be read as a kind of *ġazal*: in fact, besides the passionate love content, the letter is also composed of lines ending with the same rhyme, namely, a monorhyme verse, which is characteristic of *ġazal* poetics. Moreover, the author alludes to this poetic style in his letter by saying that he was screaming "*ġazāl/ghazàla*"[17]. Due to the Muslim slave's poor handwriting, however, it is hard to clearly split or separate the sentences in prose from the monorhyme verses.

As regards the rhetorical strategy, unlike the controversial and theologically based letter Abū l-Ġayṯ al-Darāwī would send to Baldassarre some years later (1664), the letter this slave in Malta sent contained very few or no polemical issues. Therefore, since he was not interested in engaging in a theological discussion, the well-trained dialectical "weapons" Muslims had developed for dealing with interreligious disputes since the Abbasid era are not employed here.

Indeed, interreligious disputes were a well-attested religious and intellectual practice during the Abbasid Caliphate. For example, the debate between the Caliph al-Mahdī (r. 775–785) and the Nestorian Patriarch Timothy I (d. 823), which took place in Baghdad in circa 821, should be remembered as a major case for this interreligious practice, which led to al-Mahdī's request to Timothy I to translate the *Topics*, namely the Aristotelian work on dialectics (*ǧadal*), from Syriac into Arabic[18]. Thanks to the translation of this milestone, Christians, Muslims, Jews, and other

16. According to Matar, "the letter is emotional and interspersed with poetry". Matar 2020b, p. 166. See also: Matar 2020a, pp. 256–257.
17. APUG, Ms. 1060–01, fol. 123v; APUG, Ms. 1060–01, fol. 102r.
18. Capezzone 1998, p. 18. See Khalil Samir, Nasry 2016.

religious confessions took and obtained their dialectical "weapons" for engaging in theological disputes.

According to both Leonardo Capezzone and Dimitri Gutas, the actual reason for the interest in dialectics was the need to acquire the intellectual tools which would allow a theological dispute with the *zandaqah* (Manicheans) as well as Christians and Jews[19]. On the one hand, the *kalām* was a well-established paradigm and a transversal intellectual practice belonging to each religion, through which theologians (*mutakallimūn*) developed their disputes[20]; on the other hand, the main intellectual tool for an interreligious dispute was the dialectic, which was – according to the epistemological framework developed by Islamic philosophers like al-Fārābī and Ibn Rušd – a theoretical method founded on uncertain but commonly accepted premises and typically practised by theologians.

In addition to the argumentations based on dialectics, Islamic civilisation developed a further approach towards interreligious discourse and otherness. This approach – marked by uncertain borders and linguistic ambiguity – does not rely on dialectic but instead engages interreligious encounters through the poetics of the missing beloved, rejected love, and nostalgia. Within these poetics of love and nostalgia, the interreligious discourse often emerged in homoerotic and male-to-male poetry, where a man – better still if he was a young man – of another religion was pictured as the object of desire.

Abū Nuwās (756–815) is definitely a foremost example of this trend. In his poetry, the intersection between interreligious discourse, the picture of otherness, and male-to-male love are depicted as a lifelong state of euphoria in which the foolish poet also appropriates the religious and cultural dimension of his beloved one. Symbols and rituals themselves became objects of desire for the crazy (*mağnūn*) Muslim poet, who dreams of being the bread and chalice of his beloved Christian monk[21].

According to several scholars, this Arabic male-to-male courtly love has long been a genre of poetry flourishing in the whole Arabic speaking

19. Capezzone 1998, pp. 13–20; Gutas 1998, pp. 66–69; see also Charfi 1994, pp. 44–56.
20. Capezzone 1998, pp. 14–15.
21. Capezzone 2020, pp. 226–227; see also Capezzone 2007, pp. 7–82, (see here Capezzone's edition and translation of Abū Nuwās' poem no. XXXII, pp. 120–121 – with the references to the bread and chalice – and the poems XXX and XXXI, pp. 116–119 in which the interreligious theme is linked to the homoerotic courtly love.)

world: such an extensive amount of literature related to the topic – found in many other literary genres like juridical, poetical, mystical, historical, biographical, and others – cannot be found in any other form of world literature. According to Thomas Bauer, "there is no other pre-modern literature in which homoerotic texts are as numerous and as central as they are in classical Arabic"[22]. Consequently, this amount of homoerotic literature led an orientalist like Bernard Lewis to state that "there are times and places in Islamic history when the ban on homosexual love seems no stronger than the ban on adultery in, for example, Renaissance Italy or seventeenth century France"[23].

Scholars warn us, however, that a broad dissemination of the homoerotic literature should not lead us to presuppose that sexual acts between persons of the same sex were tolerated. Such acts were, on the contrary, banned by religious and juridical authorities[24]. Therefore, the boundaries between reality and fiction were anything but clear. For instance, little is known about the supposed reality of the ambience of "permanent Saturnalia"[25] in the poetry of Abū Nuwās: Were life experiences the source of his poetry, or was it mere fiction? It is difficult to give a right answer, and it cannot be confirmed whether the perpetual self-destructive passion Abū Nuwās narrates in his poems was a true part of his lifestyle[26].

This kind of courtly love poetry was still widely popular during the Ottoman era, and even the male-to-male dimension was a common poetic Islamic trend of the period[27]. As El-Rouyaheb has pointed out, such poetry should be interpreted as follows: the homoerotic poetry was neither evidence of the toleration of homosexuality within the Ottoman borders nor merely a rhetorical exercise. The male-to-male poetry reflects a juridical distinction Islamic societies made between chaste love, including whenever it was lived with passion and open emotion, and love expressed

22. Bauer 2014, p. 108.
23. Lewis 2001, p. 26; I found the quotation thanks to El-Rouyaheb 2005b, p. 10; El-Rouyaheb 2005a, p. 3.
24. Bürgel 1996, p. 254; see the discussion in El-Rouyaheb 2005b, pp. 11–13; El-Rouyaheb 2005a, pp. 76–79.
25. Hamori 1974, p. 47. Quotations are found in: Capezzone 2020, p. 208.
26. Capezzone 2020, pp. 208–209.
27. Andrews, Kalpakli 2005, pp. 39–43 (with examples regarding poems dedicated to boys). See also: Kuru 2015, pp. 81–102, in English translation: Kuru 2020a, pp. 43–63; Kuru 2020b, pp. 133–145.

through sexuality[28]. This means that chaste love was tolerated even when directed at a person of the same sex. Thus, the main Islamic dichotomy was not focused on heterosexuality or homosexuality but on chaste or sexual love ("between passionate infatuation and sexual consummation")[29], not only in classical Islamic poetry but also in the Ottoman period up until at least the 19th century.

Therefore, it should not surprise us that this kind of poetics can also be found in the letter the Muslim slave in Malta sent to Baldassarre. In fact, even though the constant subtext of the writing is the intra/interreligious theme – namely Baldassarre's conversion – the poetics of the letter belongs to the framework of the courtly love poetry, and the topoi of nostalgia and sadness for the absence of the beloved one are the main poetic framework of this passionate letter.

The Content and its Translation

The letter begins with the "moro Schiavo in Malta" referring to Baldassarre by the honorary title of the one who "is already honoured in this world and will be in the other, God willing" ("huwa fī l-dunyā saʿīd wa-fī l-āḫirah in šāʾ Allāh šahīd/in questo mondo già onorato, e nell'altro piacendo Dio, glorioso")[30]. After becoming aware of Baldassarre's forsaking Islam, the Muslim slave refers to himself as deadened due to the love he feels for his master ("kātib al-ḥurūf [allaḏī] huwa min ḥubbi-ka mazǧūf/lo scrittore di questa sempre vostro amore intisichito") and as being unable to slee and constantly remembering him ("huwa min hubbi-ka lā yanāmu wa-yaḏkuru-ka fī l-quʿūd wa-l-qiyām/mai dorme per vostro amore, e

28. El-Rouayheb 2005a, pp. 1–8, see also p. 153; regarding the legal questions see also Andrews, Kalpakli 2005, pp. 270–303; and: Ze'evi 2006, pp. 48–76.
29. El-Rouyaheb 2005b, p. 14; According to El-Rouyaheb, "Belletrists and scholars simply did not operate with a concept of homosexuality, and thus managed to combine a severe condemnation of sexual intercourse between males with a toleration and even idealization of chaste pederastic love". El-Rouyaheb 2005a, p. 79. See also a well-known passage from Michel Foucault on the difference between the ancient ban regarding the acts of sodomy and the modern concept of the homosexual as a character: Foucault 1976, pp. 58–59.
30. APUG, Ms. 1060–01, fol. 123r; APUG, Ms. 1060–01, fol. 101r. See Lange 2015, pp. 55–56.

sempre fa di voi menzioni vegliando"). He is fervently hoping that God will one day reunite them ("*Allāh šamila-nā*/Dio ci unirà"). And then, referring to the awfulness of the distance between them, he writes: "*mā amarr firāqu-kum wa-mā aẓlam al-dunyā ʿalayya wa-awḥaš*/ò quanto amara è la vostra lontananza, e il mondo quanto è oscurato, e fatto orribile, perche da noi allontanato"[31].

The above sentences the Muslim slave wrote to Baldassare in the opening part of his letter are the main courtly love topoi in Islamic poetry: the illness caused by a passionate love and the rhetoric of sadness due to the absence and distance of the beloved one. The Muslim slave is picturing himself as affected by the "malady of love"[32], and, as I have pointed out, the poetics in the letter should not be read as something peculiar in early modern Islamic literary culture.

Sorrow leads the imprisoned Muslim to make use of irony to explain the reason for his master's absence, perhaps also as a way to hold off his never-ending sadness. Why does his beloved master Muḥammad/Baldassarre does not send him any news? A particular problem is definitely keeping him from writing. But what can be that reason be? The slave makes use of desperate irony in *ghazal* as follows:

> *qallat qarāṭīsu-kum*
> *am ǧaffa ḥibru-kum*
> *am ġāba kātibu-kum*
> *am aqlāmu-kum kisar*
> *am al-rasūl ʿaṣā-kum*
> *am risālatu-kum*
> *min qabl an taʾtī ilāy-nā ballala-hā al-maṭar*
> *in kāna ḏanb^{an} fa-naḥnu al-tāʾibūn la-kum wa-ḏanb man tāba ʿinda llāh muḫtabar*[33]

And according to Baldassarre's Italian translation:

> È forsi perso il vostro carattere, o si è seccato l'inchiostro; forsi non si trova il vostro segretario, o le vostre penne son rotte, o gl'ambasciadori non obediscono al vostro commando, mentre aspettavamo

31. APUG, Ms. 1060–01, fol. 123r; APUG, Ms. 1060–01, fol. 101r.
32. Biesterfeldt, Gutas 1984, pp. 21–55.
33. APUG, Ms. 1060–01, fol. 123r (vertically on the left side of the manuscript).

> per tanto tempo, come si aspetta la pioggia, necessaria dal Cielo: se è stata colpa nostra, noi ne dimandiamo perdono, e Dio rimette la colpa a chi ne dimanda il perdono[34].

The Muslim slave then continues his letter with a metaphor: as Muslims can use earth (*tayammum*) for the dry ritual purification when no water is available, instead of performing the ablutions by washing their bodies (*wuḍū'*), this letter is no more than a replacement for a personal meeting with Baldassarre: "wa-hāḏā kitab-ī nāṭiq[an] 'an ṣubābah wa-fī 'adam al-mā' al-tayammum ǧā'iz". Baldassarre translates this without disclosing the meaning of the ritual and thus not giving any clear meaning to the whole sentence – as well as the metaphor – to a Catholic audience: "questa mia Lettera supplisce al tuono della mia voce, come il tocco della pietra supplisce alla mancanza dell'acqua"[35].

The Muslim sender of the letter goes so far in expressing love for his master as to suggest he would worship Baldassarre if this were allowed. With a hint of idolatry (*širk*), he employs an unmistakable word for pointing to the religious worship he directs towards his master: *al-suǧūd*, which is the prostration Muslims perform towards the Kaaba during their daily prayers. The complete sentence the Muslim wrote to Baldassarre is the following: "law kān yanbaġī al-suǧūd li-maḫlūq la-kunt ya-sayyid anā awwal man yasǧud" (if it were possible to prostrate towards a creature, I would be the first, oh master, in prostrating), which Baldassarre translates as follows: "se lecita fusse l'adoratione ad alcuna creatura, io sarei il primo, o mio signore, che v'adorassi"[36]. Translating the word *al-suǧūd* and the verb *yasǧud* (*saǧada*) by *adoratione* and *adorassi* (worship, to worship), Baldassarre intends to emphasise the religious meaning of an act (prostration) – which may not have been fully understandable to an Italian Catholic reader – even more clearly.

The Muslim goes on addressing Baldassarre employing additional religious words. He says: "naẓara ilà waǧh al-ḥabīb na'īm" (looking at the face of the beloved is Paradise, translated by Baldassarre as follows: "il vedere la faccia del mio amato signore è un Paradiso")[37]. The word

34. APUG, Ms. 1060–01, fol. 101v.
35. APUG, Ms. 1060–01, fol. 123v; APUG, Ms. 1060–01, fol. 101v.
36. Ibid.
37. Ibid.

the Muslim slave employed for indicating Paradise was less common than the expected *ğannah*. In fact, instead of using *ğannah*, he refers to Paradise with the word *na ʿīm* (delight, bliss)[38] which can be found in several suras, like Qur. V:65, X:9, XXII:56, as *ğannat al-na ʿīm* (Garden of Delight). According to Louis Gardet's entry in *The Encyclopaedia of Islam*, a *ḥadīṯ* attributed to Ibn ʿAbbās states that the Garden of Delight is the highest level of Paradise[39]. Therefore, by including this word in the letter, the Muslim writer would have stressed how blissful and delightful it was to be with his master.

He was prepared to do anything for his beloved master: using his blood in the absence of ink, tearing off his own skin to use instead of paper, using his own bones in the place of a pen; if he were allowed to flee, he would immediately go to Baldassarre. But imagining bodily mutilations was still not enough for him and wanting to be sure of suitably expressing just how desperate he was, the Muslim slave quotes "the best of stories" (*aḥsan al-qiṣaṣ*, Qur. XII:3, *sūrat Yūsuf*) – and the longest story devoted to a single prophet in the Qurʾān – comparing his tears to what Jacob felt after losing his son Joseph[40]. The words in a monorhyme *ġazal* by the Muslim and Baldassarre's Italian translation are as follows:

> *Bakaytu ʿalà faqd al-ḥabīb tāʾssufan*
> *kamā bakà Yaʿqub iḏ ġāba Yūsufan*[41]

This is translated by Baldassarre as follows:

> ho pianto con sospiri al ricordo del mio amato,
> come pianse Giacob nella perdita di Gioseppe[42]

But including a reference to the story of Jacob and Joseph may not have only been a way to compare his tears to those of Jacob. In fact, it may be read with a double meaning. On the one hand, there is an explicit analogy with Jacob's sadness who saw Joseph taken away to Egypt by the other brothers; according to this first and clear reading, the Muslim

38. Lange 2015, pp. 38, 50
39. Gardet 1965, p. 450
40. Matar 2021b, p. 257.
41. APUG, Ms. 1060–01, fol. 123v.
42. APUG, Ms. 1060–01, fol. 102r.

sender would have drawn a parallel between Jacob and his own state of separation from a beloved person. On the other hand, the reference to Jacob and Joseph may have implied a further meaning between the lines, if the following verses in Qur. II:131–133 are considered:

> His Lord said to him [Abraham], "Devote yourself to Me". Abraham replied, "I devote myself to the Lord of the Universe", and commanded his sons to do the same, as did Jacob: "My sons, God has chosen [your] religion for you, so make sure you devote yourselves to Him, to your dying moment". Were you [Jews] there to see when death came upon Jacob? When he said to his sons, "What will you worship after I am gone?" they replied, "We shall worship your God and the God of your fathers, Abraham, Ishmael, and Isaac, one single God: we devote ourselves to Him"[43].

According to this hidden meaning, the Muslim slave may have addressed a warning to Baldassarre, which can be read as follows: "remember", he says, "you shall worship your God, as your fathers did, and die worshipping him".

Baldassarre's quite literal approach to the translation does not entail a full transposition of the cultural and religious otherness within the text, as the case of prostrating shows. But omitting, deleting, or changing certain words should not be read as a form of censorship; on the contrary, even though Jesuits recommended not keeping profane books like Petrarch's and Ariosto's in the library and discouraged the reading of such "libri osceni"[44], Baldassarre does not hesitate to translate the many love passages in the letter. As a former Muslim, he fully understood that genre of Arabic poetry, which a century and a half later would be identied by the Jesuit Juan Andrés as the source of the French and Italian courtly love in his monumental work *Dell'origine, progressi e stato attuale d'ogni letteratura* (1782–1799)[45].

The way Baldassarre removes the otherness from within the text seems to be due to the prerequisite of making the Islamic cultural and religious world more comprehensible. He was aware that some aspects pertaining

43. *The Qur'an: A New Translation by M. S.A., Abdel Haleem*, p. 15.
44. Mancini 2020, pp. 165–166.
45. Benigni 2017, p. 114. On the relation between Islamic and Western courtly love, see also Mansub Basiri 2011, pp. 17–24.

to Islam may have been hard to grasp for a Catholic reader who was not skilled regarding the subject matter. Therefore, in this case he does not appear to have any interest in stressing the theological/heresiological issues with and differences from Catholic morality.

For instance, Baldassarre inexplicably translates a reference to visiting the Kaaba and circumambulating it ("*yazūru al-Ka'bah wa-yaṭūfu*") with "che abbellisce la Mecca, e si fa celebre"[46], deleting the text in the Arabic version and putting the Italian translation in brackets. As a further example, the Muslim slave says that two marvellous things like King Solomon's flying carpet (*bisāṭ Sulaymān*) or Caesar's kingdom (*mulk al-akāsir*) would be nothing more than a mosquito's wing compared to the vision of the object of his desire. Besides the now familiar love language, it is interesting to note here that, while Baldassarre correctly translates *mulk al-akāsir* by "imperio di Cesare" – a well-known title even in the Ottoman Empire, which the sultans used to address to themselves[47] – he employs the phrase "potere di Salomone" in the place of *bisāṭ*[48]. In this way, Baldassarre only removes the reference to an unfamiliar cultural and literary theme from the text and, at the same time, preserves the conceptual meaning regarding the actuality, according to which nothing compares to the nearness to his beloved master, no matter how marvellous and great things are.

Along with the already mentioned elimination (and erroneous Italian translation) of the sentence regarding the Kaaba – a minor editing which allows us to read the words all the same – the Arabic letter contains an additional perceptibly deleted sentence. In fact, Baldassarre deletes the reference to the prophet Muḥammad after the praise to God, placed in the very beginning of the Arabic text. This time, however, Baldassarre surprisingly and perplexingly keeps the textual reference to the Prophet in the Italian translation ("Lode à Dio solo e la salute di Dio à Maometto nostro Signore")[49], without any emendation of the sentence. Why did Baldassarre not delete the praise to Muḥammad in the Italian text as he did in the Arabic version? Did Baldassarre himself make the deletion?

46. APUG, Ms. 1060–01, fol. 123r; APUG, Ms. 1060–01, fol. 101r.
47. On "the romanization of Turkish rulers in Ottoman imperial propaganda", see Tommasino 2018b, pp. 79–103, pp. 95–96.
48. APUG, Ms. 1060–01, fol. 123v; APUG, Ms. 1060–01, fol. 102r.
49. APUG, Ms. 1060–01, fol. 123r; APUG, Ms. 1060–01, fol. 101r.

If it was not Baldassarre, then who removed this reference? A definite answer cannot be given; one can only raise questions about how and why a quite literary translation of a letter full of love and nostalgia from Arabic into Italian contains omissions and deleted sentences.

Continuing the reading of the letter, the Arabic version becomes less clear with the Muslim slave starting to allude to Baldassare's family, country, and former life, perhaps with the aim of instigating nostalgia in his master's heart as well. Then, once again, the Muslim slave goes on to describe his miserable circumstances due to Baldassarre's absence. Even eating, drinking, and sleeping are becoming harder for him: "al-akl wa-l-šurb fa-li-ağli-ka wa-l-nawm ṣāhir yubātu yantaẓirū ilà qudumi-ka ʿalayhi", which according to Baldassarre's translation reads: "che non mangia, ne beve per vostro amore, ne dorme vegliando tutta la notte, aspettando la vostra venuta"[50]. Overcome by discouragement and despair, as a final request the Muslim slave asks Baldassarre to let him join him in Messina or wherever else he may be (*aradtu an tabīʿa-nā fī Masinā aw bilād uḫrā*/"o facendomi stare in Messina, o altrove")[51].

Nearing the end of his letter, the Muslim sender has a further expression of idolatry towards Baldassarre referring to him as he who created him (*wa anta ḫalaqta-nī*), using a verb (*ḫalaqa*) the Qurʾān often uses when describing God's act of creation. He then makes a clear reference to the Prophet Muḥammad: "innī saʾaltu-ka bi-l-nabī Muḥammad ḫayr al-anām wa-sayyid al-šufaʿāʾ", surprisingly translated correctly by Baldassarre this time: "vi prego per l'amor di Maometto, che è bene di tutti, e capo di tutti i Profeti"[52].

How Baldassarre – or anybody else – deals with some aspects of Islamic otherness is far from clear in the translated letter. In this case, however, the role played by the translation is clear: transferring the otherness of Islam into a Catholic Western context, which many Jesuits already did when dealing with different cultural contexts. Of course, Baldassarre was not the first or the only Jesuit to carry out such a cultural activity since he was part of an already well-established Jesuit tradition of translations, which flourished in those years and continued to do so up until the

50. APUG, Ms. 1060–01, fol. 124r; APUG, Ms. 1060–01, fol. 103r.
51. Ibid.
52. Ibid.

suppression of the order, not only as regards non-European texts but also within the sphere of the European languages[53]. In this way, the Jesuits were able to decipher a wide number of languages, which – after the discovery of the New World – resulted in being many more than the 72 biblical languages listed in the story of the Tower of Babel[54].

In his essay on the Jesuits and the practice of translation, Peter Burke has drawn a parallel between the concept of "cultural translation" – formulated by Edward Evans-Pritchard and the British anthropological school – and the Jesuit practise of accommodation[55]. In fact, by undertaking the translation of Arabic texts with Islamic content, Baldassarre was translating several Islamic concepts (the ritual of the Kaaba, ablution, the carpet of Solomon, etc.) and a peculiar Islamic poetics into an Italian-speaking Catholic context. What he carried out was undeniably a cultural translation, which should be read, however, keeping in mind some of Talal Asad's enlightening suggestions concerning inequality in the power of languages due to the "asymmetrical tendencies and pressures in the languages of dominated and dominant societies"[56]. Regarding cultural translation and its addressees, Asad states that: "The translation is addressed to a very specific audience, which is waiting to read *about* another mode of life and to manipulate the text it reads according to established rules, not to learn *to live* a new mode of life"[57]. Asad's reflections on asymmetry, the inequality of languages, and translation could also apply to Baldassarre and the Muslim slave, due to the asymmetrical position between these two men. Baldassarre was a former Muslim ruler who converted to Christianity, he was a free man and going to be a priest in a society where Catholicism was dominant. He translated a letter written by an educated Muslim slave – who was, instead, living as a member of a minority group among Catholics – for a Catholic readership that was interested in reading about Islamic culture and religion, but not in living that way.

53. Burke 2007, pp. 24–32; see also Taneja 2012, pp. 267–275; Brockey 2019, pp. 389–409.
54. See the Jesuit António Vieira's sermon given in 1657 regarding the many languages discovered in Brazil and quoted in Brockey 2019, p. 403.
55. Burke 2007, p. 24.
56. Asad 1986, p. 164
57. Ibid, p. 159.

6. Conclusion

The asymmetrical position between the two characters of this story does not devalue the peaceful content of the writing. The Muslim's letter – together with Baldassarre's Italian translation – are priceless documents pertaining to interreligious relations. Moreover, the relevance of the letter is related to the underlying story, namely, a case of apostasy (*riddah*) of a Muslim ruler who was renowned as a tireless anti-Christian preacher among the Muslim slaves in Malta. Confused by his radical change in religion, the Muslim slave chose the approach of love for dealing with such a sensitive issue, avoiding hate speech and allegations of apostasy, as well as any kind of religious controversy. The Muslim's letter consisted of alternating prose and *ġazal*, using the homoerotic courtly love poetry that still flourished during the Ottoman period. Missing his master and his presence by his side, the Muslim slave does not seem to be interested in theological matters regarding apostasy. He obviously included religious and Qur'anic themes in the letter, but they act as poetic allegories for depicting his enormous sadness – with the possible exception that may be read between the lines as a second meaning of the sentence on Jacob and Joseph.

The love themes permeating the whole letter were noted even by Domenico Brunacci himself in the biography, who wrote without surprise for the passionate love (*d'amore*) language[58]:

> In tanto il sopradetto Dottore Maomettano all'avviso, che Diego Baldassarre fosse giunto à Malta, corse subito a fargli riverenza, e ben seppe usare espressioni corrispondenti à quelle, che seppe inviarle nella lettera riferita di stima, d'amore, d'ossequij al suo Signore e Padrone, ma insieme di speranza d'haverlo à ristituire al suo Regno[59].

Thanks to Brunacci's biography of Baldassarre and to a small work by the spiritual father in Malta Francesco Navantieri[60], we know how the story ended. After receiving the letter and before travelling to Rome,

58. On Islam and its relationship with sodomy as a form of heresy according to early modern Christian thought, see Lavenia 2015, pp. 103–130; in English translation: Lavenia 2020, pp. 65–88; Lavenia 2021, pp. 155–173.
59. Brunacci, *Vita*, 103, 142v.
60. APUG, Ms. 1060–02, fols. 130r-v.

Baldassarre chose to go back to Malta for a personal meeting with the anonymous Muslim (the *Dottore Maomettano*, according to Brunacci), rather than writing a response. Once the Muslim slave saw his master landing in Malta, he acted as he wrote in the letter, namely with love and respect. But, after a face-to-face theological dispute with his beloved master Baldassare, the Muslim finally converted to Christianity[61]. According to Brunacci, Baldassarre said the following to the now-former Muslim: "Sarete sempre non mio schiavo, ma mio vero Fratello" (You will always be not my slave, but my true Brother)[62].

Obviously, as Matar states, the Muslim slave in Malta was searching for Baldassarre's help[63]. In conclusion, however, it can be stated that nostalgia and sadness due to the distance which kept him apart from his beloved master Baldassarre are the main characteristics of this writing, which can be read as a beautiful example of interreligious literature in the Mediterranean area in the early modern age.

References

Andrews, W. G., Kalpakli, M. (2005), *The Age of Beloveds: Love and the Beloved in Early-Modern Ottoman and European Culture and Society*, Duke University Press, Durham and London.

APUG, Ms. 1060–02. https://gate.unigre.it/mediawiki/index.php/Index:BLMM_1060_02.djvu (transcribed by Emanuele Colombo)

APUG, Ms. 1060–01, fols. 101r–103v. https://gate.unigre.it/mediawiki/index.php/Index:BLMC_s.d._1060_01–101.pdf (transcribed by Federico Stella).

APUG, Ms. 1060–01, fols. 123r–124v. https://gate.unigre.it/mediawiki/index.php/Index:BLMC_1060_01.pdf (transcribed by Nabil Matar).

Asad, T. (1986), *The Concept of Cultural Translation in British Social Anthropology*, in J. Clifford, G. E. Marcus (eds.), *Writing Culture: The Poetics and Politics of Ethnography*, University of California Press, Berkeley-Los Angeles-London, pp. 141–164.

Bauer, T. (2014), *Male-Male Love in Classical Arabic Poetry*, in E. L. McCallum, M. Tuhkanen (eds.), *The Cambridge History of Gay and Lesbian Literature*, Cambridge University Press, Cambridge, pp. 107–124.

61. Brunacci, *Vita*, 103, 141v–146r.
62. Brunacci, *Vita*, 103, 144v.
63. Matar 2021b, pp. 256–257.

Benigni, E. (2017), *Dante and the Construction of a Mediterranean Literary Space: Revisiting a 20th Century Philological Debate in Southern Europe and in the Arab World*, in "Philological Encounters", 2, pp. 111–138. https://doi.org/10.1163/24519197-00000017

Biesterfeldt, H. H., Gutas, D. (1984), *The Malady of Love*, in "Journal of the American Oriental Society", 104, 1, pp. 21–55. https://doi.org/10.2307/602641

Bono, S. (1998), *Conversioni di musulmani al cristianesimo*, in B. Benassar, R. Sauzet, *Chrétiens et Musulmans à la Renaissance: Actes du 37e colloque international du CESR (1994)*, Honoré Champion Éditeur, Paris, pp. 429–445.

Brockey, L. M. (2019), *Comprehending the World: Jesuits, Language, and Translation*, in "Archivum Historicum Societatis Iesu", 88, 2 (fasc. 176), pp. 389–409.

Brogini, A. (2006), *Malte frontière de chrétienté (1530–1670)*, École Française de Rome, Rome.

Brunacci S. J., Domenico (1692), *Vita del ammirabile P. Baldassarre Loiola de Mandes della Compagnia di Gesù. Prodigio della Divina Grazia*, ARSI, *Vitae*, 103–104.

Bürgel, J. C. (1996), *Literatur und Wirklichkeit*, in "Asiatische Studien", 50, pp. 245–257. https://doi.org/10.1515/9783110936186-010

Burke, P. (2007), *The Jesuits and the Art of Translation in Early Modern Europe*, in P. Burke, R. Hsia (eds.), *Cultural Translation in Early Modern Europe*, Cambridge University Press, Cambridge, pp. 24–32.

Capezzone, L. (1998), *La politica ecumenica califfale: pluriconfessionalismo, dispute interreligiose e trasmissione del patrimonio greco nei secoli VIII–IX*, in "Oriente Moderno", 17(78), 1, pp. 1–62. https://doi.org/10.1163/22138617-07801002

Capezzone, L. (2007), *Scenari d'amore pre-cortese, a Baghdad*, in Abū Nuwās, *Così rossa è la rosa*, Saggio introduttivo, traduzione e note di L. Capezzone, Carocci, Rome, pp. 7–82.

Capezzone, L. (2020), *«Fonderei la mia fede alla fede dei Greci»: Abū Nuwās e la poetica degli amori interreligiosi*, in A. Perrotta, L. Mainini (eds.), *Confini e parole: Identità e alterità nell'epica e nel romanzo*, Atti del Convegno, 21–22 settembre 2017 Sapienza Università di Roma, Sapienza Università Editrice, Rome, pp. 207–232.

Charfi, A. (1994), *La fonction historique de la polémique islamochrétienne à l'époque Abbaside*, in S. Khalil Samir, J. S. Nielsen (eds.), *Christian Arabic Apologetics during the Abbasid Period (750–1258)*, Brill, Leiden, pp. 44–56.

Colombo, E. (2011), *Baldassarre Loyola de Mandes (1631–1667), prince de Fez et Jésuite*, in B. Vincent, J. Dakhlia (eds.), *Les Musulmans dans l`histoire de l`Europe*, Éditions Albin Michel, Paris, Vol. I, pp. 159–193.

Colombo, E. (2013), *A Muslim Turned Jesuit: Baldassarre Loyola Mandes (1631–1667)*, "Journal of Early Modern History", 17, pp. 479–504. https://doi.org/10.1163/15700658-12342378

Colombo, E. (2020), *Conversioni religiose in Calderón de la Barca:* El Gran Príncipe de Fez (1669), in "Drammaturgia", 16, 6, pp. 49–79.

De Castries, H. (1922), *Les sources inédites de l'Histoire du Maroc*, Ernest Leroux Éditeur, Paris, Vol. 2/1, pp. 203–240.

De Castries, H. (1928), *Trois princes Marocains convertis au Christianisme*, in *Memorial Henri Basset*, Librairie Orientaliste Paul Geuthner, Paris, Vol. 1, pp. 141–158.

El-Rouyaheb, K. (2005a), *Before Homosexuality in the Arab-Islamic World, 1500–1800*, The University of Chicago Press, Chicago-London.

El-Rouyaheb, K. (2005b), *The Love of Boys in Arabic Poetry of the Early Ottoman Period, 1500 –1800*, in "Middle Eastern Literatures", 8, 1, pp. 3–22. https://doi.org/10.1080/1366616042000309157

Fani, S., Farina, M. (eds.) (2012), *Le vie delle lettere: La Tipografia medicea tra Roma e l'Oriente*, Mandragora, Florence.

Fiume, G. (2009), *Schiavitù mediterranee. Corsari, rinnegati e santi di età moderna*, Bruno Mondadori, Milan.

Foucault, M. (1976), *Histoire de la sexualité I. La volonté de savoir*, Gallimard, Paris.

García-Arenal, M. (2009), *Ahmad al-Mansur: The Beginning of Modern Morocco*, Oneworld, London.

García Goldáraz, C. (1944), *Baltasar Loyola Mandes, S.I.: Hijo del rey de Fez. Extracto de la tesis de doctorado en la facultad de misionologia de la Universidad Gregoriana*, Imprenta Aldecoa, Burgos.

Gardet, L. (1965), *s.v.* «Djanna», in *The Encyclopaedia of Islam*, 2nd ed., vol. 2, Brill-Luzac, Leiden-London, pp. 447–452

Girard, A. (2017), *Teaching and Learning Arabic in Early Modern Rome: Shaping a Missionary Language*, in J. Loop, A. Hamilton, C. Burnett (eds.), *The Teaching and Learning of Arabic in Early Modern Europe*, Brill, Leiden, pp. 189–212

Gutas, D. (1998), *Greek Thought, Arabic Culture: The Graeco-Arabic Translation Movement in Baghdad and Early 'Abbāsid Society (2nd–4th/8th–10th centuries)*, Routledge, London.

Hajji, M. (1976–1977), *L'activité intellectuelle au Maroc à l'époque sa'dide*, Dar el-Maghrib, Rabat.

Hamori, A. (1974), *On the Art of Medieval Arabic Literature*, Princeton University Press, Princeton.

Khalil Samir, S. Nasry, W. (2016), *The Patriarch and the Caliph: An Eighth-Century Dialogue between Timothy I and al-Mahdī*, Brigham Young University Press, Provo.

Kuru, S. S. (2015), *Il genere del desiderio: L'amore per i bei ragazzi nella letteratura ottomana della prima età moderna*, in U. Grassi, G. Marcocci (eds.), *Le trasgressioni della carne: Il desiderio della carne nel mondo islamico e cristiano, secc XII–XX*, Viella, Rome, pp. 81–102.

Kuru, S. S. (2020a), *Generic Desire: Homoerotic Love in Ottoman Turkish Literature*, in U. Grassi, *Mediterranean Crossings: Mediterranean Crossings: Sexual Transgressions in Islam and Christianity (10th–18th Centuries)*, Viella, Rome, pp. 43–63.

Kuru, S. S. (2020b), *Male Discourses of Gender and Sexuality: How History Omits the Ottoman Elites' Love of Literature*, in "Journal of the Ottoman and Turkish Studies Association", 7, 2, pp. 133–145. https://doi.org/10.2979/jottturstuass.7.2.09

Lange, C. R. (2015), *Paradise and Hell in Islamic Traditions*, Cambridge University Press, Cambridge.

Lavenia, V. (2015), *Tra eresia e crimine contro natura: sessualità, islamofobia e inquisizioni nell'Europa moderna*, in in U. Grassi, G. Marcocci (eds.), *Le trasgressioni della carne: Il desiderio della carne nel mondo islamico e cristiano, secc XII–XX*, Viella, Rome, pp. 103–130.

Lavenia, V. (2020), *Between Heresy and "Crimes against Nature": Sexuality, Islamophobia and the Inquisition in Early Modern Europe*, in U. Grassi (ed.), *Mediterranean Crossings: Mediterranean Crossings: Sexual Transgressions in Islam and Christianity (10th–18th Centuries)*, Viella, Rome, pp. 65–88.

Lavenia, V. (2021), *Contaminating Infidels, Burnt Bodies, and Saved Souls: Sodomy and Catholicism in the Early Modern Age*, in E. Fischer, X. von Tippelskirch (eds.), *Bodies in Early Modern Religious Dissent Naked, Veiled, Vilified, Worshipped*, Routledge, London and New York, pp. 155–173.

Lebessou, L. (1910), *Le seconde vie d'un sultan du Maroc*, in "Études", 123, pp. 488–498.

Ledóchowski, W. (1937), *De Mahumetanorum conversione rite paranda et promovenda*, in "Acta Romana Societatis Iesu", 8, 3, pp. 784–792.

Lewis, B. (2001), *Music from a Distant Drum: Classical Arabic, Persian, Turkish and Hebrew Poetry*, Princeton University Press, Princeton.

Mancini, L. (2020), *L'ordine e i libri: fonti per la storia dell'uso delle biblioteche della Compagnia di Gesù*, in E. P. Ardolino, A. Petrucciani, V. Ponzani (eds.), *What Happened in the Library? Cosa è successo in biblioteca? Lettori e biblioteche tra indagine storica e problemi attuali. Reader and Libraries from Historical Investigations to Current Issues*. International Research Seminar. Seminario internazionale di ricerca Roma 27–28 settembre 2018, Associazione Italiana Biblioteche 2020, Rome, pp. 157–171.

Mansub Basiri, I. (2011), *Due motivi orientali della lirica romanza*, in "La parola del testo", 14, 1–2, pp. 17–24.

Matar, N. (2021a), *Mediterranean Captivity through Arab Eyes, 1517–1798*, Brill, Leiden.
Matar, N. (2021b), *Two Muslim Converts to Catholicism in Arabic Sources, 1656–1667*, in "The Seventeenth Century", 36, 2, pp. 253–269.
Pizzorusso, G. (2004), *I satelliti di Propaganda Fide: il Collegio Urbano e la Tipografia poliglotta. Note di ricerca su due istituzioni culturali romane nel XVII secolo*, in "Mélanges de l'École française de Rome", 116, 2, pp. 471–498.
Pouzet, L. (1983), *Motivations et contributions des Jésuites dans les etudes islamiques*, in *Meeting of Jesuits in Islamic Studies: Proceedings and Paper, Sayyidat al-Bi'r, Lebanon, 15–19 June 1983*, s.n., Rome, pp. 157–169.
The Qur'an: A New Translation, trans. M. S. A. Abdel Haleem, Oxford University Press, New York 2004.
Santus, C. (2019), *Il «turco» a Livorno. Incontri con l'Islam nella Toscana del Seicento*, Officina Libraia, Rome.
Taneja, M. (2012), *Translation as a Dialogue between Cultures: The Jesuit Experience*, in I. Arellano, C. Mata Induráin (eds.), *St Francis Xavier and the Jesuit Missionary Enterprise: Assimilations between Cultures / San Francisco Javier y la empresa misionera jesuita: Asimilaciones entre culturas*, Servicio de Publicaciones de la Universidad de Navarra, Pamplona, pp. 267–275.
Tommasino, P. M. (2018a), *Bulghaith al-Darawi and Barthélemy d'Herbelot: Readers of the Qur'an in Seventeenth-Century Tuscany*, in "Journal of Qur'anic Studies", 20, 3, pp. 94–120. https://doi.org/10.3366/jqs.2018.0353
Tommasino, P. M. (2018b), *Roman Prophet or Muslim Caesar: Muḥammad the Lawgiver before and after Machiavelli*, in L. Biasiori, G. Marcocci (eds.), *Machiavelli, Islam and the East: Reorienting the Foundations of Modern Political Thought*, Palgrave Macmillan, Cham, pp. 79–103.
Ze'evi, D. (2006), *Producing Desire: Changing Sexual Discourse in the Ottoman Middle East, 1500–1900*, University of California Press, Berkeley, Los Angeles, and London.

Federico Stella graduated with a degree in the history of philosophy at Sapienza University of Rome and obtained a PhD in Oriental Studies at the same University. Currently, he is a postdoctoral researcher at the University of Naples L'Orientale with an ERC Synergy Grant for a project *The European Qu'ran. Islamic Scripture in European Culture and Religion 1150–1850*. His main interests are Islamic philosophy and the history of Christian-Muslim relations.

Chapter 11

Peace and Justice: A Catholic Palestinian Response to the Israeli-Palestinian Conflict

Paolo Maggiolini

Abstract

The 1970s and the 1980s were characterised by the unfolding of multiple processes of transformation and reconfiguration of the Israeli-Palestinian political and religious landscapes. For Christian Palestinians, these years saw the indigenisation of the upper hierarchies of most of the established churches in Jerusalem and the inauguration of fresh theologies, with the gradual circulation of new cultural products designed to stimulate local Christians' awareness during the Israeli occupation and the First Intifada. Of the many initiatives and protagonists in these decades, the chapter concentrates on the Catholic dimension by reconsidering some of the statements and letters from the Justice and Peace Commission, complementing this analysis with a brief focus on the theological reflection of Michel Sabbah (Mīšīl Ṣabbāḥ), the first Arab Patriarch for the Roman Catholic (Latin) community. These cultural products were aimed at promoting a stronger consciousness of local Christians' vocation and role at the local level, while stimulating a better understanding of their condition at the international level in the light of demands for peace and justice for all the inhabitants of this land.

Keywords: Christian Palestinians, First Intifada, Latin Patriarchate of Jerusalem, churches in Jerusalem, Justice and Peace Commission in Jerusalem.

1. Introduction

The analysis of the Christian Arab Palestinians' presence and their intellectual engagement with the Israeli-Palestinian political context requires a willingness to embrace complexity, refusing simplistic and mono-dimensional assessments.

Christian Palestinians in the Holy Land live in an intrinsically multivocal landscape, with its many religious orders and churches both from the East and the West[1]. This has endowed them with material and symbolic capital. Christians benefitted from the numerous church institutions and missionary activities by gaining income, employment, and education. They also achieved access to many international Christian networks, further improving their capacity to navigate this complex political and security scenario. Nevertheless, these "opportunities" have sometimes been transformed into barriers and obstacles. For many decades, ecclesiastical fragmentation and competition between the churches have multiplied controversies and struggles, preventing local Christians from expressing their positions and views with a single voice. Similarly, the non-indigeneity of the majority of the upper hierarchies of the churches in Jerusalem has often multiplied internal tensions, particularly in the Orthodox dimension between Greek and Arab elements.

At the sociopolitical level, Christian Palestinians face the challenging situation of being a demographic minority both in Israel and Palestine, albeit with different contextual conditions. As Arab, Palestinian, and Christian in a land of conflict and diverging nationalist projects, they have been constantly called upon to steer between their religious and national senses of belonging. In Israel, the advocacy for their rights as a religious community distinct from Jews and Muslims has the potential to open a line of negotiation with state authorities independently of the conflict. Nevertheless, this scheme has always posed to Christians the risk of becoming politically irrelevant[2] or, worse, being transformed into an instrument of a divide-and-conquer strategy. Israeli state authorities have frequently pressured them to profile themselves solely on the basis of their religious affiliation in order to separate them from the rest of

1. O'Mahony 2009, p. VIII.
2. McGahern 2012, p. 178.

the Arab Palestinian population[3]. While such an approach has partially served the churches' interests for the defence of their activities and institutions, at the individual level Christian Palestinians have always experienced the same treatment as their Muslim brothers[4]. Furthermore, this situation has also fostered tensions between Muslims and Christians in towns like Nazareth, Haifa, and Akko (Acre)[5].

By cultivating their attachment to Arab and Palestinian culture, they were able to overcome the strict limits of their communities to play an active role in the most important Palestinian sociocultural and political dynamics with an impact far more significant than their numbers might lead one to expect. This attitude and its results are proved by their strong engagement with the struggle for Palestinian liberation. However, this approach has also resulted in the risk of publicly veiling and dimming their specific instances, especially from the perspective of an external audience. This situation reverberates in the intra-Christian tension between the opportunity to maintain or challenge traditional Arab cultural norms on the one hand and the desirability of demarcating community boundaries vis-à-vis Muslims and nurturing cultural ties with the West on the other[6]. This kind of dilemma has always simmered within the local Christian community to clearly emerge at the end of the Second Intifada.

Today, Christian Palestinians seem to still be oscillating between three main different positions. Part of the community remains strongly attached to the traditional position of PLO secular nationalism. Another component seems to be moving towards forms of religious and communal renewals that parallel that of Islamists. Finally, others are showing disengagement from the Israeli-Palestinian sociopolitical context, seeking refuge in quietism and piety[7].

Clearly, local Christians' extra effort to constantly reconfigure their presence is also determined by their worrisome demographic situation. Low birth rates and high emigration for economic reasons and individual desires to live far from the conflict have gradually reduced their number in Israel and Palestine. In the West Bank, Gaza and East Jerusalem area,

3. Bialer 2005, pp. 139–140.
4. Tsimhoni 2002, p. 127.
5. Kårtveit 2014, p. 5.
6. Ibid., p. 3.
7. Lybarger 2007, p. 780.

Christians accounted for 12% of the population in 1914, but today they represent less than 1.2%, numbering between 49,000 and 51,800 people. In East Jerusalem, they number about 10,000, namely, 1% of the overall population, while in the West Bank they number 39,000 and in Gaza 1000. In Israel, their number is around 120,000, representing 8% of Israel's Arab Palestinians, 75% of the Israeli Christian citizens and thus just 2% of the total population[8]. Nonetheless, thanks also to the churches' presence, Christians have never succumbed to the logic of numbers and to the idea of being categorised as a minority predestined to disappear or to become just a symbolic living testimony in the Christian Holy Land.

Hence, Christian Palestinians are a reflection of one of the most vivid expressions of Middle Eastern Christianity with its capacity to reconcile liminality, indigeneity, and decreasing demographic trends in a land rich in diversity where the continuous intermingling of local, regional, and international dimensions has produced a multifarious intermestic political and religious field. The starting point of new intellectual and theological elaborations of the late 1970s and the 1980s was precisely such considerations with the aim of stimulating individual and community ponderation of the significance of being indigenous Christians of the Holy Land with strong bonds with the Universal Church and a role to play in a time of conflict and occupation.

2. State-Church Relationships between the 1967 War and the First Intifada

After the 1967 War, Christian institutions focused on expanding their international networks and connections, while repositioning their presence and role within the new reality of the Occupied Territories and a reunited Jerusalem under the Israeli regime. State-church relationships continued to be inspired by the traditional path of appeasement and sectoral collaboration that had been initiated after 1948. Nevertheless, it is also important to mention that, already in the late 1960s, some episodes of friction occurred[9]. For example, in 1972, the Greek Catholic (Melkite) Archbishop Joseph Raya (Yūsuf Rāyā) led a demonstration to protest the

8. *Is Peace Possible?* 2019, p. 9. Kårtveit 2014, p. 4.
9. Bialer 2005, p. 127.

expulsion of the inhabitants from Kafr Birʿim and Iqrit in Upper Galilee that had occurred in 1948[10]. He ordered all churches in his eparchy to remain closed on Sundays as a sign of protest. Although limited to Israel, Raya's activism was already exposing the situation of the Arab Palestinian community that can be described as in crisis during those years and deeply afflicted by demographic decline due to emigration[11].

To a large extent, the Israeli attitude at this time was part of a broader approach to the Arab Palestinian population that can be described as "liberal". By allowing the development of the religious community life of Christians and Muslims, Israel sought to foster new divisions among them and to consolidate a system of control and co-optation to quell political activism and inter-community solidarity[12]. It also pursued the goal of discouraging the formation of a united Christian front, especially in Jerusalem. Hence, the emergence of new Christian ecumenical initiatives in particular raised Israeli concerns.

For example, an article published by The Jerusalem Post in June 1984 openly questioned this new attitude of the churches[13]. Their activism and vocal support for an indigenous church strongly committed to local politics was dismissed as a product of the clergy's willingness to appease the local Christians. In this view, Israel was the only true friend of the church, while the Muslim majority was only interested in instrumentalising it and would soon abandon Christians when its goal was achieved.

At the same time, Israel's interest in preserving its positive relationship with the churches was also due to their vast patrimonial properties, especially that of the Greek Orthodox Patriarchate. Israel aimed to develop good relations with them to have the possibility to lease as much church-owned land as possible[14]. This last aspect has always been particularly controversial and, since 1967, it fostered new tensions with the Palestinian Christian laity, reviving old tensions and creating new divisions, especially within the Orthodox sphere.

Such a modus vivendi began to change during the late 1970s. The Likud's electoral victory in 1977 and the expansion of religious Zionism

10. Marteijn 2020, p. 262.
11. Dumper 2002a, p. 105.
12. Bialer 2005, pp. 140–141.
13. Shapiro 1984, p. 5.
14. Dumper 2002a, p. 113.

since 1973–1974 prompted the acceleration of the reconfiguration of this land under the sole ideal and image of Jewish identity[15]. In particular, the Likud seized the opportunity to control the Israeli Lands Administration, the Ministry of Justice, the Ministries of Religious Affairs and of Housing to make Jerusalem the main stage of this new project[16]. Integrally part of this strategy, the Likud also gave new energy to the implementation of Jewish settlements, already initiated few years before, providing open room to fervent militant organisations, such as the Temple Mount Foundation, to manoeuvre[17]. Accordingly, the churches in Jerusalem began to perceive Israeli authorities as being less motivated to maintain their good relations with them. In this regard, Israeli support for the Christian fundamentalist movement of the International Christian Embassy in Jerusalem, openly pro-Zionist, increased concerns and suspicions[18].

Hence, the churches' new attitude in the late 1970s towards Israeli authorities was not just a reaction motivated by self-defence interests but attested to a maturation of a different sensibility concerning the pastoral duty of the church in a context of conflict and occupation. The protagonists of this transformation were young indigenous priests and pastors along with members of the local Palestinian laity who had first-hand experience of the hard political reality under the occupation and of Western Christianity's relatively poor knowledge of it. From the late 1970s, and more openly during the First Intifada, a new generation of Christian Palestinians mainly affiliated with the Roman Catholic, Melkite, Lutheran, and Anglican churches began to directly engage with daily social and political issues[19]. Their dedication was based on the conviction that it was not only necessary to improve the material and religious assistance that the churches always provided to their communities, but also to develop a new intellectual and theological knowledge to help Christians navigate the complex landscape of the occupation.

Their commitment was also facilitated by the gradual indigenisation of a large part of local ecclesiastical leadership. This process began with the Anglican Church that elected an Arab bishop, Faik Haddad (Fāʾiq

15. Omer, Springs 2013, p. 99.
16. Dumper 2002a, pp. 76–77.
17. Ibid., p. 117.
18. Dumper 2002b, p. 55.
19. See, for example, Chacour 1990 and Ateek, Ellis, Reuther 1992.

Ḥaddād), in 1976. It then continued with the Lutherans, with the appointment of their first Palestinian bishop, Daoud Haddad (Dāwud Ḥaddād), in 1979. Afterwards, the dynamic progressed with the appointments of Archbishop and Patriarchal Vicar in Jerusalem Lutfi Laham (Luṭfī Laḥḥām) (Greek Catholic) in 1981, of Bishop Samir Kafity (Samīr Qafʿītī) (Arab Anglican) in 1984, and of Latin Patriarch Michel Sabbah (Mīšīl Ṣabbāḥ) in 1987.

This indigenisation process not only changed the ecclesial composition of the churches but also further stimulated the development of a new theology. This result was achieved thanks to the formulation of a Palestinian contextual theology (*lāhūt maḥāllī filasṭīnī*) by the al-Liqa' Center (1982), led by Geries Khoury (Ǧurays Ḫūrī), and a Palestinian liberation theology (*lāhūt taḥrīr filasṭīnī*), thanks to the dedication of Naim Ateek (Naʿīm ʿAtīq)[20] and the work of the Sabeel Ecumenical Liberation Theology Center (1990). These two institutions, along with the theological contribution of religious leaders such as Bishop Riah Abu Al-Assal (Riyāḥ Abū l-ʿAsal) (Anglican), Archbishop Elias Chacour (Ilyās Šaqūr)[21] (Greek Catholic), Patriarch Michel Sabbah (Latin), Fr. Rafiq Khoury (Rafīq Ḫūrī)[22] (Latin), opened the field for a new collective Christian intellectual and theological enterprise for rethinking the role and content of Palestinian Christians' presence and vocation in the name of peace and justice. Their theological efforts gave new voice to local Palestinian Christians and stimulated reflection that still endures today. They also represented a means to try to recompose the Churches' fragmented presences and connect their multiple facets.

Integrally part of such developments, the 1970s also saw the foundation of the Justice and Peace Commission (*Laǧnat al-ʿadl wa-l-salām*) in Jerusalem. Although less famous than the religious leaders mentioned above, this institution is a good example of the crucial evolution experienced by some of the local churches in Jerusalem, especially among Catholics. More interestingly, it was an initiative not simply operating in parallel with those of Christian communities and their church institutions but was integrally part of the Catholic Church presence in Jerusalem. Its

20. Ateek, Ellis, Reuther 1992.
21. Chacour 1990.
22. Khoury 2020.

foundation was a product of a wider and gradual reconfiguration of such a presence in the spirit of Vatican II, and its cultural products perfectly served this goal, embracing both clergy and laity.

Within this framework, 1970 was a crucial year. On the one hand, Patriarch of Jerusalem Giacomo Giuseppe Beltritti promoted the reform of the local school system, supporting the creation of a Diocesan Commission for Religious Education in 1973. The Commission's members were representatives of different Catholic orders and institutions. Its mission was to develop teachings and methodologies able to produce and disseminate new knowledge concerning the challenges of the church at that time and especially in Jerusalem. The secretary, Rafiq Khouri – one of the proponents of Palestinian contextual theology – devoted himself to drafting a new catechism expressive of the needs, interests, and wishes of Christian Palestinians, engaging with the topics of dialogue with Muslims, ecumenism, and the meaning of living in Jerusalem and the Holy Land[23]. On the other hand, in 1970, the idea of establishing a Justice and Peace Commission in Jerusalem on the model of that operating in Rome and in other Western countries also began to be considered. Its foundation would have symbolised for the Holy Land the realisation of Pope Paul VI's invitation to dedicate efforts to the promotion of justice, peace, and human rights according to a Roman Catholic perspective, as indicated by his Motu Proprio *Iustitiam et Pacem* of January 1967. For this purpose, in 1970, Joseph Grémillion, Secretary of the Pontifical Commission for Justice and Peace in Rome, made a first visit with the aim of assessing the possibility of establishing such an institution in the Holy Land[24]. The visit had such positive results that the following year, the Apostolic Delegate in Jerusalem, Pio Laghi, recommended the creation of a Secretariat and a commission to take on responsibility for its activities.

The Commission was ecumenical from the beginning and aimed at becoming a point of contact and debate between all Catholics in the Holy Land. After a first transitional period, it began to function in 1974, being composed of 10 to 12 members representing the different Catholic churches in Jerusalem and their various levels, men and women as part of

23. Tsimhoni 1993, p. 122.
24. The information on the first years of the Justice and Peace Commission in Jerusalem was supplied by Fr Frans Bouwen.

the laity and clergy with various professions and roles. The importance of this Commission was that it represented the first and only place where lay people could meet and express their voices within the Catholic Church, establishing a direct liaison with the Pontifical Council for Laity in Rome and other institutions having the same purpose at the international level. Furthermore, the Commission became a place where it was possible to discuss and monitor the daily political and socioeconomic situation in Israel-Palestine and the Middle East from the perspective of justice, peace, and human rights. From this standpoint, the issue of the housing scarcity and increasing emigration were considered strategic from the start. Therefore, the Commission became a centre for planning activities and a resource to recount the challenges and aspirations of Christian Palestinians without being subject to external or foreign narratives. Finally, it was also intended to become a focal point for promoting bridges between Muslims and Christians.

After a period of internal reflection and debate, aimed at avoiding the public display of its activities to prevent Israeli suspicions about its Palestinian members, the innovative attitude of this new initiative became openly manifest in May 1980 with publication of its first statement, *Christians' Faith and Political Consciousness*. This text provided a local Catholic political and religious understanding of Christian Palestinians in their daily lives within the Holy Land, inviting them to participate and perform active roles.

3. The First Intifada and the Churches in Jerusalem

The outbreak of the First Intifada and its early activity gave a decisive acceleration to the dynamics recalled above. They defined some of the push and pull factors that influenced the position and role of local churches in Jerusalem during these events. They explain how and why Christian Palestinians, both from the clergy and laity, began to develop and disseminate a new theological understanding of the Christian presence under the occupation. They also illuminate the reasons behind the development of a more evident sociopolitical engagement of clergy and laity, a greater coordination between church religious leaderships, and a resolute commitment to repositioning the churches' presence in the wake of the Oslo Accords and the diplomatic negotiations for a final agreement[25].

Traditionally, the beginning of the First Intifada is dated 9 December 1987. It is often said that the Palestinians' uprising was mainly sparked by the combination of two events: a car crash on December 8, that killed four men and seriously injured another seven, and the clashes of the following day when a twenty-year-old, Ḥātim al-Sīsī, was killed when Israeli authorities tried to prevent the gathering of Palestinians coming from all over Gaza to the Ǧabaliyyah camp, where three of the four dead men had lived[26]. In reality, the Palestinians' uprising was much more than a simple spontaneous outburst of grievance and rage. It was the apex of a prolonged period of rising mobilisation in the Occupied Territories that had involved all Palestinians since the 1970s[27].

The Intifada thus confirmed and consolidated the Palestinians' shared awareness of their unique situation and nationalist sentiments under the Israeli occupation[28]. It was thanks to the already existing Palestinian grassroots activism and broad network of multiple initiatives and committees that the Intifada lasted for the next five consecutive years, transiting into a new dimension only after the Oslo Accords (1993).

Therefore, many events and factors contributed to this process both at the local and regional levels. Unquestionably, the 1967 War was the turning point. The defeat of the Arab armies fostered the development of a purely Palestinian nationalist movement under the banner of the Palestinian Liberation Organization (PLO) led by Yasser Arafat (Yāsir ʿArafāt). The war also created the daily reality of the Israeli occupation, with the majority of Palestinians directly under the military rule of Israel. It was exactly the combination of these two new situations, to which the impact of the post-1967 Israeli strategies should be added. These strategies defined the multifaceted landscape in which the Intifada and Palestinian Christians' new theological efforts took place.

First, the 1987 uprising and its specific characteristics were partly a result of the historical vicissitudes experienced by the PLO during these

25. Dumper 2002a, p. 118.
26. Farsoun, Aruri, 2018, p. 208.
27. Alimi 2007, p. 1.
28. Ibid., p. 47.

decades. Since the end of the 1970s, the PLO began to encounter increasing challenges to its image as the sole effective protagonist of the Palestinian national struggle. This dynamic pushed local Palestinian activism to grow and expand with the aim of directly advocating for Palestinians' rights in their daily life under the occupation. In this framework, the negotiations between Egypt and Israel, culminating with the Camp David Accords (1978–1979), were particularly important. They did not simply foster new frustrations in the Palestinian camp but appeared to Palestinians as an open denial of their rights, driving the PLO into a difficult diplomatic position. In particular, the Camp David Accords stimulated an initial attempt to launch a local initiative for representing the entire Palestinian population in the Occupied Territories, thus refusing any possible political accommodation of their presence without their direct involvement.[29] Such concerns increased when a few years later the Israelis launched a campaign, supported by Ariel Sharon, to eliminate the PLO presence in the Territories (1981) and the PLO was evicted from Lebanon following the Israeli invasion (1982).

Second, and more importantly, shortly after 1967, the extension to the Occupied Territories of the British Mandate Defence Regulation of 1945 gave a free hand to Israeli military authorities to assert their power and control over Palestinians[30]. Their individual and collective liberties were thus seriously limited or curtailed. At the same time, since the late 1970s Israeli authorities also dedicated themselves to relinking the West Bank and the Gaza Strip to Israel, extending its economic and communication infrastructure. These policies did not lead to the integration of Palestinians but rather increased their sense of difference and marginalisation. In addition, the increasing number of new settlements and the growing confrontation between Palestinians and the Jewish settlers' bloc widely fuelled contentious politics in the Territories[31]. In just the three years before the Intifada, 17 new settlements were built in the West Bank and the Gaza Strip, bringing the number of settlers to an average of 60 to 80,000[32]. The growing influence of the Jewish settler movement and its

29. Tsimhoni 1993, p. 168.
30. Alimi 2007, p. 34.
31. Omer, Springs 2013, pp. 96–98.
32. Gelvin 2014, p. 225.

religious zeal did not simply increase the pressure of the Israeli occupation but imposed on Christians the challenging test of reconciling their faith in the Bible with their present condition under the Israeli occupation. This dynamic infused them with a strong sense of urgency also because of the support that the settlers' view received from certain Christian Western milieus[33]. Moreover, during the same years, the Palestinian citizens of Israel began to protest and demonstrate for their rights, spotlighting their condition of isolation and marginalisation as second-class citizens in the country. This fostered unity between the many different contextual conditions under which Palestinians were dwelling. Finally, the unilateral declaration of the annexation of East Jerusalem (1980) and the Golan Heights (1981) were a further provocation, stimulating Palestinians to organise and coordinate their activities. Therefore, the gradual erosion of PLO credibility combined with the increasingly harsh attitude of Israeli authorities fostered grassroots activism. These dynamics also served to corroborate Palestinians' awareness of their specific and urgent situation.

It is not by chance that precisely in the second half of the 1970s Palestinians in Israel and the Occupied Territories began to manifest the first signals of growing unity in defence of their rights. First, in 1976 Palestinian protests spread all across historical Palestine against the Israeli decision to expropriate thousands of *donums* of Palestinians' lands, mainly in Galilee. This decision motivated Palestinians in Israel to react with strikes and protests. The National Committee for the Protection of Lands was convened, and it began to inform all Palestinians about the intransigence of the Israeli authorities' decision. On 30 March a vast demonstration was organised during which six Palestinian citizens of Israel were killed. Since then, this event has been commemorated by the name "Land Day", becoming an integral part of the Palestinian commemorative political calendar and a crucial expression of Palestinian unity. Interestingly, among the protagonists of the 1976 protests and demonstrations was Fr. Shehade Shehade (Šaḥādah Šaḥādah), Chairman of the National Committee for the Protection of Lands in Israel. By combining his pastoral duties with activism, Fr. Shehade was among the first of a new generation of priests to become active during the 1970s not simply

33. Robson 2010, p. 47.

in the name of Christians but for the rights of all Palestinians, employing nonviolent resistance.

Consequently, beyond the contingent sparks of 1987 cited above, the First Intifada did not erupt out of nowhere. Just months before the outbreak of the First Intifada, Palestinians were already involved in open confrontations with the Israeli army and Jewish settlers, as the cases of the Balāṭah camp or Qalqīliyyah confirm[34]. Without such experiences and levels of mobilisation the First Intifada would probably not have been possible. This was confirmed by the immediate formation of the United National Command of the Uprising (UNCU) in December 1987, which issued its first leaflet in January 1988. Having a fluid structure without formal leadership but a systematic approach to the coordination of protests and demonstrations, the UNCU was able to capitalise on the experiences of the previous years, limiting the use of violence, confronting Israeli authorities on a daily basis and reassuring the population through the dissemination of its communiqués that the ongoing struggle was being politically guided[35].

But the pre-Intifada period also witnessed the gradual consolidation of another trend of Palestinian activism. The eruption of the uprising sanctioned the rise of a more militant and violent approach to the struggle with Israel that since then has been represented by Hamas and the Islamic Jihad. This would exert a strong influence on the history of the conflict and on the intra-Palestinian balances of power. For Christians, the announcement of the foundation of Hamas represented one of the many signs of the need to create new bridges with the Muslim population in the spirit of collaborating in a shared awareness of the equal belonging of Christians and Muslims to the Palestinian national community.

In the years before the outbreak of the Intifada and during its proceedings, Christians' new theological production thus became important not only to show Christians' commitment to the ongoing events and to stimulate their peaceful engagement, but also to promote ecumenism and interfaith dialogue with the aim of promoting solidarity and equality among all Palestinians, regardless of their faith and ideological orientation.

34. Alimi 2007, p. 116.
35. Ibid., p. 135.

Therefore, these years were crucial for the history of the churches' and Christians' engagement in multiple respects and can be considered a veritable watershed in Christian Palestinian history[36]. While Christians have always played a role in Palestinian sociopolitical dynamics on the basis of their own affiliation with or proximity to the already existing political organisations, a new form of participation emerged with the Intifada. It prompted their direct participation as Christians as fully part of the Palestinian nation. This was a result of the gradual indigenisation of most of the churches in Jerusalem and a more pronounced ecumenical and interritual attitude that the Intifada finally consolidated. One of the main characteristics of the new Palestinian Christian leaders of the time was that they were distinctive for being more antagonistic towards Israeli authorities. In some cases, this new attitude took a very radical stance, as with the case of the Greek Catholic Vicar Hilarion Capucci, who had already been imprisoned in 1974. But the vast majority of their contributions were developed within the field of theological reflection, ecumenical dialogue, and peace activism in support of the protests. Concerning the theological dimension, it is interesting that the al-Liqa' Center published the document *Theology and the Local Church* precisely in 1987, while Naim Ateek issued *Justice and Only Justice: A Palestinian Theology of Liberation* in 1989. These can be considered the first attempts to systematise all debates about and elaborations of Palestinian liberation theologies developed between the late 1970s and early 1980s[37]. They also document the efforts to develop an image of indigenous Christianity strongly attached to this land, its history, and political vicissitudes.

Therefore, it is not strange that once the Intifada broke out, Christians and their churches soon entered the fray. It is important to stress that their participation was not meant to defend Christians alone or their respective communities but the rights and national cause of all Palestinians. Among the many examples of their involvement, one can find some symbolic events that fostered Christians' identification with the Intifada. First, shortly before the uprising, the mayor of Bethlehem, Elias Freij (Ilyās Furayğ), with the support of the churches in Jerusalem, decided to cancel the traditional reception for Christmas. The transformation of Christmas

36. Christiansen 2004, p. 309.
37. Khoury 2020.

1988 into a day of mourning, which UNCU called "a day of national mourning", was particularly important to prove the commitment of the churches and Christians to the Intifada[38].

This demonstrative act was repeated from 1987 to 1989[39]. Michel Sabbah in particular supported and promoted the boycott of official ceremonies associated with religious celebrations. Furthermore, he did not refrain from inviting the Catholic community to focus on present political challenges and suffering also by praying and fasting as, for example, emerges from his message for Christmas 1988[40]. Sabbah's support for the Intifada did not go unnoticed by the Israeli authorities. They strongly criticised his posture and role during the uprising. For example, in 1992 the Religious Affairs Ministry directly condemned his attitude, warning him to go on "to function as a politician and representative of the intifada leadership, rather than as a man of the cloth"[41].

Moreover, following the occupation of St. John's Hospice of the Greek Orthodox Patriarchate by Jewish settlers in April 1990, the established churches agreed to a 24-hour closure of the Holy Sepulchre in open dissent from the Israeli authorities' attitude to the event.

Equally important for Christians' identification with the Intifada were the fatalities of members of their communities during the first two years of the uprising. In July 1988, a Christian resident of the Old City of Jerusalem, Niḍāl al-Rabaḍī, lost his life. In February 1988 Ḫālid al-Tarazī, a Christian boy from Gaza, was apprehended during a demonstration and died while being interrogated. During the same months, another two Christians were killed in Bayt Sāḥūr and Bayt Ǧālā. Their deaths became the symbol of Christians' commitment to the Intifada[42]. Furthermore, in 1989 the predominantly Christian town of Bayt Sāḥūr became one of the biggest stages for the non-violent campaign of resistance in support of the Intifada. Its tax revolt, the throwing away of Israeli identity documents and the attempt to replace Israeli products with Palestinian and Jordanian goods became a powerful symbol, at the local and international levels,

38. Greenberg 1988.
39. Coffey 2016, p. 107.
40. Sabbah 1988, p. 268.
41. Ackerman 1999, p. 3.
42. Tsimhoni 1993, p. 168.

of the Palestinians' peaceful struggle[43]. The experience of Bayt Sāḥūr is particularly relevant because, during their protests, the town repudiated religious markers and stood united in denouncing Israeli occupation as a threat to all Palestinians and not to a specific community[44]. At the same time, during these events, the local church did not hesitate to show its support for the people of Bayt Sāḥūr, succouring and taking them to hospitals when the curfews were in place[45].

The religious leaderships of the established churches became more vocal during 1988. The rapid sequence of the events just briefly cited pushed them to directly enter the fray, making their position and vision heard. This was also possible because the Intifada fostered cooperation and common commitment among church leaderships. This new attitude culminated in 1989 with the *Statement by the Head of the Christian Communities in Jerusalem*. In this document, the leaders of the established churches in Jerusalem denounced the injustice to and oppression of the Palestinian people and solidarised explicitly with their sufferings and aspirations. The statement was not only an unprecedented demonstration of cooperation and coordination amongst the heads of the local churches, it was also an extraordinary act of innovation. In this regard, the Greek Orthodox Patriarch's full participation in this initiative was particularly significant. Diodoros not only joined the other ecclesiastical heads but also broke with the Orthodox Patriarchate's traditional strategy of proximity to state authorities, especially after the St. John's Hospice episode of 1990. This new attitude was crucial in a period that also saw Orthodox Palestinians' activism reviving. The Intifada did not simply stimulate their old demands concerning the control of church properties but made Orthodox Palestinians reconfigure them within the wider national struggle. In 1992, an Arab Initiative Committee passed a resolution emphasising that the church lands should no longer be considered the exclusive domain of Greek-Cypriot clergy but an integral part of Palestinian heritage and therefore an issue involving the future of their homeland[46].

43. Kårtveit 2014, p. 93.
44. Bowman 1990.
45. Coffey 2016, p. 107.
46. Dumper 2002a, p. 120.

4. Writing for Peace and Justice: The Justice and Peace Commission in Jerusalem and Michel Sabbah

Christian Palestinians' new cultural production of the 1980s was an important achievement in the effort to reinvent the role of Christianity in the conflict because it was a collective and ecumenical enterprise from the start. It departed from the firm conviction of the need to stimulate local Christians to connect with their history and present condition through their faith. The path for attaining such a goal was twofold. First it was meant to push for their commitment to local public life in the spirit of their faith. In parallel fashion, it was dedicated to reconciling Christian Palestinians with passages from the Old Testament used by Jewish and Christian fundamentalists to reclaim the land[47]. This intellectual production was thus an act of resistance against religious exclusivity and chauvinism, establishing an indissoluble bond between peace and justice. It was also important evidence of the willingness not to succumb to the difficult political situation briefly described above. The aim was for them to become agents of transformation for Christian communities and the logics leading Israeli-Palestinian politics. On the one hand, this goal took the form of an attempt to rebut the Christian Zionist interpretation of the Scriptures, as Naim Ateek and Mitri Raheb (Mitrī al-Rāhib) theologically highlight[48]. On the other hand, it focused on developing a Christian understanding of the relationship between justice and peace within the context of the Israeli-Palestinian conflict, as in the case of Sabbah[49].

Two keywords define this effort: contextualisation and liberation. Contextualisation meant illuminating historical moments and contemporary sociopolitical dynamics through biblical interpretation[50]. Liberation was both an invitation and a goal at the same time. Liberation was aimed at overcoming unjust policies, their *raisons d'être* and rationales[51]. The starting point was to recognise the liberating essence of faith. From this standpoint, the theology of liberation was distinctive for its prophetic

47. Omer 2015, p 377.
48. Calder 2018, p. 108.
49. D'Orfeuil 2002, p. 203.
50. Khoury 2020, pp. 39–42.
51. Patierno 2015, p. 447.

interpretation of biblical passages according to their consistency with Jesus' revelation[52].

Such theologies gave birth to two different fields. One focused on "resistance"[53] where Muslims and Christians live together against the Israeli occupier. The other was based on "co-existence"[54] where Christians, Jews and Muslims are called upon to create the conditions to live peacefully together. Within this framework, this cultural production evolved and consolidated during the following decades until today. It mainly concentrates on four clusters of topics: individual and collective liberation, reconciliation, witness, and ecumenical and interfaith dialogue[55].

With respect to the Justice and Peace Commission in Jerusalem and to Michel Sabbah[56], the analysis of their cultural production needs to take into consideration some important elements. First, both are expressions of the Catholic Church in Jerusalem, with different roles, statuses, and authority. The Commission was, and still is, an institution where the clergy and laity from different rites and orders cooperate with the objective of monitoring Christian Palestinians' wishes, needs, challenges, and priorities in relation to the Israeli-Palestinian and Middle Eastern context, informing and updating Christian religious authorities in Jerusalem and abroad. Hence, the foundation of the Commission was a first result in the effort to promote a new contextual theological understanding. From 1988 until 2008, Michel Sabbah was the head of the Latin Patriarchate, therefore an authoritative religious leader in the Holy Land. He was among the new Arab religious leaders that, since the early 1980s, were committed to reconfiguring the role of the church in the Israeli-Palestinian context. By combining his Palestinian origins, ecclesiastical status, and theological vision, he was able to play a significant role in the Intifada, becoming a spokesperson for Christians and Palestinians at large. Although he always refused to be associated with party politics, his commitment to conveying

52. Omer 2015, p. 379.
53. Marteijn 2020, p. 276.
54. Ibid., p. 276.
55. Ibid., p. 271.
56. The Justice and Peace Commission's statements were collected during field work in Jerusalem in 2015. Not all documents have been preserved in all languages, especially those in Arabic. Where possible, the following analysis has been developed comparing the different available texts.

messages of peace, justice, and reconciliation, and to denouncing everyone's responsibilities for the present condition in the Holy Land, inevitably made his speeches and statements deeply political, winning much support and admiration but also many critics.

Based on their respective roles and statuses, the dissemination and circulation of their contents inevitably differed, both in terms of potential impact and outreach. The Commission initially limited the distribution of its statements and letters to protect Palestinian members and to avoid arousing Israeli suspicion. When it began to circulate its contents, it mainly disseminated them through Catholic networks, like other commissions abroad or the bulletins of the Patriarchate. This makes it difficult to evaluate the impact on and how much its production was known to a Muslim audience. Nevertheless, it remains an important source of information and still represents a vocal manifestation of Catholicism in the Holy Land. Given his role as the head of the Latin Patriarchate directly nominated by the Holy See, Sabbah had all the means he needed to make his messages resonate within the Holy Land and at the international level, well beyond the Catholic community. His skills, role, activism, and status made his cultural production particularly authoritative and vibrant.

Beyond these specificities, he and the Commission also shared many traits. They had similar goals and dealt with the same topics, being part of a common path for the reconfiguration of the Catholic Church's presence in the Holy Land. Furthermore, their cultural production was intrinsically multilingual, being authored and disseminated mainly in English, French, Italian, and of course Arabic. Multilingualism has always been one of the many features of the multivocal Christian presence in the Holy Land. It has also been a constant necessity to bring together such a diverse network of initiatives and presences. But during the Intifada, this quality was also a powerful resource for reaching out to many different audiences in Israel-Palestine and abroad.

After a series of meetings between 1975 and 1979, the Commission published its first statement in 1980: *Christian Faith and Political Consciousness*, circulating in Arabic with the title *Īmānunā al-masīḥī wa-l-wa'ī al-siyāsī*. This document is distinctive not only for its unique content but also for its structure and approach. It presents its arguments by alternating questions and elucidations with the aim of stimulating personal and group reflection and meditation. Among the many crucial passages of this statement, it is important to stress three aspects. First, as is evident from the title, the document seeks to correlate and connect faith and politics, contextualising this relation within the present condition of Christians living in Israel-Palestine. This was a very innovative approach for Catholicism in the Holy Land. In fact, it opens by pointing out that "the political problem that our Palestinian people are enduring faces us constantly and challenges us. It is a question which is also posed to our faith, in the knowledge that faith is a living force which embraces all aspects of our lives, both privately and publicly"[57]. Accordingly, Palestinian Christians should not remain silent or ignore the present condition, trenching themselves within the secure boundaries of their private life or communities, but need to accept their role and responsibility. By recalling the Church's traditional teaching on the relation between faith and politics and the fact that they are never disconnected and cannot be separated, the Commission explains that "it is the very vision of faith that demands Christian commitment to political activity", not just for the benefit of a specific community or denomination, but for the sake of all people living within this area[58]. This exhortation from the Commission provides more evidence of the gradual unfolding of the Vatican II in this context. Moreover, it is a clear sign of discontinuity with the traditional position of the Roman Catholic Church in Israel-Palestine. This position was characterised by a twofold approach. On the one hand, the Roman Catholic Church has constantly committed itself to defending Catholic interests in this land, namely, the holy places and the prerogatives of the Catholic community. On the other hand, it has always invited Roman Catholics to avoid intermingling with the conflict.

In this statement the Commission instead invites Christians to play their role and explains that "[…] the objective conditions that we live in – together with his [the Christian's] brothers and sisters, the sons of the Palestinian people, confirm him in this commitment". Faith, political commitment, and shared suffering are the ingredients that substantiate solidarity and push Christians to fully integrate into public life, because "[…] the teaching in Christ does not separate us from anyone, regardless of his belief". This solidarity is a sharing in suffering, but it is also

57. *Christian Faith* 1980, p. 1.
58. Ibid., p. 2.

a sharing in the "struggle" and "hope"[59]. The document subsequently focuses on the Church in Jerusalem, posing the question "Is the Church neutral?" In the Arabic version, this is presented together with the image of the Church on the fence. The authors point out that "throughout human history the Church had its martyrs, those who died not only for their faith but also for the service of their brothers. Each of us is also called today to follow this tradition of giving witness to the truth"[60]. In this section, the document introduces readers to the issue of peace and justice on the basis of the Constitution on the Church in the Modern World, *Gaudium et Spes* (1965). With such a reference, it makes these two principles the focal points for stimulating and guiding Christians' and the Church's faith and political commitment to the present condition in the Israeli-Palestinian context.

Some years later, in August 1983, the Commission circulated a second important document titled *Muslims and Christians on the Road Together*, in Arabic under the title *Muslimūn wa-masīḥiyyūn maʿan ʿalā l-ṭarīq*. Taking on some of the main points developed in its first statement and contextualising the reflections of *Nostra Aetate* (1965) in the Israeli-Palestinian situation – as evinced by an excerpt from the Vatican II declaration – this document proposes to elaborate on the relationship between Muslims and Christians. It asks how they can envisage constructing a common future together and how they can live in harmony and peace, despite differences[61]. In this document, the Commission dedicates itself to delineating a common field of coexistence and shared awareness for developing dialogue and creating a new mentality[62]. In this framework, this statement proceeds to describe the many elements that bind Muslims and Christians together. Jerusalem is presented as the clearest representation of the possibility of building together a common future in harmony, as the presence of the Dome of the Rock and the Church of the Resurrection teach[63]. Given the timing of this statement, the centrality that Jerusalem holds in this text is particularly significant. In 1980, Israel had just passed the so-called Jerusalem Law, symbolically annexing its eastern part,

59. Ibid., p. 3.
60. Ibid., p. 4.
61. *Moslems and Christians* 1983, p. 1.
62. Ibid., p. 40.
63. Ibid., p. 35.

declaring the whole city its capital. The Commission shines a light on Jerusalem as the focal point from which to construct a new mentality of collaboration and solidarity between Muslims and Christians open to all the inhabitants of this land. Based on such premises, the document then invites Muslim and Christian Palestinians to be "courageous" and "sincere" in responding "to the demands of the present"[64]. Such an attitude should develop from a common awareness that "the painful experiences of the last years have already united us in a community of suffering and resistance"[65]. In the conclusion, after having described the liberating quality of faith, the declaration delivers an invitation to "others to search with us [Muslims and Christians] for new ways of advancing together, to adopt a new perception of things and create a new mentality"[66]. It then states that "if these pages are concerned with the dialogue between Palestinians, Muslim and Christian, we want to stress that dialogue remains open to all, no matter what their religion or conviction may be"[67]. In particular, this passage refers to Palestinians upholding secularist views and to Jews, both believers and non-believers. It is thus important evidence of the new attitude and consciousness that this cultural production sought to convey and stimulate within the Christian population, reconfiguring the role of Christianity with the public in the spirit of a dialogue that involves all the inhabitants of this land for constructing a common future of peace and justice.

After these two documents, the Commission embarked on an intellectual reflection on the Israeli-Palestinian context and the Middle East that still endures today. Its activity intensified during the second part of 1988, in parallel with the growing engagement of the churches in Jerusalem. A few months after the outbreak of the Intifada, the Commission released the statement *A Grave and Urgent Situation: Six Months of Palestinian Uprising*[68]. This document is fully dedicated to the uprising and describes the deep sense of solidarity that unites Palestinians in "a new national consciousness"[69]. The statement openly condemns the Occupation, while

64. Ibid., p. 38 (in Arabic, p. 4).
65. Ibid.
66. Ibid., p. 40 (in Arabic, p. 7).
67. Ibid., p. 41 (in Arabic, p. 8).
68. *A Grave and Urgent Situation* 1988.
69. Ibid., p. 2.

praising the Palestinians' resistance. Without ignoring the fact that the Palestinians' protests were not altogether non-violent, it underlines their intentional efforts to limit the level of violence and incites them to pursue this path. The document concludes by underlining that the uprising was not reversible, calling for negotiation with the PLO and dialogue between the parties involved.

As this last document shows, during the Intifada the Commission became increasingly concerned with the dissemination of information and statements about the daily challenges Palestinians were facing under the occupation. In fact, the focus and tone of its communications are less concerned with theological reflection. Rather, they are fully devoted to the ongoing political events. For example, the Commission denounced the severe economic situation of rural areas in the Occupied Territories (November 1988), the strategy of house demolition (July 1989), defined as a "collective punishment", as "inhuman", and "completely unacceptable"[70], or the impact of curfews and blockages on education in Palestine (February 1989). This activity sought to keep international attention focused on the events in Palestine and to fight against a sort of addiction to the ongoing disorders and protests, defending a political solution to the conflict and the need to save the peace and promote it, as the statements of June 1990, *Save the Peace*, that of October 1990, *Yet Again…*, and, finally, the appeal of Christmas 1991, *For Christ is Our Peace*, prove.

As mentioned above, the Intifada saw the contribution by a crucial leader for Catholicism in the Holy Land, the Latin Patriarch Michel Sabbah. The systematic analysis of his prolific intellectual production during his service in the Holy Land goes beyond the aim of this chapter, so we will focus here on three pastoral letters written between 1988 and 1993, which are briefly presented with the aim of elucidating his contribution during the years covered by this chapter, complementing the analysis of the Commission's statements.

Michel Sabbah's first pastoral letter in August 1988 is particularly instructive. In this text, the Patriarch deals with the main factors that inform the life of Christians in the Holy Land. First, he concentrates on the issues of the Church's and Christians' commitment and participation, explaining that "the Church cannot remain silent, and the believer has no

70. *The Demolition of Houses* 1989, p. 1.

right to retrench behind religious rites and observances"[71]. The Patriarch affirms that each person has the duty to participate according to her/his role and skills with the aim of constructing peace on the basis of truth, justice, and love. Here, Sabbah underlines that the Church does not intermingle with party politics but delivers a message to all humankind, inviting everyone to respect and recognise human rights and dignity[72]. At the same time, by embracing the affirmation of Vatican II that the Church "should have true freedom [...] to pass moral judgment in those matters which regard public order when the fundamental rights of a person or the salvation of souls require it"[73], Sabbah explains the duty and right of each religious leader to promote dialogue and interchange, engaging in politics whenever human rights and dignity are violated and ignored[74].

In its conclusion, this pastoral letter openly deals with the minority condition of Christians in the Holy Land. Such a focus is particularly significant. It builds on the reflection already introduced by the Commission in 1980 and further develops it, directly taking on the issue of the relationship between numbers, spirituality, and commitment. Sabbah invites Christians to be faithful to their history and faith and to avoid thinking that because of their numbers they can ignore contingent problems and challenges, considering them issues only pertaining to the majority. He also invites Christians to "bear witness" and exert "constructive service and collaboration" and not to "run away"[75].

Within this framework, in his pastoral letter of 1990, Sabbah continues exhorting Christians to participate in and commit to the ongoing events because "you are an integral part of your society, a party to the conflict. You therefore should contribute to the solution. You cannot evade your responsibilities. You have no right to survive thanks to the sacrifices of others. Each must offer up one's own sacrifice"[76]. Such an appeal is the conclusion of a broader analysis where the Patriarch invites all believers involved in the conflict to "see in forgiveness and reconciliation a way towards justice and the obtaining of all rights. When the believer

71. Sabbah 1988, p. 193. Original in French, my translation.
72. Ibid., p. 193.
73. *Gaudium et Spes 1965*, par. 76. See also Cristiansen, Sarsar 1993, p. 14.
74. D'Orfeuil 2002, p. 79.
75. Cristiansen, Sarsar 1993, pp. 80–81.
76. Sabbah 1990, par. 52.

demands justice for himself, he should demand it also for his neighbour (cf. Mt 6,12)"[77]. Sabbah observes that "an occupied people has the right to claim its rights and to organise itself politically in the way it sees fit, in the way it has already expressed: that is, as an independent state. This is a right of natural law, and no one can take this right away"[78].

This pastoral letter clearly elucidates the profound developments achieved at the beginning of the 1990s with respect to self-perception, understanding, and the representation of the role and presence of the Church and Christian communities in the local public space and political fields. It also shows the importance of this new theological production for proposing the Scriptures as the leading force for Christians' participation and commitment. Sabbah indicates that theological and religious reflection is the main means to pursue peace, justice, and liberation, leaving the duties of governance and the management of the state to the political actors. Nevertheless, the recognition of such a division between the role of religion and that of politics should not lead to a drastic separation of them but to the recognition of a unique responsibility and mutual commitment between these two spheres.

Finally, it is worthwhile to conclude this analysis by briefly mentioning some of the most salient aspects of Sabbah's pastoral letter of 1993, probably the most theologically and politically informed among those of these years. *Reading the Bible Today in the Land of the Bible*[79] is a study of the violence in the Bible and in history[80] and shows Christians "the way to read and understand it [the Bible], in order to make it the object of meditation and prayer"[81]. It elucidates the importance of Bible criticism and the meaning and value of the Bible for each Christian, within and outside Palestine. Furthermore, it openly tackles the issue of the relation between Christian Palestinians and the Bible in a land where the Word of God is politically claimed as proof of a special entitlement and ownership over it by a part of its inhabitants.

77. Ibid., par. 44.
78. Ibid., par. 54.
79. Sabbah 1993.
80. D'Orfeuil 2002, p. 203.
81. Sabbah 1993, par. 2.

Building upon Vatican II and contextualising the teaching of *Dei Verbum* and *Nostra Aetate* in Palestinian reality[82], Sabbah concentrates on neutralising manipulations of the Word of God. Based on such a reflection, in the following years Sabbah would keep on warning against any sort of deviation in which "man replaces the goodness of God with human interest"[83].

In this pastoral letter, he analyses the relation between "ancient Biblical history and our contemporary history"[84], questioning his readers from different perspectives, both theological and political. In doing so, the Latin Patriarch not only questions the views of Christianity and Judaism, but he also deals with the relation between the former and Islam, thus involving an intra-Palestinian dimension. On the one hand, Sabbah stresses that

> to accept the Bible and believe in it does not mean that God is one's adversary, supporting the opposing side. On the contrary, to believe in it is an invitation to both sides who believe in it to see God inviting both of them to grant each other justice and reconciliation. In the present circumstances, the Bible is a word of God, a word of justice and forgiveness directed to the two peoples, the Palestinians and the Jews[85].

On the other hand, he underlines that both Christians and Muslims are undoubtedly part of the same homeland and nation. They are called to develop a common political field with an equal share in it. This pastoral letter points out Sabbah's commitment, along with that of other Palestinian religious leaders, to dedicate themselves to the effort of interpreting the Bible in the land of Israel-Palestine and contextualising its message within the developing political events. Christians should be aware of and accept their role and responsibility for promoting mutual recognition, peace, and justice. They should also be aware that no single word of their Scriptures speaks against this natural vocation.

82. Khader, Neuhaus 2006, p. 300.
83. Sabbah 2015, pp. 7–8.
84. Sabbah 1993, par. 7.
85. Ibid., par. 57.

5. Conclusion

If the events and initiatives analysed by this chapter are viewed in the light of the present condition of Christian Palestinians and the Israeli-Palestinian conflict, they could be tempted to describe them as a clear failure or act of illusion. Christian Palestinians still experience all the challenges and contradictions of their minority situation. Emigration and demographic decrease still strongly affect their presence. The Israeli-Palestinian conflict not only endures, but it is growing with the recent outbreak of war between Israel and Hamas. People talking and writing for peace and justice in this land seem overwhelmed by short-term political interests, tactical manoeuvrings, and fluctuating interest from the international community. In fact, the Israeli-Palestinian conflict most frequently attracts interest only when the struggle revives, ignoring the many attempts to promote peace and justice between the people of this land.

Nevertheless, the development of a new intellectual and theological production during the late 1970s and 1980s proved to be irreversible. It still exists, endures, and progresses. The first group of religious leaders that initiated this path stayed faithful to their initial objectives and devoted themselves to expanding this collective enterprise. During the 1990s, they were joined by a new generation that today is pushing this thinking, both intellectually and materially. Their cultural products were, and still are, disseminated among multiple audiences and in different languages, giving voice to a theological reflection on the conflict and the occupation that focuses on promoting a culture of peace and justice directly from the heart of the Holy Land. This theological production makes it possible for Christian Palestinians to circulate their own theological wisdom that is intrinsically Christian and Palestinian at the same time.

Among the many elements that deserve to be mentioned, it seems important here to conclude by pointing out how the concentration on the indissoluble bonds between peace and justice represented the starting point and the end goal for the construction of a new mentality and understanding of oneself and others. It was an act of resistance against Christians' temptation to seek refuge within their community or to isolate themselves because of their numbers, surrendering to a "minority mentality". It was also dedicated to giving Christians a contextualised understanding of the Scriptures within their present condition, providing them with new intellectual and theological resources to play their role. Moreover, it increased the visibility of the church at both local and international levels during a very significant experience in the contemporary history of Palestinians. It opened an important field of dialogue and collaboration between the many manifestations of the multivocal Christian landscape in Israel-Palestine. This theological effort created new possible bridges to connect the Holy Land with Christians in other nations and to sensitise them to the present condition of this land. Finally, it was an act of commitment to position the church and Christian community among Jews and Muslims, inviting all believers to dialogue and mutual recognition. In essence, such an intellectual enterprise aimed to introduce Arab Christian thought at the heart of the unfolding political events, overcoming the narrow boundaries of denominations and communities to reconnect local Christianity with the words of the Bible and the political situation in Palestine. It represented and still is a stimulus for a full and active Christian participation in their daily socio-political life and a voice able to refute the Christian Zionist vision and divisive narratives.

The experiences of the Justice and Peace Commission and Michel Sabbah during these years confirm that this enterprise was not only that of single individuals, religious leadership, or a community but one of a group of Palestinian Christians and their religious leaders that indicated the path to living as an integral component of the local society. Their intellectual and theological production sought to recompose the multidimensional and multivocal character of the Christian Palestinian presence, developing new individual and collective consciousness. Moreover, their statements aimed at stimulating ecumenical and interfaith dialogue, exhorting Christians to find their answers within their religious heritage and not just in secular ideologies.

The history of theological production of the Justice and Peace Commission and Michel Sabbah narrates the progressive unfolding of the Vatican II message in the Holy Land. They are emanations and local responses to the multifarious exhortations sorted out from this crucial moment in the contemporary history of the Catholic Church. The foundation of the Commission would not have been possible without it. At the same time, its work attested to Catholic Palestinians' commitment to transforming their presence by undertaking the invitations of Vatican II documents and working for solutions to the challenges stemming from the conflict and illuminating them through their faith. Michel Sabbah is at the forefront of this enterprise. He provides the example of a religious leader concerned with the possibility that Palestinian Christians could feel uneasy with some parts of the Bible because of their use by politics. His work represents an attempt to rejuvenate the faith of Christians in the Holy Land by elaborating a stronger understanding of the Bible's message, and of its connections to the state of war in this land. At the heart of this effort there is the firm conviction of the need for a new pastoral message centred on the human being and their spiritual and material needs.

In line with the teaching of Vatican II, their efforts departed from the belief of the impossibility of remaining neutral towards the conflict. Their message refuses the partisanship of politics and invites the church and Christians of the Holy Land to spend their energy and life to promote peace and to resist the violent logics of war. They are a testimony to the ongoing human quest for peace and peace.

Along with other protagonists of the time, their efforts were meant to persuade both Western Christians and Middle Eastern Muslims of the possibility of developing a Christian theological justification for a peaceful political solution to the Israeli-Palestinian conflict. Furthermore, their cultural production was aimed at disseminating new demands in the spirit of peace and justice, also for the purpose of establishing interaction with that part of Israeli society engaged with peace activism in the light of the two-state solution. In this framework, their efforts are aimed at recognising the rights of all parties involved in the conflict, struggling against the manipulation of the religious message. Accordingly, this documentation is a means of Christian Palestinians' self-narration, a constant invitation to mediate between opposing political projects, and a testament of Christians' efforts to transform the Israeli-Palestinian context in a land of justice and peace.

References

Ackerman, S. (1992), *Latin Cleric's Pro-Intifada Remarks Draw Ministry Fire*, in "The Jerusalem Post", 31 January, p. 3.

Alimi, E. (2007), *Israeli Politics and the First Palestinian Intifada: Political Opportunities, Framing Processes and Contentious Politics*, Routledge, London-New York.

Ateek, N. S., Ellis, M. E., Radford Ruether R. (1992), *Faith and the Intifada: Palestinian Christian Voices*, Orbis Books, New York.

Bialier, U. (2005), *Cross on the Star of David: The Christian World in Israel's Foreign Policy, 1948–1967*, Indiana University Press, Bloomington.

Calder, M. D. (2018), *Palestinian Christians: Situating Selves in a Dislocated Present*, in P. S. Rowe (ed.), *Routledge Handbook of Minorities in the Middle East*, Routledge, London-New York, pp. 100–114.

Chacour, E., Jensen, M. E. (1990), *We Belong to the Land: The Story of a Palestinian Israeli Who Lives for Peace and Reconciliation*, HarperCollins, San Francisco.

Christiansen, D. (2004), *Palestinian Christians: Recent Developments. The Vatican-Israel Accords: Political, Legal and Theological Concerns*, University of Notre Dame Press, Notre Dame (IN).

Coffey, Q. (2016), *The Political, Communal and Religious Dynamics of Palestinian Christian Identity: The Eastern Orthodox and Latin Catholics in the West Bank*, PhD thesis, University of St Andrews, 2016.

Dumper, M. (2002a), *The Politics of Sacred Space: The Old City of Jerusalem in the Middle East Conflict*, Lynne Rienner Publishers, Boulder (CO).

Dumper, M. (2002b), *The Christian Churches of Jerusalem in the Post-Oslo Period*, in "Journal of Palestine Studies", 31, 2, pp. 51–65. https://doi.org/10.1525/jps.2002.31.2.51

Farsoun, S. K., Aruri, N. (2006), *Palestine and the Palestinians: A Social and Political History*, Routledge, London and New York.

Gelvin, J. L. (2014), *The Israel-Palestine Conflict: One Hundred Years of War*, Cambridge University Press, Cambridge.

Greenberg, J. (1988), *An Intifada Christmas in Bethlehem Jerusalem*, in "Jerusalem Post", 25 December, p. 8.

Christian Faith and Political Consciousness. Īmānunā al-masīḥī wa-l-waʿī al-siyāsī (1980), Justice and Peace Commission Jerusalem.

Moslems and Christians on the Road Together. Muslimūn wa-masīḥiyyūn maʿan ʿalà l-ṭarīq (1983), Justice and Peace Commission Jerusalem.

A Grave and Urgent Situation: Six Months of Palestinian Uprising (1988), Justice and Peace Commission, Jerusalem.

The Demolition of Houses. Hadm al-buyūt (1989), Justice and Peace Commission, Jerusalem.

Is Peace Possible? Christian Palestinians Speak (2019), Justice and Peace Commission, Latin Patriarchate Printing Press, Jerusalem-Beit Jala.

Kårtveit, B. (2014), *Dilemmas of Attachment: Identity and Belonging among Palestinian Christians*, Brill, Leiden.

Khader, J., Neuhaus, D. (2006), *Le dialogue interreligieux en terre sainte quarante ans après Nostra Aetate*, in "Proche-Orient chrétien", 56, 3–4, pp. 299–310.

Khoury, R. (2020), *Palestinian Contextual Theology: A General Survey*, in R. Khoury, R. Zimmer-Winkel Christian (eds.), *Theology in the Palestinian Context*, Aphorisma Verlag, Berlin, pp. 9–46.

Lybarger, L. D. (2007), *For Church or Nation? Islamism, Secular-Nationalism, and the Transformation of Christian Identities in Palestine*, in "Journal of the American Academy of Religion", 75, 4, pp. 777–813. https://doi.org/10.1093/jaarel/lfm066

Marteijn, E. S. (2020), *The Revival of Palestinian Christianity: Developments in Palestinian Theology*, in "Exchange", 49, 3–4, pp. 257–277. https://doi.org/10.1163/1572543X-12341569

McGahern, U. (2012), *Palestinian Christians in Israel: State Attitudes Towards Non-Muslims in a Jewish State*, Routledge, London and New York.

Neuhaus, D. (2009), *Contemporary Jewish Israeli Views on Christianity and Christians*, in A. O'Mahony (ed.), *Christianity and Jerusalem: Studies in Modern Theology and Politics in the Holy Land*, Gardners Books, Leominster.

O'Mahony, A. (ed.) (2009), *Christianity and Jerusalem: Studies in Modern Theology and Politics in the Holy Land*, Gardners Books, Leominster.

Omer, A. (2015), *The Cry of the Forgotten Stones: The Promise and Limits of a Palestinian Liberation Theology as a Method for Peacebuilding*, in "Journal of Religious Ethics", 43, 2, pp. 369–407. https://doi.org/10.1111/jore.12101

Omer, A., Springs, J. A. (2013), *Religious Nationalism: A Reference Handbook*, Abc-clio, Santa Barbara (CA).

Patierno, N. (2015), *Palestinian Liberation Theology: Creative Resistance to Occupation*, in "Islam and Christian-Muslim Relations", 26, 4, pp. 443–464. https://doi.org/10.1080/09596410.2015.1080896

Robson, L. C. (2010), *Palestinian Liberation Theology, Muslim–Christian Relations and the Arab–Israeli conflict*, in "Islam and Christian-Muslim Relations", 21, 1, pp. 39–50. https://doi.org/10.1080/09596410903481846

Sabbah, M. (1988), *Premier Lettre Pastoral*, in "Jérusalem. Le Bulletin Diocésain du Patriarcat Latin", 54, 7–9, pp. 3–24.

Sabbah, M. (1990), *Second Pastoral Letter*, available at https://www.lpj.org/archives/second-pastoral-letter-of-patriarch-sabbah-1990.html (last accessed 24 January 2022)

Sabbah, M. (1993), *Reading the Bible in the Land of the Bible*, available at https://www.lpj.org/archives/fourth-pastoral-letter-patriarch-sabbah-reading-bible-today-land-bible-november-1993-5e45d3114195b.html (last accessed 24 January 2022).

Sabbah, M. (2015), *Religion and the Palestinian-Israeli Conflict*, in "Israel Journal of Politics, Economics, and Culture", 20/21, 4/1, pp. 7–11.

Christiansen, D., Sarsar, S. (eds.) (1993), *Faithful Witness: On Reconciliation and Peace in the Holy Land*, New City Press, Hyde Park (NY).

D'Orfeuil, Y. T. (2002), *Michel Sabbah, paix sur Jérusalem: Propos d'un évêque palestinien,* Desclée de Brouwer, Paris.

Shapiro, J. (1984), *A Dialogue of the Oppressed*, "The Jerusalem Post", 10 January, p. 5.

Tsimhoni, D. (1993), *Christian Communities in Jerusalem and the West Bank since 1948: An Historical, Social, and Political Study*, Praeger, Westport (CT).

Tsimhoni, D. (2002), *The Christians in Israel: Aspects of Integration and the Search for Identity of a Minority within a Minority*, in Ma'oz, M., Sheffer, G., *Middle Eastern Minorities and Diasporas*, Sussex Academic Press, Brighton, pp. 124–152.

Paolo Maggiolini is a Research Fellow and Adjunct Professor at the Catholic University of Milan (Italy). He is editor for the Palgrave series "Minorities in West Asia and North Africa" (MiWANA). His research mainly focuses on religion and politics in Israel, Iraq, Jordan and Palestine. His publications include *Minorities and State-Building in the Middle East: The Case of Jordan* (with Idir Ouahes).

Chapter 12

A Thousand and One Jordans: The Story of Rafedìn

Odetta Pizzingrilli

Abstract

Rafedìn – literally "the two rivers", [*bilād*] *al-rāfidayn,* the Arabic toponym for Mesopotamia – is a humanitarian project born in Amman in March 2016, with the aim of empowering Iraqi refugee women and is currently run by the Habibi Valtiberina Association. This chapter places the Rafedìn experience within the Jordanian (hi)story by presenting the different "Jordans" that succeeded one another over time (i.e., Arab-Hashemite, Palestinian, Bedouin, Jordanian), their myths and symbols, their self-representations, and their storytellers. In turn, the Rafedìn project emerges as a successful model of peaceful coexistence that has been able to carve its place within the multifaceted Jordanian society, a character of the story that could overcome the boundaries of its own frame tale[1].

Keywords: national identity formation, National identity narratives, Jordan, Iraq, Iraqi Refugees in Jordan

1. With the expression "frame tale", I refer to the official narrative(s) (*sardiyyah, sardiyyāt*) developed and promoted by the Jordanian ruling family over time and at the same time viewing Rafedìn as one if its many characters that was able to build an effective counternarrative. The frame tale is also "the story which forms the elastic border of the *Nights*", to use Sallis' words (2007, p. 154). Hence, using this expression places the discussion within the realm of narration.

1. Introduction

The imagined Jordanian community in Anderson's (1983) account constructs and reconstructs itself continuously over time: hence, the chapter addresses the Jordanian Kingdom's nation-building process as a narrative with the urban space of Amman as the designated stage of the Hashemite play(s). Starting with the kingdom's foundation, the chapter retraces the state's key moments, focusing on the ever-changing articulations of the (Jordanian) Self in the attempt at disentangling both the national narratives proposed by the ruling elite to the international community, and the civil society's self-representations. Accordingly, the chapter is divided into five sections devoted to these Jordanian historical key points and the national narratives' changes that followed. Who has been the "Other" in relation to which the Jordanian identity was formed and transformed? Who is not Jordanian? Indeed, identity is constructed in discourse and through difference[2]. What account of otherness did the Rafedìn experience propose and how did it succeed in finding its own space within the Jordanian social fabric?

2. A Hashemite Arab Jordan

Left out of the territorial definition process that started with the Ottoman *Vilayet* Law of 1864, modern Jordan is the result of a British geopolitical strategy,[3] and its theoretical grounds lay in the pan-Arab ideology of the late 19th century. This ideology was championed by the *šarīf* and *amīr* of Mecca al-Ḥusayn ibn ʿAlī al-Hāšimī (1853–1931) and based on Sāṭiʿ al-Ḥuṣrī's (1880–1968) account of *waṭan* (nation)[4]. The son

2. Derrida 1978; Butler 1997; Hall 2000.
3. No national movement emerged before or during World War I calling for the establishment of a nation in the region. Its northern inhabitants had the Syrian town of Damascus as their political centre, while the south had the Hijaz. The importance of the land was mainly derived from its location as a route for the pilgrimage to Mecca; hence, it was called, depending on the pilgrims' starting point, *mašārif al-Šām* (roads to Syria) or *mašārif al-Hiǧāz* (roads to the Hijaz).
4. Following the German account of nation, al-Ḥuṣrī could affirm that the Arab nation existed even without a state (*dawlah*) to represent it. The French and Anglo-American concepts of nation, indivisible from the national state, were indeed unsuitable for his

of Ḥusayn, ʿAbd Allāh (1882–1951), appointed emir of Transjordan by Winston Churchill (minister of the British colonies of the time) in 1921 and then the first king of the Hashemite Kingdom of Transjordan/Jordan (1946/1949) as ʿAbd Allāh I, was indeed the leader of both a nation-state and a (pan-)Arab entity, a dichotomy that characterised the Hashemite rule over Jordan throughout the entire 20th century. The first section focuses on this dichotomy and outlines how the Jordanian identity was first articulated in the city space, labelled with and visually represented by the king himself.

Rafedìn manages to exist as a piece of the mosaic of the "non-city"[5] of Amman that embodies, in its unique way, the ever-changing state policies by spatialising them through practices of inclusion and exclusion, meaning that the government changes the policies through the space. To strengthen his position, ʿAbd Allāh I, initially used the new capital[6] to enact dramatised and symbolic performances, "visual manifestations of a central government [...] slowly but steadily consolidating itself"[7], such as a ritual procession from his palace through the city centre to attend Friday prayers. In fact, as pointed out by Rogan, "rather than seeking to project the state's power through architecture, the ruling authorities used Amman as a stage upon which elaborate ceremonial spectacles were enacted to reaffirm both elements of the colonial state: British trusteeship and Hashemite rule"[8].

The above-mentioned coexistence of a macro (pan-)Arab identity with a smaller Jordanian national identity is clearly visible when looking at school textbooks, which described the Hashemite Kingdom of Jordan throughout the 1960s to children as "my small motherland which is part of my larger Arab motherland"[9]. Furthermore, in every edition of

---

goal. Finally, al-Ḥuṣrī's *waṭan* is also rooted in a more endogenous basis as is Ibn Ḫaldūn's notion of *ʿaṣabiyyah*.

5. Shami 2007.
6. Amman, resettled and established in 1878 by Circassian immigrants, became a town after 1903 (when the Hijaz railway reached the city), the Emirate's capital in 1921 (preferred to al-Salṭ, ʿAbd Allāh's first choice) and gained the title of municipality (*amānah*) in the 1950s, thus becoming the administrative and political capital of the two banks.
7. Eilon, Avon 2007, p. 81.
8. Rogan 1996, p. 103.
9. Culcasi 2016, p. 9.

the Jordanian school atlas published by the Royal Jordanian Geographic Centre (RJGC) since 1984 to 2003 – thus in spite of the 1988 disengagement of the West Bank, *fakk al-irtibāṭ* – the first map (also distributed as a stand-alone map) was "The Hashemite Kingdom of Jordan and Palestine", and presented the two territories as one borderless region – perhaps a claim to the lost land, but Culcasi defines it, through the testimonies of her interviewees, as "a reminder of the past, a relic of the tenuous and disputed status of Palestine, and of the longstanding connection between the West Bank and Jordan"[10]. Indeed, ʿAbd Allāh I called Jordan's first organised military force[11] the "Arab Legion" (*al-ğayš al-ʿarabī*) and the majority of the governmental, bureaucratic and military posts were filled by Syrian, Palestinian, Iraqi, and Hijazi immigrants[12]. Amman's population, which at first numbered no more than 2,500 people prior to 1921[13], including the Circassian (in origin and tongue) majority, merchants from the Levant and the Arabian Peninsula and also political dissidents escaping first the Ottomans and then the French[14]. Moreover, most teachers in the schools founded in the early 1950s were Syrians and urban Palestinians[15], thus the first of the many "Jordans" to be narrated is expressed through their urban Levantine linguistic features (such as the glottal stop pronunciation of *qāf* as opposed to the Bedouin variant [g]), which were at that time symbols of culture and modernity[16]. In 1948, Palestine and saving its Arab population became a constitutive element of the Hashemite political discourse. As stressed by Nevo and Pappé, with King Ḥusayn (1935–1999), protecting the Palestinians of the West Bank became "part of the *raison d'être* of

10. Culcasi 2016, p. 12.
11. Méouchy et al. 2013, p. 213.
12. See De Bel-Air 2007 and *City Migration Profile-Amman. Executive Summary* 2015.
13. Amman was still a small town of 10,000 inhabitants in the 1930s. Since then, the population grew steadily, reaching 550,000 after the Six Days War. Shami 2007, p. 214.
14. The officers of the failed Syrian government of ʿAbd Allāh's brother, Fayṣal, sought refuge from French attacks in Transjordan; they arrived in Amman aiming to establish a (pan-)Arab government, thus rejecting the very existence of a Transjordanian nation (still considered a province of the Great Syria). Meanwhile, the Transjordanians were starting to articulate their own identity.
15. It has been estimated that 8,000–10,000 people from these backgrounds came to the country soon after its foundation.
16. Suleiman 2004, pp. 115–116.

Jordan's existence as a sovereign state, and [...] an essential component of the Hashemite ideology"[17]. This led to the 1950 annexation, which was politically legitimised by Hashemite Arab nationalism[18]. But it was never officially recognised by any of the Arab League states because by making the West Bankers Jordanians, the unification of the two banks could jeopardise the Palestinian claims to independence and pose an obstacle to the refugees' right to return (guaranteed by the United Nations General Assembly Resolution 194). In 1951, ʿAbd Allāh I was assassinated while visiting *al-Ḥaram al-šarīf* in Jerusalem with his nephew Ḥusayn[19]. He had been accused of being too lenient with the Zionist enemy and its European ally, the British.

3. Towards a Bedouin Jordan

The 1957 failed coup led by Arab nationalists against king Ḥusayn resulted in the resignation of the prime minister at the time, Sulaymān al-Nābulusī (1908–1976), head of the Nationalist Socialist Party. A radical change in the national discourse was in the making, and the Jordanian nationalist trend was going to lead the political scene. Indeed, with the failure of the United Arab Republic in 1961 and especially in the 1967 War, Arab nationalism waned as a unifying ideology, the Palestinian-Jordanian dynamic drastically changed, and Jordan ended up becoming a stronger political entity[20]. This second section focuses on the Jordanian, tribal-centred frame tale written by King Ḥusayn.

"Palestinians in Jordan do not have a full understanding of nationality as a concept, their understanding is limited, that is why they still define themselves as 'West Bankers'. [...] Do you know that Palestinians call the 1970 civil war 'Black September' while we [Jordanians] call it

17. Nevo, Pappé 1994, p. 3.
18. *The Constituent Assembly: First Knesset 1949–1951. Annexation of the West Bank by the Hashemite Kingdom of Jordan*, available at http://www.jcpa.org/art/knesset6.htm (last accessed March 2021).
19. ʿAbd Allāh I's son Ṭalāl reigned only one year as he was forced to abdicate by the Parliament in 1952 due to mental illness and was succeeded by his son Ḥusayn. Ḥusayn remained in power until his death in 1999 and was in turn succeeded by his son ʿAbd Allāh II, now in power. See also Ronen 2010.
20. Innab 2016, p. 127.

'White September'? Because that was the end of it"[21]. These words by the Circassian Jordanian ʿAlī Kašt, express well how the 1970–71 clashes radically changed the power distribution between Jordanians (or "pure" Jordanians) and Palestinian-Jordanians, a label widely criticised but still very common in the country[22]. After Black September and the consequent crystallisation of a (Trans-)Jordanian, intrinsically tribal, Islamic, and Hashemite identity, the Jordanian state actually needed to rewrite its national discourse. The new Bedouin culture – music and soap operas (*musalsal badawī*) in particular – became a manifestation of this necessity and eventually part of the solution. Indeed, in Jordan, "the folk tradition [...] should not be understood as one with an ancient origin, but rather as a contemporary invention [...], which can be engaged in the construction of a unique national culture"[23]. King Ḥusayn paved the way for the cultural tribalisation of society, finding in this imagined (and more compliant with the emerging nation-state) tribalism a source of shared history and a convenient national symbol[24]. The Jordanian nationalist identity became so tribal in its essence that King ʿAbd Allāh II (b. 1962) defines the Kingdom itself his "larger tribe"[25].

The nationalist singer Samīrah Tawfīq (b. 1935) is an exemplary storyteller of the "Bedouin Jordan" tale: A Christian of Armenian descent born in a southern Syrian village to a Maltese father and a Syrian mother as Samīrah Ġasṭīn Karīmūnā, she assumed the task of reviving "Jordanian folklore with [her] voice"[26]. She sang in a language that she

21. Pizzingrilli, unpublished semi-structured interview with ʿAlī Kašt, June, 2017, Amman.
22. A conclusion drawn from the data analysis of a larger project on the identity criteria upon which the legitimacy of the Arab-Muslim states is founded, with a focus on the Jordanian and the Kuwaiti cases. The empirical part of the project consisted of over 80 open semi-structured interviews. The Jordanian sample included both "pure Jordanians" and Jordanians of Palestinian origin.
23. Al-Bakri 2020, p. 55.
24. On 31 July 1971, King Ḥusayn instituted the Council of Tribal Leaders (*maǧlis šuyūḫ al-ʿašāʾir*).
25. Speech of His Majesty ʿAbd Allāh II at the Graduation of the 26th Class of Muʾta University's Military Wing, Amman, 16 June 2013, available at: http://jordanembassyus.org/news/speech-his-majesty-king-abdullah-ii-graduation-ceremony-26th-class-muta-universitys-military (last accessed April 2021).
26. Jarrar 2019.

described in televised interviews as both a "Jordanian dialect" and a "Bedouin dialect"; a diluted dialect taught to her by Information Ministry officials, and presented as the Jordanian national dialect, in which the pronunciation of the *qāf* as [g] – which went from being the "ugly variant" to embodying the new identity of the victorious Jordanians over the Palestinians[27] – plays the pivotal role of throwing the listener into a standardised, thus fictional, Bedouin world. Since the 1970s, Jordanian *musalsalāt* (TV series) have also portrayed Bedouins as one monolithic whole, the "true autochthonous of the Jordanian nation state"[28], using actors able to speak in the same generic (thus understandable all over the Arabian Peninsula) Bedouin accent. It was a strategy to promote this new audio-visual format in the broader Arab region, while at the same time following the political agenda of "Bedouinising" all Jordanians in order to nationalise them.[29] This enhanced a differentiation between them and the Palestinian (-Jordanians)[30], with the latter being by now, after the 1970 Civil War, a national threat that had been fought first militarily and then in the battlefield of the public arena from where Palestinians were progressively excluded through new meanings of "Jordanianness" and otherness. Finally, al-Mahadin (2017) pinpoints how some Jordanian radio stations still marginalised urban *ʿAmmanī* dialect as both feminine[31] and "inauthentic" in favour of a hybrid Bedouin dialect. Nevertheless, Samīrah Tawfīq became the ultimate "Bedouin" singer, not only in Jordan but across the Arab world[32], through songs that nationalised the Bedouin space, such as *Dayratunā al-Urdūnniyyah* (Our Jordanian Tribal Land), and many others. – All these songs praise the king and celebrate the kingdom's capital: *Urdunn al-Kūfiyyah al-Ḥamraʾ* (Jordan of the red *kūfiyyah*). They were composed for her by the creators of the new cultural

27. Suleiman stress the sensitivity of the issue (i.e., viewing ethnicity/nationality as a sociolinguistic variable) that results in cases of academic self-censorship, notably among researchers of Palestinian origin. Suleiman 2004, p. 114–124.
28. Prager 2014, p. 59.
29. Massad 2001, p. 77.
30. Suleiman 2004, p. 130.
31. The urban Levantine linguistic features have been adopted and maintained over time mostly by women, who did not have to display their ethnic and national identity in the public space (from which they were excluded) but were in constant need to assert their status. al-Wer, Herin 2011.
32. Yildirim 2020.

image of the country. As for the red *kūfiyyah* (or *šumāġ*), that appeared on Jordanian currency bills, Massad (2001) underlines that in the 1970s "Transjordanian urban male youth began to assert their Jordanianness sartorially [...] following King Hussein's footsteps [who] had begun to wear it as a headgear much more frequently"[33]. Identity can indeed be sewn into one's clothing, and evidence for that is "the special attention paid to wardrobe and choreography, with Samira Tawfik's dresses, designed by Lebanese designer William Khoury, being promoted as Bedouin attire"[34]. We shall see what the seamstresses of Rafedìn create using the same fabric.

In addition to the red *kūfiyyah*, an image of the site of Petra, the newest depositary of Jordanian "authenticity" and historical "truth", have also been placed on banknotes. Notably, in the late 1970s the Lebanese singer Fayrūz (b. 1935) produced a Broadway-style musical called *Petra*, thus contributing to the creation of the image of Jordan worldwide and also legitimising – or, better, historicising – the newly invented national dish *mansaf*[35], which was presented as the typical dish of proto-Jordanians more than 2,000 years ago.

Finally, the "Bedouin frame tale" had an additional impact on the urban space. The new tribalised identity that has been sung, sewn, and spoken since the 1970s has no place in the urban setting. Hence, Amman has been excluded from the official narrative that places the authentic Jordan in the desert of Wadi Rum or in the Nabatean site of Petra, typical settings of Bedouin soap operas. Nation states' societal foundations and cultural traditions were and are projected into the past; therefore the Bedouin soap operas became the keepers of cultural heritage and, since the 1990s, a modern form of identity production[36]. Jordan followed the regional trend that confines the national heritage to classical, religious, and

33. Massad 2001, p. 75; 250.
34. Jarrar 2019.
35. It consists of goat or sheep meat stewed in a lightly spiced sauce made from dried fermented yoghurt and served on grains on a layer of flatbread. The meat is piled high, topped with the choicest cuts, often including the head, and garnished with almonds, pine nuts and chopped parsley. Wojnarowski, Williams 2020, p. 161.
36. In the 1990s, globalisation changed the market. Although Jordan is still a leader in the technical and dramatic expertise and most of the productions still take place either in the Petra or Wadi Rum region, as of today, no country holds the monopoly anymore, and most productions are made by transnational teams, meaning that they

ancient monuments (such as the Pharaonic in Egypt and the Phoenician in Lebanon) but Jordanian official discourse has been even more radical in distancing itself from the more recent Ottoman past[37], preferring distant origins as sources of legitimacy for the newborn nation state: hence, the obsession with the Nabataean civilisation that was located in what is roughly modern Jordan's territory[38]. Accordingly, the King ʿAbd Allāh II Fund for Development, in line with the Royal project of reviving Jordanian history, established the Jordan Heritage Revival Company (JHRC) in 2010, "with the objective of developing the tourism sector in Jordan by creating authentic, engaging, and entertaining experiences [...] to bring the ancient civilisations that once populated Jordanian soil to life"[39] when Amman turned into an international tourist destination[40].

4. Jordan First

This section investigates the most recent frame tale authored by King ʿAbd Allāh II (b. 1962), adding the temporal dimension to the discussion on national identity. If national identification can be temporally framed, do people identify differently with their nation's past or present? How did the country's national history, briefly retraced above, influence their current national identity? Indeed, the Jordanian national identity and the kingdom itself, historically framed in space by the East/West Bank divide, come now to deal with the temporal dimension of a shared past on which the new homogeneous "Jordanianness" pictured by ʿAbd Allāh II is based.

The king promoted different initiatives aimed at enforcing civic education and national identity: the national campaign *al-Urdunn Awwal*[an]

are no longer subjected to the national propaganda of single nation states. Massad 2001, p. 72–73; Prager 2014, p. 75.

37. The Great Arab Revolt (1916–1918) is a powerful symbol, however, and it is often reenacted to attract tourists. See this promotional video financed by the Jordan Heritage Revival Company: https://www.youtube.com/watch?v=iCgQK5JmMkc&ab_channel=VisitJordan.
38. Daher 2008, pp. 39–41.
39. From the official company website http://jhrc.jo/.
40. Shami 2007, pp. 225–231.

(2002), part of the national and civic education curriculum in schools[41], the reform program *Kullunā al-Urdunn* (We are all Jordan, 2006), and the school reform project ERfKe (The Education Reform for Knowledge Economy)[42]. By focusing on Jordan as a distinct political entity with a common (national) identity, the "Jordan First" campaign redefined the relationship between the state and its citizens. Politics and governmental narratives together redesigned the geographical and identity boundaries of Jordan's "elastic"[43] state, as they have done ever since its foundation. The 2003 *Atlas of Jordan and the World* cover delineates Jordan only to the east of the Jordan River, thereby excluding the West Bank (in contrast to previously, see above). "We are all Jordan", likely set off by the challenges produced by the huge number of Iraqi refugees who migrated to Jordan after the 2003 US invasion, aims to enhance the citizens' sense of belonging, just like "Jordan First". As with the previous initiative, it displays the map-flag logo[44] produced by the US advertising firm Saatchi and Saatchi, hired by the Hashemite Kingdom to carry out the 2002 campaign (at a cost of about 50 million USD)[45]. These latest attempts of nation-building aimed at uniting the country through billboards, pins, and bumper stickers have been largely met with indifference. But King ʿAbd Allāh II was accused of trying to erase other identities in favour of an all-encompassing Jordanian one with a renewed Arab character that endangers the status of the ethnic minorities (e.g., Circassians). Finally, the new narrative is also built on a revised Jordanian-sponsored Islamic orthodoxy, of which the 2004 *Risālat ʿAmmān* (The Amman Message)[46]

41. Majd 2017, pp. 86–88.
42. A two-phase project (2003–2007; 2007–2013) that focused on the country's labour market challenges but was also "an example of a nation-building project meant to align Jordan with a Western model". Kubow, Kreishan 2014, p. 8.
43. Massad 2001.
44. Three hands [holding one another] on a black background form the shape of the Jordanian nation which only includes the territory east of the Jordan River. The 2006 campaign only added the "We are all Jordan" slogan.
45. Culcasi 2016, pp. 13–19.
46. The Amman Message begun as a sermon delivered by Jordan's Chief of Justice, ʿIzz ad-Dīn al-Ḫaṭīb at-Tamīmī, who stressed the need to reassert Islamic values of dialogue, cooperation, and tolerance both among Muslims and between Muslims and the West. The statement that followed defines the "true nature of Islam" (and, by defining who is part of the *ummah*, clarifies who is excluded from it) and became

is an expression. This can be used to justify state policies and criminalise those who oppose them[47]. In addition, the city itself has been integrated into meta-narratives – such as Arab Islam – and urban structures underwent a process of physical Islamisation designed to make Amman reflect its Muslim heritage only, described by Rogan as a form of religious legitimation[48].

5. A Jordan of Refugees, Refugees of Jordan

This section investigates the processes of inclusion and exclusion implemented by the government over time when dealing with migrants and refugees. Such processes are indeed constructed within discourse and through difference, as "the use of national narratives in the making of nation-states is a process linked to migration and migration policy"[49]. It concludes with a focus on the Iraqi community so as to better contextualise the Rafedìn experience.

Refugees have been an integral component of the Jordanian societal mosaic since before the kingdom's very foundation (e.g., people fleeing the Balkans and the Caucasus in the late 19th century), and Jordan followed different models for refugee management over time, moving between integration (granting citizenship), separation (creating camps), (temporary) absorption, and exclusion (from accessing legal protection and public services, also based on origin)[50]. Despite having a long history of hosting a large and diverse population of forced migrants[51], Jordan – one of the countries with the highest ratio of refugees to indigenous people in the world – is not a signatory of the 1951 Geneva Convention

---

an international reference document. The text is available at https://ammanmessage.com/. King ʿAbd Allāh II discusses the significance of the Amman Message in the 23rd chapter of his 2011 book *Our Last Best Chance: The Pursuit of Peace in a Time of Peril* (Penguin, New York).

47. Browers 2011, 943–945.
48. Rogan 1986.
49. Catling 2011.
50. Davis et al. 2017, pp. 1–10.
51. The Hashemite Emirate/Kingdom has hosted millions of refugees over the years: Somalians, Sudanese, Chechens, Circassians, Armenians, Palestinians, Mandeans, Iraqis and Syrians. Stevens 2013, p. 3.

on Refugees nor of the 1967 Protocol Relating to the Status of Refugees, and it has never developed a domestic refugee law or a procedure for adjudicating asylum claims[52]. Nevertheless, the state has pledged to uphold the 1951 Convention *non-refoulement* obligations; indeed, the Memorandum of Understanding (MoU) signed by the UNHCR with Amman in 1998 (and revised in 2014), states as follows: "In order to safeguard the asylum institution in Jordan and to enable UNHCR to act within its mandate [...] it was agreed [...] that no refugee seeking asylum in Jordan will be returned to a country where his life or freedom could be threatened because of his race, religion, nationality, membership of a particular social group, or political opinion"[53]. Although the 1998 MoU sets up the framework by which UNHCR operates in Jordan, it does not recognise the potential for any local integration of refugees in the country. Indeed, the government has framed refugees' policies under the Islamic/ Bedouin/Arab guesthood narrative[54]. For instance, Gazans[55] often define themselves as *ḍuyūf* (guests) of the fatherly king[56]. Accordingly, we shall look at refugees, specifically Iraqis, so to provide a framework for the chapter's case study, as characters of the Jordanian tale. Our purpose here is to understand how their story arc is written and nevertheless modifies the main storyline, with particular attention to the labelling process, given that lexical choices construct meaning[57].

Indeed, the recent armed conflicts in Iraq and in Syria resulted in an economic (funding deficits, competition over jobs and resources,

52. Occasional reference to refugees and asylum is made in Law n. 24 of 1973 on Residence and Foreigners' Affairs dedicated to the non-nationals' entry in the country.
53. *Memorandum of Understanding between the Government of Jordan and UNHCR*, April 1998, art. 2.
54. Kelberer 2017, pp. 148–151.
55. Gazan Palestinians are doubly displaced refugees, forced to move after the 1948 conflict and after the Six-Day War. In 1948 they were issued Egyptian travel documents because Egypt was in charge of the military and administrative rule in Gaza at the time. After 1967, some fled to Lebanon, and some to Jordan. The latter (between 118,000 and 150,000) never gained citizenship. Since the 1980s, their temporary passports have needed to be renewed every 2 years and have value as an international travel document only if the receiving state allows the holder entry. See Feldman 2012, pp. 129–169 and al-Abed 2006.
56. al-Abed 2014, p. 82.
57. Hagström, Gustafsson 2019, p. 390.

infrastructure degradation) and demographic (754,528 as of April 2021 according to UNHCR[58]) shock for the country. Interestingly, the growing Syrian and Iraqi presence has changed both the self-perception of the "Palestinian-Jordanians" and their image of the "Jordanian Jordanians": "in comparison with Syrians, Palestinians are now viewed differently because there's a new enemy, a new *other*"[59]. Furthermore, Eghdamian (2016) stresses how the religious diversity of the refugee population has had an impact on the Jordanian religious minorities as well. For instance, Christian and Druze Syrian refugees, guilty of a deeper "otherness", experience a double feeling of isolation and exclusion, both by the Muslim (Jordanian) majority and by the other (Syrian) Muslim refugees. Thus, they find their places of comfort in the kingdom's monasteries and churches, as their religious identity fosters in-group solidarity, overcoming their national belonging[60]. Moreover, Hüser (2016) discusses the government's "refugees as a burden" narrative arguing that refugees have been used by the Hashemite rulers as a scapegoat for the worsening of the economic situation of the kingdom and to attract further funding from the West[61]. Indeed, the financial aid obtained by the host government is so significant[62] as to be considered "equivalents of rent". In this regard, what Kelberer (2017) calls "refugees rentierism" connects the issue with Jordan (semi-)rentier history, which also started before it became a state, and in turn with the process of legitimation[63] that this fragile and over-reliant socioeconomic system entails[64].

58. *Registered Persons of Concern Refugees and Asylum Seekers in Jordan*, 2021.
59. Pizzingrilli, unpublished semi-structured interview with Ḥakīm, Amman, 2017.
60. Eghdamian 2016, pp. 458–462.
61. Hüser 2016, pp. 79–82.
62. For the period 2017–2020, the EU's bilateral assistance to Jordan under the ENI (European Neighbourhood Instrument) amounted to approximately to €335.5–410.1 million. *European Neighbourhood Policy and Enlargement Negotiations: Jordan*, https://ec.europa.eu/neighbourhood-enlargement/neighbourhood/countries/jordan_en (last accessed April 2021).
63. Schlumberger, Bank, 2001/2002.
64. As for the co-dependence between political power, domestic sovereignty, and foreign policy see Brand 1994.

6. Fleeing Iraq

Historically, there has been a high level of spatial mobility between Iraq and Jordan. Various flows of forced Iraqi migrants have crossed Jordan over time,[65] starting in 1958 with the overthrow of the Iraqi (Hashemite) monarchy, the assassination of King Fayṣal II (1935–1958) and the turmoil that followed. Proof of the intimate proximity between the two countries long governed by two brothers is the reference, in the 1994 masterpiece by ʿAbd al-Raḥmān Munīf (1933–2004) *Sīrat madīnah: ʿAmmān fī l-arbaʿīnāt* (translated into English as *Story of a City: A Childhood in Amman*, 1996), to the funerary ceremonies held in Amman for the Faysal II's predecessor, King Ġāzī (1912–1939), that broadens the perimeters of the boy-protagonist imagined community which came to include Baghdad: "[He became aware that] they were separated from Baghdad by distance and accent, but at the same time, it was also extremely close"[66].

Another wave of Iraqi refugees arrived in 1979 due to the Iraq/Iran war, and again after the First and the Second Gulf Wars, with the Hashemite Kingdom being the only neighbouring Arab state opening its borders to Iraqis during the 1990–2003 UN sanctions. But the majority of those who arrived in 1990–1991 used the Hashemite Kingdom as a "transition space, a stepping stone"[67] to other destinations[68]. Unlike the 2003/2004 wave, limited to small numbers of wealthy businessmen and former army officials who were able to secure *iqāmah* (residency). The real challenge for the Hashemites started in 2005 as the sectarian conflict in Saddam's Iraq worsened, reaching its peak in 2007, when the Jordanian government reported the presence of 450,000 to 500,000 Iraqi nationals on its soil. Moreover, the 2005 bombing of hotels where 60 people were killed and 115 injured. Al-Qaeda in Iraq claimed responsibility, and these attacks were perpetrated by four Iraqi nationals, led the state to look at

65. Stevens 2013, pp. 1–6.
66. Sheetrit 2014, p. 38.
67. Davis et al. 2017, p. 15.
68. About 400,000 emigrated to Western countries between 1991 and 2002. In the same years, about 300,000 "Palestinians of Kuwait" were expelled from the Gulf city-state because of the OLP alignment with Saddam Hussein. This was a wave so significant as to be called "the Palestinians' third exodus". See Le Troquer, Hommery al-Oudat, 1999.

the refugees as potential security threats, and its policies changed accordingly (no access to public schools or to the national healthcare system, stricter control over the informal job market, tighter border procedures that made the intra-national circular movements between the two countries difficult) to be relaxed only in 2007, when UNHCR transferred 60% of its budget directly to the government[69]. Finally, many have fled Iraq to escape the so-called Islamic State (especially since 2014, when ISIS occupied one third of the territory of present-day Iraq) and because of the country's general instability.

To summarise, in accordance with the 1998 MoU, Iraqis can stay in Jordan, be eligible for resettlement in a third country, or repatriate. But they are "guests"[70] to be taken care of as expected within the "Arab brotherhood" and Islamic traditions; hence, permanent integration will never be an option. The government developed the model of "temporary absorption"[71], already mentioned above; thus, it provides access to state services but does not offer long-term solutions (such as granting citizenship). Clearly, the very process of refugee labelling bears a political weight and is being handled by governments rather than NGOs, it turned into a legitimising tool for exclusion and marginalisation policies[72]. Moreover, labelling has the power of forming or shaping identities, that can be both "externally ascribed or internally assumed"[73]. In Jordan, non-nationals (hence Iraqis) can be defined in at least ten different ways: UNHCR granted "refugee status", UNHCR registered "asylum seeker", UNHCR granted "prima facie group determined refugee", UNHCR "refugee" who do not resettle within six months, "economic migrant", "visitor" (with a resident permit), "overstayer" (without a resident permit, namely, guests who overstay their welcome), "circular migrant" (one who moves across the border usually in search of employment), "deregistered refugee" (someone who did not contact UNHCR offices in two months), "Arab brother/sister"[74]. Mason looks at "circular migrations" as shaped by both

69. Kelberer 2017, p. 152.
70. The term "guest" is often used by Gazans to describe themselves. See above. al-Abed 2014, p. 82.
71. Davis et al. 2017, pp. 1–10.
72. Zetter 2007, pp. 172–173.
73. Stevens 2013, pp. 17–18.
74. Ibid., p. 18.

pan-Arab ideologies of hospitality (endorsed by the Pact of the League of Arab States, 1945) that historically enabled high levels of spatial mobility between Iraq and Jordan but have showed their frailties since 2003, and the Jordanian politics surrounding the very category of "refugee"[75]. Finally, other classifications based on religion and nationality should be added to these legal categorisations, such as Muslim, Sunni, Shi'a, Christian, Kurd, Assyrian, Chaldean, etc. Regarding these various definitions, Chatelard points out that "Iraqi refugees [...] express their claims, identities, experiences, and expectations along a variety of relational categories of self-definition, and rarely along mutually exclusive normative ones"[76], as they seldom fit into strict categories because of the complexity of their experiences. The powerful political significance of labels in Jordan comes from the association of refugees with the "permanently resident" Palestinians (an identification that is problematic for the Iraqis themselves); hence the stress on guest status and temporariness, which resulted in non-nationals feeling themselves to be morally questionable (ungrateful guests who overstayed their welcome) and being viewed as a politically and socially problematic demographic (populist stances blame them for the worsening of the economic situation in Jordan). Rafedìn was born as a response to this painful condition of temporariness.

7. Rafedìn: The Story of "the Two Rivers"[77]

The Rafedìn story is indeed a story, a play of many faces, voices, and places that could exist nowhere but in Jordan. The tale of "the two rivers"

75. Mason 2011, p. 361.
76. Chatelard 2009, p. 39.
77. This section is based mainly on five open interviews carried out by the author via Zoom between February and May 2021 with Fr Mario Cornioli, an Italian *fidei donum* priest for the Latin Patriarchate of Jerusalem in the parish of St. Joseph in Jabal Amman, and founder and Country Director for Jordan of the Habibi Valtiberina Association (HAVA. See the official website: https://www.associazionehabibi.org/projects/?lang=en); Maria Paola Crisponi, Rafedìn Project Coordinator since 2016 to 2018, currently AIDOS – Associazione Italiana Donne per lo Sviluppo (Italian Association for Women in Development) Country Representative for Jordan; Ileana Alparone, trainee, member of the Rafedìn Project team since September 2020; Mārīnā, beneficiary of the Rafedìn project, in Jordan since 2018; Alā', beneficiary

(*bilād al-rāfidayn*) was born from an idea by Fr Mario Cornioli, who arrived in Jordan in 2015 from Palestine, where he lived and worked since 2002[78]. The long experience of Fr Mario in Bethlehem helped him make an emotional connection with Jordan and its people. Like a living memory of the long-lost motherland, he could understand and be understood at an intimate level once again by telling a story of peaceful coexistence printed on Italian silk fabrics and *kūfiyyah* from the Palestinian Territories[79].

When he was in Jordan, he noticed a vacuum surrounding the Iraqi refugees because most of the strategies in place were targeted at the Syrians. Consequently, he started working with the Iraqi community, at first to meet their essential needs. But emergency approaches alone soon revealed themselves to be insufficient, especially since, on average, Iraqis stay in Jordan around three to four years before resettling somewhere else. Indeed, when asked "When did you arrive in Jordan?", the vast majority of the girls, chose option C, "4+ years ago", and some chose option B "1 to 3 years ago". None chose option A :"less than 1 year/ 1 year ago". Therefore, *abūnā*[80] Mario and his congregation set up reception centres offering housing assistance in East Amman, particularly in *al-Ašrafiyyah*[81].

In the 1970s, Amman was split into two parts: the smaller eastern part, where most of refugees' camps and slums are located, and the wealthy

---

of the Rafedìn project, in Jordan since 2016. Moreover, the findings from a self-administered questionnaire consisting of 15 (mostly) closed-ended questions e-mailed to the 20 present beneficiaries of the project have been used. The interviews were conducted in Italian, English, and Arabic. The questionnaire was presented both in English and in Arabic, and all the respondents chose to use the Arabic version.

78. In Bethlehem, Fr Mario collaborates (this collaboration is ongoing) with the Hogar Niño Dios Children's Home that hosts and provides for children with severe disabilities. See the Facebook page: https://m.facebook.com/profile.php?id=363697863719097
79. The *kūfiyyah* are bought from the Hirbawi factory, in Hebron. See the official website: https://www.kufiya.org/
80. Literally "our father"; it is a title widely used in Jordan to refer to a priest; it can be used either by itself or with the priest's given name.
81. Most of the Armenian organisations are located in *Ǧabal al-Ašrafiyyah*, so much so that it is also called "the Armenian Neighbourhood" (*Ḥayy al-Arman*). Armenians arrived in Jordan when fleeing from the massacres in Turkey in the 1920s.

western area, with large family villas separated by agricultural land[82]. Following the 1967 defeat and 1970–1971 clashes, the middle-class neighbourhoods were transformed into temporary refugee camps, and new neighbourhoods have been continuously built only to be replaced by other spaces that could better embody the wealth and status of their inhabitants whose identity as urban elites have nevertheless remained attached to other cities of the region, such as Beirut, Damascus, Jerusalem. These cities are the true objects of the nostalgia of a stratified society[83] that ultimately works against consolidating an *ʿAmmanī* identity. This line of reasoning leads Shami to negate Amman identity with respect to its status as a city[84]. Moreover, in 1965, the government established the Housing Corporation (HC), which then merged with the urban development department to form the Housing & Urban Development corporation, part of the 1989 national housing strategy, "which aimed at enabling the private sector to participate and be involved in the production of housing units for certain target groups"[85].

Daher (2013) sees these initiatives as expressions of neoliberal urbanism that, despite its emancipation discourse promoting a utopian existence, lead to geographies of inequality and urban disparities[86]. Accordingly, Iraqis have been placed on the city margins and excluded from the main storyline. Exclusion and the sense of permanent temporariness that surrounds their lives, defined by both the volatile legal framework briefly

82. Shami 2007, p. 217.
83. To the already mentioned Circassians, Syrians, and Palestinians we should also add: the Lebanese fleeing their country because of the 1975 Civil War, the Palestinians and Jordanians returning from the Gulf after the 1990–91 crisis, and wealthy Iraqis who picked Jordan as their final destination in the mid-1990s.
84. Shami 2007, pp. 222–225.
85. From the Housing and Urban Development Corporation page in Jordanian government website: https://portal.jordan.gov.jo/wps/portal/Home/GovernmentEntities/Ministries/Ministry/Ministry%20of%20Public%20Works%20and%20Housing/Housing%20and%20Urban%20Development%20Corporation/!ut/p/z0/fY7B-CoJAFEV_ZfyAeCLVfjCxRCOt0GYTY402aO8N4yj094m0bnfv4XK4IKACgXLSrXSaUPZzv4ntna-jy8aP-SEPirXP02MYxWmR5EUAZ4WQgPg_mi2B-zcKsBWGke600NgRVplEPzn4YNew01r1-sJJsNzCJT7ancdDYQvULC-7zaWiLbqUn1ZN4KHQvJGrLLWzBdXHLueV-0HAST/.
86. Daher 2013, p. 105.

discussed above, and the prevailing political narrative, needed to be dealt with.

In this respect, *abūnā* Mario describes the Rafedìn project as a "healing process": "the girls", he says, "needed a place where it would be possible to share the traumatic experiences they had suffered with someone who went through the same ordeals, heal and start thinking about the future again". Both Maria Paola (Rafedìn Project Coordinator, 2016–2018) and Ileana (trainee, member of the Rafedìn project team) referred to the healing power of the Rafedìn experience; Ileana believes that the beneficiaries developed "a sense of belonging toward this safe place". Moreover, to the question "Did being part of Rafedìn improve your life in Jordan? If yes, how did it help you the most?" the vast majority of the girls chose option B: "Yes, it helped me psychologically, I feel less lonely and I have a purpose". Interestingly, few chose option A: "Yes, it helped me fit into Jordanian society". Training workshops are the key, according to *abūnā* Mario, to help these girls emerge from their limbo of depression and trauma, by giving them financial aid and, above all, job skills that would be an asset in the country of resettlement. Alā᾿ (the current beneficiary of the project) speaks fondly of the learning experience: "I didn't know anything about sewing, but *abūnā* Mario accepts everyone, even girls like me who start from zero and gives them the chance to learn. I even learned English since I came here".

The first Rafedìn workshop in 2015 was not framed in a project yet – the machinery could be bought thanks to private donations, and Rosaria, an Apulian seamstress, trained 20 girls for two weeks on a voluntary basis. This first group chose the title of the story, "Rafedìn", the Arabic toponym for Mesopotamia. An official project began in 2016 with the Association Pro Terra Sancta (ATS). funded by the Italian Episcopal Conference (CEI). Today, Rafedìn is run by the Habibi Valtiberina Association, founded and directed by Fr Mario, and it is currently financially aided by the French Embassy in Amman[87]. Initially hosted in a facility owned by the Franciscans in Jabal al-Weibdeh (Ǧabal al-Luwaybdah), the project eventually moved to the Greek-Melkite Cathedral of St. George, just a

87. Lately, within the initiative "Ramadan online craft market", the souqfann platform (https://souqfann.com/en/) financially aided by UNICEF, has hosted many projects, including Rafedìn: https://souqfann.com/en/sellers/Rafed%C3%ACn/.

few steps from Mecca Street, while waiting for the completion of the construction work of the present tailor shop, located in the church of Saint Joseph in the busy Rainbow Street, in downtown Amman. Through Rafedìn, its beneficiaries moved back from the peripheries to the city centre, from the margin of the tale to its main storyline. In four years, an all-encompassing minority (ethnic, religious, demographic) has been able to carve its place within the multifaceted Jordanian society, and the tailor shop, along with the pizzeria of the "Mar Yousef's pizza" project (begun in October 2017), became a vital component of the city of Amman. It is a meeting place for the expat community (particularly Italians, since Fr Mario started to celebrate mass in the Italian language), but it is also visited by Jordanians. Indeed, Fr Mario recalls a diversified crowd participating in the International Day of Human Brotherhood celebrations held in St. Joseph on 4 February 2021. Furthermore, because of travelling restrictions and safety concerns due to the Covid-19 emergency, live training sessions with the Italian seamstress had to be interrupted, and the girls were given a new mentor in Muḥsin, "Momo", an Egyptian Muslim tailor who "became like a grandfather to the girls", says *abūnā*.

Throughout the years, Rafedìn has professionally trained about sixty girls as seamstresses. At first, they were very young and single, but the demographic of the beneficiaries progressively changed; half of the present group are 26–35-years, with some over 35, and many are married with children. This shift perhaps highlights the criticalities of a system that fails to provide feasible solutions, thus leaving increasingly older people and families in a state of need and uncertainty. Among the girls now involved in the project many are from Qaraqosh (Qarah Qawš) or smaller towns that are also part of the Nineveh Governorate (in northern Iraq, about 32 km southeast of Mosul), and a minority are from Baghdad. They are Christians (Assyrians, Chaldeans, Chaldo-Assyrians) who fled their homes when ISIS was advancing towards the Kurdistan region through the province of Mosul, the base of most religious minorities. Quoting Mārīnā (a current beneficiary of the project): "Daesh came to our village and took our houses […]. I was in the fourth grade of high school. We had to leave because they were forcing the boys to join their army and [raping[88]] the girls. First, we went to Duhok (Dahūk) [Iraqi Kurdistan] but

88. Mārīnā did not know the word in English but was sadly able to explain the meaning.

it wasn't safe either. We tried to go back to Tesqopa (Tilsquf) [Mārīnā's hometown, in the Nineveh Governorate] but our houses had been occupied and other armed forces were shooting. Two kids died and we decided to come here".

Notably, religious minorities in Iraq were found in the margins of the hegemonic narrative since before the arrival of ISIS as they did not comply with Saddam's Arab nationalism and were excluded from the body politic due to the confessionalisation of the post-Bath Iraq[89]. Indeed, the most relevant identity criterion for almost all the girls is religion. Some chose family, but no one chose nationality/language. In this regard, Mārīnā said: "My country took from me more than it gave me. It took my brothers, my friends, my studies, everything". Mārīnā is 21 and arrived in Jordan in 2018. Her first struggle, besides settling in in an urban environment to which she was not accustomed, was with the language[90]: "In my village everyone speaks *ārāmiyyah* [Aramaic][91], so it was difficult to talk in Arabic or in English. Also, *al-laḥǧah taḫtalif* [the dialect is different] from here. When I speak with an Iraqi accent, they [the Jordanians] don't understand me, so I get confused, and I switch to English". She joined Rafedìn a year and a half after she arrived in the Hashemite Kingdom and she is deeply grateful to a place that gives her friends, a purpose, and job skills that could be useful when she finally resettles in Canada, where one of her brothers is already located.

As for the country of final destination, the vast majority of the girls expressed the will to relocate to Australia (no one chose the USA or Europe), both because of social networks already in place – meaning the existence of an established community[92] that can enhance a sense

89. Sevdeen, Schmidinger, 2019, pp. 5–7.
90. Mārīnā decided to do the interview in English.
91. The majority of the current beneficiaries are Aramaic-speaking. The Iraqi linguistic landscape is very rich and complex. Suffice it to say that many Christian dialects such as neo-Aramaic are spoken in the country (to a lesser extent in the big cities such as Baghdad, Mosul, or Basra). Assyrian neo-Aramaic, or "neo-Syriac", is spoken by Assyrian Christians, while Chaldean neo-Aramaic is spoken by the Chaldean Christian community. Collin 2009, p. 247.
92. Iraqi nationals have been settling in Australia since the 1970s, thus forming a large community. The Iraqi-born population is the 18th largest migrant community in the country, and at the end of June 2018, 87,750 Iraq-born people were living in Australia. Indeed, Iraqis were the single largest nationality granted visas under the

of belonging among new settlers[93] – and because of the advantageous Australian immigration policies. Australia is the country of final destination for Alāʾ, a 28-year-old elementary teacher who arrived in Jordan in 2016 and whose application has been repeatedly rejected by the Australian government ever since: "They will find any reason, any excuse to reject it, sometimes it is an incorrect address, another time the goods you would like to carry with you, they reject it and they do not care about the time, the money, and the hopes we put in it". Alāʾ joined Rafedìn two years after her arrival in Jordan. She heard about the project from her neighbour Mārīnā, who had just joined. "When I arrived, I was very sad because I had to leave my country and my job that I loved so much. I was alone all the time, always in my room, and I refused to eat. Mārīnā told me that this was a beautiful place where I could meet a lot of girls and that *abūnā* Mario was going to help us psychologically too. Indeed, we are a family". Alāʾ is from Baghdad, and she prefers to speak in her Baghdadi dialect (*lahğah baġdādiyyah*) and her sense of belonging to Iraq is stronger compared to Mārīnā's. She still identifies primarily as a Christian, but she is proud of coming from *balad al-ḫayrāt*, the country of good deeds, for which her uncle died as a martyr in the 1979 war against Iran (during which Jordan backed Iraq unequivocally), and that she believes is suffering "from neighbouring countries' and in general foreign involvement in its internal matters". Indeed, though Daesh did not enter Baghdad, she says, "we had to deal with its theories and ideas (*afkār dāʿišiyyah*) which spread across the city". Moreover, Alāʾ recalls the presence of militias "of unknown affiliation", probably referring to the armed groups that emerged in response to the Grand Ayatollah al-Sistānī (b. 1930) 2014 edict that called all able-bodied men to enlist in the Iraqi Security Forces (ISF) and help protect the homeland against ISIS forces. Many sub-state and non-state groups (newly established or remobilised) conglomerated under the banner of the *al-ḥašd al-šaʿbī* (HS), or Popular Mobilisation Forces (PMF), threatening in fact the government's legitimacy, territorial

---

offshore Humanitarian Program over 2005–2015, with around one in every five refugees resettled in Australia coming from Iraq. *Iraq-Born Community Information Summary*, 2016. Finally, the presence of the Australian Iraqi Muslim Society (AISM) is worth mentioning to highlight the active role of the Iraqi community in the country. See the Society website: http://iraqisociety.org.au/us/.

93. Johnston et al. 2009, p. 202.

integrity and the post-conflict security of Iraq[94]. Indeed, although the PMF are formally part of the ISF and report to the Iraqi Prime Minister, in many cases they give priority to the orders of their own leadership[95]. Alā᾽ comes "from a city, not a village", and she treasures her diversified environment of origin where she "used to live among people of many faiths and nationalities", hence the urban space, while being another source of alienation for Mārīnā, is familiar to Alā᾽. Perhaps more so, since Baghdad is one of the many layers that constitute the very identity of Amman. Settling in Jordan is still not an option for her, however. She complies with the above-mentioned governmental guest status narrative: "Jordan hosted us [*istaḍāfatnā*, same root of *ḍuyūf*, guests] and we are thankful for it". Hence, she feels she is both a guest of the fatherly king, afraid of overstaying her welcome, and part of a despised group: "Some Jordanians exploit our presence in the country: they are convinced that we are rich. Every time I go to a shop or take a taxi, as soon as the seller or the driver understands where I am from, he asks for something extra. With Syrians is different because people believe that they are in need, and they have work permits, they can work but we can't[96]". Alā᾽'s testimony adds yet another subplot to the Rafedìn story: she acknowledges her Arab supranational identity and finds it in the host society too: "Jordanians say they love us, they love Iraq because it is an Arab country, the first one to provide them with oil supplies[97]". Her understanding of Jordan and Amman, her life experiences and background, her relation to Christianity, and even her mother tongue are different from Mārīnā's. Nevertheless, Rafedìn managed to speak effectively to both and give them a safe place where they could wait for the longed-for future to finally happen, without neglecting the present.

94. O'Driscoll, van Zoonen 2017, p. 9.
95. Gaston, Derzsi-Horváth 2018, p. 10.
96. Syrians are able to obtain work permits under the Jordan Compact. See Grey Meral 2019.
97. The Jordanian energy sector is still heavily reliant on Iraqi exports.

8. Conclusion

The Rafedìn experience both fits in and disrupts the Jordanian tale. One can follow its thread throughout the entire Jordanian (hi)story, as it mirrors the main storyline, but offering a different ending. Indeed, it found a way to overcome the boundaries of the Hashemite kingdom's ever-changing discourses through the celebration of the multilayered beginnings of Amman and the many components of the Jordanian fabric. In fact, it can present the Iraqi demographic as one of the many layers of Jordanian society, not resorting to transnational ethnic or religious identities but relying on the very hi(story) of Jordan and Amman. According to Innab (2016), Amman is "in a state of permanent temporariness"[98]: the waves of refugees that crossed it (Palestinian, Lebanese, Iraqi, Syrian) modified the city's structure over time, while the ever-changing state's official narratives enhanced its temporary nature by endlessly building and rebuilding the "national". A glimpse of *ʿAmmānī* narrative can be detected, however, when "the social and urban heritage of the city is finally being celebrated and recognised for its uniqueness"[99]. Amman's plural, multicultural, and cosmopolitan nature – both in continuous reference to and penetrated by other places, religions, and customs – forms the multilayered and unique identity of its inhabitants[100], and is worthy of being the main character of the story just as it was presented in Munīf's *Sīrat madīnah.* This is the "inclusive" Amman of Rafedìn, the early 1920s Amman described by Hāšim Ġarāyibah (b. 1953) in *al-Shahbandar* (2003)[101], a city whose very essence is to "protect people coming to it from different locations"[102].

References

al-Abed, O. (2006), *Immobile Palestinians: Ongoing Plight of Gazans in Jordan*, in "Forced Migration Review", 26, available at https://reliefweb.int/report/occupied-palestinian-territory/forced-migration-review-no-26-palestinian-displacement-case (last accessed March 2021).

98. Innab 2016, p. 119.
99. Daher 2008, p. 44.
100. Hanania 2014; Sheetrit 2014.
101. See Fischione 2021, pp. 256–262.
102. Daher 2008, p. 43.

al-Abed, O. (2014), *The Discourse of Guesthood: Forced Migrants in Jordan*, in A. Fabos; R. Osotalo (eds.) *Managing Muslim Mobilities*, Palgrave Macmillan, New York, pp. 81–100.
al-Bakri, T. (2020), *Jordanian Musiqa Sha'bie: An Expression of Ethnical Authenticity in the Stream of Global Pop Music*, in "Journal of Education and Practice", 11, 23, pp. 51–63.
al-Mahadin, S. (2017), *Gendered Soundscapes on Jordanian Radio Stations*, in "Feminist Media Studies", 17, 1, pp. 108–111. https://doi.org/10.1080/14680777.2017.1261461
al-Wer, E., Herin, B. (2011), *The Lifecycle of Qaf in Jordan* in "Langage et société", 4, 138, pp. 59–76. https://doi.org/10.3917/ls.138.0059
Anderson, B. (1983), *Imagined Communities: Reflections on the Origin and Spread of Nationalism*, Verso, New York.
Brand, A. L. (1994), *Jordan's Inter-Arab Relations: The Political Economy of Alliance Making*, Columbia University Press, New York.
Browers, M. (2011), *Official Islam and the Limits of Communicative Action: The Paradox of the Amman Message*, in "Third World Quarterly", 32, 5, pp. 943–958. https://doi.org/10.1080/01436597.2011.578969
Butler, J. (1997), *Excitable Speech: A Politics of the Performative*, Routledge, London.
Catling, H. (2011), *State Construction and the Use of National Narratives*, in "E-International Relations", available at: https //www.e-ir.info/2011/08/03/state-construction-and-use-of-national-narratives/ (last accessed August 2022).
City Migration Profile-Amman: Executive Summary (2015), International Centre for Migration Policy Development (ICMPD), United Cities and Local Governments (UCLG) and United Nations Human Settlements Programme (UN-HABITAT), available at https://www.uclg.org/sites/default/files/amman_city_migration_profile_executive_summary_en.pdf (last accessed March 2021).
Chatelard, G. (2009), *What Visibility Conceals: Re-Embedding Refugee Migration from Iraq*, In: D. Chatty (ed.) *Dispossession and Displacement: Forced Migration in the Middle East and Africa*, British Academy, London, available at: https://www.academia.edu/182774/What_visibility_conceals_Re_embedding_Refugee_Migration_from_Iraq (last accessed April 2021).
Chatelard, G. (2010), *Jordan: A Refugee Haven*, in "Migration Policy Institute Online Journal", available at https://www.migrationpolicy.org/article/jordan-refugee-haven (last accessed March 2021).
Collin, R. (2009), *Words of War: The Iraqi Tower of Babel*, in "International Studies Perspectives", 10, 3, pp. 245–264. https://doi.org/10.1111/j.1528-3585.2009.00375.x

Culcasi, K. (2016), *Warm Nationalism: Mapping and Imagining the Jordanian Nation*, in "Political Geography" 54, pp. 7–20. https://doi.org/10.1016/j.polgeo.2016.05.002

Davis, R. et al. (2017), *Hosting Guests, Creating Citizens: Models of Refugee Administration in Jordan and Egypt*, in "Refugee Survey Quarterly", 36, pp. 1–32. https://doi.org/10.1093/rsq/hdx003

Daher, R. (2008), *Amman: Disguised Genealogy and Recent Urban Restructuring and Neoliberal Threats*, in Y. Elsheshtawy (ed.), *The Evolving Arab City. Tradition, Modernity and Urban Development*, Routledge, London and New York, pp. 37–69.

Daher, R. (2013), *Neoliberal Urban Transformations in the Arab city: Meta-Narratives, Urban Disparities and the Emergence of Consumerist Utopias and Geographies of Inequalities in Amman*, in "Environnement Urbain / Urban Environment", 7, pp. 99–115. https://doi.org/10.7202/1027729ar

De Bel-Air, F. (2007), *State Policies on Migration and Refugees in Jordan*, Discussion Paper Prepared for the Migration and Refugee Movements in the Middle East and North Africa. The Forced Migration & Refugee Studies Program, American University in Cairo, October 23–25, available at: https://documents.aucegypt.edu/Docs/GAPP/Francoise-de-Belair.pdf (last accessed April 2021).

Derrida, J. (1978), *Writing and Difference*, trans. A. Bass, Routledge & Kegan Paul, London.

Eghdamian, K. (2016), *Religious Identity and Experiences of Displacement: An Examination into the Discursive Representations of Syrian Refugees and Their Effects on Religious Minorities Living in Jordan*, in "Journal of Refugee Studies", 30, 3, pp. 447–67. https://doi.org/10.1093/jrs/few030

Eilon, J. B., Alon, Y. (2007), *The Making of Jordan: Tribes, Colonialism and the Modern State*, I.B. Tauris, London, 2007.

Feldman, I. (2012), *The Challenge of Categories: UNRWA and the Definition of a 'Palestine Refugee'*, in "Journal of Refugee Studies", 25, 3, pp. 129–169. https://doi.org/10.1093/jrs/fes004

Fischione, F. (2020), *"A Village That Harbours the Oppressed"? Amman and the Jordanian Novel (1980–2000)*, in P. Maggiolini, I. Ouahes (eds.), *Minorities and State-Building in the Middle East: the Case of Jordan*, Palgrave Mcmillan, London, pp. 249–272.

Gaston, E., Derzsi-Horváth, A. (2018), *Iraq After ISIL*, Global Public Policy Institute (GPPI).

Gray Meral, A. (2020), *Assessing the Jordan Compact One Year On – An Opportunity or a Barrier to Better Achieving Refugees' Right to Work*, "Journal of Refugee Studies", 33, 1, pp. 42–61. https://doi.org/10.1093/jrs/fez074

Hagström, L., Gustafsson, K. (2019), *Narrative Power: How Storytelling Shapes East Asian International Politics*, "Cambridge Review of International Affairs", 32, 4, pp. 429–455. https://doi.org/10.1080/09557571.2019.1623498

Hall, S. (2000), "Who Needs Identity?" in P. Gay, J. Evans, P. Redman (eds.), *Identity: a reader*, Sage Publications, Thousand Oaks, pp. 15–30.

Hanania, D. M. (2014), *The Impact of the Palestinian Refugee Crisis on the Development of Amman, 1947–1958*, in "British Journal of Middle Eastern Studies", 41, 4, pp. 461–482. https://doi.org/10.1080/13530194.2014.942978

Hüser, S. (2016), "The Syrian Refugee Crisis and Its Impact on Jordan: In Reference to the Regime's Structural Deficits", in M. Beck, D. Jung, P. Seeberg (eds.), *The Levant in Turmoil. Syria, Palestine, and the Transformation of Middle Eastern Politics*, Palgrave Macmillan, London, pp. 79–82.

Iraq-Born Community Information Summary (2016), Australian Government, Department of Home Affairs, available at: https://www.homeaffairs.gov.au/mca/files/2016-cis-iraq.PDF (last accessed August 2022).

Innab, S. (2016), *Reading the Modern Narrative of Amman: Between the Nation and the National*, in A. Amale, N., Akawi (eds.), *The Arab City in Representation*, Columbia Books on Architecture and the City, Chicago.

Jarrar, S. (2019), *Qāl wa-qulnā: What the Letter Qāf means in Spoken Jordanian*, "7iber", November 21, available at https://www.7iber.com/society/qal-wa-qulna-what-the-letter-qaf-means-in-spoken-jordanian/ (last accessed March 2021).

Johnston, V., Vasey, K., Markovic, M. (2009), *Social Policies and Refugee Resettlement: Iraqis in Australia*, in "Critical Social Policy", 29, 2, pp. 191–215. https://doi.org/10.1177/0261018308101626

Kelberer, K. (2017), *Negotiating Crisis: International Aid and Refugee Policy in Jordan,* in "Middle East Policy", XXIV, 4, pp. 148–165. https://doi.org/10.1111/mepo.12313

Kubow, P., Kreishan, L. (2014), *Citizenship in a Hybrid State: Civic Curriculum in Jordan's Education Reform for Knowledge Economy Era* in "Middle Eastern & African Journal of Educational Research", 13, pp. 4–20.

Le Troquer, Y., Hommery al-Oudat, R. (1999), *From Kuwait to Jordan: The Palestinians' Third Exodus*, in "Journal of Palestine Studies" 28, 3, pp. 37–51. https://doi.org/10.2307/2538306

Majd, M. (2017), *Amman: Gulf Capital, Identity, and Contemporary Megaprojects*, Routledge, London.

Mason, V. (2011), *The Im/mobilities of Iraqi Refugees in Jordan: Pan-Arabism, 'Hospitality' and the Figure of the 'Refugee'*, in "Mobilities", 6, 3, pp. 353–373. https://doi.org/10.1080/17450101.2011.590035

Massad, J. A. (2001), *Colonial Effects: The Making of National Identity in Jordan*, Columbia University Press, New York.

Méouchy, N., Neveu, N. et al. (2013), *The Hashemites and the Creation of Transjordan* in Myriam Ababsa (ed.), *Atlas of Jordan. History, Territories and Society*, Ifpo, Amman.

Nevo, J., Pappè, I. (1994), *Jordan in the Middle East. The Making of a pivotal State (1948–1988)*, Routledge, London and New York.

O'Driscoll, D., Dave van Zoonen, D. (2017), *The Hashd al-Shaabi and Iraq. Subnationalism and the State*, MERI, Erbil.

Prager, L. (2014), *Bedouinity on Stage. The Rise of The Bedouin Soap Opera "(Musalsal Badawi)" in Arab Television*, in "Nomadic Peoples", 18, 2, pp. 53–77. https://doi.org/10.3197/np.2014.180205

Rogan, E. L. (1986), *Physical Islamization in Amman*, in "The Muslim World", 76, 1, pp. 24–42. https://doi.org/10.1111/j.1478-1913.1986.tb02768.x

Rogan, E. L. (1996), *The Making of a Capital: Amman 1918–1928*, in Hannoyer, J., Shami, S. (eds.), *Amman: The City and Its Society*, CERMOC, Beirut, pp. 89–108.

Ronen, Y. (2010), *The assassination of King Abdallah: The First Political Assassination in Jordan: Did It Truly Threaten the Hashemite Kingdom of Jordan?* in "Diplomacy & Statecraft", 21, 1, pp. 68–86. https://doi.org/10.1080/09592290903577759

Sallis, E. (2007), *Sheherazade/Shahrazād: Rereading the Frame Tale of the 1001 Nights*, in "Arabic & Middle Eastern Literature", 1, 2, pp. 153–167. https://doi.org/10.1080/13666169808718200

Sevdeen, B. M., Schmidinger, T. (eds.) (2019), *Beyond ISIS: History and Future of Religious Minorities in Iraq*, London, Transnational Press London.

Schlumberger, O., Bank, A. (2001/2002), *Succession, legitimacy, and regime stability in Jordan* in "The Arab Studies Journal", 9/10, 2/1 (Fall/Spring), pp. 50–72.

Shami, S. (2007), *"Amman is not a City". Middle Easter Cities in Question*, in Çinar, A., Bender, T. (eds.), *Urban Imaginaries: Locating the Modern City*, University of Minnesota Press, Minneapolis, pp. 208–235.

Sheetrit, A. M. (2014), *The Geography of Identity: ʿAbd al-Raḥmān Munīf's Sīrat madīna: ʿAmmān fī ʾl-arbaʿīnāt*, in "Journal of Arabic and Islamic Studies", 14, pp. 27–45. https://doi.org/10.5617/jais.4637

Stevens, D. (2013), *Legal Status, Labelling, and Protection: The Case of Iraqi 'Refugees' in Jordan*, in "*International Journal of Refugee Law*", 25, 1, pp. 1–38. https://doi.org/10.1093/ijrl/eet001

Suleiman, Y. (2004), *A War of Words: Language and Conflict in the Middle East*, Cambridge University Press, Cambridge.

Wojnarowski, F., Williams, J. (2020), *Making* Mansaf*: The Interplay of Identity and Political Economy in Jordan's 'National Dish'*, in "Contemporary Levant", 5, 2, pp. 161–177, https://doi.org/10.1080/20581831.2020.1767325

Yildirim, K. (2020), *Samira Ghastin Karimona Samira Tewfik: La voce beduina del mondo arabo e l'oasi del deserto – Samira Tewfik*, Edizioni Sapienza, s.l.

Zetter, R. (2007), *More Labels, Fewer Refugees: Remaking the Refugee Label in an Era of Globalization*, in "Journal of Refugee Studies", 20, 2, pp. 172–192. https://doi.org/10.1093/jrs/fem011

Registered Persons of Concern Refugees and Asylum Seekers in Jordan (2021), ReliefWeb OCHA, 15 April, available at https://reliefweb.int/report/jordan/registered-persons-concern-refugees-and-asylum-seekers-jordan-15-april-2021 (last accessed August 2021).

Odetta Pizzingrilli obtained her PhD in Politics: History, Science, Theory at LUISS Guido Carli University (Rome) where she recently completed a post-doctoral fellowship in the History of Islamic Countries. Her research focuses on the nation/state building process of the Arab states, national identity formation, minorities and minoritisation processes. She teaches History of the Contemporary Middle East in the Humanities Department at the University of Macerata.

Index of Names

Ababsa, Myriam 336
ʿAbbūd, Salām 81–83, 87, 99
ʿAbd al-Ḥasan, Fayṣal 82
ʿAbd Allāh I (King of Jordan) 311–313
ʿAbd Allāh II (King of Jordan) 313–314, 317–319
ʿAbd Allāh, Muḥammad ʿAbd al-Ḥalīm 132
ʿAbd al-Quddūs, Iḥsān 132
ʿAbd al-Wahhāb, Muḥammad 137
Abdel Haleem, Muhammad A. S. 26, 44, 267, 276
Abduh, Muhammad (ʿAbduh, Muḥammad) 35, 49, 56
al-Abed, Oroub 320, 323, 332–333
Abel 36, 52, 58, 60, 63–64, 67
Abourabi, Yousra 181, 198
Abū l-Ġayṯ al-Darawī, Muḥammad 259–260
Abū Nuwās 120, 261–262, 273
Abu Zayd, Nasr (Abū Zayd, Naṣr) 32–33, 43, 49, 54–56, 68–69, 71
Abu-Nimer, Mohammed 2, 13, 18, 22, 43
Ackerman, Seth 291, 305
Adam 3, 21, 35–36, 44–45, 47–50, 52, 56, 58, 61–62, 64–70, 72
Adorno, Theodor W. 159, 175
ʿAdwān, Mamdūḥ 232, 238, 251
al-Afġānī, Ǧamāl al-Dīn 35
Afsaruddin, Asma 43
Agamben, Giorgio 79, 87, 91, 156, 175
Agier, Michel 166, 175
Aguadé, Jordi 205, 223
Aḥdād, Karīmah 8, 179–201
Aḥmad, Ibrāhīm 157
Akawi, Nora 335
Albers, Yvonne 251
ʿAlī ibn Abī Ṭālib 138
Alimi, Eitan Y. 286–287, 289, 305
Allen, Roger 224
Alon, Yoav 334
Amale, Andraos 335
ʿAmārah, Lamīʿah ʿAbbās 105
al-Anbārī, Šākir 131
Anderson, Benedict 333
Andrews, Walter G. 262–263, 272
Anishchenkova, Valerie 158, 175
Anṭūn, Sinān 112, 131
Aragón Reyes, Manuel 180, 198
Arberry, Arthur John 200
Arbouch, Mahmoud 189, 198
ʿĀrif, ʿAbd al-Salām (President of Iraq) 107–108
Ariosto, Ludovico 267
Aruri, Naseer 286, 306
Asad, Talal 270, 272
Ateek, Naim (ʿAtīq, Naʿīm) 282–283, 290, 293, 306
al-Aṭraš, Farīd 137
August, Timothy K. 156, 175
Ayyūb, Ḏū l-Nūn 129
al-ʿAzzāwī, Fāḍil 129, 156

Babikir, Adil 122, 124
Bader, Ali (Badr, ʿAlī) 6–7, 93, 99, 112, 124, 131, 154–178

Badran, Sammy Zeyad 190, 198
Bahoora, Haytham 130, 151
al-Bakr, Aḥmad Ḥasan (President of Iraq) 108–110
al-Bakri, Tsonka 314, 333
Bank, André 321, 336
al-Bannā, Ḥasan 37
Baram, Amatzia 84, 99
Barbaro, Ada 122–123
Bartuli, Elisabetta 224, 226
Bauer, Thomas 262, 272
Bauman, Zygmunt 168, 176
al-Bayātī, ʿAbd al-Wahhāb 156
Beck, Martin 335
Belhaj, Abdessamad 35, 43, 47–48, 56–57, 59, 65, 68, 70–71
Beltritti, Giacomo Giuseppe 284
Bender, Thomas 336
Bendourou, Omar 181, 198
Bengio, Ofra 127, 151
Benigni, Elisabetta 267, 273
Benítez Fernández, Montserrat 223
Ben Jelloun, Tahar 212, 224
Bennabi, Malek 36, 46, 49, 51, 62, 63, 71, 73
Bergson, Henri 165
Bernard, Maurice 180, 199
Bhabha, Homi 173, 176
Bialier, Uri 306
Biesterfeldt, Hans Hinrich 264, 273
Binebine, Aziz 212, 216, 224
Binebine, Mahi 216, 224
Binebine, Mohammed 216
Bishop, Elizabeth 107, 122
Blasim, Hassan (Balāsim, Ḥasan) 112, 131, 157, 178
Bono, Salvatore 256, 273
Boomgaarden, Hajo G. 155, 176
Botros, Atef 230, 244, 251
Bouarek, Tarek 190, 199
Boulay, Sébastien 224
Bourdieu, Pierre 126, 128, 150–151, 161, 176
Brand, Laurie A. 321, 333
Brel, Jacques 164
Brockey, Liam Matthew 270, 273
Brogini, Anne 256, 273
Browers, Michaelle 319, 333
Brunacci, Domenico 257–259, 271–273
Bürgel, Johann Christoph 262, 273
Burke, Peter 270, 273
al-Būṭī, Muḥammad 61, 71
Butler, Judith 310, 333

Caiani, Fabio 78–79, 99, 106, 122, 129, 151
Cain 36, 58, 63–64
Calder, Marc D. 293, 306
Calderón de la Barca, Pedro 257, 274
Camera d'Afflitto, Isabella 122–123
Campanini, Massimo 122
Campbell, Ian 130, 151
Canova, Giovanni 230, 233, 243–244, 251–252
Capezzone, Leonardo 20, 43, 254, 260–262, 273
Carré, Olivier 43
Casanova, Pascale 134, 151
Casini, Lorenzo 244, 251
Catling, Holly 319, 333
Chalabi, Fadhil 114, 122
Charfi, Abdelmajid 261, 273
Chatelard, Géraldine 324, 333
Chatty, Dawn 333
Christiansen, Drew 290, 306–307
Churchill, Winston 311
Çinar, Alev 336
Cobham, Catherine 78–79, 99, 106, 122, 129, 151
Coffey, Quinn 291–292, 306
Colombo, Emanuele 256–257, 272–274
Collin, Richard O. 329, 333
Cook, David 22, 43, 66
Corm, Georges 175–17
Correale, Francesco 214, 224
Courcelle-Labrousse, Vincent 180, 199

Cox, Emma 156, 176
Culcasi, Karem 311–312, 318, 334

Dadush, Uri 189, 198
Daher, Rami F. 317, 326, 332, 334
Darling, Jonathan 166, 176
Davis, Eric 78–79, 99, 146, 151
Davis, Rochelle 319, 322–323, 334
De Bel-Air, Françoise 312, 334
De Castries, Henri 256, 274
Derrida, Jacques 166, 176, 310, 334
Derzsi-Horváth, András 331, 334
Desrues, Thierry 180, 199
Diana, Elvira 123
Diouani, Azz–Eddine 181, 199
Di Tolla, Anna Maria 226
Donner, Fred M. 19, 43
D'Orfeuil, Yves T. 293, 300, 301
Dozio, Cristina 9, 224
Dransfeldt Christensen, Tina 209, 224
Dufourmantelle, Anne 166, 176
du Gay, Paul 335
Dulucq, Sophie 180, 199
Dumairieh, Naser 35, 41, 43, 46–47, 51, 65–66, 69, 71
Dumper, Michael 281–282, 286, 292, 306
Dunqul, Amal 10, 230, 232–233, 244–248, 250–251, 253

El Bouih, Fatna (al-Buwīh, Fāṭinah) 209, 224, 226
Eco, Umberto 233, 247, 251
Eghdamian, Khatereh 321, 334
El-Enany, Rasheed 155, 176
El Guabli, Brahim 9, 182, 199, 205, 206, 210, 212, 216, 224
Elinson, Alexander 210, 224
Ellis, Marc H. 282–283, 306
El Rhazy, Sebhallah 181, 199
El-Rouyaheb, Khaled 262–263, 274
Elsheshtawy, Yasser 152, 334
Eskander, Saad B. 149, 151
Evans, Jessica 335

Fábos, Anita H. 333
Fadel, Youssef (Fāḍil, Yūsuf) 9, 202–225
Falak, Naṣīf 92–93, 100, 130
Fani, Sara 258, 274
al-Fārābī, Abū Naṣr 7, 155, 159, 170–172, 174, 176, 261
Farağ, Alfred 232, 247, 251–252
Farina, Margherita 258, 274
Farmān, Ġā'ib Ṭu'mah 129
Farrier, David 156, 176
Farsoun, Samih K. 286, 306
Fayrūz (Ḥaddād, Nuhād Wadī') 316
Fayṣal I (King of Syria, King of Iraq) 312
Fayṣal II (King of Iraq) 322
Feldman, Ilana 320, 334
Fernández–Molina, Irene 226
Fernández Parrilla, Gonzalo 210, 225
Ferrara, Marianna 200
Fikri, Mouhcine (Fikrī, Muḥsin) 181
Fischione, Fernanda 332, 334
Fiume, Giovanna 256, 274
Foucault, Michel 156, 176, 263, 274

al-Ğalabī, Fāḍil 113–117, 123
Galletti, Mirella 106, 111, 123
Gallien, Claire 156, 176
Gandolfi, Paola 224–225
Ġarāyibah, Hāšim 332
García Goldáraz, Carlos 256–257, 274
García-Arenal, Mercedes 256, 274
Gardet, Louis 266, 274
Ğāsim, 'Azīz al–Sayyid 129
Gaston, Erica 331, 334
Gavillet Matar, Marguerite 230–233, 235, 237, 239, 242–243, 251–252
al-Ğawāhirī, Muḥammad Mahdī 105–106, 156
al-Ġazālī, Nāẓim 137
Ġāzī ibn Fayṣal (King of Iraq) 322

al-Ghazali (al-Ġazālī) 54
Gelvin, James L. 287, 306
Genette, Gérard 233–252
Girard, Aurelien 258, 274
Gogol, Nikolay 111
Gombar, Eduard 252
Gray Meral, Amanda 334
Grémillion, Joseph 284
Greenberg, Joel 291, 306
Greussing, Esther 155, 176
Guazzone, Laura 37, 43
al-Ǧurǧānī, ʿAbd al-Qāhir 54
Gustafsson, Karl 320, 335
Gutas, Dimitri 261, 264, 273–274
Guth, Stephan 177, 201, 226

Hachad, Naïma 210, 212–213, 225
Haddad, Fanar 127, 134, 138, 150–151
Ḥāfiẓ, ʿAbd al-Ḥalīm 137
Hagström, Linus 320, 335
Hajji, Mohamed 256, 274
al-Ḫālidī, Raḍwān 112
Hall, Stuart 310, 335
Ḥamad, Maḥmūd 103, 123
al-Ḥamad, Turkī 120–121, 123
Hamori, Andras 262, 274
Hanania, Marwan D. 332, 335
Hannoum, Abdelmajid 182, 199
Hannoyer, Jean 336
Hanoosh, Yasmeen 129, 131, 151–152, 156, 159–160, 177
Hassan II (King of Morocco) 8–9, 202, 204, 205, 207–209, 212, 222, 224
al-Ḫaṭṭābī, Muḥammad b. ʿAbd al-Karīm 180–181, 197
al-Ḥaydarī, Buland 105
Heath, Peter 230, 252
Hegasy, Sonja 223, 225
Herin, Bruno 315, 333
Hesse, Herman (Hīssīh, Hīrmān) 133, 152
al-Ḥillāwī, Ǧinān Ǧāsim 129
Ḫiṣbāk, ʿĀyid 83–84, 100
Hommery al-Oudat, Rozenn 322, 335
al-Huḍaybī, Ḥasan 30
Ḫuḍayr, Muḥammad 80
al-Ḫuḍayrī, Batūl 91, 100
Huntington, Samuel P. 158, 176
Ḫūrī, Šakīb 232
Ḥusayn, Hadiyyah 129
Ḥusayn ibn ʿAlī 138, 140, 143
al-Ḥusayn ibn ʿAlī (King of the Hijaz) 310–311
al-Ḥusayn ibn Ṭalāl (King of Jordan) 312–314, 316
Ḥusayn, Ṭāhā 132
Hüser, Simone 321, 335
al-Ḥuṣrī, Sāṭiʿ 310–311
Hussein, Saddam 5, 77, 81, 85–86, 91–92, 102, 104, 109–112, 115, 117, 120, 128, 160, 170, 322

Ibn ʿAbbās 266
Ibn Ḫaldūn 311
Ibn Rušd 261
Idrīs, Yūsuf 132
Innab, Saba 313, 332, 335
al-ʿIqābī, Ḥamīd 92, 100, 129
Iqbal, Muhammad 35, 49, 51, 56, 59, 61, 71–72
Ismael, Tareq 117, 123

Jabar, Faleh A. 134, 151–152
Jacob (Prophet) 266–267, 271
Jarrar, Shaker 314, 316, 335
Jay, Salim 203, 225
Jensen, Mary E. 306
Johnston, Vanessa 330, 335
Joseph (Prophet) 266–267, 271
Jung, Dietrich 335

al-Kaʿbī, Fāḍil ʿAbbās 86, 100
Kadiri, Ghalia 192, 199
Kağah Ǧī, Inʿām (Kachachi Inaam) 112–113, 120, 123, 131
Kalpakli, Mehmet 262–263, 272

Kamal, Mustapha 224
Kanafānī, Ġassān 229–230
Karami, Leila 200
Karīm, Faḫrī 133–134
Karīm, Šawqī 130
Kårtveit, Bård 279–280, 292, 306
Kashou, Hanan Hussam 105, 112, 123
al-Kawākibī, ʿAbd al-Raḥmān viii–ix, 49, 51, 71, 73
Kāẓim, Šakīb 118–119, 123
Kelberer, Victoria 320–321, 323, 335
Khadduri, Majid 20, 43
Khader, Jamal 302, 306
Khalafallah, Muhammad (Ḫalaf Allāh, Muḥammad) 49, 56
Khalil, Georges 177, 251
Khalil, Samir 260, 273–274
Khoury, Geries (Ḫūrī, Ğurays) 283
Khoury, Rafiq (Ḫūrī, Rafīq) 283, 290, 293, 307
Khoury, William 316
al-Khuli, Amin (al-Ḫūlī, Amīn) 49, 56
Kreishan, Lana 318, 335
Kruk, Remke 238, 252
Kubow, Patricia 318, 335
Kuru, Selim S. 262, 275
Kzār, Murtaḍà 130
Kzār, Nāẓim 136

Laâbi, Abdellatif (al-Laʿābī, ʿAbd al-Laṭīf) 198
Laachir, Karima 210, 225
Lachhab, Mohammed 195, 198, 201
Lançon, Philippe 161, 177
Lange, Christian 200, 262, 266, 275
Lavenia, Vincenzo 271, 275
Lebessou, Louis 256–257, 275
Ledóchowski, Włodimir 256–257, 275
Le Troquer, Yann 322, 335
Lewis, Bernard 18, 262, 275
Loyola Mandes, Baldassarre 10, 254–255, 273–274
Lybarger, Loren D 279, 307
Lyons, Malcolm C. 231, 242, 252

Madani, Mohamed 200
Maddy-Weitzman, Bruce 182, 199
Maggiolini, Paolo 11, 334
Maghraoui, Driss 200
al-Mahadin, Salam 315, 333
al-Mahdī 260, 274
Maḥfūẓ, Nağīb 132
al-Malāʾikah, Nāzik 105, 111, 124
al-Malāʾikah, Nizār 105
al-Malāʾikah, Ṣādiq 105
Mallat, Chibli 3, 13, 45, 48–52, 54, 60, 63–64, 67, 70, 72
Mancini, Lorenzo 254, 267, 275
Manduchi, Patrizia 30, 34, 43
Mamdūh, ʿĀliyah 91, 100
al-Mankūb, Salmān 136
Mansoori, Muhammad Tahir 23, 44
Mansub Basiri, Iman 254, 267, 275
al-Mansūr, Aḥmad 256, 274,
Ma'oz, Moshe 308
Markovic, Milica 335
Marmié, Nicolas 180, 199
Marteijn, Elizabeth S. 281, 294, 307
Marzouki, Ahmed 212, 225
al-Mašhadānī, Ṭāriq ʿAbd Allāh 86, 100
Masmoudi, Ikram 79–80, 83, 87, 91, 93, 100, 112, 124, 159, 176–177
Mason, Victoria 323–324, 335
Massad, Joseph A. 315–318, 335
Matar, Nabil 256, 258, 260, 266, 272, 276
Maṭar, Salīm 112, 129
al-Mawdūdī, Abū l-Aʿlà 30, 51
Mazīd, Muḥammad 86, 100
McGahern, Una 278, 307
Mehrez, Samia 145, 152
Méir-Glitzenstein, Esther 160, 177
Melis, Nicola 43
Menghini, Pietro 44, 65, 72
Menin, Laura 208–209, 219, 225
Méouchy, Nadine 312, 336

Milich, Stefan 78–79, 99–100, 152, 156, 177
Mitchell, Richard P. 37, 44
Moestrup, Elisabeth 205, 225
Mohsen, Fatima 129, 152
Mohsen-Finan, Khadija 182, 199, 214, 225
Moosavi, Amir 79, 100
Morabia, Alfred 19, 24, 44
Moukhlis, Salah 210, 225
Mouna, Khalid 180, 192, 200
Muḥammad (Prophet) 18–20, 26, 38, 43, 48, 53, 55, 64–72, 103, 268–269, 276
Muhammad VI (King of Morocco) 190, 199, 208
Müller, Jean Marie 35, 44, 47, 72
Munīf, ʿAbd al-Raḥmān 322
Muruwwah, Ḥusayn 105–106
Musa, Majd 318, 335
al-Musawi, Muhsin 79, 100
Mustafa, Shakir 112, 124
al-Mutanabbī, Abū l-Ṭayyib 111, 120, 124

al-Nābulusī, Sulaymān 313
al-Nadāwī, Ḥawrāʾ 131
Nağm, Aḥmad Fuʾād 244
Nāṣir, ʿAbd al-Sattār 87, 95, 130
al-Nāṣirī, Buṯaynah 112
Nasry, Wafik 260, 274
Navantieri, Francesco 258–259
Neuhaus, David 302, 306–307
Neveu, Norig 336
Nevo, Joseph 312–313, 336
Ngũgĩ wa Thiong'o 133
Nikro, Norman S. 225
Nooraddin, Hoshiar 144, 152
Nouss, Alexis (Nuselovici, Alexis) 162, 177
Nūrī, Šākir 131
al-Nuqrāšī, Maḥmūd 37
Nyman, Jopi 169, 173, 177

O'Driscoll, Dylan 331, 336
Ojeda Garcia, Raquel 214, 226
Oliverius, Jaroslav 230, 237, 252
Ollivry-Dumairieh, Florence 46–47, 72
O'Mahony, Anthony 278, 307
Omer, Atalia 282, 287, 293, 294, 307
Orlando, Valérie K. 209, 226
Osti, Letizia 226
Ouahes, Idir 334
Ouiddar, Nadia 182, 200

Pacifico, Antonio 6, 159–160, 165, 177
Pannewick, Friederike 78–79, 99–100, 177, 249, 251–252
Pappé, Ilan 312–313, 336
Patierno, Nicole 293, 307
Paul VI (Pope) 284
Pennell, C. Richard 180, 200
Pepe, Teresa 201, 226
Pepicelli, Renata 207–208, 226
Petrarch (Petrarca, Francesco) 267
Pierret, Thomas 22, 44
Pipes, Daniel 18
Pizzi, Paola 3, 47, 71
Pizzorusso, Giovanni 258, 276
Plato 170, 173
Potenza, Daniela 9–10, 230–231, 238, 252–253
Pouzet, Louis 256–257, 276
Prager, Laila 315, 317, 336

Al-Qadi Abd al-Jabbar (al-Qāḍī ʿAbd al-Ğabbār) 54
Qāsim, ʿAbd al-Karīm (Prime Minister of Iraq) 107–108, 136, 144, 146–147, 149–150
Qāsim, Ḥamīd 97, 100
Quṭb, Sayyid 3, 21, 29–34, 37, 42–44, 51, 72

Radford Ruether, Rosemary 306
Radi, Abdelaziz 180, 200
Radwan, Noha 231, 244, 247–248, 253

Raḥīm, Sa'd Muḥammad 83–84, 95–96, 98, 100
al-Ramlī, Muḥsin 112, 123, 130
Ranieri, Enrica 192, 200
Rašīd, Bašār 148
al-Raṣīf, Ǧāsim 82–84, 87, 95, 100
Raya, Joseph (Rāyā, Yūsuf) 280
Redman, Peter 335
Reggab, Mohamed (al-Rakkāb, Muḥammad) 203
Rhani, Zakaria 181, 198, 200
al-Rikābī, Hišām Tawfīq 83, 85, 100
Robson, Laura C. 288, 307
Rogan, Eugene L. 311, 319, 336
Rohde, Achim 84, 99
Rowe, Paul S. 306
Rucht, J. Jefri 199
Ruocco, Monica 108, 122–124, 159–160, 170, 173, 175, 177
Ruṣāfī, Ma'rūf 106
Rutherford, Jonathan 176

al-Saadi, Tania 173, 177
Sabbah, Michel (Ṣabbāḥ, Mīšīl) 11, 278, 283, 291, 293–295, 299–302, 304–305, 307–308
al-Šabīb, Ṭāhā Ḥāmid 90, 100
al-Sa'd, Aḥmad Ibrāhīm 96, 100
Sa'dāwī, Aḥmad 112, 130–131, 145, 151, 152
al-Ṣadr, Muḥammad Sādiq 144
Saeed, Hend 104, 124, 138, 152
Ṣaḫī, 'Abdullāh 6, 126, 128, 131–152
Said, Edward 72, 122, 124, 155, 167, 177
Sa'īd, Ǧawdat 3, 21, 35–73,
Sa'īd, Ḫālid 232, 249, 251
al-Sa'īd, Nūrī 105
Sakr, Rita 157, 178
Sallis, Eva 309, 336
al-Sallūm, Muḥammad 165, 177
Sallūm, Sa'd 127, 152
Šamdīn, Nawzat 94, 100
Sanchez-Garcia, Jose 182, 200
Saoudi, Nour-Eddine 226
al-Saqqa, Abd al-Akram (al-Saqqā, 'Abd al-Akram) 46
Šaqūr, Ilyās (Chacour, Elias) 282–283, 306
al-Ṣaqr, Mahdī 'Īsà 80, 88–89, 100
Šarārah, Balqīs 90, 104–124
Šarārah, Ḥayāt 5, 90, 100, 102–124
Šarārah, Muḥammad 104
Sarī', Ḥasan 147, 153
Šarīf, Māhir 22, 44
Sarsar, Saliba 300, 307
Sartre, Jean-Paul 160
Sassoon, Joseph 156, 178
Saussure, Ferdinand de 54, 72
al-Šawiyyah, 'Ādil 86, 100
al-Sayyāb, Badr Šākir 105–106
Schiavo, Viviana 35, 44
Schiferli, Victor 162, 178
Schlumberger, Oliver 321, 336
Schmidinger, Thomas 329, 336
Sciortino, Maria Grazia 159, 175, 178
Scott Meisami, Julie 251
Seeberg, Peter 335
Sellman, Johanna Barbro 178, 210, 226
Serhane, Abdelhak (Sarḥān, 'Abd al-Ḥaqq) 213, 226
Sevdeen, Bayar M. 329, 336
Shami, Seteney 311–312, 317, 326, 336
Shariati, Ali 49, 63–64, 73
Sheetrit, Ariel M. 322, 332, 336
Sheffer, Gabriel 308
Shehade, Shehade (Šaḥādah, Šaḥādah) 288
Shuiskaja, Natalia M. 130, 152
al-Sibā'ī, Muṣṭafà 22
Siddiqui, Mona 165, 178
Simon, Henri 180, 200
Šim'ūn, Samū'īl 112
Slyomovics, Susan 180, 182, 200, 208–209, 224, 226
Smolin, Jonathan 224

Solomon (Prophet) 268, 270
Soroush, Abdolkarim 49, 59–60, 83, 73
Springs, Jason A. 282, 287, 307
Starkey, Paul 152, 251
Steinberg, Amanda H. 238, 242, 253
Stevens, Dallal 319, 322–323, 336
Šukrī, Muḥammad 197
Suleiman, Yasir 312, 315, 336
Sulṭān, Ḫālid Ḥusayn 103, 114, 116–117, 121, 124
Sumaysim, Muḥammad Ṣāliḥ 107, 109, 115
Šuqayr, Ramzī 232
Surūr, Nağīb 244, 251

al-Ṭabarī (al-Tabari) 54
Taha, Mahmud Muhammad 49, 57, 59, 73
al-Ṭā'ī, Ṣāliḥ 147, 153
al-Takarlī, Fu'ād 129
Ṭalāl ibn 'Abd Allāh (King of Jordan) 313
Taneja, Maneesha 270, 276
Tawfīq, Samīrah (Karīmūnā, Samīrah Ġasṭīn) 314–315
Tesei, Tommaso 193, 200
Timothy I (Patriarch) 260, 274
Tommasino, Pier Mattia 259, 268, 276
Touhtou, Rachid 182, 200
Tramontini, Leslie 78–79, 99–100
Tripp, Charles 105, 124
Tsimhoni, Daphne 279, 284, 287, 291, 308
Turgenev, Ivan 111, 117

Van de Vate, Katherine 182, 201
van Zoonen, Dave 331, 336
Vasey, Katie 335
Veguilla, Victoria 226
Verbeke, Annelies 162
Veseli, Rudolf 252
Viviani, Paola 8, 191, 201, 220, 226

Wālī, Nağm 88, 93, 100, 129
al-Watrī, Akram 105
Weipert, Reinhard 230, 253
Wensinck, Arent Jan 184, 201
al-Wer, Enam 315, 333
Westphal, Bernard 165, 178
Williams, Jennifer 316, 336
Wojnarowski, Frederick 316, 336
Wolf, Anne 181, 201

Yachoulti, Mohammed 195, 198, 201
Yildirim, Kemal 315, 337
Yitzhak, Ronen 313, 336
Yūsuf, Sa'dī 156

al-Zahāwī, Ğamīl Ṣidqī 106
Zankanah, Hayfā' 131
Zappa, Francesco 19, 44
Zaynab bint 'Alī 142, 143
Ze'evi, Dror 263, 276
Zeidel, Ronen 4–5, 79–81, 84, 86, 89, 99–100, 128–132, 144, 150, 153
Zemanek, Petr 252
Zerhouni, Saloua 200
Zetter, Roger 323, 337
Zimmer-Winkel, Rainer 307
Zisenwine, Daniel 182, 199
Zrikem, Abdellatif (Izrīkim, 'Abd al-Laṭīf) 211–212, 226
Žvan Elliott, Katja 185, 201
al-Zuḥaylī, Wahbah 3, 21–29, 42, 44

Index of Subjects

20 February Movement (*Ḥarakat 20 fibrāyir*) 180–181

abrogation 27, 41
academia in Iraq 102–122
Amman urban politics and structure 316–317, 319, 325–328, 332
ʿĀšūrāʾ 138–139, 142–143
asylum 154, 156, 159, 163–165, 169, 320–321, 323, 337

Baʿath party 78, 81, 85, 87, 89–91, 93–94, 96–99, 108–110, 113–116, 118, 120, 126–130, 132–133, 136, 138, 146, 148, 156, 329
Badr (battle) 66–67
al-Basūs (war) 9, 66, 229–253
Bayt Sāḥūr 291–292
Bedouin nationalist discourse in Jordan 313–317

censorship in Iraq 102–103, 120
centre vs periphery in Morocco 180–182, 192
Christian Palestinians in the Holy Land 278–280, 300
Christians in the Middle East 131, 277–308, 314, 321, 324, 328–329
civilisation 158, 168, 170, 175
class conflict in Morocco 181, 183, 185, 189, 192
coexistence 154, 158, 167, 170, 174
Confederal Republic of the Tribes of the Rif 180–182, 197
Conseil consultatif des droits de l'homme (CCDH, *al-Maǧlis al-istišārī li-ḥuqūq al-insān*) 208
Conseil national des droits de l'homme (CNDH, *al-Maǧlis al-waṭanī li-ḥuqūq al-insān*) 208
contextual theology in Palestine (*lāhūt maḥāllī filasṭīnī*) 284
conversion from Islam to Christianity 256–257, 259–260, 263

al-Dāḥas (war) 66
daʿwah 23–27, 32–33, 37–38, 40
decadence in Islam 49–53, 62, 70
Déclaration du Rif 182
Derb Moulay Chérif prison 203, 211–212
deserters in Iraqi literature 85, 87–88, 92–95, 97

Egyptian revolution (2011) 244
embargo in Iraq 117
ethno-religious identities in Iraq 92, 126–150, 324, 329–330
exile 113, 122, 154–156, 161–163, 167–168, 174

field theory (Bourdieu) 126, 128, 131–135, 150, 161–162
fiqh 24, 27

First Intifada 11, 282, 285–286, 289–292, 299

al-Ġabrā᾿ (war) 66
ǧāhiliyyah 30–31, 34, 39, 238–239
gender issues in Morocco 181, 183, 185–187, 191–198, 217–223
ǧihād 17–43
graffiti in Cairo 10, 232–233, 248–249
Greek Orthodox Patriarchate of Jerusalem 11, 281, 291
Gulf Wars 127, 156, 322

Habibi Valtiberina Association 327
ḥadīṯ 53
Hashemite Arab nationalism in Jordan 310–313
Hirak Movement (*Ḥirāk al–Rīf*) 181–182
history (philosophy of) 40–43, 49, 58–64, 67, 70
(hi)story 145, 147, 149–150
historical Quranic exegesis 40–42, 45, 49, 53–70
hogra 181, 194–196, 198
homoerotic Arabic poetry 10, 255, 261–263, 271
hospitality to refugees in Europe 156, 165–166, 174
humour 155, 160, 165, 174
Ḥunayn (battle) 66–67

imagined communities 310, 322
indigenisation of Palestinian ecclesiastic leadership 282–283, 290
insāniyyah 45, 48–51, 54, 67, 70, 71
Instance d'arbitrage indépendante (IAI, *Hay᾿at al–ta῾wīḍ*) 208
Instance équité et réconciliation (IER, *Hay᾿at al–inṣāf wa–l–muṣālaḥah*) 182, 208–209
interreligious disputes 260–263

Iran-Iraq War 4–5, 77–99, 110–111, 144, 156, 322, 330
Iraqi Communist Party 87, 106–108, 117, 123, 127, 132, 134, 144, 148
Iraqi diaspora 80, 87–88, 94, 129, 132, 134, 156–158, 161–162
Iraqi Jews 160
Iraqi literary field 126, 129–130, 132, 134, 150
Iraqi poetry 105, 111, 156
Iraqi POWs 84, 86, 89–90
Iraqi refugees in Jordan 322–325
ISIS (Daesh) 96, 157, 323, 328–330, 336
Islamic humanism 45, 48–49
Islamic reformism 50, 52, 60, 68

Jesuits 10–11, 255, 257, 267, 269–270
Jewish and Christian Zionism 277–278, 281, 293, 304
Jordan First national campaign 317–319
Justice and Peace Commission (*Laǧnat al–*῾adl *wa–l–salām*) 283–285, 293–300, 304

Karbalā᾿ (battle) 138–139, 143
King Hassan II Mosque 204–205, 213–214, 218, 220–223
Kurds 131, 149
Kuwait War 4, 86, 111, 120

Latin Patriarchate of Jerusalem 294–295, 324
liberation theology in Palestine (*lāhūt taḥrīr filasṭīnī*) 284, 290, 293–294

martyrs and martyrdom 10, 19, 84, 94, 115, 203, 230, 249–251, 297, 330
Mediterranean Sea 255–256
migration literature 133, 137, 138, 155–158, 163–175

Moroccan Constitution (2011) 181, 190–191
Moroccan Family Code (2004) 185, 190–191
Moroccan Rif 180–182, 197–198
Muslim Brotherhood 22, 30, 37, 68

Nahḍah 20–22, 35, 50
nation building in Jordan 310, 318
National Committee for the Protection of Lands in Israel 288
nonviolence in Islam 2–4, 17, 21, 25, 34–43, 45–71
nostalgia 137, 236, 256, 260–263, 269, 272

Palestine 105, 156, 161, 277–308, 312–315, 320–321, 322, 324, 326, 332, 334–335
Palestine Liberation Organization (PLO) 11, 279, 286–288, 299
Paradise 189, 194, 236, 265–266
patriarchal violence in Moroccan society 191–192, 194–197, 214, 217–218, 220, 223
political activism of Palestinian Christian churches 290–292
post-2003 Iraq 79, 87–88, 91–99, 130, 322–323
poverty issues in Morocco 185–192, 195, 220
prison writing in Morocco 203–207, 209–214, 223

Rafedìn project 324–332
reconciliation process in Morocco 182, 205–210, 222–223
refugee crisis 7, 154–159, 167
refugees in Jordan 319–321, 325
religious fundamentalism in Morocco 186, 192–195, 218
Russian literature 108, 111, 116–117

semiotics in Quranic exegesis 49, 53–65, 67, 69–70
Sīrat al-Zīr Sālim
(manuscript versions of) 230–233, 235, 237, 243, 250
(mediation in) 233–237–240, 250
(printed editions of) 231–235, 239, 242–244, 250
(rewritings and adaptations of) 232, 244, 247–249
Skhirat coup attempt (1971) 207
social justice 103–104, 122, 170
sovereignty of God 30, 32–35
state-sponsored Iraqi literature 79, 81–86, 91, 94–95
sunnah 40
Syrian uprising (2011) 71

Tazmamart prison 207, 210–213, 216
testimonial literature in Morocco 205–214, 222–223
Thawra or Sadr City 128, 132–133, 135–137, 144–149
the Amman Message (*Risālat* ʿAmmān) 318
translation as a mediation practice 11, 255, 258–259, 263–270
trauma 112, 156, 158, 168

Uḥud (battle) 67
United National Command of the Uprising (UNCU) 289, 291
US occupation of Iraq 117, 127, 129–130, 135, 144
utopia 155, 163, 169–175

Western Sahara conflict 204–205, 214–218, 222–223

Years of Lead (*sanawāt al–raṣāṣ*) 8, 198, 202–207, 219, 222–223
Youth of Daraya 46

www.ingramcontent.com/pod-product-compliance
Lightning Source LLC
Chambersburg PA
CBHW050835230426
43667CB00012B/2011
* 9 7 8 1 8 0 0 5 0 3 8 5 4 *